THE FIRST BIOGRAPHY OF JESUS

The First Biography of Jesus

Genre and Meaning in Mark's Gospel

Helen K. Bond

WILLIAM B. EERDMANS PUBLISHING COMPANY

GRAND RAPIDS, MICHIGAN

Wm. B. Eerdmans Publishing Co.
4035 Park East Court SE, Grand Rapids, Michigan 49546
www.eerdmans.com

Hardcover edition 2020
Paperback edition 2024

Printed in the United States of America

30 29 28 27 26 25 24   1 2 3 4 5 6 7

ISBN 978-0-8028-8447-3

Library of Congress Cataloging-in-Publication Data

Names: Bond, Helen K. (Helen Katharine), author.
Title: The first biography of Jesus : genre and meaning in Mark's gospel / Helen K. Bond.
Description: Grand Rapids, Michigan : William B. Eerdmans Publishing Company,
    2020. | Includes bibliographical references and index. | Summary: "Argues that Mark's
    author used the genre of biography to extend the gospel from an earlier narrow focus
    on the death and resurrection of Jesus so that it included the way of life of its founding
    figure"— Provided by publisher.
Identifiers: LCCN 2019050666 | ISBN 9780802884473 (pbk.)
Subjects: LCSH: Bible. Mark—Criticism, interpretation, etc. | Jesus Christ—
    Biography—History and criticism. | Classical biography—History and criticism. |
    Biography as a literary form. | Jesus Christ
Classification: LCC BS2585.52 .B65 2020 | DDC 226.3/066—dc23
LC record available at https://lccn.loc.gov/2019050666

To Keith, Katriona, and Scott
with love—as always
and
Joan Sandra Scott Raffan (1938–2017)

Looking back, it becomes clear that various kinds of philosophical, spiritual, and ethical Lives are the main artery of ancient biography. It starts with the figure of Socrates, represented as embodying his own ethical teaching, and continues with Hellenistic interest in the life and lifestyle of both ancient sages and contemporary philosophers. The canonical and apocryphal gospels, located at the side of the main Graeco-Roman tradition, are striving towards a complete Life of Jesus, making him a living model as much as a teacher. The ostensibly political Lives of Plutarch are in substance ethical biography, using great historical figures to make clear the consequences in a person's life of virtue and vice. The comic variety, such as the *Life of Aesop* and Lucian's biographical satires, is equally concerned with ethics. Diogenes Laertius shows most interest in the lives of his philosophers, while their doctrines receive more perfunctory treatment. In Late Antiquity, the continuing Pythagorean and incipient Neoplatonic life-writing testify to the persistent centrality of the spiritual kind of biography.

—Tomas Hägg, *The Art of Biography* (Cambridge: Cambridge University Press, 2012), 387

Contents

Acknowledgments

Many people have contributed to the writing of this book. Some have changed my thinking in significant ways while others have offered encouragement, support, and friendship along the way.

I would like to thank Michael Thomson at Eerdmans, who had faith in the proposal even when it was little more than a scrappy outline, and latterly Trevor Thompson, who saw it through the press. Richard Burridge has been unfailingly supportive and helpful during this project; thanks especially to him for sharing with me a pre-publication copy of the third edition of *What Are the Gospels?* Craig Keener, too, has shared my biographical interests, and I'm hugely grateful to him for sending me proofs of his excellent new study *Christobiography: Memory, History, and the Reliability of the Gospels*, now also published by Eerdmans.

In academic life, good colleagues are not always easy to come by, so I feel particularly fortunate to note my thanks to colleagues at Edinburgh, especially the Biblical Studies team—Paul Foster, Matthew Novenson, Philippa Townsend, Larry Hurtado, David Reimer, Timothy Lim, Suzanna Millar, and, most especially, Anja Klein and Alison Jack. Mona Siddiqui keeps me laughing on the Glasgow line and Robert McKay, Louisa Grotrian, and the office staff provide a jovial start to the day. Nathanael Vette put the bibliography into the Eerdmans house style and prepared the indexes, for which I'm very grateful. I'd also like to thank friends from Classics, especially Lloyd Llewellyn Jones (now of Cardiff), who alerted me to Tomas Hägg's brilliant book several years ago, to Sandra Bingham, who kindly read and commented on Chapter 2, and to Kim Czajkowski and Margaret Williams, who remind me there is more to ancient literature than Christian texts. I'd also like to thank my fellow editors on the *Jesus in the First Three Centuries* project (Bloomsbury Academic, 2019)—Chris Keith, Christine Jacobi, and Jens Schröter—for making me see that everything, in the end, is reception.

Thanks also go to the various gatherings—scholarly and otherwise—who have heard and commented on the ideas presented here: the research seminars and invited lectures at Edinburgh, Chester, St. Andrews, Exeter, Humboldt University (Berlin), Durham, the Manson Memorial Lecture at Manchester (2017), and SNTS

ACKNOWLEDGMENTS

2018 (Athens); and the more general meetings of the Irish Biblical Association, Aberdeen Theological Society, and the Bishop of Brechin's Study Day. Thanks to all of those who asked questions or emailed afterward—each and every one helped to sharpen my thinking in one way or another.

Most of all, I'd like to mention the people who just don't care whether I ever write any books. To my parents, Evelyn and John, for keeping me in Midget Gems and providing an inexhaustible supply of love and stability. To Katriona and Scott, for letting me see the world through your wonderful blend of curiosity, kindness, and general mayhem. And to Keith, for being amazingly supportive and tolerant. A final word goes to my mother-in-law, Joan Raffan, who died while I wrote this. The wife–mother-in-law relationship is perhaps one of the most difficult to navigate, but I always felt truly lucky to have you. You will always be in our hearts.

Abbreviations

AB	Anchor Bible
ABD	*Anchor Bible Dictionary*. Edited by David Noel Freedman. 6 vols. New York: Doubleday, 1992
ABG	Arbeiten zur Bible und ihrer Geschichte
AJP	*American Journal of Philology*
ANRW	*Aufstieg und Niedergang der römischen Welt: Geschichte und Kultur Rom sim Spiegel der neueren Forschung*. Part 1, *Von den Anfängen Roms bus zum Ausgang der Republik*, and Part 2, *Principat*. Edited by Hildegard Temporini and Wolfgang Haase. Berlin: de Gruyter 1972–
ARW	*Archiv für Religionswissenschaft*
ASE	*Annali di Storia dell'esegesi*
AThR	*Anglican Theological Review*
AYB	Anchor Yale Bible Commentaries
BBR	*Bulletin for Biblical Research*
BETL	Bibliotheca Ephemeridum Theologicarum Lovaniensium
BHT	Beiträge zur historischen Theologie
Bib	*Biblica*
BibInt	*Biblical Interpretation*
BS	The Biblical Seminar
BSac	*Bibliotheca Sacra*
BTB	*Biblical Theology Bulletin*
BZNW	Beihefte zur Zeitschrift für die neutestamentliche Wissenschaft
CBET	Contributions to Biblical Exegesis and Theology
CBQ	*Catholic Biblical Quarterly*
CR:BS	*Currents in Research: Biblical Studies*
CJ	*Classical Journal*
ClQ	*Classical Quarterly*
DCLS	Deuterocanonical and Cognate Literature Studies
DJG	*Dictionary of Jesus and the Gospels*. Edited by Joel B. Green, Jeannine K. Brown, and Nicholas Perrin. 2nd ed. Downers Grove, IL: IVP Academic, 2013.
ExpTim	*Expository Times*
FRLANT	Forschungen zur Religion und Literatur des Alten und Neuen Testaments

G&R	*Greece and Rome*
HSCP	*Harvard Studies in Classical Philology*
HTR	*Harvard Theological Review*
Int	*Interpretation*
JAAR	*Journal of the American Academy of Religion*
JBL	*Journal of Biblical Literature*
JECS	*Journal of Early Christian Studies*
JETS	*Journal of the Evangelical Theological Society*
JGRChJ	*Journal of Greco-Roman Christianity and Judaism*
JJS	*Journal of Jewish Studies*
JRASup	Supplements to the *Journal of Roman Archaeology*
JRS	*Journal of Roman Studies*
JSHJ	*Journal for the Study of the Historical Jesus*
JSJ	*Journal for the Study of Judaism in the Persian, Hellenistic, and Roman Periods*
JSJSup	Supplements to the *Journal for the Study of Judaism in the Persian, Hellenistic, and Roman Periods*
JSNT	*Journal for the Study of the New Testament*
JSNTSup	Supplements to the *Journal for the Study of the New Testament*
JSOT	*Journal for the Study of the Old Testament*
JSP	*Journal for the Study of the Pseudepigrapha*
JTS	*Journal of Theological Studies*
LCL	Loeb Classical Library
LEC	Library of Early Christianity
LNTS	The Library of New Testament Studies
LSTS	The Library of Second Temple Studies
MH	*Museum Helveticum*
Neot	*Neotestamentica*
NIDB	*The New Interpreters Dictionary of the Bible.* Edited by Katharine D. Sakenfeld. 5 vols. Nashville: Abingdon, 2009.
NovT	*Novum Testamentum*
NovTSup	Supplements to *Novum Testamentum*
NTM	New Testament Monographs
NTS	*New Testament Studies*
PACE	*Project on Ancient Cultural Engagement*
RAC	*Reallexikon für Antike und Christentum.* Edited by Theodor Klauser et al. Stuttgart: Hiersemann, 1950–
SBB	Stuttgarter biblische Beiträge
SBLDS	Society of Biblical Literature Dissertation Series
SBLRBS	Society of Biblical Literature Resources for Biblical Study
SBLSymS	Society of Biblical Literature Symposium Series
SBS	Stuttgarter Bibelstudien

Abbreviations

SBT	Studies in Biblical Theology
SEÅ	*Svensk Exegetisk Årsbok*
SemeiaSt	Semeia Studies
SJT	*Scottish Journal of Theology*
SNTSMS	Society for New Testament Studies Monograph Studies
SNTW	Studies of the New Testament and Its World
SWBA	Social World of Biblical Antiquity
TANZ	Texte und Arbeiten zum neutestamentlichen Zeitalter
TDNT	*Theological Dictionary of the New Testament.* Edited by G. Kittel and G. Friedrich. Translated by G. W. Bromiley. 10 vols. Grand Rapids: Eerdmans, 1964–76
TAPA	*Transactions of the American Philological Association*
TJT	*Toronto Journal of Theology*
TS	*Theological Studies*
TSAJ	Texte und Studien zum antiken Judentum
WUNT	Wissenschaftliche Untersuchungen zum Neuen Testament
ZNW	*Zeitschrift für die Neutestamentliche Wissenschaft*

Introduction

> The first step in the interpretation of any writing, whether ancient
> or modern, is to establish its literary genre. . . . A decision about the
> genre of a work and the discovery of its meaning are inextricably inter-
> related; different types of texts require different types of interpretation.
>
> —Graham Stanton[1]

A s a schoolgirl in the 1980s, I have a particularly vivid recollection of writing an essay for a religious studies exam. In answer to the deceptively simple question, "What are the gospels?" I began with the confident assertion, "The gospels are *not* biographies" (the "not" was emphatically underscored several times in different colors). Quickly I marshaled my thoughts, ready to outline the prevailing view that the evangelists were compilers and editors rather than authors, that the transmission of Jesus tradition within the early Christian communities had more in common with folklore than any kind of literary processes, and that the gospels were, in consequence, a unique phenomenon in the history of literature. More than thirty years later, I still remember that essay. What sticks in my memory is not any difficulty I might have had in setting out the scholarly consensus that I had so diligently learned, nor even my rather smug conviction that I knew the "right" answer and that my essay would score well. What struck me quite forcibly as I wrote that opening sentence was that, at heart, I did not believe a word of it.

Completely unknown to me at the time was the fact that my naïve teenage misgivings were shared by a growing number of scholars. The form-critical view that the gospels were a "unique" form of literature was particularly open to challenge. Studies of the social world of early Christianity increasingly stressed that the new movement flourished precisely because of its ability to utilize Greco-Roman cul-

---

1. G. Stanton, "Matthew: βίβλιος, εὐαγγέλιον, βίος?," in *The Four Gospels, 1992: Festschrift for Frans Neirynck*, ed. F. van Segbroeck with C. M. Tuckett, G. Van Belle, and J. Verheyden (Leuven: Leuven University Press, 1992), 1187.

ture; if it made use of contemporary travel routes, trade networks, and associations, why not also literary conventions (as Paul had done in his letters)? At the same time, literary theorists argued that it made no sense to claim that a work belonged to a "unique" genre—such a work would be impossible to understand! The task of assigning an appropriate genre to the gospels rapidly became a burning issue in New Testament research, and various analogies were brought forward for consideration. Did the gospels have most in common with biographies? Histories? Novels? Greek drama? Apocalyptic texts? Soon a clear front-runner emerged: the gospels were best seen as ancient biographies, or *bioi*.[2] In Germany, this view was particularly associated with Detlev Dormeyer, Hubert Frankemölle, Hubert Cancik, and Klaus Berger.[3] Within the English-speaking world, David Aune's *The New Testament in Its Literary Environment* (1987) offered a robust defense of the case, and Richard Burridge's monograph *What Are the Gospels? A Comparison with Graeco-Roman Biography* (1992) seemed to settle the matter. By the mid-1990s there was a measure of broad agreement that what we have in the first four books of the New Testament are *bioi*, or lives of Jesus. In a complete reversal of the former position, the "correct" answer to my schoolgirl question was now, "The gospels *are* biographies."

Strangely, however, scholars have been slow to capitalize on this important discovery. It is true that certain aspects of ancient *bioi* have been used to illuminate specific features of the gospels: their portrayal of the disciples, their ethical outlook, their readership and circulation, and (most recently) the question of their historical reliability.[4] Furthermore, it is now common for gospel commentaries to include a section on "genre" as part of the general introduction (though the *contents* of the commentaries—in terms of the questions they ask and the assumptions they make—often seem strangely unaffected by whatever genre the scholar has assigned to the work). But the practical results of the identification of the gospels as *bioi*— the payoff—seems disappointingly meager. Certainly, it does not seem to have revolutionized gospel interpretation in the manner promised by those caught up in the heady debates of the 1980s.

Why this should be is difficult to say, though I suspect that three developments within the discipline diverted scholarly attention elsewhere. First was the rise of

2. Scholars sometimes prefer to use the Greek *bios/bioi* in place of the English "biography/biographies" to stress the fact that we are referring to ancient works that are often quite different from their modern counterparts. Although I have not slavishly followed this practice, readers should be aware that, except where indicated differently, I am referring to *ancient* biographies.

3. For fuller discussion, see below, pp. 29–30.

4. See further below, pp. 35–37.

narrative criticism, which broadly coincided with the debate over genre and similarly appealed to those who were interested in the text as a literary product. A curious tendency among biblical narrative critics, however, and one that sets them at odds with most secular literary critics, is to show virtually no interest in genre.[5] Where the topic is raised, it is simply assumed that the gospels are (short) stories with little to separate them from their modern counterparts in terms of their plot, characters, settings, and so on.[6] What might have been a fruitful opportunity to look at the literary art of a set of *ancient biographers* (rather than *authors* more generally) was therefore lost, and the generic identification—at least for these scholars—became irrelevant.

Second, the 1980s and 1990s witnessed the rise of the so-called third quest for the historical Jesus. As our most significant sources, the identification of the gospels as *bioi* might have played an important role in this historical pursuit: scholars might have looked at the relationship between other *bioi* and historical events, at the way in which biographers typically used their sources, and at the extent to which imaginative fiction was acceptable within the genre. And yet they did not. Instead, the third quest coincided with a reinvigorated interest in "orality" and the evangelists' "oral heritage," interests that tended to focus attention on the "traditioning process(es)" *behind* the gospels rather than on the texts themselves.[7] Even the recent trend toward understanding the gospels as articulations of the social memories of various early Christian groups, though a welcome shift away from an atomistic search for "authentic" material within gospel *pericopae*, has tended to focus attention on the formation of cultural memories within groups of Christ followers somewhat at the expense of seeing the gospels as distinctive literary creations.

---

5. "Genre" as a topic is not even raised in the introductory works by M. A. Powell, *What Is Narrative Criticism?* (Minneapolis: Fortress, 1990), or J. L. Resseguie, *Narrative Criticism of the New Testament: An Introduction* (Grand Rapids: Baker Academic, 2005). On the uniquely biblical nature of "narrative criticism," see Powell, *What Is Narrative Criticism?*, 19–21.

6. The ground for this was laid in large measure by the pioneering work of D. Rhoads and D. Michie, *Mark as Story* (Philadelphia: Fortress, 1982), where Mark's Gospel was read as a short story. M. A. Tolbert is unusual in paying a great deal of attention to genre, though she concludes that Mark is best understood as an ancient novel; *Sowing the Gospel: Mark's World in Literary-Historical Perspective* (Minneapolis: Fortress, 1989), 55–79.

7. The title of James D. G. Dunn's important book, *Jesus Remembered*, vol. 1 of *Christianity in the Making* (Grand Rapids: Eerdmans, 2003), perfectly encapsulates this particular approach. Credit for the current interest in "orality" is usually given to W. H. Kelber's *The Oral and the Written Gospel: The Hermeneutics of Speaking and Writing in the Synoptic Tradition, Mark, Paul and Q* (Philadelphia: Fortress, 1983), which led to a privileging of orality against the written ("frozen") text; for further discussion, see below, pp. 86–88.

And third, the last couple of decades have seen a trend toward identifying scriptural echoes and allusions within the gospels (usually referred to rather anachronistically as the study of the "Old Testament in the New"). There was nothing unusual about a biographer peppering his account with literary allusions: Greco-Roman authors commonly displayed their knowledge of Homer and the other "greats" of the classical tradition, and Philo wrote biographies of a number of Jewish heroes, each of which drew heavily on the scriptural tradition. And yet, once again, the identification of the evangelists as biographers tends to be eclipsed: the model is not so much that of a *biographer*, or even a creative author, but of a Jewish *scribe* painstakingly weaving together strands of scriptural texts.[8] Any light that Greco-Roman *bioi* might offer in terms of ancient practices of "intertextuality" is sidelined in favor of an exclusive focus on the Jewish texts alone.

The effect of these three developments within New Testament studies (and doubtless others too) is that the identification of the gospels as biographies was quickly ousted from what should have been a central and decisive position and relegated to little more than a footnote. Many scholars presumably thought that there was little more to say: holding a broadly Aristotelian view in which everything can be reduced to a system of classification, the identification of genre was simply an end in itself.[9] The gospels are *bioi*: problem solved, time to move on.

My own view, in contrast, is that reading the gospels as ancient biographies makes a profound difference to the way that we interpret them. As literary critic John Frow points out, "far from being merely 'stylistic' devices, genres create effects of reality and truth, authority and plausibility, which are central to the different ways the world is understood in the writing of history or of philosophy or of science, or in painting, or in everyday talk."[10] Genres, in other words, are not arbitrary or accidental; material cannot simply be transposed from one genre to another without loss of meaning. In the careful selection of a particular genre, authors choose specific ways to organize their thoughts, to create connections and patterns of causality between events, and actively to shape the worlds they present. As soon as we acknowledge that the gospel writers had literary aspirations (even if not of the highest level), genre matters. Indeed, the fact that we are

8. A rare exception to this general observation is S. Porter, "The Use of Authoritative Citations in Mark's Gospel and Ancient Biography: A Study of P.Oxy. 1176," in *Biblical Interpretation in Early Christian Gospels*, vol. 1, *The Gospel of Mark*, ed. T. R. Hatina (London: T&T Clark, 2006), 116–30.

9. On the problems of Aristotle's taxonomic approach, see J. Frow, *Genre* (London: Routledge, 2006), 24, 55–59.

10. Frow, *Genre*, 2.

dealing with *bioi* should be the starting point for all gospel discussion. It is only when we understand something of ancient *bioi* that we can start to understand what the evangelists wanted to communicate, and why they chose this specific literary genre to do it.

The Present Volume

The purpose of this book is to explore exactly what it means to say that Mark's Gospel is an ancient biography. I admit that my title is intentionally provocative: although Mark's is the *earliest* extant example of a Christian "life of Jesus," we have no way of knowing whether he was in fact the first to adapt his material to this particular literary form. More likely, others had already made some moves in this direction (a topic we shall explore in greater depth in Chapter 3). Yet the fact remains that Mark has no known precursor in his literary endeavors, and whether or not he can claim to be the *first* biographer of Jesus, his work was certainly the most successful of those early attempts.

I regard Mark's literary activities as a very specific *reception* of the Jesus tradition. What we have here is not a passive transmission of earlier material, an attempt to compile and preserve stories and sayings for posterity, arranged broadly in the manner of an ancient "life." Mark's project, I suggest, was far grander in its conception. It was an attempt actively to reappropriate and reconfigure selected material from the mass of unstructured, ahistorical sayings and anecdotes in circulation at the time into a formal, literary creation. By imposing a *biographical* structure onto traditional material, Mark simultaneously gave it a historical framework. His work was thus the conscious shaping of a normative Christian past, intimately connected to the life of the founding figure, in such a way that it spoke to his own present as he and his audience sought to articulate their own sense of identity within the Roman world.[11] I will argue that Mark's work extended the Christian "gospel" so that it was no longer limited to the death and resurrection of Jesus, but encompassed Jesus's ministry too. Mark's *bios*, therefore, takes its place not only within an emerging and still-embryonic Christian "book culture," but also as an attempt to formulate a distinctive Christian identity based on the countercultural way of life (and death) of its founding figure.

11. When the gospels are considered sui generis, the "mechanisms" of group identity are assumed to lie elsewhere—among the nameless Christ followers who have shaped and passed on tradition. When they are seen as distinct literary creations, however, the impetus for group-shaping (even if drawing on well-known traditions) lies to a greater extent with those who crafted them.

INTRODUCTION

My approach in this study is both literary and historical. I imagine the gospel to have been written by a reasonably educated, creative author, who consciously selected and adapted his material. His adoption of a simple, "popular" style should not blind us to his theological insight, sensitivity, and literary sophistication.[12] More specifically—and this is what sets the present study apart from more conventional "narrative" readings—I aim to read Mark's work according to the literary conventions of ancient biographical literature. As we shall see in subsequent chapters, ancient biographies were very different to modern ones, with their own conventions in terms of how they display character, their (frequently) episodal structure, and their (commonly) ethical interest. It is only when we understand these literary conventions that we can come close to understanding Mark's work in its original setting. The closest analogies to Mark, I will argue, are Greek lives of philosophers: for example, Xenophon's *Memorabilia*, Philo's *Life of Moses*, the anonymous *Life of Aesop*, Lucian's *Demonax*, Philostratus's *Life of Apollonius of Tyana*, or Diogenes Laertius's *Lives of Eminent Philosophers*. While none of these provides an exact parallel to Mark (or to one another for that matter), various aspects of each of them may well prove instructive. Consequently, a great deal of space in Chapters 3–6 is given over to comparative work, noting both where Mark conforms to general biographical expectations and where he does not. My interest here lies not only in imagining what our author was trying to do (insofar as this can ever be known),[13] but also in how his earliest audiences might have received and understood his work.

12. Some might prefer that I referred to the *implied* author here, as an acknowledgment of the fact that we know nothing about this person other than what is gleaned from the text itself. This is often a valid distinction (especially in modern literature), but it seems to me that any discrepancy between the "real" author and the "implied" one is likely to be very slight in a text such as Mark's Gospel—there is no reason to think that the authoritative narrator that we encounter throughout the work holds different opinions from the flesh-and-blood author; see Powell, *What Is Narrative Criticism?*, 5, who accepts that this distinction is only "minimal" in the gospels. B. J. Malina stresses important differences between a modern "author" and an ancient one (though to my mind rather too forcefully); see "Were There 'Authors' in New Testament Times?," in *To Set at Liberty: Essays on Early Christianity in Its Social World in Honor of John H. Elliott*, ed. S. K. Black (Sheffield: Sheffield Phoenix, 2014), 262–71.

13. Some might be a little perturbed by my interest in establishing Mark's authorial activity. Ever since the New Criticism of the 1940s declared the death of the author in reaction to the excessively biographical approach that preceded it, critics have held a more chastened attitude toward "authorial intent." Most narrative critics today, however, reject the extremes of New Criticism, allowing some degree of (implied) authorial intentionality; see Powell, *What Is Narrative Criticism?*, 4–5; Resseguie, *Narrative Criticism*, 22–23. None of this, how-

6

A word of caution is in order here: as part of a deeply creative activity, genre is fluid and malleable, unstable and open-ended. This was particularly so in the early imperial period, when experimentation, innovation, and hybridity tended to be the norm. Despite the impression we sometimes take from the ancient grammarians, there was no one "blueprint" for how an author should set about his craft. Biographies range wildly from the serious and educational to the far-fetched and imaginative, with everything in between. Most can be situated somewhere between *encomium* and history, though many quite effortlessly integrate features from other genres—tragedy, novels, poetry, letters, and so on. Still, an ancient biography, much like its modern counterpart, "operated within a set of conventional and highly organized constraints on the production and interpretation of meaning."[14] *Bioi* are socially circumscribed, creating generically specific "worlds" of meaning, and drawing on conventional features, expectations, and *topoi*. Greek "lives" in particular, though written for different purposes, commonly exhibit a number of similarities in terms of structure and moral exhortation.[15] When I talk about "ancient *bioi*" or the "biographical tradition" within this book, therefore, I do not mean to reduce ancient *bioi* to a rigid literary genre, but to point to characteristics that feature commonly within surviving examples.

Time, Place, and Author

Like all literature, biographies reflect the age in which they are written. On a general level, this is fairly obvious. Nineteenth-century biographers tended to present the lives of Great Men—statesmen, soldiers, adventurers, or writers. Readers today,

---

ever, is to dispute the "messy" nature of ancient book production, or the vagaries and perils of textual transmission, especially in the earliest decades of emerging Christianity; on this topic, see M. D. C. Larsen, "Accidental Publication, Unfinished Texts and the Traditional Goals of New Testament Textual Criticism," *JSNT* 39 (2017): 362–87, though I am far more convinced than Larsen that some kind of "initial text" of Mark existed, a view reinforced by regarding Mark as a self-consciously literary *bios* (Larsen sees it rather as "unfinished textual raw material"; 378).

14. Frow, *Genre*, 10; more specifically relating to New Testament texts, see R. A. Burridge, *What Are the Gospels? A Comparison with Graeco-Roman Biography*, 3rd ed. (Waco: Baylor University Press, 2018), 25–52, and S. Adams, *The Genre of Acts and Collected Biography* (Cambridge: Cambridge University Press, 2013), 1–5.

15. Science fiction writer N. Gaiman defines genre in terms of what would leave a reader cheated or disappointed at the end if it were not there: "The Pornography of Genre, or the Genre of Pornography," *Journal of the Fantastic in the Arts* 24 (2013): 401–7. In the case of Greek *bioi*, it is presumably the broad focus on a life and moral instruction.

however, have more democratized tastes—popular topics include the lives of ordinary people, women, domestic servants or slaves, and the concept of a "life" might be extended to cover cities and even commodities (salt, for example, or cod). And while moralizing was a central feature of nineteenth-century biography, modern authors are decidedly reluctant to pass judgment on others. In broad terms, then, biography is not only produced by a particular age and culture but is also a reflection of it. A nineteenth-century biography of Charles Dickens or Florence Nightingale would be very different from its modern counterpart, and each of these works would tell us just as much about the intellectual and cultural age in which it was written as the historical character at its center.[16]

If we are to understand a text, particularly one from a distant culture, we need to be attuned to its historical context. Any piece of writing contains far more meaning than that expressed solely by the words on the page. Texts assume and evoke cultural knowledge, and without this any reading is hazardous. Once again, genre plays an important role here in alerting readers to what range of readings are probable, even likely, and setting constraints and limits on those that are not. Certain genres tend to be used in certain situations, subtly arousing a set of unconscious expectations. As John Frow notes, "The generic framework constitutes the unsaid of texts, the organisation of information which lies latent in a shadowy region from which we draw it as we need it; it is information that we may not know we know, and that is not directly available for scrutiny."[17] The difficulty for any modern interpreter of Mark's *bios*, of course, lies in what is "unsaid," the vast store of cultural assumptions that Mark's audience instinctively brought to bear on their understanding of his work. We cannot hope ever to be able to put ourselves in the position of those earliest audiences, but it is possible to say some things about Mark's general setting.

In line with a growing scholarly consensus, my working assumption throughout this book is that Mark's *bios* was written in the early to mid-70s CE,[18] that is, after

16. On this general point, see T. Hägg, who also notes the ephemeral nature of (most) biographical subjects, *The Art of Biography in Antiquity* (Cambridge: Cambridge University Press, 2012), 69.

17. Frow, *Genre*, 83. See also 93: "To speak of genre is to speak of what need not be said because it is already so forcefully presupposed."

18. Some have argued for a very early date for Mark: see, for example, J. A. T. Robinson, *Redating the New Testament* (London: SCM, 1976); E. E. Ellis, "The Date and Provenance of Mark's Gospel," in Van Segbroeck et al., *The Four Gospels, 1992*, 801–15; and J. G. Crossley, *The Date of Mark's Gospel: Insight from the Law in Earliest Christianity* (London: T&T Clark, 2004). Others put it in the late 60s, at the height of the Jewish-Roman war: see, for example, M. Hengel, *Studies in the Gospel of Mark* (London: SCM, 1985), 14–28, and

the catastrophic Jewish war with Rome, the civil war of 69, and the Flavian accession to the imperial throne. Although I am well aware of the problematic nature of the ancient sources, the traditional Roman provenance has always seemed to me to have much to recommend it.[19] It accounts for the air of persecution that hangs so heavily over this work, persecution that broke out brutally and unexpectedly under Nero in 65 CE, and might well have continued to threaten the community of Christ followers after the war.[20] A knowledge of the Flavian triumph, celebrated in Rome in 71, might also explain the "anti-triumph" motif that several scholars have detected in Mark's account of the crucifixion.[21] And, as far as the current project is concerned, a Roman origin has the added advantage of situating our author at the heart of a dynamic literary culture. Nothing in the present work, however, *depends* upon a Roman provenance, and readers who are more inclined toward Syria or elsewhere need not be alarmed.[22]

A. Y. Collins, *Mark: A Commentary* (Minneapolis: Fortress, 2007), 11–14. A post-70 date, however, commands most support nowadays. For a representative sample, see D. Lührmann, *Das Markusevangelium* (Tübingen: Mohr Siebek, 1987), 222; P. J. J. Botha, "The Historical Setting of Mark's Gospel: Problems and Possibilities," *JSNT* 51 (1993): 27–55; J. Marcus. "The Jewish War and the *Sitz im Leben* of Mark," *JBL* 113 (1992): 441–62; H. N. Roskam, *The Purpose of the Gospel of Mark in its Historical and Social Context* (Leiden: Brill, 2004), 89–92; E.-M. Becker, "Dating Mark and Matthew as Ancient Literature," in *Mark and Matthew I, Comparative Readings: Understanding the Earliest Gospels in Their First-Century Setting*, ed. E.-M. Becker and A. Runesson (Tübingen: Mohr Siebeck, 2011), 123–43; and J. Kloppenborg, "*Evocatio Deorum* and the Date of Mark," *JBL* 124 (2005): 419–50. After discussing recent scholarship, J. R. Donahue concludes that "more and more scholars are dating it after AD 70 and somehow in response to the Jewish War of AD 66–70 and the destruction of the temple"; "The Quest for the Community of Mark's Gospel," in Becker and Runesson, *Mark and Matthew I*, 817–38.

19. For a recent attempt to defend a Roman origin, see B. J. Incigneri, *The Gospel to the Romans: The Setting and Rhetoric of Mark's Gospel* (Leiden: Brill, 2003).

20. See in particular Mark 4:17; 8:34; 10:37–40; and 13:9–13; also B. M. F. van Iersel, "The Gospel according to St. Mark—Written for a Persecuted Community?," *Ned TTs* 34 (1980): 15–36, and, more recently, H. N. Roskam, *The Purpose of the Gospel of Mark* (Leiden: Brill, 2004), 27–74. Recently the whole Neronian persecution has been called into question; see B. D. Shaw, "The Myth of the Neronian Persecution," *JRS* 105 (2015): 73–100. Certainly the evidence for linking the deaths of Peter and Paul with this event is not strong, but the fact of the persecution itself (as outlined by Tacitus) seems robust; see C. P. Jones, "The Historicity of the Neronian Persecution: A Response to Brent Shaw," *NTS* 63 (2017): 146–52.

21. Josephus gives what may well have been an eyewitness account of this event in *Jewish War* 7.119–62. On the "anti-triumph" motif, see below, pp. 238–41.

22. Syria seems to be the strongest alternative to Rome nowadays; see the detailed discus-

The author of the *bios* remains something of an enigma. Scholars commonly maintain that the names by which the gospels are now known were only assigned to them in the second century, largely in the fight against heretics.[23] However, as Martin Hengel has pointed out, the earliest Christian communities would have needed some way of identifying their texts—and distinguishing between them—from very early on. Once "Matthew" was composed, how did his church refer to "Mark"? And how were Luke's many "narratives" (*diēgēseis*, Luke 1:1) or John's book (*biblion*, John 20:30) distinguished from one another? Although we lack very early papyrological evidence, it is noteworthy that while the order of the gospels might vary, the ascriptions linking them to particular authors never differ, even when they derive from widely divergent geographical areas—a feature that suggests that the names under which we know these texts go back to the earliest period.[24] Furthermore, while it is easy to see why the second-century church might have ascribed gospels to "John" and "Matthew" (names that easily implied their authors were apostles), it is more difficult to account for "Mark" and "Luke." Neither were disciples of Jesus, and neither could claim eyewitness authority. At least from the early second century, supporters of Mark were forced to derive his authority from a supposed connection with Peter (see the comments of Papias preserved in Eusebius, *Ecclesiastical History* 3.39.15–16) and to detect a reference to him in 1 Pet 5:13.[25] All of this inclines

---

sions in Marcus, "Jewish War" and Roskam, *Purpose*; also T. Wardle, "Mark, the Jerusalem Temple and Jewish Sectarianism: Why Geographical Proximity Matters in Determining the Provenance of Mark," *NTS* 62 (2016): 60–78. A Syrian origin is simply presupposed by the essays in *Redescribing the Gospel of Mark*, ed. B. S. Crawford and M. P. Miller (Atlanta: SBL Press, 2017). In the end, it is simply not possible to infer provenance from the gospel itself. As J. M. Smith notes, as part of an argument for an intentionally wide distribution of the gospel, "the material in Mark is ambiguous enough to enable social reconstructions that would fit in any number of cities in any number of parts of the Mediterranean world in the first century"; *Why Βίος? On the Relationship between Gospel Genre and Implied Audience* (London: T&T Clark, 2015), 157. Rather less constructively, D. N. Peterson sees the whole attempt to locate Mark as futile; *The Origins of Mark: The Marcan Community in Current Debate* (Leiden: Brill, 2000).

23. This view is very common; see for example C. M. Tuckett, "Mark," in *The Oxford Bible Commentary*, ed. J. Barton and J. Muddiman (Oxford: Oxford University Press, 2000), 886, and J. Marcus, *Mark 1–8: A New Translation with Introduction and Commentary*, AYB (New York: Doubleday, 2000), 30.

24. Hengel, *Studies*, 66–67.

25. For a full discussion, see C. C. Black, *Mark: Images of an Apostolic Interpreter* (Edinburgh: T&T Clark, 2001). On Mark's possible connection with Peter, see below, p. 108.

me toward the supposition that our *bios* was indeed written by someone with the common Roman name of Marcus.[26]

One further point is worth considering. If the gospels circulated widely, as the use of Mark by both Matthew and Luke implies, we might expect them to be known by the *place* from which they emerged—the "life of Jesus" from Rome, or Antioch, or elsewhere. Instead, Mark's work (and those that he inspired) are all linked with a specific individual, a fact that seems to reflect a general assumption that the *bios* is the work of a creative author.[27] Unlike most ancient biographers, Mark did not set out his credentials for writing in his opening preface (a point we shall come back to in Chapter 3), yet some information about the work's author must have been passed down orally, or in some paratextual form, at least at first.[28] Early audiences would have wanted to know the identity of the author and his qualifications for writing such an account, particularly if it differed in some respects from their own more familiar traditions.[29] This information, however, has now been lost. All we can say with any certainty is that the *bios* was probably written by a church leader named Marcus, an educated man of some standing in his local Christ-following community. Our findings here are admittedly rather meager, but at least provide a measure of historical and cultural context within which to situate our earliest "life of Jesus."

Overview

How, then, are we to proceed? Our first task is briefly to chart the scholarly debate over the last century regarding Mark's genre, from being regarded as a unique form of literature in the early twentieth century to the present view that it is an example of an ancient *bios*. My intention here is not to be exhaustive

26. So also a number of German scholars, for example R. Pesch, *Das Markusevangelium* (Freiburg: Herder, 1976), 1:9-11; D. Luhrmann, *Das Markusevangelium* (Tübingen: Mohr Siebeck, 1987), 5-6. As Hengel observes, Christian writings are rarely anonymous; most bear the name of a real author (e.g., Paul, Clement, Ignatius), and where the author hides his or her identity it is more common to take refuge behind the authority of one of the great teachers of old (e.g., Paul or Peter). As he rightly notes, it is very unlikely that Theophilus did not know the identity of the person who wrote the gospel dedicated to him; Hengel, *Studies*, 72-74.

27. So also R. A. Burridge, "About People, by People, for People: Gospel Genre and Audiences," in *The Gospels for All Christians: Rethinking Gospel Audiences*, ed. R. Bauckham (Grand Rapids: Eerdmans, 1998), 125-30. Also Collins, *Mark*, 129.

28. For further discussion, see below, pp. 97-98.

29. Hengel, *Studies*, 74-83.

(the literature is huge and other studies cover this topic more than adequately already), but rather to chart the broad contours of the discussion, and to see what assumptions and concerns have driven participants. I should perhaps note at this point that my purpose in this book is not to *prove* that Mark wrote a biography, but to see how such a generic assumption might affect its interpretation. If the resulting reading helps to strengthen the generic identification, then so much the better.

Next, we need a firm understanding of ancient biographies. As we shall see, biography enjoyed something of a heyday in the first century and we are lucky that so many examples have survived. The task of the second chapter, then, is to sketch out the broad expectations and conventions of *bioi* around the time that Mark's Gospel was written, from the earliest *encomia* of Isocrates and Xenophon to the fully developed *bioi* of near contemporaries Suetonius, Tacitus, Plutarch, and Lucian. There has been a surge of interest in biography among classicists in recent decades, and a growing determination to study them on their own terms rather than regarding them as simply poor examples of historiography—all of which makes the task of offering an up-to-date survey very much easier. In this chapter, we shall look at the emergence of biography as a discrete literary genre, at its distinctive features, at the reasons why people wrote biographies, and at the close connection between biography and morality. We shall look at how ancient biographies construct character and the moment at which character was often most clearly revealed—by the subject's death. In all of this, we shall pay particular attention to the closest analogies to the gospels, the Greek lives of philosophers. The chapter will conclude with a few reflections on biographical fact and fiction, a topic that will help us to understand the degree of latitude that biographers were allowed as they set about crafting their chosen "lives."

The third chapter considers a set of general topics relating to *how* Mark wrote. Crucial here is a discussion of the evangelist's level of education and style of writing, along with an attempt to situate him at the very beginning of an emerging Christian "book culture." I shall consider what we know of Mark's earliest readers, and how the biography of a founding figure could help to forge a specific Christ-following identity. More specifically, I shall analze Mark's structure and use of anecdotes, comparing both with other *bioi* and noting how interpreting these features within their correct literary context challenges several widely held form-critical assumptions. Although my focus is on Mark's final text, it is worth considering our author's use of earlier sources here, both oral and written, though I do not hold out much hope of ever recovering them. Finally, I shall consider Mark's lack of a preface and his muted authorial voice, asking how these aspects of the work would have struck an ancient audience.

The next two chapters are concerned with characterization, both that of Jesus (Chapter 4) and of others (Chapter 5). Ancient characterization tends to "show" rather than "tell," and Chapter 4 demonstrates the way in which features such as miracles, conflict with opponents, and the so-called messianic secret lay out both Jesus's identity *and* character. Throughout the early chapters, the Markan Jesus displays many of the qualities prized by elite males—he is a force to be reckoned with, authoritative, self-controlled, and generous, one worthy of his adoption as God's Son (1:9–11). At the same time, however, he not only teaches but also embodies a new honor code, one based on suffering and service rather than public esteem. Mark clearly presents Jesus as a person to be imitated—this comes across both through the constant call to "follow" him and is even embedded within the structure of the book itself. But how far are followers expected to go? And why does Mark refrain from giving even the briefest physical description of his hero? Could this also have something to do with his exemplary nature?

All of this, however, raises a problem: If Jesus is both the central character of the biography and the model of Christian discipleship, where does that leave other characters? Chapter 5 looks at the way an ancient audience might have made sense of secondary characters, paying attention to the techniques of *synkrisis* (comparison) and the use of vignettes as *exempla*. We shall look at how Mark creates character through the juxtaposition of scenes, not only in the case of peripheral characters, but also within more complex units (such as the passages surrounding "King Herod" in the middle of the work, or the high priest/Pilate toward the end). Most importantly, we shall need to pay attention to the twelve disciples: How do we explain what seems to be their ambiguous portrait? Is Mark's use of them polemical or pastoral, or do they have another function? And what of the "minor" characters who populate the passion narrative once the Twelve have fled? In this chapter, perhaps more than any other, we shall see the effects of reading Mark's work as an ancient biography rather than a modern short story.

Finally, Chapter 6 considers Mark's striking account of Jesus's death. Rather than searching the text for indications of scriptural models (a version of the Suffering Righteous One, perhaps, or Isaiah's Suffering Servant), I read Mark's concluding chapters as an account of a philosopher who dies in accordance with his teaching, particularly the countercultural teaching of chapters 8–10. I assume that our author *began* with Jesus's shameful and servile death on the cross, and that the whole biography was carefully structured in order to present Jesus as a philosopher who goes to his death in accordance with his teaching. The Jesus who instructed his followers to deny themselves and to become like servants to others (8:34; 10:43–44) will himself take this teaching to its logical end, in obedience to the will of God. But what does Jesus's death achieve for Mark? And to what extent is it paradigmatic for believers?

And why does Mark end his work as he does? Here again, comparison with other *bioi* may offer some answers.

With all of this in mind, we are ready to move on to the first chapter and an analysis of the modern scholarly debate on gospel genre. As a way into this whole question, however, it may be instructive to go right back to the very beginning, and to ask what clues the very first Christ followers give us to the way they understood these pivotal texts.

CHAPTER 1

Mark as a *Bios*

Genre matters to the reading of every text.

—John Frow[1]

When scholars argued in the 1970s and 1980s that the gospels were *bioi*, they were only advocating a view that had been taken for granted within Christian circles for almost nineteen hundred years. What is more surprising, perhaps, is that anyone should ever have doubted that the gospels were biographies. In this first chapter, we shall look at the debate over the genre of the gospels, noting the way in which various issues have played into the dispute, not least assumptions over the nature and formation of the gospels, the evangelists' level of education, and often rather rigid conceptions of ancient *bioi* themselves. We shall pay attention not only to the academic arguments but also to the social contexts in which they were debated, in the conviction that scholars are no more insulated from prevailing cultural trends and attitudes than anyone else.

From the Ancients to Votaw

At first glance, it is rather surprising that no one in the ancient world ever refers to the gospels as *bioi*. The reason for this, however, may be quite straightforward: almost from the very beginning, these particular "lives" were known as "gospels" (*euangelia*).

The term "gospel" is not, of course, a literary genre. The term, often in the plural, was used in the Greco-Roman world to refer to the proclamation of significant news or imperial proclamations—to announce a military victory, the accession of a new emperor, or an emperor's benefactions—and would be the occasion for civil rejoicing. On the famous Priene Calendar, for example, Augustus can refer to his

---

1. J. Frow, *Genre* (London: Routledge, 2006), 28.

own birthday as "the beginning of good news (*euangelia*) for the world."[2] When Paul talks about "the gospel" he has in mind Christian preaching concerning the death and resurrection of Jesus. Although his language can vary, he appears to appeal to a body of shared tradition such as we find in 1 Cor 15:3b–5: "that Christ died . . . that he was buried, that he was raised on the third day in accordance with the scriptures, that he appeared to Cephas, then to the twelve." Although he can sometimes uses the word in a similar way, Mark's great innovation was to include the life, ministry, and teaching of Jesus within his understanding of "gospel" (1:1, 14, 15; 8:35; 10:29; 13:10; 14:9).[3] Still for him, however, as for Paul, the term referred primarily to *oral proclamation.*

At some point over the next few decades, however, the term underwent a shift of meaning so that it now referred not only to oral preaching but quite specifically to books about Jesus. Clear evidence for this change does not appear until the mid-second century, when Justin Martyr, Irenaeus, and Clement of Alexandria all begin to use the term "gospel" to refer to written lives of Jesus (both those that were later considered canonical and those that were not).[4] There are good reasons, however, to assume that this usage goes back significantly earlier. Marcion seems to have referred to his abridged copy of Luke as a "gospel," and references in 2 Clement, Ignatius, and the Didache, though not quite as clear as we might like, do nevertheless seem to suggest that their authors now associated the term "gospel" with written books as well as oral proclamation.[5] James Kelhoffer has recently argued—persuasively in my opinion—that the change came about sometime between the writing of Matthew

2. See *Orientis Graeci Inscriptiones Selectae*, ed. W. Dittenberger (Leipzig, 1903–5), 2:458, cited by C. A. Evans, "Mark's Incipit and the Priene Calendar Inscription: From Jewish Gospel to Greco-Roman Gospel," *JGRChJ* 1 (2000): 67–81. See also Josephus, *Jewish War* 4.618, 656. On the meaning of the term *euangelion* in contemporary literature, see J. P. Dickson, "Gospel as News: εὐαγγελ- from Aristophanes to the Apostle Paul," *NTS* 51 (2005): 212–30.

3. The most strikingly "Pauline" use of the word is at 16:7.

4. Justin, *Dialogue with Trypho* 10.2, 100.1; Irenaeus, *Against Heresies* 3.1.1; Clement of Alexandria, *Stromata* 1.21 (352).

5. H. Koester argues that the use of the word "gospel" to refer to a written text was a specific response to Marcion; "From the Kerygma-Gospel to Written Gospels," *NTS* 35 (1989): 361–81; so also R. H. Gundry, "Εὐαγγέλιον: How Soon a Book?," *JBL* 115 (1996): 321–25. See the surveys of other literature in M. Hengel, *Studies in the Gospel of Mark* (London: SCM, 1985), 67–72; G. Stanton, "Matthew: βίβλιος, εὐαγγέλιον, βίος," in *The Four Gospels, 1992*, ed. F. van Segbroeck, C. M. Tuckett, G. van Belle, and J. Verheyden (Leuven: Leuven University Press, 1992), 1190–95; and J. A. Kelhoffer, "'How Soon a Book' Revisited: ΕΥΑΓΓΕΛΙΟΝ as a Reference to 'Gospel' Materials in the First Half of the Second Century," *ZNW* 95 (2004): 1–34.

and the composition of the Didache (which appears to describe Matthew's work as a "gospel"), that is, in the very late first century.[6] Such a usage can be explained quite naturally from Mark's opening line: "The beginning of the gospel of Jesus Christ, Son of God." Whether Mark intended "the beginning" (*archē*) to include only the prologue or the whole of the book (a point we shall return to in Chapter 3), his opening incipit applied the term "gospel" to a written text, and (whether consciously or not) set in motion a train of thought that would eventually identify the term "gospel" with a particular type of literary work.[7] As it circulated among Christian churches and was read out at gatherings, Mark's *bios* would have quite naturally become known as a "gospel," a term that could equally easily be applied to Matthew, and then by analogy to Luke and John.[8]

This early shift in meaning has important implications for our study. The reason why no one in the early church describes the earliest lives of Jesus as *bioi* is presumably because from very early on they became known by a term that had quickly acquired theological significance within Christ-following circles—that is, "gospels."

One other term is worth noting. In the early second century, Papias claimed that Mark wrote down Peter's "memoirs" (*apomnēmoneumata*), and soon after Justin Martyr could refer to the "memoirs of the apostles" (*apomnēmoneumata tōn apostolōn*) being read out at the Eucharist.[9] Both authors were keen to link the gospels

6. Kelhoffer, "'How Soon'"; for discussion of the relevant texts in the Didache (specifically 8.2, 11.3–4, and 15.3–4), see 16–29. Stanton pushes things back even further still, arguing that the innovator was actually Matthew: when the Matthean Jesus refers to "*this* gospel of the Kingdom" (24:14, 26:13), Stanton argues, he has in mind his own, distinctive, and now written, version of Jesus's life; "Matthew," 1193–95. This is not impossible, though it is perhaps safer to go with Kelhoffer's more cautious dating.

7. Hengel, *Studies*, 83 perhaps overstates the case by suggesting that Mark's work represented a "revolutionary innovation," but it certainly seems instrumental in this change. See also D. E. Aune, *The New Testament in Its Literary Environment* (Philadelphia: Westminster, 1987), 17; U. Schnelle, *The History and Theology of the New Testament Writings* (Minneapolis: Fortress, 1998), 161 (who cites Hengel approvingly).

8. Curiously, perhaps, neither Luke nor John uses the noun *euangelion*, though Luke uses it twice in Acts and the verb ten times. Neither author has much to say about the genre of his work: in the preface to his first volume, Luke calls his work a "narrative" (a *diēgēsis*) of events—a general term that could cover any kind of written account. John refers to his efforts as a book or scroll, *biblion* (20:30), again a rather general term that leaves the precise genre of his work unspecified.

9. Justin, *First Apology* 67; the term is a favorite of Justin's, being used again in *First Apology* 66.3 and 67.3, and thirteen times in his *Dialogue with Trypho*, for example at 103.8 and 106.3.

with the reliable recollections of Jesus's first followers, and the term "memoirs" was clearly a useful one in that regard. Yet it is interesting that precisely the same word was used to designate Xenophon's biography of Socrates, known as his *Memorabilia* (= *apomnēmoneumata*).[10] Although "memoirs" was a rather loose literary genre, the use of the same term to refer to both Xenophon's collection of anecdotes relating to Socrates and to what were now known as Christian "gospels" does suggest that Papias and Justin, and presumably others, assumed that they belonged to the same category of broadly biographical literature.

The strongest piece of evidence that Mark was indeed read as a *bios*, however, comes from the way in which his work was received and expanded by Matthew and Luke. Both later authors added a genealogy to the earlier account, and both included elaborate birth stories that, in keeping with biographical expectations, act as precursors to the adult man. Luke even added a childhood story in which the twelve-year-old Jesus outshone the rulers of his day with his wisdom and scriptural interpretation (2:41–51). Both gospels too, in line with general expectations, include more detailed accounts of events following Jesus's death, now adding resurrection appearances to the Markan story of the empty tomb.[11] Assuming the general validity of the "two-document hypothesis," the fact that two later authors—quite independently—added elements that enhanced the biographical nature of the earlier text strongly suggests that they (and presumably most other audiences) understood that earlier text as a *bios*. They might have considered Mark's work to be deficient in a number of aspects—aspects that they themselves could easily remedy—but it was recognizably an attempt at a *bios* all the same.

And this general assumption seems to have continued into modern times. The establishment of Markan priority in the mid-nineteenth century encouraged a flood of "Lives of Jesus," based on what was now known to have been the earliest (and therefore, it was supposed, most reliable) of the gospels. While many of these tell us more about the concerns of their own age than the object of their study, their authors all took it for granted that the gospels were broadly biographical, albeit poor examples of the genre. Ernest Renan, for example, remarks that the gospels

10. Justin knew Xenophon's work; see *Second Apology* 11.2–3; for discussion, see Hengel, *Studies*, 65–67.

11. The rhetorical handbooks known as the *progymnasmata* suggest discussing "events after the death"; see M. W. Martin, "Progymnasmatic Topic Lists: A Composition Template for Luke and Other Bioi?," *NTS* 54 (2008): 18–41, esp. the table on 22. Even if neither evangelist was fully conversant with the rhetorical handbooks (a point we shall discuss in Chapter 3), their knowledge of other *bioi* may have suggested that more detail could be added at this point.

"are neither biographies after the manner of Suetonius, nor fictitious legends, after the manner of Philostratus; they are legendary biographies. I place them at once alongside of the legends of the saints, the lives of Plotinus, Proclus, Isidore, and other compositions of the same sort, in which historical truth and the desire to present models of virtue are combined in divers degrees."[12]

A full articulation of the case for regarding the gospels as *bioi*, however, was left to C. W. Votaw in two lengthy articles published in the *American Journal of Theology* in 1915. The Chicago professor compared the gospels to other "popular" biographies of intellectual leaders, specifically Plato and Xenophon on Socrates, Arrian on Epictetus, and Philostratus on Apollonius of Tyana. Votaw pointed out that each of these authors presented a selective and idealized account of the teaching of their hero, and that their interest was not so much antiquarian (that is, to provide a historical account) as to present their subject's way of life as relevant to their own times (that is, as one to be appreciated and emulated). In this broad aim, Votaw found significant parallels to the gospels, concluding that they too were biographical accounts written not simply to preserve tradition but to "accomplish practical results in the moral-religious sphere."[13]

Votaw's insights were hugely significant and deserved much fuller critical study. This, however, would have to wait for several decades. Scholars were on the brink of a new approach to the gospels that would advocate a very different understanding of both their composition and literary genre—form criticism.

The Eclipse of Biography

In Germany, the seeds of change had already been sown. Noting their rather primitive style, Franz Overbeck argued that the gospels had much more in common with oral folklore and sagas than with contemporary literature. He coined the term "Ur-literatur," meaning that the gospels were not designed for a wide literary audience, but rather for simple Christian congregations who were more interested in their content than their aesthetic merits. In Overbeck's view, it was only with the patristic writers that Christian authors began to participate in the popular literary genres of their day.[14] In a similar manner, Adolf Deissmann distinguished between what he

12. E. Renan, *The History of the Origins of Christianity. Book 1: Life of Jesus*, trans. from the 13th French ed. (Woodstock, Ont.: Devoted Publishing, 2016; orig. 1890), 23.

13. C. W. Votaw, "The Gospels and Contemporary Biography," *American Journal of Theology* 19 (1915): 223.

14. F. Overbeck, "Über die Anfänge der patristischen Literatur," *Historische Zeitschrift* 12 (1882): 417–72.

called "Kleinliteratur" (popular literature) and "Hochliteratur" (the high literature of the cultured elite). The gospels, he suggested, were examples of "Kleinliteratur" and were similar in style to the many unassuming papyrus documents emerging at the time from Egypt—basic letters, contracts, and popular literary efforts that provided a window onto the lives of ordinary people with only a rudimentary level of education.[15] Together, the views of Overbeck and Deissmann encouraged a distinction between consciously literary works indebted to a particular generic tradition, produced by and for educated circles ("Hochliteratur"), and works destined for the lower classes whose prime function was to act as depositories for oral material ("Urliteratur" or "Kleinliteratur"). This distinction would prove fundamental to the form critics, who would drive an even broader wedge between the gospels and the more literate compositions of their contemporaries.

The person who would do most to sever the identification of the gospels as ancient *bioi* was the form critic K. L. Schmidt. In a contribution to Herman Gunkel's Festschrift in 1923, titled "The Place of the Gospels in the General History of Literature," he tackled the question of gospel genre head on.[16] Dismissing Votaw's parallels as merely superficial, he stressed the differences between the gospels and Greco-Roman biography. Authors of the latter, he argued, present themselves as self-conscious litterateurs; their works describe the descent, family, education, and development of their hero; their portraits include a physical description, a note of character and personality, and an attempt to give a sense of the subject's motives, emotions, and private thoughts.[17] Philostratus's *Life of Apollonius of Tyana*, for example, has great literary pretensions: the authorial "I" is present throughout, the author gives a clear indication of the nature of the work and his use of sources, and strives for both completeness and a good literary style.

The gospels, he argued, are very different. Schmidt's own work on the frame-

15. A. Deissmann, *Light from the Ancient East: The New Testament Illustrated by Recently Discovered Texts of the Graeco-Roman World*, trans. L. R. M. Strachan (London: Hodder and Stoughton, 1927; German orig. 1908). Other critiques from this period include those of E. Norden, *Die antike Kunstprosa vom vi Jahrhundert vor Chr. bis in die Zeit der Renaissance* (Stuttgart: B. G. Teubner, 1978; orig. pub. 1898), 2:480–81; and P. Wendland, *Die Urchristliche Literaturformen*, 2nd ed. (Tübingen: Mohr Siebeck, 1912), who anticipated a number of form-critical points.

16. K. L. Schmidt, *The Place of the Gospels in the General History of Literature*, trans. B. R. McCane (Columbia: University of South Carolina Press, 2002; German orig. 1923); the English translation has a useful introduction by J. Riches.

17. We shall see later that Schmidt's overview of ancient *bioi* was rather too monolithic— few *bioi* exhibit all of these features, and it is rare to have much psychological development; see Chapter 2.

work of Mark's Gospel had convinced him that the evangelist was responsible only for the connecting material, and not for the units of tradition (or *pericopae*) themselves.[18] These units of tradition were essentially the *kerygma* of the early church—lively, oral preaching material that had been shaped according to the needs of various congregations and largely preserved in cultic settings. The contribution of the evangelists was simply to gather material together. Thus for Schmidt, as indeed for all the form critics, Mark and his followers were not creative authors, but collectors, compilers, and editors. The uneducated nature of most believers in this early period, along with their intensely apocalyptic outlook, meant that it would be some time before Christians engaged in anything other than simply preserving tradition. The gospels for Schmidt were to be relegated to the level identified by Deissmann as "Kleinliteratur." The closest analogies, therefore, were not consciously literary works such as biographies, but rather collections of folktales and oral sayings, similar to the Homeric literature or the stories found in the Pentateuch. Schmidt summed up his views succinctly: "*a Gospel is by nature not high literature, but low literature; not the product of an individual author, but a folk book; not a biography, but a cult legend.*"[19]

Rudolf Bultmann was even clearer. For him, the gospels were without parallel, "a unique phenomenon in the history of literature."[20] Mark in particular, as the first to be written, was "an original creation of Christianity."[21] The gospels were, in short, sui generis—in a class of their own, or unique.

Not everyone of course agreed with the form critics, and some scholars, particularly those outside Germany, offered rather less radical views of gospel formation.[22] But the form critics were to set the tone of the debate for the next half a century: it could no longer be asserted without qualification that the gospels were biographies.[23]

In many respects, the views of the form critics suited the spirit of their time. By

18. K. L. Schmidt, *Der Rahmen der Geschichte Jesu: Literarkritische Untersuchungen zur ältesten Jesusüberlieferung* (Berlin: Trowitzsch, 1919).

19. Schmidt, *Place of the Gospels*, 27 (italics original).

20. The quotation is from R. Bultmann, "The Gospels (Form)" (trans. R. A. Wilson), in *Twentieth Century Theology in the Making*, ed. J. Pelikan (London: Fontana, 1969–70), 1:86–92; see also R. Bultmann, *A History of the Synoptic Tradition*, trans. J. Marsh (Oxford: Blackwell, 1968), 371–74.

21. Bultmann, *History*, 74; see also 347–48.

22. See, for example, the works of C. H. Dodd, *History and the Gospel* (New York: Scribner's, 1938), and B. H. Branscomb, *The Gospel of Mark* (London: Hodder and Stoughton, 1937), xix (who seems blissfully unaware of developments in mainland Europe).

23. S. Walton gathers quotations from representative authors during this period in "What

the 1920s and 1930s, Europe had experienced both the Great War and the period of intense social and economic upheaval that followed it. Unsurprisingly, societal changes were to have a profound effect on literary endeavors, not least on the writing of biography. The highly moralistic, almost hagiographic, biographies of the Victorian era were giving way to "new biography" (to use Virginia Woolf's term). An interest in the heroic public deeds of famous individuals was now replaced by an intense preoccupation with psychology and an often irreverent wit, as exemplified by the work of Lytton Strachey. Rather than presenting their subjects as exemplary models of virtue, biographers were now far more interested in exposing their subject's nature in all its variety and irrationality. Sigmund Freud showed the important role that psychology, early upbringing, and sexual proclivities might have on a person's life, and ensured that an exploration of these topics would quickly be seen as central to any biographical endeavor.[24]

The debate, of course, centered on whether the gospels were *ancient* biographies (as Schmidt made clear), but people are always more easily persuaded of the truth of something if it coheres with their own experience. If the gospels could hold their own against Victorian biography, the same was not true of the very different type of biography emerging in the 1920s and 1930s. With their almost complete disinterest in Jesus's inner personality, psychology, and private life, the gospels fit less readily with what most people meant by "biography." More positively, perhaps, the form critics could find support for their position within the guild of literary criticism. In an effort to resist a rigid understanding of genre in terms of a prescriptive taxonomy, literary critics of the period were inclined to think in terms of there being only one genre, which encompassed all literary creations, or of an endless multiplicity of genres, with every work being in some sense unique, or sui generis.[25] Within this intellectual climate, the claim that the gospels were distinctive and set apart from other types of literature was not unduly remarkable.

A further point to note is that the claim that the gospels are "unique" has always had a particular appeal to scholars of a more conservative persuasion—a unique

Are the Gospels? Richard Burridge's Impact on Scholarly Understanding of the Genre of the Gospels," *CBQ* 14 (2015): 83–85.

24. For an overview of biography through the ages, see A. Shelston, *Biography* (London: Methuen, 1977); N. Hamilton, *Biography: A Brief History* (Cambridge, MA: Harvard University Press, 2007); and H. Lee, *Biography: A Very Short Introduction* (Oxford: Oxford University Press, 2009). For an excellent collection of individual studies written by biographers, see E. Homberger and J. Charmley, eds., *The Troubled Face of Biography* (London: Macmillan, 1988); also instructive here is V. Woolf, *The Art of Biography—A Collection of Essays* (London: Reed Books, 2011; orig. 1927).

25. See Frow, *Genre*, 26–28, who links this development to post-Romanticism and the work of Friedrich Schlegel.

form for a unique message. While many of these scholars would have had little sympathy with the highly radical views of the form critics, the idea that the gospels were unlike anything else in the surrounding culture was an attractive one. It is hardly surprising that some chose to accept this particular form-critical argument even while rejecting the broader framework to which it belonged. (And perhaps part of the enduring appeal of the sui generis position is that it posits a uniqueness at the heart of the Christian gospels.) Thus, the view established itself that the gospels were without analogy in the ancient world, that they represented a spontaneous creation of a new literary form with few precursors—in short, a completely new genre.

As the twentieth century wore on, however, a number of form-critical assumptions began to be challenged, several of which had a bearing on the gospel genre. In terms of social class, it became increasingly apparent that the earliest Christians were not confined to the lower ranks of society, as Deissmann in particular had argued, but that the movement was largely urban and "dominated by a socially pretentious section of the population."[26] Some undoubtedly belonged to lower socioeconomic levels, but others might have belonged to the ranks of free craftspeople, artisans, and small traders. Others still might have been reasonably affluent, owning houses and slaves and possessing the ability to travel (in this regard we might think of wealthy converts in Corinth such as Chloe or Stephanas). Such people might have been educated themselves, or at least had access to literary texts through friends or slaves. At all events, they would have had no difficulty in understanding and appreciating the literary conventions of their day.

Furthermore, it became increasingly apparent that the form critics were operating with a rather romantic view of "primitive" folk communities, drawn from nineteenth-century studies that were themselves being challenged.[27] Although literacy rates were

---

26. So, for example, E. A. Judge, *The Social Pattern of the Christian Groups in the First Century* (London: Tyndale, 1960), 60. Subsequent studies tended to reinforce this judgment—see G. Theissen, *The Social Setting of Pauline Christianity* (Philadelphia: Fortress, 1978); W. Meeks, *The First Urban Christians: The Social World of the Apostle Paul* (New Haven: Yale University Press, 1983), 51–73; R. L. Rohrbaugh, "Methodological Considerations in the Debate over Social Class Status of Early Christians," *JAAR* 52 (1984): 519–46; and R. Stark, "The Class Basis of Early Christianity: Influences from a Sociological Model," *Sociological Analysis* 47 (1986): 216–25—though a number of recent studies have argued for a rather less elevated group; see for example J. J. Meggitt, *Paul, Poverty and Survival* (Edinburgh: T&T Clark, 1998) and B. Longenecker, "Socio-Economic Profiling of the First Urban Christians," in *After the First Urban Christians: The Social Scientific Study of Early Christianity Twenty-Five Years Later*, ed. D. Horrell and T. Still (London: T&T Clark, 2009), 36–59.

27. So H. Gamble, *Books and Readers in the Early Church: A History of Early Christian Texts* (New Haven: Yale University Press, 1995), 20.

extremely low in the first century, it would be wrong to characterize the early Christian context as an "oral society." Theirs was a world that knew of books and writing. The sheer volume of papyrus letters from the first century indicates that written communication was by no means unusual. Jews in particular had a long and rich written tradition and a practice of gathering together in weekly meetings or at festivals to hear those texts read out, interpreted, and made relevant to their daily needs.[28] Nor should we assume that apocalyptically minded groups eschewed literature: the wealth of Jewish apocalypses from this period, not to mention the abundance of texts from Qumran, showed that apocalyptic expectation was no bar to the production of texts.

Perhaps the form-critical view to be challenged most decisively over the last few decades, however, has been their assumption that the evangelists were little more than compilers and editors. By the mid-twentieth century, redaction critics were increasingly arguing that Mark's Gospel was consciously shaped by an intelligent author with a specific theological agenda, a view that would be enhanced significantly by narrative critics from the 1970s onward. It soon became clear that rigid distinctions between "Klein-" and "Hochliteratur" were no longer useful. The evangelists might not have the elegance and artistry of a Tacitus, a Suetonius, or a Plutarch, but that did not mean that their work had no literary value or artistic merit.

Wider structural changes within universities played their part too. By the 1970s, the expansion of higher education in the Anglophone world led to the rise of departments of religion in the United States and of religious studies in the United Kingdom. Scholars now increasingly found themselves operating not simply in traditional "New Testament" departments but in much more interdisciplinary contexts, sharing space with sociologists, anthropologists, and philosophers. It is probably no great coincidence that this period saw a resurgence of the old "history of religions" school (*Religionsgeschichtliche Schule*), with its emphasis on the degree to which early Christian writings were the products of their religious, cultural, and socioeconomic milieus. A number of classic works were now translated into English for the first time, among them Wilhelm Bousset's *Kyrios Christos* and William Wrede's *The Messianic Secret*.[29] Along with the rise of sociological approaches to

---

28. See J. Assmann, "Form as a Mnemonic Device: Cultural Texts and Cultural Memory," in *Performing the Gospel: Orality, Memory and Mark; Essays Dedicated to Werner Kelber*, ed. R. A. Horsley, J. A. Draper, and J. M. Foley (Minneapolis: Fortress, 2006), 78. For fuller discussion of the ideas in this paragraph, see below, pp. 78–80.

29. W. Bousset, *Kyrios Christos: A History of the Belief in Christ from the Beginnings of Christianity to Irenaeus*, trans. J. E. Steely (Nashville: Abingdon, 1970; German orig. 1913); W. Wrede, *The Messianic Secret*, trans. J. C. G. Grieg (Cambridge: Clarke, 1971; German orig. 1901).

the biblical texts, these developments situated early Christianity firmly within a realistic ancient Mediterranean context. Scholars now envisaged members of the new faith participating in the world around them, aware of the prevailing cultures, and responding and adapting to external pressures. Viewed through this lens, the idea of the "uniqueness" of Christian documents seemed faintly quaint and anachronistic. If Paul had been happy to communicate with newly founded churches through the common literary form of letters, why should the evangelists have been any different?

Simultaneously with all these developments, literary theorists were becoming increasingly interested in the topic of genre, and their findings were spreading to biblical critics. It gradually became clear that the idea of a unique genre made no sense. Texts need to employ conventional methods to communicate meaning; they can adapt and transform what they use (and frequently do), but the idea that any written piece could hope to convey ideas through an entirely new genre seemed unlikely. The primary purpose of the gospels was surely to communicate—and an entirely novel form would have been unintelligible to Christ followers and outsiders alike. The old form-critical view that the gospels were a unique literary phenomenon was becoming unsustainable.

By the 1970s and 1980s, then, a new intellectual climate had emerged in which scholars began to look for generic antecedents to the gospels. Votaw's essays on the gospels as biographies were republished,[30] but was the Greco-Roman world the best place to look for analogies? Given the *Jewish* context out of which Christianity developed, the most obvious place to start the search was within the Jewish world itself. Yet parallels here were far less compelling than we might expect.

A Jewish Background?

The Hebrew Bible contains what we might call "biographical episodes" structured around certain key figures—Abraham (Gen 12–25), Jacob (Gen 25–26), Joseph (Gen 37–50), Moses (Exod–Deut), David (1 Sam 16–2 Sam 5), and Elijah/Elisha (1 Kgs 17–2 Kgs 13). Yet in all of these cases, the biblical authors' interests focus less on the characters themselves as the part they play in the wider story of God's relationship with Israel.[31] And although there are a number of books bearing the

---

30. C. W. Votaw, *The Gospels and Contemporary Biographies in the Greco-Roman World* (Philadelphia: Fortress, 1970).

31. So Aune, *Literary Environment*, 36–45; G. Strecker, *History of New Testament Literature*, trans. C. Katter with H.-J. Mollenhauer (Harrisburg, PA: Trinity Press International, 1997; German orig. 1992), 106–7; also A. D. H. Mayes, "Biography in the Ancient World:

name of individuals, both in the Hebrew Bible and the Apocrypha (Ruth, Esther, Judith, and Tobit), none of these provides a particularly close match for the gospels—they tend to focus on a particular incident in the protagonist's life, rather than the story of their career and death. The prophetic books, too, despite bearing the names of individual prophets, are largely concerned with preserving the words of God rather than providing us with accounts of the prophets' lives. The central theme of the entire Jewish Scriptures is God and God's saving relationship with Israel; human characters are important only insofar as they play a role within this wider story.

A similar phenomenon is at work within rabbinic literature. Although sayings and stories attributed to individual rabbis are plentiful, there is never any attempt to provide a sustained account of the lives and activities of individual sages. The focus of those who compiled the rabbinic corpus was on the Torah and scholarly attempts to extricate its meaning, not on the rabbinic teachers themselves. As Philip Alexander notes, none of the sages held the same place within rabbinic tradition as Jesus did within Christian thought, and attempts to raise their lives to a higher level of visibility would have seemed misplaced.[32] Thus rabbinic literature gives us no real parallels to the gospels. Nor did those gathered by the Dead Sea at Qumran write a biography of their "Teacher of Righteousness" (much to the frustration of modern scholars).

Jewish analogies to the gospels only really begin to appear in postbiblical times. Martyr texts, for example, became popular after the persecution of Antiochus IV Epiphanes in the second century BCE. Most famous here is the account of the Maccabean martyrs in 2 Macc 6:18–7:42, a story written to encourage Jews to remain faithful to their ancestral traditions. The genre of the testament, or prolonged deathbed scene, also comes to prominence in this period. The first-century *Life of Adam and Eve*, for example, is a midrashic account of certain episodes in the lives

---

The Story of the Rise of David," in *The Limits of Ancient Biography*, ed. B. C. McGing and J. Mossman (Swansea: Classical Press of Wales, 2006), 1–12. For a more positive assessment of the biographical features of these accounts, however, see K. Baltzer, *Die Biographie der Propheten* (Neukirchen-Vluyn: Neukirchener Verlag, 1975).

32. P. Alexander, "Rabbinic Biography and the Biography of Jesus," in *Synoptic Studies*, ed. C. Tuckett (Sheffield: JSOT Press, 1984), 19–50. A number of scholars sought parallels in Jewish synagogue practices, suggesting that the gospels grew up in the context of early Christian worship and were designed as lectionary readings throughout the liturgical year. P. Carrington, for example, suggested that Mark was based on a Jewish liturgical calendar, and M. Goulder and E. Guilding presented similar theories for Matthew and John, respectively. The difficulties with this approach, however, are outlined by Aune, *Literary Environment*, 26–27.

of the first humans, and includes deathbed recollections and instructions, involving repentance and a return to paradise.[33] Another first-century text is the Palestinian *Lives of the Prophets*, a work that offers encomiastic sketches of the lives of twenty-three prophets (the three major and twelve minor, along with Daniel and a number who do not have their own book, such as Elijah and Elisha). In each case, the author gives the prophet's name, place of origin, manner of death, and place of burial. Six of the prophets were martyred, though the author does not reflect upon this theologically, nor is he interested in the prophets as ethical teachers. When he pauses to tell an anecdote, it tends to be a miracle or a prophecy, and it is usually connected to the site of the prophet's burial. In fact, the main purpose of the collection seems to have been to provide a list of the burial sites of the prophets and (where appropriate) their memorials. This may have been part of the same impetus to commemorate the dead that led Herod I to construct an expensive white marble memorial at the entrance to David's tomb (Josephus, *Jewish Antiquities* 16.182).[34] At all events what we have here is an emerging interest in the lives—and particularly the deaths—of characters from Israel's past, not only for the part they play in the story of God's dealings with Israel, but to some extent as characters in their own right.[35]

Perhaps the closest Jewish parallel to the gospels is Philo's *Life of Moses*. The Alexandrian philosopher wrote a number of biographies of the patriarchs. Those on Abraham and Joseph are marked by a heavy use of allegory and were probably intended for a Jewish audience. The *Life of Moses*, however, is quite different in method and style. It is addressed to gentiles, and although Philo notes that the great Lawgiver had his detractors (*Life of Moses* 1.1–2),[36] the work is less interested

---

33. For the text (now extant in later Greek and Latin versions), see M. D. Johnson, "*Life of Adam and Eve*: A New Translation and Introduction," in *The Old Testament Pseudepigrapha*, ed. J. H. Charlesworth (New York: Doubleday, 1985), 2:249–95; see also the review article of W. Zemler-Cizewski, "The Apocryphal Life of Adam and Eve: Recent Scholarly Work," *AThR* 86 (2004): 671–77.

34. So D. R. A. Hare, "*The Lives of the Prophets*: A New Translation and Introduction," in Charlesworth, *The Old Testament Pseudepigrapha*, 2:379–99. Luke 11:47//Matt 23:29 refer to building tombs for prophets at this period, and the list of ways in which prophets were executed in Heb 11:37 (stoned, sawn in half, and beheaded) seems to reflect similar traditions and interests to those present in the *Lives of the Prophets*.

35. The first part of the *Ascension of Isaiah* (chapters 1–5, excluding 3.13–4.22, often referred to as the *Martyrdom of Isaiah*), if dependent on an earlier Jewish source, may reflect a similar interest in the death of a prophet. The book in its present state, however, is clearly Christian and generally dated to the early second century.

36. The comment regarding detractors may simply be a literary convention, one that neatly supplies Philo with an excuse for writing his biography.

in rebutting misapprehensions than in presenting an idealized account of its hero. As Louis Feldman notes, Philo presents "an official biography of Moses," one that reveals him as an ideal king, Lawgiver, high priest, and prophet (*Life of Moses* 2.2–7), and that indirectly praises the Jewish faith through its most famous figure.[37]

There are a number of important similarities here with Josephus's retelling of the Scriptures in his *Jewish Antiquities*. Although couched in a historical framework, the narrative (at least until the reign of Herod I) is largely a series of quasi-biographies, each crafted around a specific patriarch, prophet, or king. Josephus draws on Hellenistic tropes and conventions in describing his heroes' characters. Almost without exception they are of good birth, handsome, and precocious. They also exhibit the four cardinal virtues—wisdom, courage, temperance, and justice—along with piety and wealth.[38] Readers are to see that the founders and leaders of the Jewish faith are every bit as impressive as their Greek or Roman equivalents. Josephus's tendency to minimize the role of God in favor of highlighting the actions of his heroes also injects a much more biographical feel into the narrative when compared with the biblical original.[39] Rather than the "story of Israel," we are presented with a subtly different account of the "great men of Israel's past."

All of the Jewish texts mentioned in the last few paragraphs have been thoroughly influenced by Hellenistic literary conventions, with Philo being the most thoroughgoing example.[40] Jews of course borrowed heavily from Hellenism in this period, and it is natural to find authors looking to Greco-Roman models for their work. The clearest Jewish analogies to the gospels emerge once Hellenistic literary conventions begin to exert an influence, particularly the genre of biography. It is not surprising, then, that large numbers of scholars have seen the closest generic precedent for Mark not so much within Jewish literary genres as within Greco-Roman biography.

Before we leave the question of Jewish antecedents, and for the sake of clarity,

37. See L. H. Feldman, *Philo's Portrayal of Moses in the Context of Ancient Judaism* (Notre Dame: University of Notre Dame Press, 2007); the quotation here is from p. 7.

38. See the summary in L. H. Feldman, *Studies in Josephus' Rewritten Bible* (Leiden: Brill, 1998), 546–51.

39. See again Feldman, *Studies*, 568. It is also worth at least noting Josephus's autobiography, the *Life*, which was added as an appendix to the second edition of his *Jewish Antiquities*, published around 100 CE. Heavily apologetic, the work was composed largely in response to a hostile account of Josephus's war record put out by his rival Justus of Tiberias. For more on the *Life*, see S. Mason, *Life of Josephus* (Boston: Brill, 2003).

40. His work shows an indebtedness to early Greek models, particularly Isocrates and Xenophon (on both, see the next chapter), and bases Moses's ideal qualities on those advocated by Plato, *Republic* 5.473D. See Feldman, *Philo's Portrayal*, 7.

it is useful to distinguish here between *content* and *genre*. There is no doubt that the Jewish Scriptures have exerted a profound influence on the *content* of the Jesus story, both on the gospels themselves and, at an earlier stage, on the traditions that the evangelists inherited. Mark clearly drew on broad scriptural themes of monotheism, election, and covenant, and developed ideas and images from the prophetic literature and elsewhere. The Jewish roots of his portrait of Jesus are not in dispute. It is in terms of his selection of an appropriate literary *genre*, however—in the specific literary format of his work—that Mark turned his sights to the wider Greco-Roman world.

The Return of Greco-Roman Biography

Over the last few decades, the view that the gospels are a type of ancient biography has gradually gained ground. Early work was hampered by attempts to link the gospels with one particular strand of biographical tradition. Moses Hadas, Morton Smith, and Helmut Koester, for example, argued that the gospels were "aretalogies" (narrative accounts of the miraculous deeds of a god or hero),[41] while Philip Shuler identified the gospels as *encomia* (eulogies).[42] Another early pioneer was Charles Talbert, who came at the problem from a rather different direction. In *What Is a Gospel?* (1977), he attempted to undermine the form-critical objections to identifying the gospels as biographies,[43] concluding that Mark was indeed a particular type

41. M. Hadas, *Hellenistic Culture: Fusion and Diffusion* (New York: Columbia University Press, 1959), chap. 13; M. Hadas and M. Smith, *Heroes and Gods: Spiritual Biographies in Antiquity* (New York: Harper and Row, 1965); also H. Koester, "One Jesus and Four Gospels," *HTR* 61 (1968): 230–36; and M. Smith, "Prolegomena to a Discussion of Aretalogies, Divine Men, the Gospels and Jesus," *JBL* 90 (1971): 174–99. Quite apart from the problematic notion of a "divine man," which lies at the heart of this, however, there is little evidence that "aretalogy" formed a distinct genre; for evaluation of this position, see H. C. Kee, "Aretalogy and Gospel," *JBL* 92 (1973): 402–22.
42. P. L. Shuler, *A Genre for the Gospels: The Biographical Character of Matthew* (Philadelphia: Fortress, 1982). Reviewers of Shuler's work tended to see his focus on encomiastic biography as too narrow. Many of the features he identified as crucial to the encomium were shared in fact by biographical literature more broadly (for example techniques of amplification and comparison); and while praise was certainly a feature of the gospels, the central purpose of eliciting *faith* seemed to require a broader category than was offered by encomium; see, for example, Stanton, "Matthew: βίβλιος, εὐαγγέλιον, βίος," 1198–99.
43. C. H. Talbert, *What Is a Gospel? The Genre of the Canonical Gospels* (Philadelphia: Fortress, 1977). Drawing largely on the work of Bultmann, he identified three "pillars" undergirding the form-critical view: (1) that the gospels exhibit a mythical worldview; (2) that

of ancient biography, "written to defend against a misunderstanding of the church's savior and to portray a true image of him for the disciples to follow."[44] Reviews of Talbert's work were mixed,[45] but his short book captured the scholarly imagination and served to relaunch the question of gospel genre in a decisive way.[46]

The 1980s saw a number of contributions to the topic, particularly in Germany, with 1984 standing as something of a high-water mark. This year saw two publications by Hubert Cancik. In the first, "Die Gattung Evangelium," Cancik pointed to the differences between modern biographies and ancient *bioi*, noting that the latter tended to have strongly pedagogical aims, often presenting the life and character of the protagonist as something to be imitated. Anecdotes, sayings, fictitious embellishments, and often martyrdom were all commonly used to further the biographer's aims. While Jewish audiences would have also connected the life of Jesus to those of the prophets, Cancik concluded that gentiles would have simply read Mark's work as a *bios*, albeit a rather exotic one. In a second article, Cancik compared Mark with Lucian's *Demonax*, noting similarities in terms of the two works' structure and aims.[47] The same year, two articles appeared in the influential *Aufsteig und Niedergang der Römischen Welt*. In an article on Hellenistic genres in the New Testament, Klaus Berger concluded that the closest analogy to the gospels were ancient *bioi*,[48] while Detlev Dormeyer and Hubert Frankemölle analyzed the development of the term "gospel" in the New Testament and later writings, surveyed the generic labels attached to the gospels throughout the centuries, and offered some observations on Mark as an ancient *bios*.[49]

---

they emerged in a cultic setting; and (3) that they emerged from communities with a world-negating outlook inconducive to literary productivity. He argued that the first two pillars could apply equally to other biographies, while the third was untrue.

44. Talbert, *What Is a Gospel?*, 134.

45. The severest criticism came from D. E. Aune, who accused him of charging into unfamiliar territory; "Review of C. H. Talbert," in *Gospel Perspectives*, 2:9–60.

46. Other early works on biography include J. Drury who, in a published lecture, referred to Mark as a "rough, abrasive biography": "What Are the Gospels?," *ExpTim* 87 (1976): 324–28.

47. H. Cancik, "Die Gattung Evangelium: Das Evangelium des Markus im Rahmen der antiken Historiographie," in *Markus—Philologie*, ed. H. Cancik (Tübingen: Mohr Siebeck, 1984), 85–113; H. Cancik, "Bios und Logos: Formgeschichtliche Untersuchungen zu Lukians 'Demonax,'" in Cancik, *Markus*, 115–30.

48. K. Berger, "Hellenistische Gattungen im NT," *ANRW* II 25.2:1031–1432.

49. D. Dormeyer and H. Frankemölle, "Evangelium als literarische Gattung und als theologischer Begriff. Tendenzen und Aufgaben der Evangelienforschung im 20. Jahrhundert, mit einer Untersuchung des Markusevangeliums in seinem Verhältnis zur antiken Biogra-

In the United States, Vernon Robbins compared Mark with Xenophon's *Memorabilia*, detecting in both works similar cycles of relationships and conversations from the calling of the disciples to the death of the teacher. Although there are also significant differences between the two texts, Robbins concluded that the "basic impulse that underlies Xenophon's *Memorabilia* and the Gospel of Mark is the portrayal of a religio-ethical teacher manifesting his adult role through interaction with those around him."[50] Some years later, in an important survey, *The New Testament in Its Literary Environment* (1987), David Aune identified the gospels as a modified form of *bioi*; Hellenistic in terms of form and function, but Jewish in terms of content. He stressed the complexity and flexibility of *bios* as a genre and showed that—despite their idiosyncrasies—the gospels could be situated comfortably within the parameters of ancient biographical conventions.[51]

Perhaps the most significant contribution to the discussion, however, came from a British scholar, Richard Burridge, in 1992.[52] While other studies tended to compare a gospel with one specific biography, or to range freely over biographies generally, Burridge compared the gospels to ten roughly contemporary *bioi* (five from before the probable date of the gospels, and five from after). Each was analyzed under four headings: (1) its opening features, (2) its subject, (3) its external features—meter, length, structure, scale, literary units, use of sources, and methods of characterization—and (4) its internal features—setting, topics/motifs, style, tone,

phie," *ANRW* II 25.2:1543–1704. See also Frankemölle's *Evangelium—Begriff und Gattung: Ein Forschungsbericht* (Stuttgart: Katholisches Bibelwerk, 1988).

50. V. Robbins, *Jesus the Teacher: A Socio-Rhetorical Study of Mark* (Philadelphia: Fortress, 1984).

51. Aune, *Literary Environment*, esp. 46–76; see also "The Gospels as Hellenistic Biography," *Mosaic* 20 (1987): 1–10. More recently, Aune has argued that Mark wrote in reaction to Greco-Roman biography rather than as a simple emulation of it, that it is, in effect, a parody of the biographical genre; D. E. Aune, "Genre Theory and the Genre-Function of Mark and Matthew," in *Mark and Matthew I, Comparative Readings: Understanding the Earliest Gospels in Their First-Century Setting*, ed. E.-M. Becker and A. Runesson (Tübingen: Mohr Siebeck, 2011), 145–75. There is no doubt that Mark promotes the countercultural social and religious values of first-century Christians (a fact we shall come back to several times in subsequent chapters), but "parody" itself is not a genre, and it is perfectly possible to satirize the standards of society while still employing a well-known genre to do it (the *Life of Aesop* is a case in point).

52. R. A. Burridge, *What Are the Gospels? A Comparison with Graeco-Roman Biography* (Cambridge: Cambridge University Press, 1992). In subsequent notes, I shall refer to the third edition (Waco: Baylor University Press, 2018), which helpfully retains the original pagination.

MARK AS A *BIOS*

quality of characterization, social setting and occasion, and authorial intention and purpose.[53] Not all of these features were present in every example, but there was enough similarity throughout the group as a whole to be able to demonstrate a "family resemblance." The strength of Burridge's approach was to show that in order to be classified as *bioi* the gospels do not have to cohere in every respect with a chosen biography (or even a group of biographies); all they need is to be broadly within the range of acceptable variables.

What distinguished a *bios*, for Burridge, was its concentration on the life (and usually the death) of one individual. After this, however, there could be a great deal of variety. An author might choose to adopt a broadly chronological approach or a topical one, or a mixture of the two. A biographer might aim for even coverage throughout the life or might choose to emphasize one particular period at the expense of others. This would naturally be the most notable feature of the life, for example Tacitus's account of Agricola's victory at Mons Graupius (which takes up 26 percent of the narrative), or Xenophon on Agesilaus's Persian campaign (a substantial 37 percent). A common argument against identifying the gospels as *bioi* is the space and importance given to Jesus's death (particularly in Mark),[54] but Burridge showed that several *bioi* placed an equally strong emphasis on their hero's death: Plutarch described the death of Cato at length, as did Cornelius Nepos in his account of Atticus, while Philostratus devoted a quarter of his narrative to the trial and death of Apollonius of Tyana.[55] There was clearly a great deal of flexibility in the manner in which ancient biographers went about their craft; viewed from this angle, the gospels fit comfortably within the acceptable range of variables within the genre as a whole.

Integral to Burridge's approach is his attention to genre theory. He stresses that genre is not a fixed entity, slavishly obeying set rules and rigid requirements, but rather something fluid and elastic—a "flexible set of expectations," ready to be molded in a variety of ways by a creative author. Genre is a "dynamic and flexible grouping whose boundaries and labels shift."[56] We should not expect every feature of Mark to line up perfectly against a biographical "ideal," any more than a work by Plutarch, Suetonius, or any other author would do so. It is in the nature of writing,

---

53. See particularly Burridge, *What Are the Gospels?*, 105–23.

54. So M. Edwards, "Gospel and Genre: Some Reservations," in *The Limits of Ancient Biography*, ed. B. C. McGing and J. Mossman (Swansea: Classical Press of Wales, 2006), 51–75.

55. The exact figures are 17.3 percent for the death of Cato, 15 percent for Nepos, and (when we include the hero's trial) 26.3 percent for Apollonius. See Burridge, *What Are the Gospels?*, 133, 160, and 163.

56. The quotations are from Burridge, *What Are the Gospels?*, 54, 47. So also Aune, "Genre Theory."

and of creative authors, that they will play with a genre, sometimes pushing it to its limits. Furthermore, we should not be surprised to find some generic crossover. By New Testament times, the boundaries between different types of prose narrative had become a little blurred. Nestled in the intersection between "history, encomium and moral philosophy," *bioi* might easily take on features from any of these complementary genres.[57] We should hardly be surprised to find that scholars have detected features of these other genres within the gospels: Mark's plot may occasionally contain motifs drawn from Greek tragedy,[58] ancient novels, history, or apocalyptic literature. None of these features, however, alters the fact that the gospel most readily finds a home in the broad spectrum of works collectively termed "biography."[59] All they show is an author who did not feel bound by any particular convention and who was happy to draw on a range of material and traditions.

Research subsequent to Burridge has tended to reinforce his conclusions.[60] That is not to say, of course, that all have been convinced. Several scholars continue to have reservations, preferring to see Mark as some kind of historical mono-

---

57. Burridge, *What Are the Gospels?*, 54, 67. For similar sentiments, see also Aune, "Genre Theory," 149–52; J. Fitzgerald, "The Ancient Lives of Aristotle and the Modern Debate about the Genre of the Gospels," *Restoration Quarterly* (1994): 209–21; C. B. R. Pelling, "Breaking the Bounds: Writing about Julius Caesar," in *The Limits of Ancient Biography*, ed. B. C. McGing and J. Mossman (Swansea: Classical Press of Wales, 2006), 256; and the introduction by the editors in McGing and Mossman, *Limits*, ix–xx.

58. So, for example, B. H. M. G. M. Standaert, *L'Evangile selon Marc: Composition at Genre Litteraire* (Nijmegen: Stichting Studentenpers, 1978); A. Stock, *Call to Discipleship: A Literary Study of Mark's Gospel* (Wilmington, DE: Michael Glazier, 1982); M. A. Beavis, *Mark's Audience: The Literary and Social History of Mark 4.11–12* (Sheffield: JSOT Press, 1989).

59. Aune perceptively notes that most criticisms of the *bioi* theory come from those who hold too inflexible an idea of genre; "Genre Theory," 167.

60. D. Frickenschmidt, in a virtually comprehensive philological study, compared the gospels to 142 biographical works from the same time period and concluded, similarly to Burridge, that the gospels belonged to the same literary family; *Evangelium als Biographie: Die vier Evangelien im Rahmen antiker Erzählkunst* (Tübingen: Francke, 1997). See also A. Dihle, "The Gospels and Greek Biography," in *The Gospel and the Gospels*, ed. P. Stuhlmacher (Grand Rapids: Eerdmans, 1991), 361–86 (though with some misgivings); and C. Bryan, *A Preface to Mark: Notes on the Gospel in Its Literary and Cultural Settings* (New York: Oxford University Press, 1993), 9–64. For surveys of work since 1992, see Burridge's second edition of *What Are the Gospels?*, 96–104; also Walton, "What Are the Gospels?," 81–93; and most recently the introductory essay to Burridge's third edition of *What Are the Gospels?*, 1.1–112.

graph,[61] a novel,[62] or something less determinate.[63] But the pendulum has certainly swung decisively in favor of seeing the gospels as ancient biographies. A number of introductions to the New Testament now present the gospels to students as biographies. Those using Bart Ehrman's hugely popular New Testament textbook, for example, will read that "the Gospels are best seen as a kind of Greco-Roman (as opposed to modern) biography."[64] The *Blackwell Companion to the New Testament* pronounces the gospels to be "a subgenre of the ancient Greco-Roman biography, or *bios*."[65] And not only the scholarly *Anchor Bible Dictionary* (1992) but both the revised *New Interpreters' Bible Dictionary* (2007) and the second edition of the *Dictionary of Jesus and the Gospels* (2013) note that the gospels are seen by most

61. Although writing about Luke-Acts, G. Sterling identifies an oriental "apologetic historiography" to which Josephus's *Jewish Antiquities* also belongs; *Historiography and Self-Definition: Josephus, Luke-Acts and Apologetic Historiography*, NovTSupp 64 (Leiden: Brill, 1991). A. Y. Collins regards Mark as "an apocalyptic historical monograph" in the manner of 1 Enoch, Daniel, the Qumran pesharim, and Josephus; see *Is Mark's Gospel a Life of Jesus? The Question of Genre* (Milwaukee: Marquette University Press, 1990). More recently, E.-M. Becker has identified the gospel as Greco-Roman historiography; *Das Markus-Evangelium im Rahmen Antiker Historiographie* (Tübingen: Mohr Siebeck, 2006); C. C. Black recognizes Mark as a *bios*, but sees this as a "species of the genus *historia*"; "Mark as Historian of God's Kingdom," *CBQ* 71 (2009): 64–83.

62. M. A. Tolbert sees it as a popular Hellenistic novel or romance; *Sowing the Gospel: Mark's World in Literary-Historical Perspective* (Minneapolis: Fortress, 1989). M. E. Vines, on the other hand, wants to find the background to Mark in Jewish literature and concludes that the gospel is a (Jewish) novel; *The Problem of Markan Genre: The Gospel of Mark and the Jewish Novel*, Academia Biblical 3 (Atlanta: Scholars Press, 2002).

63. N. Petersen argues that the gospels do not all belong to the same genre; it is more helpful, he suggests, to think of "plot type," such that Mark (for example) is an example of a "concealment/recognition type" ("Can One Speak of a Gospel Genre?," *Neot* 28 [1994]: 153). M. Edwards, too, doubts that Mark is a *bios*, regarding not only the amount of space devoted to the passion but also the number of miracles in Mark as problematic; "Gospel and Genre: Some Reservations," 51–75. And J. Marcus suggests that Mark is a "dramatization of the good news that was originally staged in the context of a Christian worship service"; although features from drama, *bios*, and biblical histories all feature within the work, Marcus contends that it is essentially "a new creation because of its close links with the Christian liturgical setting"; *Mark 1–8*, AYB (New Haven: Yale University Press, 2002), 69.

64. B. Ehrman, *The New Testament: A Historical Introduction to the Early Christian Writings*, 5th ed. (Oxford: Oxford University Press, 2012), 84.

65. D. C. Duling, "The Gospel of Matthew," in *The Blackwell Companion to the New Testament*, ed. D. Aune (Oxford: Wiley-Blackwell, 2010), 300.

as ancient biographies.[66] Also worthy of note is the fact that recent studies by classicists have accepted the gospels into the "canon" of ancient *bioi*. Tomas Hägg, for example, in his magisterial *The Art of Biography in Antiquity* (2012), devotes a chapter to the gospels. While he notes that Mark in particular displays a couple of unusual features, Hägg argues that the gospels are no more deviant or special than any other biography from the time.[67] Similarly, a number of recent edited collections on biography in the classical world have contained at least one essay on the gospels.[68] While talk of a "consensus" in New Testament studies is always risky, the view that the gospels are best understood as ancient *bioi* has certainly become a dominant scholarly position.

The Last Twenty-Five Years

As noted in the introduction to this volume, however, what might be thought to be one of the most spectacular "discoveries" in recent years—a finding rich with interpretive possibilities—seems to have fallen rather flat. With the exception of

66. W. Vorster, "Gospel, Genre," *ABD*, 2:1077–79; D. Aune, "Gospels," *NIDB*, 2:637–39, writes, "Several factors have convinced many that the Gospels are indeed a distinctive type of Greco-Roman biography" (638); R. A. Burridge, "Gospel, Genre," *DJG*, 335–42, writes, "Since the end of the twentieth century the biographical understanding of the Gospel genre has become the accepted scholarly consensus" (340). Of course, both Aune and Burridge were heavily involved in the debate over gospel genre, but the fact that they were chosen to write these articles gives an indication of the prominence of their views. For a (rather too) guarded assessment, see W. R. Telford, who suggests that "attempts to identify the genre of Mark . . . in terms of its literary antecedents or ancient literary parallels, have produced mixed results" (though he does note that identifying Mark with Greco-Roman biography is a "popular approach"); *Writing on the Gospel of Mark* (Dorchester: Deo, 2009), 9.
67. Hägg, *Art of Biography*, 148–86.
68. The inclusion of the gospels might well be expected in McGing and Mossman, *Limits*, with its specific interest in exploring works on the fringes of the biographical genre (both culturally and chronologically); but see also R. Ash, J. Mossman, and F. B. Titchener, eds., *Fame and Infamy: Essays for Cristopher Pelling on Characterization in Greek and Roman Biography and Historiography* (Oxford: Oxford University Press, 2015), where the essay by T. Morgan pays particular attention to the gospels; and K. De Temmerman and K. Demoen, eds., *Writing Biography in Greece and Rome: Narrative Technique and Fictionalization* (Cambridge: Cambridge University Press, 2016), where a discussion of the gospels forms a significant part of the chapter by D. Konstan and R. Walsh.

a handful of studies, the rich potential of situating the gospels within Greek *bios* literature seems to have remained largely untapped.[69] Of course, those who led the debate were quick to build on the new generic identification: Aune's original work included a chapter-length appreciation of Mark's Gospel in the light of its biographical genre;[70] Dormeyer presented Mark's work as a fusion of Greco-Roman biography and the idealized biographical vignettes of the historical books and prophets of the Jewish Scriptures (specifically Moses, David, Solomon, Elijah, and Isaiah);[71] and Burridge used genre to highlight gospel Christology and, more recently, to emphasize the ethical dimensions implicit within the gospels.[72] Richard Bauckham drew on genre for his important argument that the gospels were intended for wide circulation, against the prevailing opinion that they were written for particular "communities."[73] And Craig Keener and Edward Wright have edited a collection of essays that focus on the historical reliability of ancient *bioi*.[74] It is now common for gospel commentaries to include a section on "genre" as part of the introductory comments; many conclude that *bios* is the best fit, though it is not always clear what difference this generic decision has

69. For a thorough review of works published in the last twenty-five years, see Burridge, *What Are the Gospels?*, 3rd ed., I.1–112. Burridge's interest here is to show that the *bios* theory has largely been persuasive, though his chapter indirectly illustrates how little the theory has been built upon. I am grateful to Professor Burridge for allowing me to see a prepublication copy of this chapter.

70. See Aune, *Literary Environment*, esp. chap. 2 (on Mark).

71. D. Dormeyer, *Das Markusevangelium als idealbiographie von Jesus Christus, dem Nazarener* (Stuttgart: Verlag Katholisches Bibelwerk, 1999; 2nd ed., 2002).

72. R. Burridge, *Four Gospels, One Jesus? A Symbolic Reading*, 2nd ed. (Grand Rapids: Eerdmans, 2005; first published 1994) explored the Christology of the gospels for a general audience; see also his useful comments in "Reading the Gospels as Biography," in McGing and Mossman, *Limits*, 31–49; on ethics, see R. Burridge, *Imitating Jesus: An Inclusive Approach to New Testament Ethics* (Grand Rapids: Eerdmans, 2007).

73. R. Bauckham, ed., *The Gospels for All Christians: Rethinking Gospel Audiences* (Grand Rapids: Eerdmans, 1998), 9–48; see also Burridge's article in the same volume, "About People, by People, for People: Gospel Genre and Audiences," 113–45. Bauckham has stressed the need to understand the gospels as *bioi* in a number of publications; see, for example, *Jesus and the Eyewitnesses: The Gospels as Eyewitness Testimony* (Grand Rapids: Eerdmans, 2006), and *Testimony of the Beloved Disciple: Narrative, History, and Theology in the Gospel of John* (Grand Rapids: Baker Academic, 2007).

74. C. S. Keener and E. T. Wright, eds., *Biographies and Jesus: What Does It Mean for the Gospels to Be Biographies?* (Lexington: Emeth, 2016). For more on this topic, with further literature, see below, pp. 66–71.

made to the work's interpretation.[75] Some even attempt to read specific gospels as *bioi*, though the results are often uneven.[76] All in all, the list of scholarship is not particularly long for an issue that seemed so pressing only a few decades ago, and it is still possible (not to mention largely unremarkable as far as reviewers were concerned) to write a long book on gospel origins without devoting any attention to their genre at all.[77]

It does seem, then, that the "so what?" question has still to be explored: What difference does it make to say that Mark wrote a *bios*, rather than a history, a theological treatise, or a letter? What clues does the generic identification provide with respect to the composition and purpose of Mark's work? These are the questions that will occupy the rest of this book. First, however, we need a fuller appreciation of ancient *bioi*. What was distinctive about these works, and what were their typical features?

75. On Mark, see, for example, R. H. Stein, *Mark*, Baker Exegetic Commentary on the New Testament (Grand Rapids: Baker Academic, 2008), 19–21. In general, John's Gospel tends to fare better here (perhaps because there is less form-critical baggage to displace); see, for example, C. S. Keener, *The Gospel of John: A Commentary* (Peabody, MA: Hendrickson, 2003), 1:3–34, and A. T. Lincoln, *The Gospel according to John* (Peabody, MA: Hendrickson, 2005), 14–17.

76. B. Witherington reads Mark as a biography, though in my view not always consistently; *The Gospel of Mark: Socio-Rhetorical Commentary* (Grand Rapids: Eerdmans, 2001).

77. See, for example, Francis Watson, *Gospel Writing: A Canonical Perspective* (Grand Rapids: Eerdmans, 2013), and the critique by R. Bauckham, "Gospels before Normativization: A Critique of Francis Watson's *Gospel Writing*," *JSNT* 37 (2014): 198–99. Other useful studies of the gospels as *bioi* include: Bryan, *Preface to Mark*; D. B. Capes, "*Imitatio Christi* and the Gospel Genre," *BBR* 13 (2003): 1–19; K. Keefer, *The New Testament as Literature: A Very Short Introduction* (Oxford: Oxford University Press, 2008), 23–29; and A. T. Lincoln, *Born of a Virgin? Reconceiving Jesus in the Bible, Tradition and Theology* (Grand Rapids: Eerdmans, 2013).

CHAPTER 2

Ancient *Bioi*

A biography relates the significance of a famous person's career (i.e., his character and achievements), optionally framed by a narrative of origins and youth, on the one hand, and death and lasting significance on the other.

—David Aune[1]

All human societies have told stories of heroes. From the Epic of Gilgamesh to the wanderings of Odysseus, the daring deeds and accomplishments of great men (and very occasionally women) have been held up for the admiration and emulation of ordinary folk. Shared stories of national heroes strengthen the bonds of kinship, tribe, and ethnicity; they create a sense of security in the face of social or political unrest; and articulate the qualities and values deemed important by the group. It was not until the Hellenistic era, however, that a distinctively biographical style of writing began to develop, enjoying a "golden age" in the late Hellenistic and early imperial periods. The aim of the present chapter is to provide an overview of these ancient *bioi*: How did the genre emerge from the writing of history more generally? What reasons might an author have for crafting a biography? How do *bioi* construct character, and for what purpose? How important are death scenes in this literature? And where do authors draw the line between truth and fiction? Only when we have a secure grasp of all of this will we be able to turn to consider Mark's *bios*.

The Emergence of Biography

The origins and development of biography as a literary form have been debated at length, though both, to some extent, remain obscure. The fragmentary state of our knowledge of much ancient literature means that precise lines of evolution are

---

1. D. E. Aune, *The New Testament in Its Literary Environment* (Philadelphia: Westminster, 1987), 27.

difficult to draw.[2] Luckily for our purposes, however, a precise account of the origins of *bioi* is unnecessary; all we need to note are some of the major trajectories that led to the type of biography with which Mark would have been familiar.

The first stirrings toward a distinctively biographical manner of writing can be seen as early as the fifth century BCE. By now, the Greeks had developed a keen interest in foreign lands and other peoples, and the historian Herodotus began to include character depiction in his works—thus earning him acclaim as the "father" of both history *and* biography.[3] Even the rather more austere Thucydides permitted himself occasional biographical digressions and showed a distinct interest in the psychological effects of events on human behavior.[4] A growing sense of the "individual" at this period, together with a concern to commemorate great lives (often in funerary contexts), found expression not only in literature but in a range of other media, including art and sculpture.[5] By the fourth century, Aristotle and his followers (the Peripatetics) began to use anecdotes from the lives of great men as illustrations of virtue and vice.[6] Aristotle's student, Theophrastus, tried to classify character traits, just as his school had done with animals and plants, and composed biographical vignettes to illustrate each one.[7] Scholars pieced together lives of the poets, largely drawn from anecdotes found within their works, or those of their contemporaries,[8]

---

2. For discussion, see A. Momigliano, *The Development of Greek Biography* (Cambridge, MA: Harvard University Press, 1971); P. Cox Miller, *Biography in Late Antiquity: A Quest for the Holy Man* (Berkeley: University of California Press, 1983), 3–16; and T. Hägg, *The Art of Biography in Antiquity* (Cambridge: Cambridge University Press, 2012), 67–98.

3. On Herodotus's dynamic conception of character and interest in exploring ethical truths, see E. Baragwanath, "Characterization in Herodotus," in *Fame and Infamy: Essays for Christopher Pelling on Characterization in Greek and Roman Biography*, ed. R. Ash, J. Mossman, and F. B. Titchener (Oxford: Oxford University Press, 2015), 17–35.

4. Aune gives a number of examples of Thucydidean digressions: Kylon (1.126.3–12); Pausanias (1.128–34), and Themistocles (1.138); *Literary Environment*, 29.

5. I use the term "individual," of course, not as we would understand it today, but to indicate a recognition that people might have an identity beyond their family and kin; see the discussion in C. B. R. Pelling's introduction to his edited work, *Characterization and Individualism in Greek Literature* (Oxford: Clarendon, 1990), especially v–vii.

6. On the peripatetics, see Hägg, *Art of Biography*, 67–98. Although interested in anecdotes, Aristotle and his followers never produced full biographies. See G. L. Huxley, "Aristotle's Interest in Biography," *Greek, Roman and Byzantine Studies* 15 (1974): 203–13.

7. Theophrastus, *On Character*; the work contains sketches of thirty character traits (see further below).

8. Only fragments of these works now remain. See M. R. Lefkowitz, "The Euripides *Vita*,"

and at a much lower educational level popular romances told of heroes such as Aesop, Alexander the Great, and Homer.[9]

The honor of writing the first biography, however, is usually given to Isocrates, who in his account of Evagoras (written around 370 BCE) claimed to be the first to turn the funeral eulogy into prose. Technically speaking, his work is an *encomium*, an invitation to admire a great man and to preserve his memory, but its clear focus on one human life is a significant movement on the way to a distinguishable type of biographical literature. His Athenian contemporary, the soldier and rhetorician Xenophon, composed both the *Cyropaedia*, a rather fantastical account of the education of Cyrus the Great of Persia, and the *Agesilaus*, in which he presented the Spartan as a model king—energetic, modest, accessible, genial, and attentive to his friends.

Shortly afterward, Isocrates's (putative) student Theopompus outdid Herodotus by composing an entire history dominated by the personality of the main character. His *Philippica* was a huge, unwieldy work in fifty-eight books, which, though full of far-flung digressions, focused primarily on the life and works of Philip II. Polybius was full of disdain for a work that built history around one man rather than Greece (*Histories* 2.8.10), but Theopompus's concern was less with great historical events than with the feelings and motives of major characters—both Philip himself and other actors in the story. The work was marked by a strongly moral approach to history; the focus on Philip was not led simply by curiosity about a great man, but by a concern for a great leader's strengths and weaknesses in the face of temptations. Despite labeling Philip the finest man ever produced by Europe in his *proem*, Theopompus did not hesitate to judge his actions throughout the book, bestowing either praise or, much more commonly, censure as he deemed appropriate.[10]

Theopompus's magnum opus became the standard work on Philip for a long time to come. It also introduced a quasi-biographical approach to historiography that was to have a profound effect on many of his successors. In the first century

---

Greek, Roman and Byzantine Studies 20 (1979): 187–210, for an account of the development of one of these.

9. Hägg, *Art of Biography*, 99–147. Although the earliest versions of these anonymous "texts" date from the Roman period, it is likely that they circulated much earlier in an open, fluid form. On the *Alexander Romance* as an "open text," see D. Konstan, "The 'Alexander Romance': The Cunning of the Open Text," *Lexis* 16 (1998): 123–38.

10. On Theopompus, see I. A. F. Bruce, "Theopompus and Classical Greek Historiography," *History and Theory* 1 (1970): 86–109; G. Shrimpton, "Theopompus' Treatment of Philip in the 'Philippica,'" *Phoenix* 31 (1977): 123–44; and M. R. Christ, "Theopompus and Herodotus: A Reassessment," *ClQ* 43 (1993): 47–52.

BCE, Dionysius of Halicarnassus, a great admirer of Theopompus, included discussions of the lives and achievements of public figures, along with their virtues and vices, in his *Roman Antiquities*.[11] And in the late first century CE, Josephus rewrote the Jewish Scriptures in his *Jewish Antiquities* as a series of lives of great men.[12]

What these works remind us is that the boundaries between various genres in antiquity were highly porous and flexible. It is not always clear where to set the dividing line between biography and history, or biography and *encomium*, and features more properly associated with rhetoric, moralizing, or polemic might be found in any of them.[13] It is also worth noting that the Hellenistic age was a time of great literary productivity throughout the whole eastern Mediterranean, a time of novelty, flexibility, and experimentation.[14] Gradually, however, *bioi* did emerge as something distinguishable from history, though ancient theorists were often slow to reflect on the new genre.[15] Plutarch famously distinguishes between the two, declaring in the opening to his study of Alexander that "it is not histories that we are writing but lives." The difference, he suggested, was that histories concerned themselves with famous actions and events, while the revelation of a man's character in a life was often more appropriately achieved through smaller details (*Alexander* 1.1–2). The distinction is a good and useful one, though reality was not always quite so clear-cut.

Arguably the life that had the greatest impact on the development of Greek biography was that of Socrates, with Xenophon's *Memorabilia* serving in particular as a model for much later biographical literature. While Plato never actually wrote a biography of his teacher, Tiberius's astrologer Thrasyllus put together four of his works recounting various aspects of Socrates's last hours (the *Ethyphro, Apology, Crito,* and *Phaedo*), effectively creating a narrative account of the great philosopher's trial and death.[16] The prominence of Socrates ensured that "the philosopher"

11. See, for example, 5.48.2–4 (on Publicola) and 8.60–62 (on Coriolanus).

12. See above, p. 28.

13. So R. A. Burridge, *What Are the Gospels? A Comparison with Graeco-Roman Biography*, 3rd ed. (Waco: Baylor University Press, 2018), 62–63.

14. J. Fitzgerald, "The Ancient Lives of Aristotle and the Modern Debate about the Genre of the Gospels," *Restoration Quarterly* (1994): 210–11.

15. For a collection of (rare) reflections by ancient biographers on their craft, see S. Adams, "What Are *bioi/vitae*? Generic Self-Consciousness in Ancient Biography," in *The Oxford Handbook of Ancient Biography*, ed. K. De Temmerman (Oxford: Oxford University Press, 2020).

16. See Diogenes Laertius, *Lives of Eminent Philosophers* 3.56–61; 9.45. Antisthenes, another pupil of Socrates, also wrote an account of the great teacher, though this no longer survives.

would be a common and well-regarded biographical subject, and some of the more well known, such as Plato, Pythagoras, and Diogenes the Cynic, enjoyed several biographies both in the Hellenistic and Roman periods. In the second century CE, Lucian of Samosata could write in glowing terms of his own teacher, Demonax, while composing a sneering parody of the ridiculous life and death of the sophist Peregrinus. By the early third century, Philostratus had penned the lengthy *Life of Apollonius of Tyana*, and Diogenes Laertius had gathered together his *Lives of Eminent Philosophers*. The latter's ambitious project charted the development of philosophy itself from its Greek origins down through successive individual philosophical lives, in effect creating "a geneaology of philosophy, positioning each philosopher in his particular place on the family tree."[17]

Latin biography, when it appeared in the late Republic, tended to dwell less on philosophers and more on public figures, those who upheld the structures of society: emperors, statesmen, and generals. These lives (or *vitae*)[18] worked well with the traditional Roman interest in ancestors, public honor, the tracking of the *cursus honorum* (the course of a man's military and political posts), and funeral orations.[19] By early imperial times, however, there was another reason for the growing prominence of biographical literature: the emergence of the *princeps*. Although little Latin historiography from this period has survived, there appears to have been a narrowing of focus away from the deeds of the people of Rome in general to those of the emperor alone. Historians could still write about foreign wars and generals, but the magnetic pull of the emperor meant that all contemporary history ultimately chronicled *his* glory. As Christina Shuttleworth-Kraus notes, there was a shift from "history about Rome to history-about-Rome-as-embodied-in-the-emperor."[20] Even Tacitus, though he chose the ultra-republican format of annals (a yearly progression designed to mirror the annual rotation of the consuls), could hardly avoid the fact that his work becomes little more than a sequence of biographies of successive emperors. In his section on Tiberius, he famously frequently omits his name, simply

17. W. James, "Diogenes Laertius, Biographer of Philosophers," in *Ordering Knowledge in the Roman Empire*, ed. J. König and T. Whitmarsh (Cambridge: Cambridge University Press, 2007), 146.

18. The word "biography" (from the Greek *biographia*) was not used until the fifth century CE. Greeks referred to their literary endeavors as *bioi*, while Romans called them *vitae*. Both not only meant "life" or "career" but also incorporated a wider sense of the subject's "way of living."

19. On Roman political biography, see Hägg, *Art of Biography*, 187–238.

20. C. Shuttleworth Kraus, "From Exempla to Exemplar? Writing History around the Emperor in Flavian Rome," in *Flavius Josephus and Flavian Rome*, ed. J. Edmondson, S. Mason, and J. Rives (Oxford: Oxford University Press, 2005), 183.

referring to his subject as "he."[21] Similar features mark the works of Appian and Dio Cassius, presenting what Christopher Pelling has referred to as a "biostructuring" of the narrative.[22] Eventually, and whatever the personal opinion of the historian, Caesar became the focal point for all historical and political discourse.

Many Latin *vitae* from the early imperial period onward are found as part of collections of biographies of great men. The earliest surviving Latin biographies are portions of Cornelius Nepos's encyclopedic *On Famous Men*. Although the entire work comprised at least sixteen books, only the section "On Famous Generals" now survives, along with a handful of other lives. Written in the dying days of the Republic, Nepos presented a range of renowned Mediterranean figures in order to serve as role models for his own day. The short sketches gathered together very different men from a variety of cultures under specific headings (generals, historians, etc.) and encouraged his audience to reflect on their virtues (or lack thereof). Nepos could not boast any great literary style, but he was a thoughtful and painstaking compiler, and perhaps the originator of the grouped political biographies that would prove so popular in this era.[23]

Writing in Greek a century and a half later, in the renaissance of Roman literature that followed the assassination of Domitian in 96 CE, Plutarch's *Parallel Lives* seem to have been inspired by Nepos. While the latter juxtaposed a series of lives under one heading, however, Plutarch's great genius lay in carefully selecting pairs of lives (typically one Roman, one Greek). And while Nepos's lives were little more than sketches, Plutarch's were on a much larger scale, treating his subjects' lives in some depth. The *Parallel Lives* proved highly popular among the educated and leisured classes, and twenty-two pairs still remain.[24] In a similar vein, Suetonius established the imperial biography. His *Lives of the Caesars* charted the lives of twelve

21. Kraus, "From Exempla to Exemplar," 185.

22. C. B. R. Pelling, "Breaking the Bounds: Writing about Julius Caesar," in McGing and Mossman, *Limits*, 258.

23. For useful discussions of Nepos, which seek to rehabilitate him as a thoughtful political biographer, see R. Stern, *The Political Biographies of Cornelius Nepos* (Ann Arbor: University of Michigan Press, 2012); R. Stern, "Shared Virtues and the Limits of Relativism in Nepos' *Epaminondas* and *Atticus*," *CJ* 105 (2009): 123–36; M. M. Pryzwansky, "Cornelius Nepos: Key Issues and Critical Approaches," *CJ* (2009): 97–108; and J. Beneker, "Nepos' Biographical Method in the Lives of Foreign Generals," *CJ* 105 (2009): 109–21.

24. On Plutarch, see D. A. Russell, "On Reading Plutarch's Lives," *G&R* 13 (1966): 139–54, and *Plutarch* (London: Duckworth, 1973); J. Geiger, "Nepos and Plutarch: From Latin to Greek Political Biography," *Illinois Classical Studies* 13 (1988): 245–56; C. B. R. Pelling, *Life of Antony* (Cambridge: Cambridge University Press, 1988); T. Duff, *Plutarch's Lives: Exploring Virtue and Vice* (Oxford: Oxford University Press, 1999); and Hägg, *Art of Biography*, 239–81.

successive Roman emperors from Julius Caesar to Domitian, treating his subjects in a broadly topical manner well suited to displaying their characters. Augustus stands out as an exemplary emperor, a worthy *princeps*, thoroughly deserving his posthumous deification. We might ask why Suetonius began with Julius Caesar, given that he was never strictly speaking a *princeps*. The reason may be that Suetonius's master Hadrian, like Augustus, owed his position largely to his adoption by his predecessor; starting with Julius Caesar's dictatorship, then, strengthened parallels between Augustus and Hadrian, not only flattering the reigning emperor but implicitly bolstering his claim to the throne as well.[25] Or perhaps, as John Henderson suggests, Suetonius intended the lives of both Augustus and Julius Caesar as programmatic, illustrating both positive and negative imperial qualities.[26]

The idea that a biography might be used to explain a man's behavior or to justify a particular outlook (often one shared by the author) was a common one. At first glance, Nepos's biography of his friend Atticus appears rather uneventful, yet that is precisely the point. Set against the turmoil of the triumvirate and no great lover of Octavian's rise to power, Nepos wrote to praise Atticus's lack of political engagement. His hero turned his back on public life, refused to take sides in the civil wars, and consciously preferred to weather the storm in comfortable retirement with his literary and antiquarian pursuits. For Nepos, these were the right choices, indeed the only ones that could have preserved the old republican way of life.[27] Tacitus, too, in his biography of Agricola, written in 97–98 CE, presents him as a paragon of civic and military professionalism and personal integrity, showing how good men can conduct themselves even during the rule of bad emperors. Although the work is a fitting tribute to Tacitus's father-in-law, it is not hard to detect a degree of self-interest here: Tacitus himself had also done well under Domitian. The work shows that, by keeping their heads down

25. So D. Wardle, *Suetonius: Life of Augustus* (Oxford: Oxford University Press, 2014), 9. Plutarch also composed lives of Galba and Otho, leading Wardle to suggest that he may have wanted to cover the first one hundred years of the principate, perhaps from 31 BC to 69 CE, thus marking off the Flavian dynasty as a new beginning (Wardle, *Suetonius*, 8).

26. J. Henderson, "Was Suetonius' Julius a Caesar?," in *Suetonius the Biographer: Studies in Roman Lives*, ed. T. Power and R. K. Gibson (Oxford: Oxford University Press, 2014), 81–110.

27. On Atticus in particular, see F. Millar, "Cornelius Nepos, 'Atticus,' and the Roman Revolution," in *Rome, the Greek World, and the East*, vol. 1, *The Roman Republic and the Augustan Revolution*, ed. G. M. Rogers and H. M. Cotton (Chapel Hill: University of North Carolina Press, 2002), 346–73, and Stern, "Shared Virtues." Nepos's *Atticus* is the first *bios* in antiquity to be published during its subject's lifetime—the account of Atticus's death belongs to a second edition (1.9.1).

and carrying out their assigned tasks in a dignified and self-controlled manner, men like Agricola—and Tacitus himself—had ultimately served the Roman state more usefully than any of the flashier Stoic opposition, men who had earned great praise by taking their own lives.[28]

Other authors, however, could use biography in a more subversive manner, with the figure of Cato the Younger (95–46 BCE) acting as a particular magnet for treasonous sentiments. As a Stoic who preferred to kill himself rather than accept Julius Caesar's offer of clemency, Cato's life attracted a large body of literature, from supporters and opponents alike. Thrasea Paetus (one of the Stoic opposition) withdrew from public life under Nero and wrote a life of Cato (Plutarch, *Cato the Younger* 37.1), while Arulenus Rusticus wrote a life in praise of Paetus in the time of Domitian and was promptly executed.[29]

As will already be apparent, one of the most striking features of ancient biographies was their variety. As David Aune points out, an ancient biographer was faced with a range of options, depending not only on his literary purpose but also on the nature of the subject, the available evidence, and his own literary abilities. Biographies might occupy a variety of positions on a number of sliding scales from the serious to comedic, from praise of the subject to blame, and from the heavily didactic to the largely entertaining. The structure of the work might also vary: some authors preferred a broadly chronological arrangement while others favored a topical approach; some cast their work as a continuous narrative while others were content with little more than a jumble of anecdotes.[30] And while most *bioi* occupied a place somewhere between history and *encomium*, their flexible borders meant that features associated with other genres could easily be absorbed.[31] Despite this variety, however, two features of ancient biographical writing stand out clearly: first, a concern to commemorate a great life, and second, a moralistic desire to learn from it. This second concern deserves more attention.

---

28. On Tacitus's *Agricola*, see D. Sailor, "The Agricola," in *A Companion to Tacitus*, ed. V. E. Pagan (Chichester: Wiley-Blackwell, 2012), 23–44; A. J. Woodward with C. S. Kraus, *Tacitus: Agricola* (Cambridge: Cambridge University Press, 2014); and B. C. McGing, "Synkrisis in Tacitus' *Agricola*," *Hermathena* 132 (1982): 15–25. On Tacitus's own advancement under Domition, see his *Histories* 1.1.3 and *Annals* 11.11. It is interesting to note that Tacitus's only biographical endeavor is not of an emperor.

29. For reconstructions of the work of Thrasea Paetus (which was used by Plutarch in his work on Cato), see J. Geiger, "Munatius Rufus and Thrasea Paetus on Cato the Younger," *Athenaeum* 57 (1979): 48–72. On accounts of Cato's end, see below, pp. 57–59.

30. See the useful discussion in Aune, *Literary Environment*, 34–35. We shall return to the question of structure in Chapter 3.

31. So Burridge, *What Are the Gospels?*, 62–63.

Biography and Morality

The educational system, for both Greeks and Romans, was based on the idea of imitation (or *mimēsis*). This manifested itself both in the sphere of literary composition, where students were encouraged to imitate great works from the past in order to achieve excellence in their own endeavors, but also in the sphere of morality, where attention to the lives of great men served as models of moral excellence.[32] Quintilian was of the opinion that the lines set for young boys to copy out should convey moral lessons (*Institutes of Oratory* 1.1.35–36), and that the teacher should also set a good example by his own behavior (2.2.8). Similarly, Dio Chrysostom argued that Socrates had learned from Homer, not by meeting him, but by imitating what he knew of his words and deeds (*Discourses* 55.4–5).[33]

Short stories illustrating virtue or vice (known as *exempla* in Latin, *paradeigmata* in Greek) had appeared as early as Homer and continued to be a regular feature of Greek and Roman narrative technique. From the early Augustan period onward, however, a growing preoccupation with exemplarity began to emerge. In the literary realm, Varro had composed a (now lost) work with seven hundred *imagines* (or portraits) of famous men, both Greeks and Romans, each one accompanied by a prose text and an epigram in verse.[34] In a similar vein, Augustus set up a line of statues of famous figures from Roman history and legend along the sides of his new forum, each inscribed with his offices and achievements. The figures were intended to serve as examples, illustrating conduct appropriate not only to Augustus himself but also to subsequent *principes* (Suetonius, *The Divine Augustus* 31). Philosophers, too, commonly illustrated virtues to be emulated and vices to be avoided through the use of historical *exempla*. Seneca and other Stoics were particularly drawn to the didactic use of *exempla* in their constant fight against the moral weaknesses of their contemporaries; on one occasion Seneca sent books to his friend Lucilius with profitable topics already marked (*Moral Epistles* 6.5). Historians also made good use

32. See the useful discussion in E. A. Castelli, *Imitating Paul: A Discourse of Power* (Louisville: Westminster John Knox, 1991), 59–87; although focused on Luke-Acts, see also W. S. Kurz, "Narrative Models for Imitation in Luke-Acts," in *Greeks, Romans, Christians: Essays in Honor of Abraham J. Malherbe*, ed. D. L. Balch, E. Ferguson, and W. A. Meeks (Minneapolis: Fortress, 1990), 171–89. On imitation in composition, see Dionysius of Halicarnassus, *On Imitation*; Quintilian, *Institutes of Oratory* 10.2; and Longinus, *On the Sublime* 13.

33. I owe these references to D. Capes, "*Imitatio Christi* and the Gospel Genre," *BBR* 13 (2003): 3–7.

34. Pliny, *Natural History* 35.11; Aulus Gellius, *Attic Nights* 3.10. See Millar, "Cornelius Nepos," 362.

of moral illustrations. Tacitus, for example, declared that the first duty of history is "to ensure that merit shall not lack its record and to hold before the vicious word and deed the terrors of posterity and infamy" (*Annals* 3.65), and his work is full of examples to instill a sense of virtue in his readers and to guide them through their own moral difficulties.[35]

Exempla had always been particularly prized in the world of oratory. Their use had been advocated by Aristotle, and their skillful deployment was a frequent topic of discussion in the works of grammarians and rhetoricians.[36] Under Tiberius, Valerius Maximus compiled his hugely popular *Memorable Doings and Sayings*, a collection of almost one thousand historical *exempla* drawn from both Rome and foreign nations, and grouped under a number of general headings (religion, false religiosity, omens, courage, etc.). Young men in the rhetorical schools drew on them for illustrations to use in their speeches, but equally importantly the work provided a "cheat's guide" to the moral values of classical times. In an era of social mobility and uncertainty, the collection of *exempla* provided a comprehensive reference book for a rising class of entrepreneurs and "new men," offering models for contemporary behavior.[37]

Within the biographical tradition, there was always a strong sense of learning through observing the lives of others. Biographies, in a sense, were *exempla* writ large.[38] This was already clear to Isocrates, who addressed Evagoras's son Nicocles in the following manner:

For those who do not choose to be slothful, but desire to be good men, it is easy to imitate the character of their fellow-men and their thoughts and purposes—

35. The quotation from Tacitus is from Moore and Jackson, LCL 249. On *exempla*, see H. W. Lichfield, "National Exempla *Virtutis* in Roman Literature," *HSCP* 25 (1914): 1–71; A. J. Malherbe, *Moral Exhortation: A Greco-Roman Sourcebook* (Philadelphia: Westminster, 1986), 135–38; C. Skidmore, *Practical Ethics for Roman Gentlemen: The Work of Valerius Maximus* (Exeter: University of Exeter Press, 1996), 3–27; and W. Turpin, "Tacitus, Stoic *exempla*, and the *praecipuum munus annalium*," *Classical Antiquity* 27 (2008): 359–404.

36. Aristotle, *Rhetoric* A2.1356a35–b6. See further Cicero, *On Invention* 1.49 and *Rhetoric for Herennius* 4.62.

37. On Valerius Maximus and his work, see W. M. Bloomer, *Valerius Maximus and the Rhetoric of the New Nobility* (Chapel Hill: University of North Carolina Press, 1992); Skidmore, *Practical Ethics*; and H. J. Walker, *Valerius Maximus: Memorable Deeds and Sayings; One Thousand Tales from Ancient Rome* (Indianapolis: Hackett, 2004), esp. xiii–xxiv.

38. Diogenes Laertius's *Lives* is one of the few exceptions to this; as noted above, his work is more interested in tracing the lineage of philosophy itself rather than providing models to emulate.

those, I mean, that are embodied in the spoken word. For these reasons especially I have undertaken to write this discourse because I believed that for you, for your children, and for all the other descendants of Evagoras, it would be by far the best incentive, if someone should assemble his achievements, give them verbal adornment, and submit them to you for your contemplation and study. For we exhort young men to the study of philosophy by praising others in order that they, emulating those who are eulogized, may desire to adopt the same pursuits, but I appeal to you and yours, using as examples not aliens, but members of your own family, and I counsel you to devote your attention to this, that you may not be surpassed in either word or deed by any of the Hellenes. (*Evagoras* 76–77)[39]

Isocrates's purpose was not only to highlight the moral excellence of the philosopher-king but also to present his son with a portrait of an ideal ruler worthy of emulation.[40] Equally clear in this regard was Plutarch; the subjects of his *Parallel Lives* ranged from Greek mythology to republican Rome, but the purpose behind them was always the same: readers would, he hoped, learn how to live good and virtuous lives themselves—a pursuit he found contagious: "I began the writing of my *Lives* for the sake of others, but I find that I am continuing the work and delighting in it now for my own sake also, using history as a mirror and endeavouring in a manner to fashion and adorn my life in conformity with the virtues therein depicted" (*Aemilius Paulus* 1).[41]

Not surprisingly perhaps from the author of the *Moralia* (a set of seventy-eight moral essays), most of Plutarch's subjects are examples of moral excellence (*aretē*), providing a repertoire of examples to guide the actions of men in public life. Some however, such as Antony or Demetrius, were weak, illuminating lives of vice (*kakia*), and serving as cautionary tales. Plutarch can easily justify the inclusion of anti-heroes: "Perhaps, then, it is no bad thing to include in our examples of *Lives* one or two pairs of those who have behaved recklessly or have become conspicuous for evil in positions of power or in great affairs . . . it seems to me that we will be more enthusiastic in our admiration and imitation of good lives if we examine bad and blameworthy lives as well."[42] The point was not that the audience should imitate the hero's specific deeds: they were not being called to found cities or to lead others into battle. Plutarch himself had only limited experience of (and often little

39. Van Hook, LCL 373. For a similar sentiment, see Xenophon, *Agesilaus* 10.

40. Hägg, *Art of Biography*, 30.

41. See the similar sentiment in *Pericles* 1–2. Tacitus also writes of honoring Agricola by following his example; *Agricola* 46.

42. This and the previous quotation are from *Demetrius* 1.4–6; translated by Pelling, *Antony*, 11.

sympathy with) the trials of public life.[43] Rather, readers were to learn to emulate the *virtues* displayed in these historical situations—the hero's loyalty, piety, courage, self-control, moderation, and so on.

Of particular interest to the present study are the lives of philosophers. Naturally enough, most biographies of philosophers were written by their followers, with the clear intention of setting out the life and teaching of their leader and encouraging others to follow his example (though some might be polemical or even derisory, such as Lucian's *The Passing of Peregrinus*). Here again two aims tend to dominate, those of remembrance and imitation, both of which are set out clearly in the opening to Lucian's account of Demonax: "It is now fitting to tell of Demonax for two reasons—that he may be retained in your memory by men of culture as far as I can bring it about, and that young men of good instinct who aspire to philosophy may not have to shape themselves by ancient precedents alone, but may be able to set themselves a pattern from our modern world and copy that man, the best of all philosophers whom I know about" (*Demonax* 1–2). Interestingly, Demonax's philosophy is not so much contained within a body of teaching—he does not give public lectures or engage in philosophical dialogue—but in his *mode of life*, expressed most clearly in his freedom from ambition and boldness of speech (his *eleutheria* and *parrēsia*).[44] Readers are to take note of Demonax's virtuous conduct and to emulate it in their own lives. Similarly, in the final chapters to his *Life of Pythagoras* (27–33), Iamblichus presents not only Pythagoras himself but the actions of the whole school as the embodiment of virtue. As Whitney Shiner observes, readers are to see here the clearest examples for their own actions.[45]

Biographies of philosophers established a meaningful relationship between the living and the dead. In effect, describing the life and teaching of a philosopher brought the revered man back to life and allowed him to be introduced to a whole new audience who might also begin to revere his memory and to model their lives on his. This personal connection between philosopher and pupil is expressed well by David Capes: "one could become a 'disciple' or 'follower' without personal association with a great teacher. Through the study and imitation of their words and deeds contained in writings about them (particularly those that

---

43. So Russell, "On Reading," 141; Hägg, *Art of Biography*, 277.

44. D. Clay, "Four Philosophical Lives" (Nigrinus, Demonax, Peregrinus, Alexander Pseudomantis), in *ANRW* II 36.5:3426. Whether Demonax is indeed a "philosophical fiction," as Clay maintains, is not particularly relevant to this issue.

45. W. T. Shiner, *Follow Me! Disciples in Markan Rhetoric* (Atlanta: Scholars, 1995), 83–88.

are well composed), one can know what kind of teachers they are and ultimately become like them."[46]

A similar concern for imitation can also be found in Jewish biographies. In Philo's *Life of Moses*, the patriarch consciously sets himself up as an example to be imitated (*Life of Moses* 1.158–59), and his remarkable career provides a model of virtue for his readers. Philo notes that Moses "exemplified his philosophical creed by his daily actions. His words expressed his feelings, and his actions accorded with his words, so that speech and life were in harmony, and thus through their mutual agreement were found to make melody together as on a musical instrument" (1.29). Josephus's retelling of Jewish history in the *Jewish Antiquities* (which, as we have seen, is cast as a series of biographies) contains frequent calls to imitate his numerous positive examples. The witch of Endor, for instance, receives fulsome praise from Josephus, who advises his audience "to take this woman for an example and show kindness to all who are in need" (*Jewish Antiquities* 6.342).[47] King Ahab's sorry end is presented as a lesson on the inevitability of Fate (8.418–20), while Antipater's intrigues against the dying Herod are related in full "in order that it may be an example and warning to mankind to practice virtue in all circumstances" (17.60).[48] Indeed, Josephus makes it quite clear in his preface to the *Jewish Antiquities* that the work aims to teach by example the benefits of obeying God's Law (1.14–15).

There was always a certain tension between regarding the subject of a *bios* as a unique, historically determined individual and yet at the same time offering that life as a paradigm for others. Both Philo and Josephus, for example, held Moses in the highest esteem, as someone chosen by God for a particular purpose: Philo talks of him as the perfect man (*Life of Moses* 1.1), loved by God as few others (2.67), even "named God and King of the nation" (*theos kai basileus*; 1.158). Josephus is rather more careful to avoid anything that looks like a deification of Moses, yet even he devotes three books to the Jewish Lawgiver and casts him (in a similar manner to Philo) as the ideal philosopher-king and Stoic sage, whose birth and death were

46. D. B. Capes, "*Imitatio Christi* and the Gospel Genre," *BBR* 13 (2003): 7.

47. Thackeray and Marcus, LCL 210.

48. Marcus and Wikgren, LCL 410. See elsewhere in *Jewish Antiquities* 6.347; 8.24, 193, 196, 251–52, 300, 315; 9.44, 99, 173, 243, 282; 10.37, 47, 50; 12.20, 241; 13.5; 17.97, 109–10, 245–46; 18.291; the theme is picked up again in *Against Apion* 2.204, 270. Exemplarity is common throughout the Jewish tradition—see also 2 Macc 6:27–31, or Ben Sira's praise of famous men in chapters 44–50 of his work (especially the casting of Solomon as the model sage in 47:13–18). See also Luke's presentation of the positive example of Barnabas with the negative ones of Ananias and Sapphira (Acts 4:34–5:11).

attended by wondrous circumstances.[49] Despite their encomiastic treatments of Moses, both writers are clear that the life of this great man could act as a moral example for their own contemporaries. Nor did it matter that an exemplar was from the remote (even mythical) past; biography tended to collapse the distinction between past and present, so that examples of virtue (or of vice) were assumed to have a universal application.

At the heart of biography was a concern with *character*, or what Plutarch calls "the signs of the souls in men" (*Alexander* 1.3). By laying out the subject's way of life, virtues and vices would be displayed for all to see.[50] But how exactly was character conceived?

Character

In comparison to their modern counterparts, characters in the works of ancient authors can often appear superficial and lacking in development. In large part this was due to a sense that a person's character (or *ēthos*) was innate, predetermined by one's ancestors and breeding (*eugeneia*), and manifesting itself in a natural temperament (or *phusis*).[51] Of course, this was not the full story, and the ancients acknowledged the importance of external influences, including parents, teachers, companions, and society in general. Moreover, a person could *choose* to live well, to habituate himself to making the right moral choices, and so become a good person. Indeed, there would be no point in the prolific use of *exempla* in the early imperial period if such were not the case. From boyhood onward, philosophers and popular moral

---

49. On Josephus's portrait of Moses, see L. H. Feldman, *Josephus' Interpretation of the Bible* (Berkeley: University of California Press, 1998), 374–442. Feldman suggests that Josephus may have been reacting against Philo's "near deification" of Moses (376).

50. This is explicit in Xenophon, *Agesilaus* 1; Tacitus, *Agricola* 1; Lucian, *Demonax* 67.

51. Useful discussions of character can be found in D. A. Russell, "On Reading," *G&R* 13 (1966): 139–54; C. Gill, "The Question of Character Development: Plutarch and Tacitus," *ClQ* 33 (1983): 469–87; C. B. R. Pelling, "Aspects of Plutarch's Characterization," *ICS* 13 (1988): 257–74; A. Billault, "Characterization in the Ancient Novel," in *The Novel in the Ancient World*, ed. G. L. Schmeling (Leiden: Brill, 1996), 115–29; S. Halliwell, "Traditional Greek Conceptions of Character," in *Characterization and Individuality in Greek Literature*, ed. C. B. R. Pelling (Oxford: Clarendon, 1990), 32–59; C. B. R. Pelling, "Childhood and Personality in Greek Biography," in Pelling, *Characterization*, 213–44; and A. Smith, "Tyranny Exposed: Mark's Typological Characterization of Herod Antipas (Mark 6:14–29)," *BibInt* 14 (2006): 259–93.

thinkers encouraged their contemporaries to reflect on their moral character, to strive to eradicate ingrained defects, and to live virtuous lives.[52]

When it comes to depicting character in ancient literature, a work's genre was of paramount importance. While tragic figures such as Antigone, Ajax, or Medea might exhibit lifelike individuality and psychological depth,[53] the same was not generally true of the characters encountered in biography or history, where they often tended toward the static, and even on occasion stereotypical. The reason for this lies in the fundamentally moral purpose of these two closely related genres. Christopher Gill's work on the distinction between personality and character is useful here. Gill suggests that writers with an interest in "personality" try to understand their subjects in a morally neutral way, to appreciate them as individuals, to empathize with them—in effect, to get "under their skin." Those interested in "character," however, treat their subjects as possessors of good or bad qualities, and see their task as one of moral evaluation in which they apportion praise or blame.[54] Given their interest in ethics, it is no surprise to find that most biographers tend toward the "character" end of the spectrum. The aim was not so much to provide a rounded portrait of a real person as to lay out the subject's way of life to scrutiny, to expose his virtues and vices, and to invite the audience to evaluate his actions and to learn from them. Thus biographical subjects tend to embody a range of ethical qualities—loyalty, courage, moderation, or their opposites.

A good example here is Plutarch, whose lengthy biographies in the *Parallel Lives* often acknowledge considerable complexity in his subjects. His depiction of Antony, for example, particularly in its final stages, reaches great psychological depth as it explores the way in which the Roman leader's noble and brilliant nature was torn apart.[55] Yet even here, there is little sense of a real man; Antony's character traits are surprisingly "integrated," to use Christopher Pelling's expression:[56] individual qualities cluster together seamlessly to produce a coherent character, with none of

52. For references, see Gill, "Question of Character Development," 470.

53. Even here, we should not overestimate the degree to which these characters change and develop. Aristotle's view that tragedy could exist without characters but not without plot is a sobering judgment (*Poetics* 6.7–21), and one that should prevent us from importing more psychological realism into these figures than the texts warrant. On character in Greek drama, see S. Goldhill, *Reading Greek Tragedy* (Cambridge: Cambridge University Press, 1986), 168–74; and P. F. Easterling, "Constructing Character in Greek Tragedy," in Pelling, *Characterization*, 83–99.

54. See Gill, "Question of Character Development"; and his later essay, "The Character-Personality Distinction," in Pelling, *Characterization*, 1–31.

55. For discussion, see Pelling, *Life of Antony*, 14–15.

56. Pelling, "Aspects," 263.

the idiosyncrasies and paradoxical combinations that define flesh-and-blood people. A similar phenomenon can be found at the beginning of the life cycle. Plutarch's moral essays show a great interest in the critical transition from childhood to adulthood and the crucial importance of educational influences, yet his treatment of these topics in the *Lives* seems strangely banal and uninformative, with subjects largely reflecting only those traits that will manifest themselves in later life. Once again, we are left with a sense of integration, as if contradictory and inconsistent traits have been ironed out. There is, of course, a good reason for this. As Pelling notes, the more regular the combination of traits, the easier it is to extract morals and the more generally applicable these morals will be.[57]

Of all subjects, biographies devoted to philosophers or teachers might allow a greater measure of idiosyncrasy or "quirkiness." Unlike kings, generals, and statesmen, there were fewer conventions for how philosophers ought to behave. Diogenes Laertius took great delight in highlighting the unusual features of some of his philosophers—for example, the stout Pittacus's refusal to use a lamp in the dark (*Lives* 1.4.8), Xenocrates's slowness and clumsiness (4.2), Aristotle's slender calves and love of rings (5.1.1), Theophrastus's readiness to do a kindness to anyone (5.2), or Zeno's fondness for green figs and basking in the sun (7.1.1).[58] Yet his work is unusual: his many philosophers do not primarily serve as examples to readers (many of the accounts in any case are extremely brief)—rather, they function as links in a "family tree" of philosophy. Where a philosopher's way of life is more clearly held up as a model to be imitated, however, we encounter the same tendency toward integrated characters, usually depicting the subject as the embodiment of a variety of virtues. Lucian's Demonax, for example, is presented as a model of outspokenness, freedom from ambition, and sound judgment.[59] And while the Bible credits Moses only with humility (Num. 12:3), Philo is extravagant in heaping virtues upon him—not only the traditional wisdom, courage, temperance, and justice, but also honesty, piety, and asceticism. In short, as the perfect Lawgiver he possessed "all the virtues fully and completely" (*Life of Moses* 2.8).

In the composition of their *bioi*, authors drew on predetermined *topoi* and ste-

---

57. Pelling, "Aspects," 267. Plutarch's characters derive their complexities in large part from the paired structuring, which invites comparative reading; see M. de Poureq and G. Roskam, "Mirroring Virtues in Plutarch's Lives of Agis, Cleomenes and the Graachi," in De Temmerman and Demoen, *Writing Biography*, 163–80.

58. See James, "Diogenes Laertius," 135–36.

59. On Demonax, see M. Beck, who argues for a limited amount of "personality" in Lucian's description; "Lucian's *Life of Demonax*: The Socratic Paradigm, Individuality, and Personality," in De Temmerman and Demoen, *Writing Biography*, 80–96.

reotypical lists of virtues and/or vices. Training in how to represent character began in elementary school and continued into advanced levels of education. Pupils were trained in *prosōpoeia*, the art of imitating the character of a particular speaker. They might imagine the speech of a general to his victorious troops, or the kind of things a man pretending to be rich might say and do. Theophrastus's *On Characters* displayed a range of thirty largely negative character traits for students to absorb and emulate (though whether he wrote them specifically for this purpose is unclear).[60] In all of this, the emphasis was on the typical: how a person in any situation might behave, what set of characteristics he or she might display, and how these might indicate moral character. The stereotypes were well known, though how creatively they were used depended on the individual biographer's literary art.

The formation of character in biography, however, involved one further aspect that is often overlooked. Unlike novelists, who were free to invent character in any way they pleased, ancient biographers dealt with real-life people who existed already, prior to the biographers' literary endeavors, perhaps in a variety of literary and cultural traditions. Koen De Temmerman illustrates this with the example of Apuleius's Lucius, who is a purely fictional character with no independent existence outside *The Golden Ass*. Everything that can be known about Lucius comes from Apuleius's narrative, and so as a literary character he can be said to be "complete."[61] The same, however, cannot be said about biographical subjects. Whether emperors, generals, or philosophers, these lives had generally been documented, or at least remembered, in a variety of ways, and competing traditions continued to exist alongside the new biography. Unless he or she intended to offer a radically new portrait of an individual, then, the biographer was not entirely free to invent the subject's character. It may be pared down to basics, rubbed smooth, and "integrated," but in most cases it had broadly to conform to what was generally known about the person in question. Moreover, an ancient audience would generally have approached a biography with a set of presuppositions drawn from what was widely known about the subject. Thus biographical character could never be "complete" in the manner of characters found in ancient novels. Readers of biographies inevitably related what they heard of the subject's character to what they knew already. As De Temmer-

---

60. Strikingly (at least to modern readers), Theophrastus's interest is solely in the "type" of behavior linked to a particular characteristic, and there is no discussion whatsoever of what might have led a person to act in such a way. For further details on character in ancient education, see W. M. Wright, "Greco-Roman Character Typing and the Presentation of Judas in the Fourth Gospel," *CBQ* 71 (2009): 544–59.

61. K. De Temmerman, "Ancient Biography and Formalities of Fiction," in De Temmerman and Demoen, *Writing Biography*, 8–9.

man puts it, "Their image of Aesop or Demonax at the end of the reading process depends not necessarily only on characterization in the text itself but possibly also on an interplay of wider, cultural, literary and historical factors implicating these characters from the moment they start reading the very first page."[62]

Character in biography, then, tended toward the stereotypical and "flat," often highlighting virtues (or vices) already acknowledged to belong to the subject, or at other times presenting a different set of attributes in an attempt to rehabilitate the subject (we might think here of Philo's attempt to counter those who would slander Moses; *Life of Moses* 1.2–3). It is true that ancient audiences may not have "identified" with these possessors of moral qualities in the same manner in which modern readers empathize with the protagonists of nineteenth-century novels, with their deep exploration of individuals' inner lives, feelings, and contradictions.[63] Yet *bioi*, and indeed the whole *exempla* tradition, encouraged a certain level of "identification" with the subject and the situations in which he found himself, along with an ability to extract the moral qualities at the heart of events and to apply them to one's own life. Listeners were invited to compare themselves with these characters,

62. De Temmerman, "Ancient Biography," 11.

63. A number of scholars have argued that *identifying* with characters in a text is a profoundly post-Romantic thing to do; this is true, but it should not be pushed too far. See M. A. Talbert, "How the Gospel of Mark Builds Character," *Int* 47 (1993): 347–57; P. Mehrenlahti, "Characters in the Making: Individuality and Ideology in the Gospels," in *Characterization in the Gospel: Reconceiving Biblical Criticism*, ed. D. Rhoads and K. Syreeni (Sheffield: Sheffield Academic, 1999), 49–72; S. S. Elliott, "'Witless in Your Own Cause': Divine Plots and Fractured Characters in the Life of Aesop and the Gospel of Mark," *Religion and Theology* 12 (2005): 397–418; S. D. Moore, "Why There Are No Humans or Animals in the Gospel of Mark," in *Mark as Story: Retrospect and Prospect*, ed. K. R. Iverson and C. W. Skinner (Atlanta: SBL Press, 2011), 71–93. Rather differently, F. W. Burnett argues for "degrees of characterization," moving from agent, to type, to character. He cautions that we should be wary of assuming a close connection between biblical characters and those in the classical world, urging that "ancient audiences and readers constructed much fuller characters than is usually thought" ("Characterization and Reader Construction of Characters in the Gospels," *Semeia* 63 [1993]: 13; see also C. Bennema, "A Theory of Character in the Fourth Gospel with Reference to Ancient and Modern Literature," *BibInt* 17 [2009]: 375–421, who draws on Burnett). In my view, this approach tries too hard to bridge the gap between ancient literature and modern, psychological characterization; moreover, it does not take the exemplary function of *bioi* seriously enough (despite noting that characterization is often genre specific, Burnett remains agnostic on the question of gospel genre [8–9]; Bennema declares the gospels to be both sui generis and *bioi* [379]). *Modern* readers may well fill in the gaps created by often sparsely drawn characters in psychologically meaningful ways, but that does not mean that ancient audiences did the same.

and to gauge how well their own actions measured up to the virtues on display. To that extent, at least, biographical characterization promoted contemplation, self-reflection, and ultimately transformation.

Of all the events of a person's life, that which perhaps exerted the most fascination for biographers was death. That moment of transition—the almost sacred transfer from existence to nothingness—was often seen as the point when a man's true character might at last be revealed. We should not be surprised, then, to find that death scenes occupied an important place in several *bioi*.

Depictions of Death

Death and dying were part of everyday experience in the ancient world. It was all too visible in the shockingly high mortality rates, the effects of poor sanitation and nutrition, epidemics, and natural disasters.[64] Violent death might come in the shape of thieves and muggers, warfare and officially sanctioned public executions, or the gory spectacles that took place in the arena.

Death was of course inevitable, but some people might choose to go out in a blaze of glory, and both Greeks and Romans developed strong concepts of what kind of deaths were considered honorable. To die like Achilles on the battlefield, or valiantly defending one's homeland against foreign tyranny, was a sure way to attain fame and immortality.[65] Similarly, Iphigenia's readiness to sacrifice her own life for the freedom of her country demonstrated the nobility of her spirit.[66] The preemi-

64. There is a large literature on death in antiquity; see for example V. M. Hope, *Death in Ancient Rome: A Sourcebook* (London: Routledge, 2007), and D. G. Kyle, *Spectacles of Death in Ancient Rome* (London: Routledge, 1999). On noble death traditions in particular, see H. A. Musurillo, *The Acts of the Pagan Martyrs: Acta Alexandrinorum* (Oxford: Clarendon, 1954), 236–46; A. Ronconi, "Exitus illustrium virorum," *RAC* 6 (1966): 1258–68; D. Seeley, *The Noble Death: Graeco-Roman Martyrology and Paul's Concept of Salvation* (Sheffield: JSOT Press, 1990), esp. 83–141; A. J. Droge and J. D. Tabor, *A Noble Death: Suicide and Martyrdom among Christians and Jews in Antiquity* (San Francisco: HarperSanFrancisco, 1992); A. Y. Collins, "The Genre of the Passion Narrative," *ST* 47 (1993): 3–28; G. Sterling, "Mors philosophi: The Death of Jesus in Luke," *HTR* 94 (2001): 383–402; J.-W. van Henten and F. Avemarie, *Martyrdom and Noble Death: Selected Texts from Graeco-Roman, Jewish and Christian Antiquity* (London: Routledge, 2002); R. Doran, "Narratives of Noble Death," in *The Historical Jesus in Context*, ed. A.-J. Levine, D. C. Allison, and J. D. Crossan (Princeton: Princeton University Press, 2006), 385–99.

65. Homer, *Iliad* 9.410–16; 19.95–121. In a similar vein, see the long line of military heroes honored by Athenian funeral orations in van Henten and Avemaire, *Martyrdom*, 16–19.

66. See Euripides's *Iphigenia at Aulis*, esp. lines 1368–401; luckily for Iphigenia, she was

nent example of a noble death, however, was that of Socrates in 399 BCE, particularly as it was depicted in Plato's *Phaedo*. Socrates did not die on the battlefield, but privately in prison, surrounded by family and friends. When the fateful hour arrived, he was ready for death and drained the cup of hemlock in one go. Strikingly, the manner of his death was in perfect harmony with his philosophical teaching and his way of life: he embraced his unjust death steadfastly and with dignity, thinking freely and speaking openly even in the midst of imprisonment; his death was in accordance with God's will (*Apology* 29d; *Crito* 43b), and after drinking the poison his soul blissfully migrated to another world (*Apology* 40b–41c). Socrates could be used to exemplify a number of important Roman virtues, and his demise was to exert a powerful influence on the concept of the noble death throughout this period, especially among the Stoics who advocated an indifference to death and the importance of a praiseworthy exit.[67]

The Roman elite seem to have had a particular preoccupation with death. The turbulent political climate around the end of the Republic and then again under the "bad" emperors (notably Nero and Domitian, whose reigns saw a series of forced executions and voluntary suicides) had drawn particular attention to the manner of a man's exit.[68] An important figure here was Marcus Porcius Cato (the Younger). Hearing in 46 BCE that Julius Caesar's victory now seemed inevitable, Cato resolved to die rather than accept the sovereignty of his enemy. Through his voluntary death, Cato established himself as the preeminent symbol of the Republic, and the one faithful proponent of the *libertas* that would disappear under

---

saved at the last moment. Pompeius Trogus tells of the Athenian king Codrus who, learning from an oracle that only his death would prevent a Dorian victory, entered the enemy camp in disguise and was slain. The Athenians were thus freed from war "by the power of a leader offering himself to death for the salvation of the fatherland" (the works of Popeius Trogus are preserved in an epitome made by Jarcus Junianus Justinus in the third century CE; Justinus, *Epitome of Pompeius Trogus* 2.6.16–21; trans. Doran, "Narratives of Noble Death," 387).

67. For a useful introduction to Plato's account of Socrates's death, see H. Tarrant, *Plato: The Last Days of Socrates* (London: Penguin, 2003), 99–115; also C. Gill, "The Death of Socrates," *ClQ* 23 (1973): 25–28. On the influence of Socrates in this period, see K. Döring, "Sokrates bei Epiktet," in *Studia Platónica: Festschrift für Hermann Gundert zu seinem 65; Geburtstag am 30.4.1974*, ed. K. Döring and Wolfgang Kullman (Amsterdam: Grüner, 1974), 195–226; also J. P. Hershbell, who notes the frequent references to Socrates in the works of Seneca, Epictetus, and Plutarch: "Plutarch's Portrait of Socrates," *Illinois Classical Studies* 13 (1988): 365–81; and Turpin, "Tacitus, Stoic *exempla*."

68. Momigliano, *Development*, 72; Hägg, *Art of Biography*, 236–38. For an account of political opponents from Cato to the reign of Tiberius, see W. Allen Jr., "The Political Atmosphere of the Reign of Tiberius," *TAPA* 72 (1941): 1–25.

autocracy.[69] Accounts of his end proliferate in Roman literature, though the extent to which it was seen as virtuous depended on the political outlook of the writer.[70] Many saw him as a Roman Socrates, and indeed Cato himself seems to have deliberately modeled his demise on the Athenian's sublimely serene end. According to Plutarch's lengthy account, for example, Cato gathered his friends at his country residence at Utica and calmly discussed Stoic philosophy with them the night before his death. Retiring to bed, he took with him "Plato's book on the immortality of the soul" (presumably the *Phaedo*) along with his sword. Despite the failure of his first attempt, Cato tore open his wounds and finally died in the presence of his companions (*Cato the Younger* 66–73). Although Plutarch himself remained unconvinced by this elaborate exit, others considered it an honorable and principled end, his final hours combining philosophical awareness, self-control, and a certain theatricality.[71]

Shades of both Cato and Socrates color the accounts of the deaths of the "Stoic opposition" under Nero, particularly those granted what Tacitus calls "free choice of death" (*liberum mortis arbitrium*; *Annals* 11.3)—men who were condemned to die but who, due to their elevated social status, were granted the opportunity to choose their own death and to end their lives in the company of their friends and relatives.[72] All receive the news that they are to take their own lives in the evening; all are comforted by their shocked friends and relatives; and all end their lives with a libation. If Cato read Plato on the eve of his death, Thrasea Paetus discussed the nature of the soul before taking hemlock, his courage contrasting strongly with his

69. On Cato, see C. Edwards, "Modelling Roman Suicide? The Afterlife of Cato," *Economy and Society* 34 (2005): 200–22. It is important to note that death at one's own hands did not necessarily carry any sense of disgrace in the ancient world. As long as one's reasons were good, it could be seen as necessary, noble, and heroic. For a full discussion of suicide in antiquity, see Droge and Tabor, *Noble Death*.

70. Although Caesar attacked him, Cicero saw Cato as a Stoic sage, and for Seneca and Lucan he became a symbol of moral and political freedom. For a comparison of texts, see R. J. Goar, *The Legend of Cato Uticensis from the First Century BC to the Fifth Century AD: With an Appendix on Dante and Cato* (Brussels: Latomus, 1987).

71. On Plutarch's account of Cato's end see A. V. Zadorojnyi, "Cato's Suicide in Plutarch," *ClQ* 57 (2007): 216–30. Zadorojnyi argues that Plutarch's less than laudatory account of Cato's suicide was due to both his anti-Stoic agenda and a sense that philosophy was not something to be derived from books alone. Interestingly, Cato's Plutarchian partner, Phocion, studied at the Academy with Plato and Xenocrates (*Phocion* 4.2; 27.1–3) and dies in a manner truly reminiscent of Socrates (*Phocion* 38.5).

72. This practice is first heard of in 131 CE according to Appian, *Civil Wars* 1.26, but became common practice only under the principate; see Edwards, "Modelling," 205.

tearful audience (Tacitus, *Annals* 16.34.1). Here we have an explicit recycling of motifs from the death of Socrates, motifs that lend a nobility not only to the forced suicide itself but also to the virtuous characters of the men involved. For Tacitus, and presumably many others, these men are to be regarded as "Roman Socrates," men whose dignified deaths were perfectly in keeping with their honorable lives.[73]

A striking feature of Roman heroes from the civil war and early empire is that their glorious deaths often occur in the context of failure and defeat. As Carlin Barton observes, heroic figures in this period tend to be drawn from the disgraced and redeemed rather than the unspoiled and triumphant.[74] This is true not only of Socrates, Cato, and members of the "Stoic opposition," but for a range of other figures too, and the works of Livy and other early imperial writers are full of examples. We might think of the legendary Mucius Scaevola, for example, who, after being captured while sneaking into the Etruscan camp and attempting to kill the king, is said to have restored his honor (and secured his freedom and a peace treaty) by putting his sword hand into the altar fire and watching impassively as it burned.[75] Or Publius Decius Mus, who, seeing his men suffer heavy losses in battle, dedicated himself to the infernal gods and through his death spurred the Romans on to victory.[76] Or Vulteius and the six hundred supporters of Caesar, who, finding themselves on a raft in the Adriatic, surrounded by many thousands of Pompey's men, chose to kill themselves at dawn rather than surrender to the enemy.[77] Closer to Mark's time, when defeat by Vitellius seemed inevitable in 69 CE, Emperor Otho committed suicide to save the nation from the ravages of further civil war.[78] In all of these stories, extreme courage and even death allow the hero to be restored to glory and honor in the face of humiliation and disgrace.

Stories of noble deaths seem to have been drummed into Roman boys from their youth, stirring their souls to the great Roman virtues of courage, manliness,

73. J. Ker, *The Deaths of Seneca* (Oxford: Oxford University Press, 2009), 56–57. As noted earlier, however, Tacitus seems to have held a rather different view of the martyrs when he wrote the *Agricola*, where their self-inflicted deaths are now viewed as pointless.

74. C. A. Barton, "Savage Miracles: The Redemption of Lost Honor in Roman Society and the Sacrament of the Gladiator and the Martyr," *Representations* 45 (1994): 41–71.

75. The story is in Livy, *History of the Roman People* 2.12–14; on Martial's poems about a gladiator playing the part of Scaevola, see Barton, "Savage Miracles," 41–44.

76. Livy, *History of the Roman People* 8.9.1–8.10; see Doran, "Narratives of Noble Death," 387–89. Van Henten and Avemarie, *Martyrdom*, 19–21, link this story to Roman traditions of *devotio*, or dedication by a general of himself or the enemy's army (or both) to the gods of the underworld.

77. Lucan, *Civil War* 4, ll. 447–581.

78. Tacitus, *Histories* 2.46–56; Martial, *Epigrams* 6.32.

and virtue.[79] The portrait of the good and wise man who stands up to a tyrant even at the expense of his life became a stock motif in the rhetorical and philosophical schools of the day.[80] For some, these stories had only a metaphorical significance, inspiring them to remain true to their beliefs whatever opposition they might encounter. Thus Plutarch advocates that in hard times his readers should reflect upon Socrates's example, mentally reenacting it and allowing his virtues to shape their own.[81] Others, however, took these accounts much more literally, even allowing them to provide a blueprint for their own deaths. Nero's advisor Seneca, for example, clearly took these accounts to heart, and when he was forced to commit suicide in 65 CE his own exit was clearly shaped by these *exempla* (see the account in Tacitus's *Annals* 15.60–64).[82]

Collections of "deaths" appear to have been common in the first century. Pliny the Elder, for example, gathered together a number of sudden deaths, or *repentinae mortes* (*Natural History* 7.180–86), while Valerius Maximus included a series of unusual deaths in his own work (*On Extraordinary Deaths* 9.2). Of particular interest is a genre of literature known as the *exitus illustrium virorum*, the exits/deaths of illustrious men.[83] Unfortunately, no examples of *exitus* literature survive, but there are two references to it in the work of Pliny the Younger. In the first, Pliny laments that the sudden death of Gaius Fannius had left his "finest work" unfinished. Apparently, "he was bringing out a history of the various fates of people put to death or banished by Nero." Pliny continues: "His accuracy in research and purity in style (which was midway between the discursive and historical) were evident in the three volumes he had already finished, and he was all the more anxious to complete the series when he saw how eagerly the first books were read by a large public" (*Letters* 5.5.3). The book, then, seems to have been a popular series of (presumably aristocratic) deaths at the hands of Nero, recounted in prose and direct speech.

79. So Seneca, *Moral Epistles* 24.6.

80. See for example Horace, *Epistles* 1.16.73–78; this image likely derived from the examples of the early Greek philosophers Zeno of Elea and Anaxarchus of Abdera, on whom see below, pp. 63–64.

81. Plutarch, *On the Tranquility of the Mind* (*Moralia* 475D–475F).

82. On the several representations of Seneca's death, which include the briefer report in Suetonius (*Nero* 35.5) and the rather more hostile account in Dio Cassius (*Roman History* 62.25.1–3), see Ker, *Deaths.*

83. On this literature, see F. A. Marx, "Tacitus und die Literatur der exitus illustrium virorum," *Philologus* 92 (1937): 83–103; Ronconi, "Exitus"; Ker, *Deaths,* 41–62; and Hägg, *Art of Biography,* 236–38. On earlier Greek accounts of the deaths of famous men (often called *teleutai*), see Collins, "Genre," 5–13, and Sterling, "Mors philosophi," 384–86.

In the second passage, Pliny declares his intention to attend a recitation that day by his friend and patron Titinius Capito, who was writing on the deaths of famous men. Some of these men, he says, were very dear to him, and attending the recital has something of the air of attending their funerals (*Letters* 8.12). Like that of Fannius, Capito's work also seems to have been a series of vignettes, each dealing with the death of an individual at the hands of a harsh emperor. Some of the deaths—at least those of victims known to Pliny—presumably occurred under Domitian when writing eulogies for them would have been a capital offense.[84] Capito's purpose, then, was doubtless both to commemorate these men and to restore them to dignity. Thus the works of both Capito and Fannius—and perhaps *exitus* literature in general—sought to rewrite the reigns of "bad" emperors through a celebration of the nobility and virtues of their victims. In the age of freedom associated with the reigns of Nerva, Trajan, and Hadrian, the stories of these men could also be turned into an implicit eulogy for the new regime.[85]

Given this intense interest in death as the supreme indicator of a man's *ēthos*, it is no surprise to find biographers paying particular attention to their subject's final hours.[86] Not all biographers record their hero's death, but by far the majority do; indeed, ancient rhetoricians advocated including not only the subject's death but "events after death" too (which might include any unusual occurrences, the funeral

84. So Tacitus, *Agricola* 2.1; Herennius Senecio was put to death by Domitian because of his book *Life of Helvidius* (Tacitus, *Agricola* 45.1). Pliny himself published a short work on Helvidius, though wisely only after Domitian's death (*Letters* 9.13.1).

85. So Musurillo, *Acts*, 241. It is often suggested that Tacitus was dependent upon *exitus* literature (perhaps even the work by Fannius) in his long series of death scenes under Nero in *Annals* books 15–16 (see Marx, "Tacitus"; Ker, *Deaths*, 41–62). Tacitus fears that his readers may become bored with so many "exits of citizens, however noble" (16.16.1), though it does not deter him from continuing in the same vein. The accounts of deaths might be seen as interrupting the annalistic structure of the work (earlier, under Tiberius, he had refrained from such a list; 4.71.1), but their purpose seems to be to commemorate the dignity of each of those who died. The nobility of their deaths lends dignity to a dark period in Roman history and justifies his claim in the preface to his *Histories* that the good examples of his age included "exits equal to the glorious deaths of the ancients" (*Histories* 1.3).

86. Plutarch records the deaths of all but two of his subjects (Camillus and Flamininus). Diogenes Laertius records the deaths of fifty-eight of the eighty-eight philosophers featured in his *Lives*; those lacking accounts of deaths, however, tend to be extremely short (for example Anaximander or Anaximenes in book 2, Crates in book 4, or Archytas and Alcmaeon in book 8). Philostratus often omits details of his subject's deaths (and births) in the *Lives of the Sophists*; however, he claims that his lengthy account of Apollonius of Tyana would not be complete without an account of the philosopher's death (*Life of Apollonius of Tyana* 8.29).

and burial, the holding of games, etc.).[87] A "good death" could be the crowning point of a virtuous life; conversely, a shameful death was a sure sign of a rogue. An illustration of this principle can be found in Suetonius's *Lives of the Caesars*. The "good" emperor Augustus dies quietly at home with his wife, the peace and control of his passing reflecting the peace and stability that he has brought to the empire, and his supreme dignity is maintained to the end. His is the noblest of imperial deaths, a final testament to his virtuous character.[88] In contrast, Nero commits suicide with the help of his secretary Epaphroditus (*Nero* 49.3–4). What makes his death abhorrent and shameful is not the fact that it is self-inflicted (suicide, as we have seen, could be extremely noble in the right circumstances) but Nero's sniveling and unmanly behavior. He fainted at the news that Galba and the Spanish provinces had revolted (42.2), refused to engage with events except in an extravagantly theatrical manner, took fright at a variety of portents and dreams (46), and at the end, abandoned by friends and enemies alike, wept in terror and lacked the courage to take his own life until the very last moment. When dead, Suetonius adds, his protruding eyes and startled expression filled all who saw him with horror (49.4). Similarly, Julius Caesar and Caligula were both assassinated, but while Caesar stood up to his attackers, bravely dying with dignity (*The Divine Julius* 82.2), Caligula is said to have fallen to the ground, writhing as swords were thrust into his private parts, and to have left ghosts in his home (*Gaius Caligula* 58–59).[89] Clearly the *manner* in which one approached death was more important than the form that the death took; as Valerie Hope puts it, "how you died mattered more than what killed you."[90] A calm, courageous, dignified acceptance of one's fate marked a good death, while loss of control, frenzied begging for mercy, and an unwillingness to face one's end marked its opposite.

87. On the link between the theorists and biographers, see M. W. Martin, "Progymnasmatic Topic Lists: A Compositional Template for Luke and Other *Bioi*?," *NTS* 54 (2008): 18–41. Whether or not these lists were strictly adhered to, they provide a *general* sense of what was expected.

88. On Suetonius's account of Augustus's death, see M. Toher, "The 'Exitus' of Augustus," *Hermes* 140 (2012): 37–44; on Suetonius's death scenes more generally, see R. Ash, "Never Say Die! Assassinating Emperors in Suetonius' Lives of the Caesars," in De Temmerman and Demoen, *Writing Biography*, 200–216.

89. Such tropes are found throughout ancient biography. In Cornelius Nepos, for example, Epaminondas faces death with bravery in battle, while Phocion displays bravery in the face of an unjust end. Tacitus, too, completes the virtuous portrait of his father-in-law with a noble death, in which the aged general's bravery and peaceful acceptance contrast strongly with the agony of his loved ones (43.1–2).

90. Hope, *Death*, 10; so also Barton, "Savage Miracles," 50–51 (with examples).

Of particular interest to the present study are the deaths of philosophers where, in general terms, a good death signaled an endorsement of the philosophers' way of life. In a detailed analysis of the monumental work of Diogenes Laertius, Sergi Grau observes that "like a hero in battle, a wise man is not fully confirmed until the moment of his death."[91] Philosophers offered practical guidance on how people should conduct their lives, and it was only to be expected that they should put those principles to good use in their own lives. The philosopher thus became the supreme example of his own doctrine. As Eleni Kechagia puts it, "Their lives, and also the critical last act of their lives, that is, their death, can justifiably be seen as representative of their theories."[92] What was crucial for a philosopher was that his end should be in keeping with his teaching, that death was simply an extension of the principles by which he lived. A good death, a blissful even joyful exit in extreme old age, underscored not only the integrity of the philosopher but also the truth and consistency of his teaching. Conversely, a bad death, from disease or a ridiculous accident, undermined both the philosopher and the authenticity of his doctrine. Both extremes are well illustrated in the works of Lucian. His own teacher, Demonax, died peacefully in old age, exerting control over his own death and retaining his wisdom and humor to the end (*Demonax* 65). In contrast, his *Peregrinus* satirizes a pointless philosophical death, the showy end of a man preoccupied only with acquiring personal fame and glory (*The Passing of Peregrinus* 35–39).[93]

A variant on the good death in extreme old age was the philosopher who met a violent end, defending his philosophical convictions to the last. Grau refers to such men as "martyrs of philosophy," people who stood firm despite torture and eventual execution at the hands of tyrants.[94] Paradigmatic here was Zeno of Elea, who stood firm against the tyrant Nearchus, or Anaxarchus of Abdera, who defied Nicocreon, claiming that the "real" Anaxarchus could not be touched by bodily torture.[95] Despite Plato's description of his blissful exit, Socrates also belongs here

91. S. Grau, "How to Kill a Philosopher: The Narrating of Ancient Greek Philosopher's Deaths in Relation to Their Way of Living," *Ancient Philosophy* 30 (2010): 348; see also E. Kechagia, "Dying Philosophers in Ancient Biography: Zeno the Stoic and Epicurus," in De Temmerman and Demoen, *Writing Biography*, 181–99; Burridge, *What Are the Gospels?*, 160–62.

92. Kechagia, "Dying Philosophers," 182.

93. Similarly, Lucian's satire on the death of Alexander (*Alexander* 59–60) presents a man who seeks a glorious death with divine approval, but who is rewarded with gangrene and worms. At the end, doctors discover that he has been wearing a wig, a detail that suggests that he has been deceiving all along.

94. Grau, "How to Kill," 371.

95. Both are described by Diogenes Laertius in his *Lives of Eminent Philosophers*; on Zeno, see 9.26–29; on Anaxarchus, see 9.58–59.

as one condemned to drink hemlock by the Athenian court on the charge of atheism and corrupting the city's youth. Very few philosophers were remembered in
unambiguously positive ways, and the deaths of Socrates, Zeno, and Anaxarchus
only enhanced their paramount status as men who remained true to their beliefs
to the very end. Although condemned to execution by tyrannical regimes, their
praiseworthy deaths more than obliterated their ignominious sentences, and ensured that both the manner of their deaths and their teaching would be preserved
for posterity.

This interest in death was shared by the Jewish world. Josephus frequently tells
of the noble deaths of Jewish heroes, whether great men such as Samson (*Jewish
Antiquities* 5.3–17) or Saul (6.344–50), or the freedom fighters at Masada (*Jewish
War* 7.389–406).[96] Indeed the whole Jewish nation, he claims, would gladly die
rather than see their ancestral laws trampled upon (*Jewish War* 2.174, 184–203;
Against Apion 2.232–35). In a rather different vein, Philo presents Moses's death as
a glorious departure into heaven, an exchange of mortality for immortality, "trans-
forming his whole being into mind, pure as the sunlight" (*Life of Moses* 2.288).[97]
But perhaps the noblest Jewish deaths belong to the Maccabean martyrs of the
second century BCE. The book of 2 Maccabees tells the story of Eleazar, an old
and noble scribe, who courageously refused to eat profane meat and calmly went
to his death rather than betray his principles. The hero is cast as a Jewish Socrates,
offering a "noble example of how to die a good death willingly and nobly for the
revered and holy laws" (2 Macc 6:18–31, here v. 28).[98] Similarly, the horrific torture
and deaths of a mother and her seven sons tell of noble endurance under extreme
trial (2 Macc 7:1–41), along with Razis, an elder from Jerusalem, who took his own
life rather than surrender to Nicanor's men (2 Macc 14:37–46).[99] Written in the first
or second century CE, 4 Maccabees offers a philosophical reflection on these earlier
martyrs, heightening their desire for death and claiming that reason, as informed
by the Jewish Law, can control the passions. Instead of military victory (which is

96. This is not to deny a certain ambivalence in Josephus's own attitude toward suicide
(compare his speech at Jotapata, which is critical of self-killing; *Jewish War* 3.361–82). But
Eleazar's speech at Masada draws on ideas from Plato's *Phaedo*, presenting the decision to
die as a noble act of freedom, a nobility that impresses the Romans when they come upon
the scene (7.406). See J. Klawans, *Josephus and the Theologies of Ancient Judaism* (Oxford:
Oxford University Press, 2013), who sees the whole account as a "cautionary tale" (132).

97. Colson, LCL 289. On the extraordinary death of Moses, both in Philo and other
roughly contemporary Jewish literature, see Feldman, *Philo's Portrayal*, 220–33.

98. See discussion in J. A. Goldstein, *II Maccabees: A New Translation, with Introduction
and Commentary* (New York: Doubleday, 1983), 285.

99. For texts and discussion, see Doran, "Narratives of Noble Death."

not mentioned at all), the author claims that the tyrant was conquered and the land purified by the martyrs' nobility, courage, and endurance. What distinguishes these Jewish accounts from their Greco-Roman counterparts, however, is a strong sense that the martyrs will be vindicated and rewarded beyond death, along with a quasi-sacrificial sense that the deaths of the innocent will arouse God's mercy and intervention.[100]

When it came to death scenes, what mattered most was the way the story was told. The difference between a good or a bad death might amount only to a few details—the addition of a courageous concern for one's friends and family, a calm demeanor, and the suppression of excessive fear and weeping. Plato's *Phaedo* is a good illustration of this. As Christopher Gill points out, hemlock poisoning led to vomiting, choking, spasms, and eventual paralysis; however the "historical Socrates" departed this life, we can be quite sure that it was not in the idealized manner described by Plato.[101] What the account does, however, is to bring Socrates's death into line with his life and teaching, thus illustrating the essential truth of his philosophy. Often of course a biographer could not have known the exact details of a subject's end, particularly those last intimate moments, and so would be forced to invent a fitting exit. Even Suetonius, writing about some of the most documented men of his day, has a dearth of actual facts and relies both on invented details and an artistic patterning across the whole sequence of death scenes.[102] At other times a biographer might find conflicting accounts in his sources. This is hardly surprising: a man's friends and enemies might describe the same events in significantly differing ways as each attempted to impose meaning on what they had witnessed. Sometimes, however, accounts differed enormously. Cornelius Nepos, for example, knew of various accounts of the death of the Athenian naval commander Thermistocles; some said that he died in prison, but Nepos himself preferred to follow Thucydides, who claimed that he died of a disease in Magnesia (2.10). Diogenes Laertius was well aware that several of his philosophers had attracted competing accounts of their ends; rather than choose between them, he preferred to report them all. Thus

100. On the Maccabean martyrs, see Droge and Tabor, *Noble Death*, 69–76; van Henten and Avemarie, *Martyrdom*, 45–49, 62–76; on various views of the afterlife in first-century Judaism, see Klawans, *Josephus*, 92–115.

101. Gill, "Death of Socrates." In the case of Livy's Decius Mus, mentioned on p. 59 above, it is not clear that he even took part in the battle! See Doran, "Narratives of Noble Death," 385.

102. So R. Ash, "Never Say Die!"; see also D. Hurley, "Rhetorics of Assassination: Ironic Reversal and the Emperor Gaius," in Power and Gibson, *Suetonius the Biographer*, 146–58; for similar features in Diogenes Laertius, see Kechagia, "Dying Philosophers."

we are told that various accounts of Diogenes's death were in circulation: some said he was seized with colic after eating raw octopus, others claimed that he was bitten on the foot while dividing an octopus between his dogs, and a third version (favored by his friends) was that he held his breath in a deliberate attempt to end his life (*Lives* 6.2.76–77).[103] Philostratus, too, indicates that there were differing accounts of Apollonius's end.[104] In most cases, of course, the biographer would simply choose whichever account best suited his purposes, or would even make up his own. Xenophon, for example, seems to have rejected accounts that described the death of Cyrus in battle in favor of having his hero die at home in his palace (a death better suited to his purposes in the *Cyropaedia*).[105]

The ancients were quite well aware of all these limitations and constraints in the reporting of death, and they allowed for much artistic license. Cicero maintained that historians have a right when describing death to "adorn it rhetorically and trag-ically" (*Brutus* 11.42). Last words were particularly susceptible to "improvement," and few biographers worth their craft could resist the temptation to assign an appo-site and revealing final quotation (a point we shall return to in Chapter 6).[106] But what about the rest of the subject's life? How far was historical accuracy prized here?

Biographical Fact and Fiction

We might well suspect that the moralizing purpose of most biographies led to a certain amount of distortion and idealization. At the very least, the biographer had to be selective, choosing from all available sources only those sayings and events that cohered with the portrait that he wished to develop. This is stated explicitly by Lucian in the closing lines of his *Demonax*, where he notes that he has "made but a small selection of the material available" but hopes it may nevertheless "serve to give readers some idea of this great man's character" (67). Plutarch, too, was well aware that real lives are not composed solely of virtue or vice, but admits in one of his exemplary lives that he strove to make the most of his subject's positive

103. See also the various accounts in *Lives* of the ends of Menedemus (2.142–43), Hera-clides (5.89–91), Chrysippus (7.184–85), Pythagoras (8.39–40), Empedocles (8.67–75), and Zeno of Elea (9.26–28).

104. Philostratus, *Life of Apollonius of Tyana* 8.30–31.

105. Xenophon, *Cyropaedia* 8.7; on Cyrus's death in battle, see Ctesias, *Persica* 7 and Herodotus, *Histories* 1.214 (though both describe different battles!). See further, S. R. Bassett, "The Death of Cyrus the Younger," *ClQ* 49 (1999): 473–83.

106. For a wide-ranging survey, see J. M. Smith, "Famous (or Not So Famous) Last Words" (paper given to the Markan Literary Sources Section, SBL Annual Meeting, Atlanta, 2016).

attributes while quietly dispensing with those that detracted (*Cimon* 2.4–5).[107] For most biographers, the tendency to caricature, exaggerate, and idealize must have been difficult to resist. And while some (such as Plutarch or Suetonius) were clearly interested in historical research and reliability,[108] others (such as Xenophon in his *Cyropaedia* or Philostratus in the *Life of Apollonius of Tyana*) were happy to draw on what can only be regarded as legendary material.[109]

Cicero cited Polybius in support of his view that while historians had to stick to the truth, a biographer could take rather more liberties with the facts (*Letters to Friends* 5.12).[110] This general assumption has been reinforced by Christopher Pelling's investigations of historical accuracy in Plutarch.[111] He finds that the bi-

---

107. For further discussion, see Russell, "On Reading," 143.

108. C. S. Keener carefully compared Suetonius's portrait of Otho with that sketched by Tacitus in his *Histories* and concluded that Suetonius aimed at historical accuracy. Of course, the interpreter needs to take into account certain conventions of the genre (a biographer is less likely than a historian to give speeches or details of wars), but by and large Suetonius's historical information is no less impressive than that of Tacitus (and similar things could be said for Plutarch). Keener went on to conclude that what was true of Suetonius was true of other ancient biographies, and that the genre as a whole tended to put a high value on historical accuracy; "Otho: A Targeted Comparison of Suetonius' Biography and Tacitus' History, with Implications for the Gospels' Historical Reliability," *BBR* 21 (2011): 331–56. See also his "Assumptions in Historical-Jesus Research: Using Ancient Biographies and Disciples' Traditioning as a Control," *JSHJ* 9 (2011): 26–58; and more recently *Christobiography: Memories, History, and the Reliability of the Gospels* (Grand Rapids: Eerdmans, 2019). As will be apparent from the following paragraphs, I am rather less inclined than Keener to regard historical accuracy as a particular concern of most biographers.

109. In contrast to Keener (see previous note), J. B. Chance compared the gospels with four works that stood somewhere between *bios* and the novel: the *Ninus Romance*, Xenophon's *Cyropaedia*, Philostratus's *Life of Apollonius of Tyana*, and the *Alexander Romance*. Each of these works exhibits a high level of fiction and at times what appears to be a complete lack of concern for historical fact. Chance concluded from this that fictional elements were an integral part of ancient *bioi*, and that those found within the gospels were due to the nature of the biographical narrative itself; "Fiction in Ancient Biography: An Approach to a Sensitive Issue in Gospel Interpretation," *Perspectives in Religious Studies* 18 (1991): 125–42. (We might add here the much later *Augustan History* [*Historia Augusta*], a collection of biographies from the late fourth or early fifth century, much of which seems almost entirely fictional.) Yet once again, this is too one-sided a reading, as the following paragraphs will demonstrate. On fiction in the biographies of early Greek poets, see M. R. Lefkowitz, "Patterns of Fiction in Ancient Biography," *The American Scholar* 52 (1983): 205–18.

110. On this point, see also Momigliano, *Development*, 55–56.

111. C. R. B. Pelling, "Truth and Fiction in Plutarch's *Lives*," in *Antonine Literature*, ed.

ographer was willing to use a story even when its accuracy had been disproved on chronological grounds, such as Solon's meeting with Croesus (*Solon* 27.1). Plutarch is far less critical in his use of sources if a particular story suits his purposes, such as accounts of the extravagance of Antony or his infatuation with Cleopatra. He adds circumstantial detail and bends the truth, either to highlight a certain character trait (for example Antony's passivity) or to improve the flow of his narrative (Caesar's trips to Greece and Rome, for example, are tidied up). Finally, the same events are recounted rather differently in different lives (examples might be the debates of December 50/January 49 as variously recounted in the lives of *Pompey*, *Caesar*, and *Antony*; the Lupercalia incident of 44 as found in *Antony* and *Caesar*; and Antony's behavior at Philippi as narrated in *Antony* and *Brutus*). Pelling sums up his findings in the following manner: "So what do we conclude about Plutarch's attitude to the truth? He does not always behave as we would, certainly; he tidies and improves, and in some cases he must have known he was being historically inaccurate. But the process has limits, and the untruthful tidying and improving is never very extensive. The big changes, the substantial improvements tend to come where he could generally claim—'yes, it must have been like that.'"[112] There are limits to Plutarch's "creative reconstruction": he might enhance a subject's role in a particular event, but only so far as it might help to draw out his character, and not to such an extent that it falsifies the central thrust of the life. Where there are gaps in his sources, particularly in relation to childhood, he generally feels no compunction to fill them for the sake of completeness.[113] His aim above all is not to mislead his readers, but to delineate character in the clearest possible terms.[114]

Similar findings characterize a recent collection of essays edited by Koen De Temmerman and Kristoffel Demoen on the topic of "fictionalization" in ancient biography. In the first chapter to the volume, De Temmerman notes that the border between history and fiction tends to be blurred in most types of literature, but that biography is particularly prone to slip into fiction. This is partly due to the

---

D. A. Russell (Oxford: Oxford University Press, 1990), 19–52; also Pelling, *Life of Antony* (Cambridge: Cambridge University Press, 1988), in various places.

112. Pelling, "Truth and Fiction," 41; for similar sentiments, see also Pelling, *Antony*, 35. As Pelling observes, Plutarch is more interested in history in certain lives (e.g., *Caesar*) than others (e.g., *Antony*); "Truth and Fiction," 29.

113. See also Pelling's "Childhood and Personality in Greek Biography," in Pelling, *Characterization*, 213–44.

114. For a similar assessment of Cornelius Nepos, see Pryzwansky, "Cornelius Nepos," esp. 99–100. As she notes, scholars nowadays tend to appreciate Nepos on his own terms and are more inclined to regard him as a skilled biographer rather than a "failed historian."

genre's encomiastic aims, but it is also because "biography is almost always having to conjecture, interpret and reconstruct actions, private moments, motivations and attitudes."[115] De Temmerman rightly argues that we need to move beyond any easy opposition between "truth" and "fiction." Biographies take their place on a spectrum with the lives of the poets and Xenophon's *Cyropaedia* at one end and Plutarch and Suetonius at the other; some take historical accuracy more seriously, but none are free from some degree of fictionalization. Indeed, the process of constructing a narrative always lends a certain element of fiction to the account, even when authors include elaborate claims to diligent research. This expresses itself in a range of areas, from invented speeches to fictive accounts of birth and childhood; from intertextual allusions to other characters with whom the author wants to associate his subject to imagined details at the hero's death.

In many respects, this should hardly surprise us: precisely the same challenges and constraints face even the most diligent of modern biographers. We are familiar in the modern world with the "research biography" in which the author/scholar has spent a great deal of time researching the minutiae of his or her chosen subject. We expect these often lengthy tomes to be "factual" and "historically accurate"; in fact, it would seriously diminish the biography's standing if reviewers could easily point to inaccuracies. And yet even here there are limitations. Much depends on the way material is put together, the juxtapositions, links, or breaks that the biographer imposes on her material. Imputing a subject's inner feelings and motives is perhaps the most difficult of all. As Hilary Spurling, prize-winning biographer of Ivy Compton Burnett and Henri Matisse (among others), notes, "In order to convey . . . factual material, the biographer will generally and I think inevitably, be forced to stoop to fiction. . . . Any reconstruction which is not to be purely external, and therefore superficial, must be quite largely made up. What you are doing, after all, is creating a character."[116] Even modern biography, then, however scrupulously researched, is not simply the transmission of certain well-researched facts; it too requires an imaginative element that turns words on a page into something living.

A further complication surrounds the use of anecdotes, or *chreiai* (a topic to which we shall return in the next chapter). Anecdotes are indispensable to biographers; indeed, many *bioi* are little more than a collection of short stories and

---

115. De Temmerman, "Ancient Biography," 4.

116. H. Spurling, "Neither Morbid nor Ordinary," in *The Troubled Face of Biography*, ed. E. Homberger and J. Charmley (London: Macmillan, 1988), 116. Similar sentiments are expressed by V. Glendinning, "Lies and Silences," in the same volume, particularly 49, and by H. Mantel in her BBC Radio 4 Reith Lectures (2017).

witty sayings. The problem, however, as Richard Saller points out, is that by their very nature anecdotes were frequently of indeterminate origin, spread about by gossips or storytellers, or pressed into the service of orators or moralists as *exempla*. Anecdotes are typically fluid, even when written down; while the main point may retain a certain stability, other elements such as setting, incidental characters, and even the identity of the main protagonist are subject to almost infinite variety. None of this was of any great concern to the biographer: what mattered was that the anecdote exposed something of the subject's character, often in a concise and pithy manner. Once again, there are correspondences here with the modern concept of the "apocryphal" story, which, irrespective of whether it actually happened, perfectly captures something of a person's nature. We are generally quite happy to repeat such stories, even if we doubt that they have any basis in fact. Did Churchill really take to the London Underground to ask ordinary people what they thought about standing up to Hitler? Did George Washington really admit to cutting down his father's cherry tree? Neither have any basis in fact, but both perfectly illustrate the kind of things these great men might have done and so are worth repeating.[117] Questions of historical accuracy—both now and in antiquity—are secondary to the anecdote's ability to say something profoundly true about the subject's character.

Many ancient biographers knew their subjects personally. Cornelius Nepos was on friendly terms with Atticus, Tacitus had a good relationship with his father-in-law, and Lucian had spent his formative years with his teacher, Demonax.[118] Yet even here we need to be cautious. Despite his close personal connection to Agricola, Tacitus was quite willing to bend historical facts in the interests of both highlighting his father-in-law's abilities and making his own political points.[119] And scholars have so frequently noticed that Lucian casts his teacher in his own image that there are some who would doubt his very existence.[120] Firsthand acquaintance clearly gave the biographer an excellent source of stories and information on which to draw, but it was only to be expected that the resulting life would be marked by

117. There appears to be no evidence for Churchill's trip on the London Underground (which was recently dramatized by the film *Darkest Hour*, 2017); the story of Washington and the cherry tree was deliberately invented by one of his first biographers, Mason Locke Weems (*The Life of Washington*, 1800), as an early display of the future president's virtues.

118. Bryan also notes that Suetonius was Hadrian's secretary and friends with Pliny and was able to appeal to his own observations (*The Divine Augustus* 7.1; *Nero* 57.2; *Domitianus* 12.2) or hearsay (*Gaius Caligula* 9.3; *Otho* 10; *The Divine Titus* 3.2), *Preface*, 47–48.

119. On the historical value of the *Agricola*, see D. Sailor, "The Agricola," 39–41.

120. So for example D. Clay, "Lucian of Samosata."

the biographer's own interests and agenda, not to mention a frequently one-sided emphasis on the hero's exemplary virtues.[121]

All this means that while biography was closely related in many ways to history, and often took "historical" subjects as its focus, we need to be careful about assuming that biographers were interested in history for its own sake. Their purpose was not to provide an accurate list of all that their subject did and said, but to lay bare the essence of the man, to re-create a living character. As Plutarch realized, this often involved the minutiae of life, and where precise facts were no longer available, the biographer had to rely on conjecture, interpretation, and imaginative reconstruction. All of this is summarized well by Tomas Hägg in his exhaustive treatment of ancient *bioi*: "ancient life-writers did not encounter among their contemporaries the same demands for documentary truth as their modern colleagues do, nor did for that matter ancient historiographers.... Conversations are allowed to be fictitious, and insight is readily granted into the acting characters' feelings, thoughts, and motives, as long as some kind of verisimilitude is maintained. The establishment of any form of higher truth—be it poetic, psychological, philosophical, or religious— overrules demands for the truth of facts."[122]

The Preserve of the Elite?

All the works considered so far in this chapter were written by highly literate authors, many with connections to the very highest levels of society. Readers might well be asking themselves what any of this has to do with Mark's Gospel, which, on any reading, is unlikely to have derived from elite circles.

Unfortunately, most "middle-brow" literature from the imperial period has not survived (in fact, biblical scholars may be surprised to find that many of the works mentioned above survive only in a handful of later copies). It is reasonable to suppose, however, that there was something of a "trickle-down" effect. People would have been exposed to literature in a variety of settings: dramatic performances at festivals, public readings of poetry at the games, recitations of literary

121. Interestingly, eyewitness testimony is often regarded by modern biographers as problematic. A. Thwaite writes, "among the mass of available evidence, it is usually the survivors' memories I find least valuable, especially when someone has been dead fifty years or so. The people that remember them have repeated their memories so often that, like the words in the children's game Chinese Whispers, they bear little real meaning"; "Writing Lives," in Homberger and Charmley, *Troubled Face*, 17.

122. Hägg, *Art of Biography*, 3–4. A similar sentiment is expressed by Momigliano, *Development*, 57.

works, lectures in public colonnades, speeches in law courts (which were held in the open), storytellers, and street-corner philosophers.[123] Thus the rhetorical and literary conventions of the educated elite would have effortlessly percolated down to the lower levels of society. Even with only a basic level of education, an intelligent and thoughtful writer would be perfectly able to mimic the genres with which he had come into contact, and even to ape some of their standard conventions and practices. And, we can assume, many in his audience would have understood what he was doing.

Popular tastes may well be reflected in the *Acts of the Alexandrian Martyrs*, a group of largely fictitious accounts focusing on confrontations between Alexandrian leaders (particularly gymnasiarchs) and various emperors. Dating from the first to the third centuries CE, the works clearly reflect tensions between different ethnic groups in Alexandria: emperors are caricatured as crude dictators, unduly influenced by Jews, freedmen, and women, in stark contrast to the Alexandrian martyrs who display their nobility in the face of justice and torture. Although fragmentary, the *Acts* were clearly composed of a lively collection of dialogues, trial scenes, and grisly executions.[124]

One biography that may well have derived from lower cultural circles is the *Life of Aesop*. Circulating widely, though anonymously, and in a variety of recensions, the work recounts the life of the slave Aesop who constantly outwits his master and wins his freedom, but finally loses his life after insulting the citizens of Delphi.[125] Grammatiki Karla identifies many features of "popular aesthetics" in the work:

123. The "trickle-down" effect is assumed by most scholars, including Aune, *Literary Environment*, 12–13; G. Strecker, *History of New Testament Literature*, trans. C. Katter with H.-J. Mollenhauer (Harrisburg, PA: Trinity Press International, 1997; German orig., 1992), 109; H. Gamble, *Books and Readers in the Early Church: A History of Early Christian Texts* (New Haven: Yale University Press, 1995), 18; P. J. Achtemeier, "Omne Verbum Sonat: The New Testament and the Oral Environment of Late Western Antiquity," *JBL* 109 (1990): 7, 20; M. A. Beavis, *Mark's Audience: The Literary and Social History of Mark 4.11–12* (Sheffield: JSOT Press, 1989), 8–9; C. Bryan, *A Preface to Mark: Notes on the Gospel in Its Literary and Cultural Settings* (New York: Oxford University Press, 1993), 17–18. On the prevalence of storytellers in Roman society, see A. Scobie, "Storytellers, Storytelling, and the Novel in Graeco-Roman Antiquity," *Rheinisches Museum für Philologie* 122 (1979): 229–59.

124. On these texts, which are sometimes referred to as the *Acts of the Pagan Martyrs*, see Musurillo, *Acts*, especially 247–58; van Henten and Avemarie, *Martyrdom*, 21–23; and more recently A. Harker, *Loyalty and Dissidence in Roman Egypt: The Case of the Acta-Alexandrinorum* (Cambridge: Cambridge University Press, 2008).

125. The *Life of Aesop* is often described as an "open text" to denote the fluidity of its textual transmission and the lack of any clear single author. See n. 9 on p. 40, above.

its simple use of Koine Greek, including a heavy utilization of *kai*-parataxis and asyndeton (both features of the spoken word); its humor, which frequently derives from sexual innuendo and bodily functions; and its straightforward structure, comprising episodes of varying length that tell of Aesop's adventures and encounters.[126] The work is a social satire, presenting a world of reversals where nothing is quite as it seems. It was clearly designed to entertain but also has a didactic purpose, imparting moral truths and practical wisdom to its listeners. Although largely targeting a broadly uneducated audience, the work plays with a variety of registers, perhaps challenging those with greater learning to identify its intertextual echoes and to appreciate the work on a more sophisticated level.[127] What the work clearly demonstrates, however, is that biography in the early imperial age was by no means limited to the educated classes but had a wide popular appeal.

In the next chapter we will need to investigate Mark's level of education and that of his audience to see how his work fits into an embryonic Christian "book culture." We shall also compare the work's structure, use of sources, and authorial voice to the biographies encountered in this chapter, in an attempt to see how it fits in general terms with other roughly contemporary *bioi*. First, however, I would like to clarify one further point: Should we talk about "subgroups" within ancient *bioi*?

Subgroups and Subtypes?

It has become common among New Testament scholars to describe the gospels as belonging to a particular *type* of Greco-Roman biography. David Aune, for example, describes them as a "subtype" of biographical literature, the central feature of which is their "Judaeo-Christian assumptions."[128] In a rather different vein, Richard Bauckham and Craig Keener tend to refer to them as "historical biographies," a label that springs from an assumption that the gospel contents are broadly accurate accounts of what really happened, and that serves to distinguish them from *bioi* of a

126. G. A. Karla, "*Life of Aesop*: Fictional Biography as Popular Literature?," in De Temmerman and Demoen, *Writing Biography*, 47–64. The work's wide circulation also suggests a popular appeal (63). See also R. Pervo, "A Nihilist Fabula: Introducing the *Life of Aesop*," in *Ancient Fiction and Early Christian Narrative*, ed. R. F. Hock, J. B. Chance, and J. Perkins (Atlanta: Scholars, 1998), 77–120.

127. Karla, "*Life of Aesop*," 63–64. By labeling this work as "popular," I do not of course assume any kind of mass "popular culture" associated with wide reading; as M. A. Tolbert points out, "the clearest definition of popular literature might be *literature composed in such a way as to be accessible to a wide spectrum of society, both literate and illiterate*"; *Sowing the Gospel*, 72 (italics original).

128. Aune, *Literary Environment*, 46–47.

more fictional nature.[129] But these two classifications are not the same: one focuses on content, the other on an evaluation of historical accuracy. Each classification is useful only insofar as it relates to a discussion of contents (so Aune) or historicity (so Bauckham and Keener); if any other topic is to be considered, the taxonomy becomes meaningless.

Attempts to categorize ancient biographical literature as a whole have a long history, going back at least as early as Friedrich Leo's *Die griechisch-römische Biographie nach ihrer literarischen Form*, published in 1901. Leo famously distinguished two "types" of *bios* according to their literary form. The first group, or "peripatetic," exhibited a chronological structure and tended to focus on generals and politicians, prime examples being the individual biographies that make up Plutarch's *Parallel Lives*. The second group, or "Alexandrian," preferred a more thematic systematization, well suited for reflecting on the lives of poets and artists, the prime representative here being Suetonius (who, for Leo, was the first to apply this type of biography to emperors).[130] Following Leo, others have sought to extend this classification. Fritz Wehli, for example, suggested a threefold division: (1) lives of philosophers and poets (with the material arranged chronologically), (2) *encomia* of political leaders and generals, and (3) lives of literary characters.[131] And Klaus Berger suggested a fourfold grouping: to Leo's two types, he added *encomia* and popular novelistic biographies (such as the *Life of Aesop*).[132] All of this sounds good in theory, though there will inevitably be gray areas and uncertainties when it comes to specific works. Where, for example, should the gospels be placed in all of this? With the Suetonian type? The *encomia*? Or even the novelistic *bioi*? Good arguments could be mustered for any one of these (or even a combination).

In the 1970s, Charles Talbert devised an entirely novel classification according to *social function*. In general terms, Talbert distinguished between the didactic lives that call for emulation of their hero (by far the majority of extant *bioi*) and those that are unconcerned with providing a moral example. The first group were further

---

129. R. J. Bauckham, "The Eyewitnesses in the Gospel of Mark," *SEÅ* 74 (2009): 19–39; C. S. Keener, *The Gospel of John: A Commentary* (Peabody, MA: Hendrickson, 2003), 1:29–34.

130. F. Leo, *Die griechisch-römische Biographie nach ihrer literarischen Form* (Leipzig: Teubner, 1901). Leo's classification did extend beyond formal characteristics to some extent, particularly in his suggestion that biographies in the first group were often composed with an eye toward public performance, while those in the second were largely intended for private study.

131. F. Wehrli, "Gnōme, Anekdote und Biographie," *MH* 30 (1973): 193–208.

132. K. Berger, "Hellenistische Gattungen im Neuen Testament," *ANRW* II 25.2: 1236.

divided into five types. Type A simply provided readers with a pattern to copy (such as Lucian's *Demonax*); Type B aimed to dispel a false image of a teacher and to provide a true model to follow (such as Xenophon's *Memorabilia* or Philostratus's *Life of Apollonius of Tyana*); Type C sought to discredit a teacher (such as Lucian's *The Passing of Peregrinus*); Type D demonstrated where the "living voice" was to be found among a philosopher's successors (as illustrated by Diogenes Laertius's *Lives of Eminent Philosophers*); and Type E provided the hermeneutical key to a teacher's doctrine (as demonstrated by Porphyry's *Life of Plotinus*, which acted as an explanatory introduction to his writings). Talbert located the gospels within Type B, arguing that they both attacked rival understandings of Jesus and presented their own more accurate versions.[133] This classification sounds promising, though once again it is better in theory than in practice. Individual *bioi* may exhibit more than one of the traits identified by Talbert, and some are hard to place—where, for example, would we situate the *Life of Aesop*? Furthermore, scholars are far less inclined today than in Talbert's time to assume that the gospels have a polemical agenda, to see them attacking rival positions (whether those of Hellenistic Christ followers or Jerusalem believers)—a point we shall need to come back to later. All in all, then, Talbert's classification does not really help us to see which *bioi* are most analogous to the gospels.

In 2015, Justin Smith divided them according to their audience. He distinguished between noncontemporary and contemporary subject matter, and what he calls "focused" and "open" texts. The former were written for a distinguishable audience (such as Philo's *Life of Moses*, written for detractors of Jewish beliefs, or Tacitus's *Agricola*, written for like-minded Roman intellectuals), while the latter were written for a much broader readership (Smith locates Suetonius's *Life of Augustus* here, or Lucian's *Demonax*).[134] Yet, as Smith himself admits, such a categorization is useful only for the purpose of "addressing questions pertaining to the relationships between authors, subjects and audiences."[135] Even here it is not always easy to decide where to locate any particular biography—sometimes a work's audience cannot be determined, and some *bioi* may have been directed at multiple audiences, perhaps a primary readership and a range of secondary ones. Rather than consisting of two distinct poles, it may be better to think of a work's

---

133. C. H. Talbert, *What Is a Gospel? The Genre of the Canonical Gospels* (Minneapolis: Fortress, 1977), 91–98. All but Type D, he suggests, also have parallels among lives of rulers.

134. J. M. Smith, *Why Βίος? On the Relationship between Gospel Genre and Implied Audience* (London: T&T Clark/Bloomsbury, 2015), 55–61.

135. Smith, *Why Βίος?*, 55. Smith categorizes the gospels as "contemporary focussed," meaning that they have a primary audience in view, though not a specific community (204).

audience as a sliding scale or a spectrum, with a more specific, target audience at one end and broader, potential audiences toward the other (a point we shall come back to in the next chapter).

More recently still, David Konstan and Robyn Walsh have distinguished two major trajectories within the biographical tradition. The first might be characterized as "civic" biographies, organized around dominant social values. These derive ultimately from Xenophon's *Agesilaus* and include the biographical works of Nepos, Plutarch, and Suetonius. The fundamental concern here is to reveal the subject's character through deeds, and so the work can be organized chronologically or topically, depending on what best suits the material. The second are "subversive" biographies, and have their origins in Xenophon's *Memorabilia*, a much looser collection of anecdotes or conversations involving Socrates and various dialogue partners, organized loosely around various themes. Socrates, of course, was also a paragon of virtue, but the portrait is different from those in the first group. Socrates's character and teaching are revealed through his words: he is nonconformist, a person on the margins of society. Lacking political power, he must rely on his wit and sharp mind, faculties that constantly threaten the established social order. Biographies in this mold tend to be countercultural and subversive and include the *Life of Aesop*, the *Alexander Romance*, and the gospels.[136]

While such groupings may encourage us to compare and contrast biographies in productive ways, my own view is that, in general, such distinctions are not particularly helpful. Ancient authors themselves do not seem to have categorized different types of biography, nor is it wise in the field of literature to impose modern distinctions on creative pieces, especially ones as fluid as *bioi*.[137] In broad terms, Mark has most in common with Greek lives of philosophers, especially those (the majority) that hold up their subject as a model to be imitated. Loveday Alexander labels these "intellectual biography," by which she means "biographies of individuals distinguished for their prowess in the intellectual field (philosophers, poets, dramatists, doctors)." This would most naturally seem to include the founder of a religious group distinguished by its often countercultural teaching (or "philosophy"). Most of the comparisons in the next few chapters, therefore, will be with this type of biography, particularly Philo's *Life of Moses*, Lucian's *Demonax*, Philostratus's *Life of Apollonius of Tyana*, or Diogenes Laertius's *Lives of Eminent Philosophers*. At other

---

136. D. Konstan and R. Walsh, "Civic and Subversive Biography in Antiquity," in De Temmerman and Demoen, *Writing Biography*, 26–44.

137. T. Hägg's words are apposite here: "The more I have worked with these texts, the less I can see the point in drawing borders where the authors themselves so obviously moved over mapless terrain"; *Art of Biography*, xi; see further, 67–68.

times, however, useful comparisons might be made with early *encomia*, or the works of Cornelius Nepos, Plutarch, or Suetonius—particularly insofar as they illustrate cultural assumptions and expectations. In the following chapters, then, my basic working method will be to compare and contrast Mark with what seem to me to be the most significant parallels among other ancient *bioi*.

All biographical writing is concerned, to some extent, with two distinct biographies. There is the biographical subject, who provides the focus of the written text, but there is also the much more mysterious yet ever-present biography of the writer of the work, the person who wants this particular life to be told in this particular way. In the next chapter, I shall turn to what we know of this second, rather shadowy character.

CHAPTER 3

Mark the Biographer

Tell them I've had a wonderful life.

—Ludwig Wittgenstein, on his deathbed[1]

The biographer occupies a powerful position. He or she decides not only *who* should have a biography but also *how* that story should be told: where the account should begin, and where it ought to end; what should be included, even stressed, and what should be quietly dropped; how the material should be structured, and what tone the narrative should take. This chapter will begin to look at Mark as an ancient biographer. What can we say about him as an author? What sort of an audience did he expect to reach, and for what purpose? How does he structure his narrative, both at the macro and micro levels? To what extent was he constrained by tradition? And what are we to make of his oddly abrupt opening? First, though, it will be useful to situate Mark within the vibrant reading culture that existed in the late first century.

Profile of a Biographer

The early imperial period was a world that knew of books and writing, and knew of them in abundance. Texts of all types played a crucial role in this period: not only literary works but also inscriptions, public notices, letters, contracts, tax receipts, census records, marriage/divorce certificates, wills, brick stamps, potters' marks, and graffiti are found in great numbers throughout the whole Mediterranean region. The contents and significance of these texts must have been known and understood well beyond the small percentage of the population who had acquired any kind of an education.[2] And while literacy rates were undeniably low, the upward mobility of

1. N. Malcolm, *Ludwig Wittgenstein: A Memoir* (Oxford: Oxford University Press, 1966), 100.

2. On this, see E. Rawson, *Intellectual Life in the Late Roman Republic* (London: Duck-

78

the imperial period seems to have encouraged a situation in which reading became a feature of wider social circles more than ever before.[3] As Harry Gamble puts it, "beyond the small aristocratic circles where the leisured enjoyment of books was traditional, there were the ranks of professional rhetoricians, grammarians, and philosophers, and still others of the lower social orders who, while not well-educated, were literate to a degree and had some interest, if not in *belles-lettres*, then in lesser forms of literature."[4]

Jews, of course, had a long and rich written tradition and a practice of gathering together in weekly meetings or at festivals to hear those texts read out, interpreted, and made relevant to their daily needs.[5] Christ followers, too, were aware of the social and cultural power of written texts. Although a full Christian book culture

worth, 1985); R. S. Bagnall, *Everyday Writing in the Graeco-Roman East* (Berkeley: University of California Press, 2011); H. Gamble, "The Book Trade in the Roman Empire," in *The Early Text of the New Testament*, ed. C. H. Hill and M. J. Kruger (Oxford: Oxford University Press, 2012), 23–36; L. W. Hurtado and C. Keith, "Writing and Books Production in the Hellenistic and Roman Periods," in *The New Cambridge History of the Bible: From the Beginning to 600*, ed. J. Carleton Paget and J. Schaper (Cambridge: Cambridge University Press, 2013), 63–80; J. Kloppenborg, "Literate Media in Early Christian Groups: The Creation of a Christian Book Culture," *JECS* 22 (2014): 21–59; and C. Keith, "Early Christian Book Culture and the Emergence of the First Written Gospel," in *Mark, Manuscripts and Monotheism. Essays in Honor of Larry W. Hurtado*, ed. C. Keith and D. T. Roth (London: Bloomsbury, 2015), 22–39. On the level of literacy in the ancient world, see H. V. Harris, *Ancient Literacy* (Cambridge, MA: Harvard University Press, 1989), who puts the rate at around 10 percent; and for rates among Jews, see C. Hezser, *Jewish Literacy in Roman Palestine* (Tübingen: Mohr Siebeck, 2001). R. Thomas rightly notes that offering percentages of "literates" presupposes a definition of literacy that irons out variety and complexity. She suggests that it is more useful to talk of the uses that writing is put to and of different types of literacy; "Writing, Reading, Public and Private 'Literacies': Functional Literacy and Democratic Literacy in Greece," in *Ancient Literacies: The Culture of Reading in Greece and Rome*, ed. W. A. Johnson and H. N. Parker (Oxford: Oxford University Press, 2011), 14.

3. So T. Morgan, *Literate Education in the Hellenistic and Roman Worlds* (Cambridge: Cambridge University Press, 1998), 2, 63; also R. Cribiore, *Gymnastics of the Mind: Greek Education in Hellenistic and Roman Egypt* (Princeton: Princeton University Press, 2001), 159; M. Beard et al., *Literacy in the Roman World* (Ann Arbor: University of Michigan Press, 1991); Gamble, "Book Trade."

4. Gamble, "Book Trade," 27.

5. J. Assmann, "Form as a Mnemonic Device: Cultural Texts and Cultural Memory," in *Performing the Gospel: Orality, Memory and Mark; Essays Dedicated to Werner Kelber*, ed. R. A. Horsley, J. A. Draper, and J. M. Foley (Minneapolis: Fortress, 2006), 78; Gamble, *Books and Readers*, 19.

would emerge only in the fourth century, John Kloppenborg has shown that already by the late second century—at least in some circles—Christian identity was intimately connected with the possession of certain books, despite the low educational level of most believers in this period.[6] Even a century earlier, however, in the gospels themselves, there is a surprising stress on "writtenness." It is clear that Mark expects his work to be *read*, as his direct address to the reader in 13:14 makes clear.[7] And elsewhere the sacred Scriptures are clearly written texts: both Mark's narrator and the Markan Jesus, for example, appeal to what is *written* (*graphō*),[8] and the Markan Jesus can challenge his opponents regarding their *reading*—not hearing—of Scripture (2:25, *anaginōskō*). Building on this Markan basis, it was presumably not a huge step for Luke to present a fully literate Jesus, capable of both reading a scroll in public and expounding its meaning (Luke 4:16–21).[9] Whatever the historicity behind this scene, the image of an educated Jesus clearly spoke powerfully to emerging Christianity's social and cultural ambitions. Mark's decision to present the life of Jesus as a *bios*, then, presumably stands at the very beginning of what would quickly become an aspirational early Christian book culture.

In order to gain a fuller understanding of how Mark participated in this literary landscape, we shall need to investigate his level of education. Much has been written lately on Greek education in the Hellenistic and Roman eras, allowing us to reconstruct a fuller picture than ever before of ancient *paideia*. Moreover, by comparing the hundreds of Egyptian school texts written on papyri, ostraca, and wax tablets with the more idealized aspirations of ancient literary theorists (such as the *Institutes of Oratory* penned by the famous rhetor Quintilian), scholars have come to a more realistic assessment of what ancient education actually looked like in practice.[10] The picture that emerges is, on one hand, marked by great variety: at

6. Kloppenborg, "Literate Media."

7. It does not really matter whether Mark has in mind a private reader (so Kloppenborg, "Literate Media," 39) or a lector (so Hurtado "Oral Fixation," 338, and Keith, "Early Christian Book Culture," 37n66). Perhaps both are equally intended.

8. Markan narrator: 1:2; Markan Jesus: 7:6; 9:12, 13; 11:17; 14:21, 27.

9. For a second-century insertion of Jesus's literacy into John's Gospel, see C. Keith, *The Pericope Adulterae, the Gospel of John and the Literacy of Jesus* (Leiden: Brill, 2009).

10. Useful recent treatments include Morgan, *Literate Education*; Cribiore, *Gymnastics*; M. A. Beavis, *Mark's Audience: The Literary and Social Setting of Mark 4.11–12* (Sheffield: Sheffield Academic, 1989), 20–31; R. F. Hock, "Introduction," in *The Chreia in Ancient Rhetoric*, vol. 1, *The Progymnasmata*, ed. R. F. Hock and E. N. O'Neil (Atlanta: Scholars, 1986), 3–47; R. F. Hock and E. N. O'Neil, *The Chreia in Ancient Rhetoric*, vol. 2, *Classroom Exercises* (Atlanta: SBL Press, 2002); and the detailed discussion of educational exercises collected by G. A. Kennedy, *Progymnasmata: Greek Textbooks of Prose Composition and Rhetoric* (Atlanta:

a time before any regulation, and when teaching was entirely a private enterprise, students could be taught in any manner of ways, depending on their social or geographical circumstances, what they hoped to do with an education, the availability of teachers, parental wishes, and so on.[11] And yet, on the other hand, there is a surprisingly consistent body of *content* that stretched from Alexander's conquests right into the Roman era and beyond, in both urban and rural contexts, with very little alteration.[12] Clearly, as Teresa Morgan notes, "the contents of education were regarded as more important in the ancient world than the way they were taught."[13]

Ancient *paideia* is usually divided into three tiers, and although this undoubtedly hides what were in reality much less clear-cut divisions (particularly at the lowest stages),[14] consideration of the various levels will be useful in an attempt to pinpoint Mark's level of educational achievement. The first stage included learning the alphabet, writing one's own name, and building up syllables and words until whole sentences could be copied out.[15] Students learned to write out short texts containing nuggets of Greco-Roman wisdom, largely in the form of *chreiai* (or anecdotes) and *gnōmai* (proverbial sayings). Homer was especially popular (particularly the *Iliad*), but Euripedes and the maxims of Isocrates are attested at this level too. The memorization of these short texts not only enhanced the pupil's emerging literacy but also instilled Greco-Roman virtues and values into the child from a young age.[16] By the end of this level, a student would be capable of reading a straightforward text and copying it out, but would not have attained any great skills in composition. Those aspiring to greater levels of attainment would go on to study with a grammarian (or *grammaticus*), where great stress was now placed

SBL Press, 2003). On Jewish education (which seems to have emerged only in the late first century CE), see Hezser, *Jewish Literacy*; also "Private and Public Education," in *The Oxford Handbook of Jewish Daily Life in Roman Palestine*, ed. C. Hezser (Oxford: Oxford University Press, 2010), 465–81; and Hezser, "The Torah versus Homer: Jewish and Greco-Roman Education in Late Roman Palestine," in *Ancient Education and Early Christianity*, ed. M. R. Hauge and A. W. Pitts (London: Bloomsbury, 2016), 5–24.

11. Cribiore, *Gymnastics*, 18, 37.

12. One alteration was the introduction in early Roman times of grammatical texts into rural areas of Egypt, a practice that probably followed what had been standard practice in the cities for some time; Morgan, *Literate Education*, 60.

13. Morgan, *Literate Education*, 32; see also Cribiore, *Gymnastics*, 36–37.

14. Cribiore, *Gymnastics*, 38.

15. For overviews of this level, see Morgan, *Literate Education*, 90–151; Cribiore, *Gymnastics*, 50–53, 160–84; and Hock and O'Neil, *Chreia*, 2:1–49.

16. See the comments of Quintilian, *Institutes of Oratory* 1.1.35–36 and 1.8.5; also Theon, *Progymnasmata* 2.147–8; Seneca, *Moral Epistles* 33.7; and Plutarch, *Marriage Advice* 48.

on the mastery of language through declensions, attention to morphological tables, and the ability to recognize and to use "good" Greek.[17] The reading of short poetic texts continued to be fundamental, now with the addition of *mythoi* (fables) and *diēgēmata* (short narratives). Homer was still paramount, though a wider collection of largely poetic texts drawn from the "greats" of the Greek tradition might be gradually introduced.[18] Teachers would prepare explanations and glossaries to assist pupils as they learned to tackle ever more complex material. Upon completion of this stage, a student would be able to draft short texts, paraphrases, summonses, and letters—more than enough to meet the requirements of most administrative posts.

The culmination of the education system was the third phase, in which a student passed into the tutelage of a rhetor in preparation for a glamorous career as a lawyer or politician.[19] Often this involved moving to a city, and a great deal more expense. Pupils passed through a number of preliminary exercises, known as *progymnasmata*, arranged in ascending order of difficulty. Our earliest example, those of Aelius Theon of Alexandria, gives a sense of what was expected as young men (girls had dropped out by this stage) attempted to enhance their mental dexterity through expanding, contracting, comparing, illustrating, and commenting upon well-known literary forms. The *progymnasmata* taught the aspiring orator a fluency in expression and the ability to follow standard rhetorical arguments, while continual reading (now of prose genres too, including historical texts) not only ensured a complete saturation in Greek culture but also provided models of good writing for students to imitate in their own work.

The question is, of course, how far up this educational ladder we should situate Mark. In the past our author has tended to fare poorly. His style is certainly not of the highest level: it tends to be paratactic (where short sentences are joined together with a simple *kai*), our author is fond of the historic present, and he eschews a more literate use of subordinate clauses in favor of periphrastic tenses. Mark Edwards describes him as "narrow in vocabulary, fallible in grammar and deaf to style."[20] Mark's peculiarities have generally been described as "Semitisms" or "vulgarisms," which, it is assumed, more careful authors would have avoided. The difficulty, however,

---

17. On the contents of this level, see Morgan, *Literate Education*, 152–204; Cribiore, *Gymnastics*, 53–56, 185–219; and Hock and O'Neil, *Chreia*, 2:51–77.

18. See Cribiore, *Gymnastics*, 192–204, on what was read at this level.

19. For fuller details, see Morgan, *Literate Education*, 190–239; Cribiore, *Gymnastics*, 220–44; and Hock and O'Neil, *Chreia*, 2:79–359.

20. M. Edwards, "Gospel and Genre: Some Reservations," in *The Limits of Ancient Biography*, ed. Brian McGing and Judith Mossman (Swansea: Classical Press of Wales, 2006), 56.

lies in knowing what standard of Greek to hold Mark to. In a careful and detailed study of the "tendencies" of the Synoptic tradition, E. P. Sanders notes that several apocryphal gospels (which are generally written in a more literary style) show no reluctance to use *kai*-parataxis, and the *Protevangelium of James* positively favors the construction, despite its otherwise rather high level of Greek. The author may be imitating a Semitic style here, but if so it is a deliberate *choice*, not a sign of poor education.[21] Rather surprisingly, perhaps, Sanders observes that the use of the historic present also tends to increase in the apocryphal gospels, and that Josephus consistently changes the past tenses of 1 Maccabees to presents.[22] Both the use of *kai*-parataxis and the historic present, Sanders concludes, are simply down to personal preference. Thus their presence in Mark does not necessarily tell us anything about his level of education—it may simply have suited Mark to write in a straightforward, vernacular style.

With the appearance of rhetorical criticism in the 1980s, Mark's proposed level of educational attainment rose quite considerably. The pioneering work of Vernon Robbins and Burton Mack, along with a lengthy project at the Institute for Antiquities and Christianity at Claremont, analyzed gospel *pericopae* against those of Greek writers, especially as they are classified and explained within the *progymnasmata*.[23] No longer were Markan vignettes seen as free-floating pieces of oral tradition, but were instead said "to cluster in cleverly designed units of argumentation."[24] Of great interest was the *chreia*, or anecdote, defined by Ronald Hock as "a saying or action that is expressed concisely, attributed to a character, and regarded as useful for liv-

---

21. E. P. Sanders, *The Tendencies of the Synoptic Tradition* (Cambridge: Cambridge University Press, 1969), 190–255.

22. Sanders, *Tendencies*, 229, 253.

23. An early pioneer was R. O. P. Taylor, "Form Criticism in the First Centuries," *ExpTim* 55 (1944): 218–20. See also Hock and O'Neil, *Chreia*, vols. 1–2; V. K. Robbins, "Classifying Pronouncement Stories in Plutarch's Parallel Lives," *Semeia* 20 (1981): 29–52; Robbins, "Pronouncement Stories and Jesus's Blessing of the Children: A Rhetorical Approach," *Semeia* 29 (1983): 42–74; Robbins, "The *Chreia*," in *Greco-Roman Literature and the New Testament: Selected Forms and Genres*, ed. D. Aune, Sources for Biblical Study 21 (Atlanta: Scholars Press, 1988), 1–23; B. Mack and V. K. Robbins, *Patterns of Persuasion in the Gospels* (Sonoma, CA: Polebridge, 1989); B. Mack, *Rhetoric and the New Testament* (Minneapolis: Fortress, 1990); V. K. Robbins, ed., *The Rhetoric of Pronouncement*, *Semeia* 64 (1993); J. H. Neyrey, "Questions, Chreiai and Challenges to Honor: The Interface of Rhetoric and Culture in Mark's Gospel," *CBQ* 60 (1998): 657–81; M. C. Moeser, *The Anecdote in Mark: The Classical World and the Rabbis* (Sheffield: Sheffield Academic, 2002); and A. Damm, *Ancient Rhetoric and the Synoptic Problem: Clarifying Markan Priority* (Leuven: Peeters, 2013).

24. Mack, *Rhetoric*, 22.

ing."[25] *Chreiai* were particularly associated with philosophers, neatly capturing their characteristic teaching or behavior. In its briefest form, the *chreia* is an extremely terse narrative with no extraneous detail. The following is a good example: "Diogenes the philosopher, on being asked by someone how he could become famous, responded: 'By worrying about fame as little as possible.'"[26]

Students, however, were taught various ways of adapting the simple *chreia*, known as the *ergasia*, or elaboration. This appears to be missing from Theon, who instead offers a series of rather more straightforward "expansions" (or *epekteinōseis*).[27] But the second-century rhetor Hermogenes of Tarsus lists the eight-step method, which seems to have been widely used.[28] Students might elaborate a simple *chreia* by adding an encomium of the leading actor, by paraphrasing the story, by adding a rationale for the story's retelling, by presenting the thesis in the opposite manner, by adding an analogy or an example, by adding the weight of an authority (usually the endorsement of a great literary figure), and perhaps ending with an exhortation to heed the moral of the story.[29] Advocates of rhetorical criticism see connections between elaborated *chreiai* and the Markan *pericopae*. Other rhetorical forms that seemed to find parallels within the gospels included the *mythos* (or fable, which Theon defines as a "fictitious story giving an image of truth")[30] and the *diēgēma* (or short narrative). The presence of these forms in Mark, it was claimed, suggests a rhetorically aware, even sophisticated, author.

The identification of Greek forms within the gospel has undoubtedly been of tremendous service to Markan studies, and we shall return to them later when

25. Hock, "Introduction," 1:26. Theon distinguishes three main classes of *chreia*, each of which could be further subdivided. First are sayings *chreiai*, which make their point "in words without action"; second are "action *chreiai*," or "those which reveal some thought without speech"; and third are "mixed *chreiai,*" which contain both speech and action, though they make their point with the action. See Hock and O'Neil, *Chreia*, 1:84–89.

26. Hock and O'Neil, *Chreia*, 1:313. This is one of a catalog of *chreiai* listed at the end of the book (301–43); the longest is eight short lines of Latin (a double *chreia* linked to Aristippus and Antisthenes, §9, 305–6), though most are considerably shorter.

27. See Moeser (*Anecdote*, 81–82) for arguments that Theon originally included such a discussion. The later editing of Theon's work is discussed by Hock in "Introduction," 1:17–18 (see also 65–66), and the same author outlines the rather shorter exercise in *chreia* manipulation found in Theon on 35–41 (see also 68–74).

28. Useful discussions of *chreiai* expansion can be found at Robbins, "The Chreia," 1–23, and Damm, *Ancient Rhetoric*, 3–80.

29. For text and translation, see Hock and O'Neil, *Chreia*, 1:160–63, 175–77.

30. Kennedy, *Progymnasmata*, 23.

we consider Mark's structure. But overall it seems unlikely that Mark reached the very highest educational level, and there is nothing in his work to indicate an awareness of rhetorical expansions of the basic *chreia*. As Raffaella Cribiore notes, the expanded *chreia* could be quite accomplished in the end, a far cry from its simple, basic form.[31] And even the rather rudimentary "expansions" of the *chreia* illustrated by Theon strike me as rather more sophisticated than anything we have in Mark. We also need to remember that the lack of rhetorical expression in the gospels was a matter of some embarrassment to the church fathers.[32] Furthermore, a rhetorical education would put our author in the very top rung, socially, culturally, and financially, and while this is not impossible, it does seem unlikely that any Christ followers belonged to this elevated group at such an early date.[33] Admittedly some proponents of rhetorical criticism locate the *progymnasmata* within the second educational level rather than the third, a move that would allow our author a measure of rhetorical training without requiring him to have studied with a rhetor,[34] but, as we have seen, recent studies have rather unanimously assigned the *progymnasmata* to the third, most advanced, level. It should be borne in mind that all of the forms identified in Mark—*chreiai, gnōmai, mythoi,* and *diēgēmata*—were all well known from the earliest schooldays, that they were used with increasing complexity as the years passed, and that they would be quite familiar to someone who had completed the second level of schooling. Furthermore, there is no clear evidence that Mark was aware of the more advanced progymnasmatic exercises; there is little use of *prosōpoeia* (the art of crafting speech suitable to a character), nor does Mark display any great ability to work with encomium or invective. It is *possible* that some of the rather more basic rhetorical conventions surrounding *chreiai, mythoi,* and *diēgēmata* were sometimes taught to second-level schoolchil-

31. Cribiore, *Gymnastics*, 223.

32. Hock and O'Neil, *Chreia*, 1:94–107; on the attitude of the church fathers toward Christian writings (most of whom deny the presence of rhetoric here), see N. W. Lund, *Chiasmus in the New Testament: A Study in Formgeschichte* (Chapel Hill: University of North Carolina Press, 1942), 4–7; also L. Alexander, *The Preface to Luke's Gospel: Literary Convention and Social Context in Luke 1.1–4 and Acts 1.1* (Cambridge: Cambridge University Press, 1993), 180–81.

33. On the lack of high-ranking early Christians, see B. Longenecker, "Socio-Economic Profiling of the First Urban Christians," in *After the First Urban Christians: The Social Scientific Study of Early Christianity Twenty-Five Years Later*, ed. D. Horrell and T. Still (London: T&T Clark, 2009), 36–59. Morgan stresses just how small the proportion of people acquiring this level of education would have been; *Literate Education*, 57; so also Cribiore, *Gymnastics*, 56.

34. So Mack, *Rhetoric*, 30; Neyrey, "Questions," 658.

dren in Mark's day—Quintilian complains that grammarians were encroaching on subjects properly (in his view) the preserve of rhetors (*Institutes of Oratory* 1.9; 2.1).[35] But in general nothing about Mark's straightforward prose compels us to situate his educational level above that of someone who had worked with a *grammaticus*.

There is, however, a further consideration. Scholars have occasionally detected in Mark what looks like the use of the rhetorical technique of *synkrisis* (or comparison). Agusti Borrell, for example, identifies this technique in Mark's juxtaposition of Peter's denial with Jesus's steadfastness in front of the high priest (14:53–72).[36] This is an identification with which I have a great deal of sympathy—indeed we shall see in Chapters 5 and 6 that much of Mark's characterization is achieved through a series of comparisons that might generously be described as *synkrisis*. Yet, as we shall also note, Mark's is a rather idiosyncratic use of the device. What this may indicate is an intelligent would-be author who attended the public recitations, street-corner philosophers, and storytellers that were prevalent in Roman society, and who was able to pick up certain subtleties of style to supplement his already fairly solid education.[37]

In a rather different vein, it is frequently claimed that Mark's work displays a "residual orality," that an oral heritage has left its shape on the gospel. Proponents of this view tend to valorize oral communication at the expense of the written text, stressing that the gospel was designed to be heard, even *performed* with gestures, dramatic pauses, and audience responses.[38] Some have gone so far as to suggest that the gospel was an *oral composition*, the current textual artifact being little more

35. So Hock, "Introduction," 1:21; Hock and O'Neil, *Chreia*, 1:117–18.

36. A. Borrell, *The Good News of Peter's Denial: A Narrative and Rhetorical Reading of Mark 14:54, 66–72* (Atlanta: Scholars, 1998), esp. 119–24.

37. On the "trickle down" effect, see above, pp. 71–73. Other scholars who propose a level of acquaintance with Greco-Roman rhetorical conventions (if not formal education at this level) include Gamble, *Books and Readers*, 35; Beavis, *Mark's Audience*, 25, 29–31; and P. J. Achtemeier, "Omne Verbum Sonat: The New Testament and the Oral Environment of Late Western Antiquity," *JBL* 109 (1990): 229–59.

38. W. Kelber, *The Oral and the Written Gospel: The Hermeneutics of Speaking and Writing in the Synoptic tradition, Mark, Paul and Q* (Philadelphia: Fortress, 1983); and, in a rather moderated form, *Imprints, Voiceprints, and Footprints of Memory: Collected Essays of Werner H. Kelber* (Atlanta: SBL Press, 2013); Achtemeier, "Omne Verbum Sonat." On "performance criticism," see W. Shiner, *Proclaiming the Gospel: First Century Performance of the Gospel of Mark* (Eugene, OR: Cascade, 2001); D. M. Rhoads, "Performance Criticism: An Emerging Methodology in Second Testament Studies—Part 1," *BTB* 36 (2006): 18–33; D. M. Rhoads, "Performance Criticism: An Emerging Methodology in Second Testament

than a transcript of one particular performance.[39] Features identified as "oral" include the work's hyperbole and exaggeration, simple plots, flashbacks, themes and variations on themes, frequent repetitions, groups of three, concentric structures, chiasms, *inclusios*, recurring formulas, echoes, and regular summaries.[40] The difficulty, however, lies in working out what exactly constitutes an "oral" characteristic. Themes and variations on themes, for example, are at the heart of a good literary style. Similarly, concentric structures, chiasms, and *inclusios* are features associated with writing and are used extensively in the Jewish Scriptures.[41] Even the groups of three, so beloved of those who would look to the influence of folklore and fairy stories, can just as easily stem from the hand of a practiced writer. Pliny, for example, censures a friend for not setting out his arguments in groups of three (*Letters* 2.20). Although the rhetorical handbooks say nothing about triple groupings, Pliny's comments suggest that some writers (then as now) consider groups of three to lend a certain elegance to a written text. And as Rafael Rodriguez points out, there has to be something rather ironic about deriving "oral features" from a literary manuscript.[42]

Once again, these studies are extremely useful in reminding us that the boundaries between oral and written communication in the first century were much more fluid

Studies—Part 2," *BTB* 36 (2006): 164–84, with references; K. R. Iverson, "Orality and the Gospels: A Survey of Recent Research," *CBR* 8 (2009): 71–106.

39. P. J. J. Botha, "Mark's Story as Oral Traditional Literature: Rethinking the Transmission of Some Traditions about Jesus," *Hervormde Teologiese Studies* 47 (1991): 304–31; J. Dewey, "The Survival of Mark's Gospel: A Good Story?," *JBL* 123 (2004): 495–507; A. C. Wire, *The Case for Mark Composed in Performance* (Eugene, OR: Cascade, 2001). In a short essay, "Oral Tradition in New Testament Studies," R. Horsley also talks of the possible oral composition and regular performance of Mark's "text" (note the inverted commas); *Oral Tradition* 18 (2003): 34–36.

40. See Kelber, *Oral and Written Gospel*, 64–70; J. Dewey, "Oral Methods of Structuring in Mark," *Int* 43 (1989): 32–44; Achtemeier, "Omne Verbum Sonat," 17–19; Botha, "Mark's Story as Oral Traditional Literature," 304–31; J. Dewey, "Mark as Aural Narrative: Structures as Clues to Understanding," *Sewanee Theological Review* 36 (1992): 45–56; Bryan, *Preface*, 72–81; and the collection of essays in *Performing the Gospel: Orality, Memory and Mark; Essays Dedicated to Werner Kelber*, ed. R. A. Horsley, J. A. Draper, and J. M. Foley (Minneapolis: Fortress, 2006). These "oral features" were first identified by W. Ong, *Orality and Literacy: The Technologizing of the Word* (London: Methuen, 1982), esp. 36–56.

41. See the detailed study of Lund, *Chiasmus*, esp. 51–136.

42. R. Rodriguez, *Oral Tradition and the New Testament: A Guide for the Perplexed* (London: Bloomsbury, 2014), 63–64.

than we are accustomed to expecting today.[43] But there is nothing in Mark that would prohibit its emergence as a literary composition. Rather than betraying a "residual orality," what the list of features given above indicate is an author who knew how to tell a good story. In all probability, Mark expected his *bios* to be read out to a largely uneducated group of Christ followers. His prose is simple and direct, with a colloquial feel that might have resonated well with a mixed audience.[44] Quintilian advised his students that they may need to adapt their material for people with little or no education (*Institutes of Oratory* 3.8), and the handbooks too advise *prepon* (or *aptum*), a quality of "propriety" or "appropriateness" that takes into consideration not only the contents of the speech but also the context in which it was given.[45] Even without a rhetorical education, an author could presumably work this out for himself. And the narrative asides, or brief authorial comments, with which Mark punctuates his work presumably helped to include and reassure his audience, explaining the meaning of Aramaic words and customs, and making deeper connections within the text.[46]

Overall, Mark's writing is perfectly proficient. Rather like Cornelius Nepos,[47] the author(s) of the *Life of Aesop*,[48] Greco-Roman novels,[49] and several of the non-

43. For a critique of the positions outlined in the preceding paragraph, see B. W. Henaut, *Oral Tradition and the Gospels: The Problem of Mark 4* (Sheffield: Sheffield Academic, 1993), 96–99, 113–15; and L. W. Hurtado, "Oral Fixation and New Testament Studies? 'Orality,' 'Performance' and Reading Texts in Early Christianity," *NTS* 60 (2014): 321–40. Two earlier essays by Hurtado are also useful here: "Greco-Roman Textuality and the Gospel of Mark: A Critical Assessment of W. Kelber's *The Oral and the Written Gospel*," *BBR* 7 (1997): 91–106; and "The Gospel of Mark—Evolutionary or Revolutionary Document?," *JSNT* 40 (1990): 15–32.

44. On Mark's colloquialisms, see C. H. Turner and J. K. Elliott, *The Language and Style of the Gospel of Mark: An Edition of C. H. Turner's "Notes on Marcan Usage" Together with Other Comparable Studies* (Leiden: Brill, 1993), 3–146 (Turner sees colloquialisms lying at the heart of much of Mark's distinctive use of Greek).

45. See the useful discussion in Damm, *Ancient Rhetoric*, xix–xxx. Demetrius's advice to adopt a plain, unadorned style may also be relevant here, even if he was writing for students who had already completed the *progymnasmata* (*Style* 4.191); a straightforward style may well have been appreciated in many circles. See the discussion in D. M. Schenkeveld, "The Intended Public of Demetrius' *On Style*: The Place of the Treatise in the Hellenistic Educational System," *Rhetorica* 18 (2000): 29–48.

46. See below, p. 117.

47. Nepos was once regarded as a poor and careless writer, but his plain style is nowadays seen to appeal to a broad audience. See M. M. Pryzwansky, "Cornelius Nepos: Key Issues and Critical Approaches," *CJ* 105 (2009): 97–108, esp. 98–100.

48. On the *Life of Aesop*, see above, pp. 72–73.

49. On parallels in terms of "target audience," see R. F. Hock, "Why New Testament

canonical sources discussed above, he tailored his prose to his audience, crafting his account in what he hoped would be a vibrant and entertaining manner, suitable for a listening audience.[50] His quotations from the Jewish Scriptures would encourage those who knew the story of Israel to reflect more deeply on the figure of Jesus and his message. While we should certainly not overplay Mark's literary abilities, he was clearly a competent and reasonably skilled writer who was perfectly able to convey his ideas in the literary form of a *bios*.

Before we turn to Mark's readers, it is worth making one final point on the topic of Mark's education, one that will have a significant bearing on our analysis of the text in the next few chapters. The whole purpose of ancient *paideia*, as Teresa Morgan makes clear, was not simply to impart a set of skills, but to bestow a culture.[51] Education was a powerful institution that not only created and maintained Roman identity but that was uniquely able to offer the student access to a world of culture and a route to status and influence. Right from the elementary stages, as we have seen, children were taught to absorb the cultural norms of the empire, and to negotiate their place and worth within a highly competitive society. In view of this, we should not be surprised to find Mark promoting a portrait of a Jesus who embodies many of the values of the Greco-Roman world, who speaks with authority, silences opponents in the agonistic sphere of male public debate, and who dies for the values by which he has lived. And yet at the same time, Mark turns this culture on its head: his hero challenges the striving for greatness endemic within the Roman world, calls on followers to deny themselves, and suffers a state execution. Rather than quote from Homer, Mark cites the Septuagint, echoing and imitating the language and cadences of this Jewish work rather than the Greek authors with whom he must have been familiar.[52] Noting the presence of countercultural values in Mark, David Aune

---

Scholars Should Read Ancient Novels," in *Ancient Fiction and Early Christian Narrative*, ed. R. F. Hock, J. B. Chance, and J. Perkins (Atlanta: Scholars, 1998), 121–38. However, not all are quite so sure that the novels are aimed directly at a lower-class audience; see T. Whitmarsh, ed., *The Cambridge Companion to the Greek and Roman Novel* (Cambridge: Cambridge University Press, 2008), 7–14.

50. For similar assessments of Mark, see Gamble, *Books and Readers*, 34; E. P. Sanders and M. Davies, *Studying the Synoptic Gospels* (London: SCM, 1989), 72; Beavis, *Mark's Audience*, 44; M. A. Tolbert, *Sowing the Gospel: Mark's World in Literary-Historical Perspective* (Minneapolis: Fortress, 1989), 35–47, 70–76; Aune, "Genre," 47; Hurtado, "Oral Fixation," 339; Damm, *Ancient Rhetoric*, xxii.

51. Morgan, *Literate Education*; this is a recurring theme throughout the book, but see especially 19–21, 102–3, 236.

52. Some have found Homeric echoes in Mark; see especially D. R. MacDonald, *The Homeric Epics and the Gospel of Mark* (New Haven: Yale University Press, 2003). There are

suggests that the work was written in *reaction* to Greco-Roman biography rather than as a simple emulation of it, and that it was designed to *parody* the hierarchy of values that typically characterized contemporary *bioi*.[53] This seems to me to be rather too subtle, and to ascribe to Mark too thoroughgoing and novel a critique of Greco-Roman values. At the same time, however, Aune captures something of the tension within a biographer who challenges imperial values even as he draws on its literature to express his message, and who both embraces and distances himself from his Greek education as he tries to make sense of his Jewish past and Christ-following future.

Mark's Christ-following Readers

My assumption throughout this book is that Mark was a follower of Jesus and that he wrote largely for others who shared his commitment. Several indicators within the work suggest that the general contours of the material were known to the audience. Christian terms such as "Spirit," "baptism," "gospel," and "kingdom of God," for example, pepper the narrative with no attempt to explain them. Characters such as John the Baptist, Herod, and Pilate appear with no introduction. And the call stories, with their emphasis on instant acceptance rather than the content of the message, do not read as though they were designed to persuade complete outsiders. Our author clearly has a Jewish background: we have already seen that he quotes from the Jewish Scriptures, and it is clear that he understands Jesus's significance against the broader history of Israel. Presumably some of his audience shared this heritage, along with a former association with the synagogue (either as Jews or Godfearers). At the same time, however, Mark explains Jewish customs and beliefs (7:3–4; 12:18) and has an interest in and sympathy with the mission to the gentile world (7:24–30; 11:17; 13:10; 14:9; 15:39).[54] His decision to write a biography—a literary form that was immensely popular within the Greco-Roman world and yet

---

certainly links between the Homeric thought-world and Mark (as we shall see in the next chapter), but it is less clear that these are specifically *literary* parallels. See K. O. Sandnes for a critique of this approach: "Imitatio Homeri? An Appraisal of Dennis R. MacDonald's 'Mimesis Criticism,'" *JBL* 124 (2005): 715–32. On the complexities of cultural bilingualism in this period, see K. Ehrensperger, "Speaking Greek under Rome: Paul, the Power of Language and the Language of Power," *Neot* 46 (2012): 9–28.

53. D. Aune, "Genre Theory and the Genre-Function of Mark and Matthew," in Becker and Runesson, *Mark and Matthew*, 167–68.

54. For attempts to pin down Mark's readers more specifically, see E. Best, "Mark's Readers: A Profile," in *The Four Gospels, 1992*, ed. F. Van Segbroeck, C. M. Tuckett, G. van Belle, and J. Verheyden (Leuven: Leuven University Press, 1992), 2:839–58; D. H. Juel, *A Master of Surprise: Mark Interpreted* (Minneapolis: Fortress, 1994), 123–46.

strangely uncommon within Jewish circles—may also suggest an attempt to appeal to the sorts of people who were familiar with this type of literature.

But can we say more about how Mark expected his text to function within this group of Christ followers? In a number of recent publications, William Johnson has stressed the *sociology of reading* in the Roman world. He refers to "reading cultures" or "reading communities," rather than simply "readers," in an attempt to highlight the complex set of sociocultural factors at play whenever a text is accessed in a particular context. Reading is not simply a "neurophysiological, cognitive act," he suggests, but an "event" that is intimately associated with one's cultural background, self-identity, inherited traditions, and aspirations.[55] Johnson offers a number of examples, but two will be sufficient to illustrate his point. The first centers on Pliny the Younger, who published his *Letters* in the early second century CE. Johnson shows that through the dissemination of these letters to certain readers, Pliny creates a literary universe that offers an idealized vision of the world and places himself at the center. The ideal Roman for Pliny is one who, like himself, integrates high-minded literary pursuits with political and social duties. "Reading" and consenting to these texts, whether aurally at recitations or privately at home, is what distinguishes Pliny's group from others; it defines the members of his literary coterie as his *amici*, shows that they endorse his values, and maintains Pliny's central place within the circle.[56]

A second example comes from Aelius Gellius's *Attic Nights*, dating to the mid- to late second century CE. At first glance, the work appears to be a collection of musings and reported conversations on various literary themes with no obvious connections. It is, however, "packed with commentary on what are the right ways to speak, to think; who are the right voices from the past to attend; who are the arbiters—commentators and masters—of this rightness."[57] For Gellius, literature functions as an exclusionary device; only those with sufficient education can be admitted into the group, and those who fall short are publicly shamed (as happens to a couple of fraudulent grammarians within the work). Those who meet to read and discuss the book position themselves as the "gatekeepers" of "proper" Roman ways of speaking, thinking, and remembering the past. Most significantly, perhaps, the work's idealized scenes embody codes of behavior that members of the reading

---

55. Johnson, "Towards," esp. 600–606; see also his *Readers and Reading Cultures in the High Roman Empire: A Study of Elite Communities* (Oxford: Oxford University Press, 2010), 3–16; and the introduction to Johnson and Parker, *Ancient Literacies*, 3–10.

56. On Pliny, see Johnson, *Readers*, 32–62.

57. On Gellius, see Johnson, "Constructing Elite Reading Communities in the High Empire," in Johnson and Parker, *Ancient Literacies*, 327.

group are to follow. Thus the text "actively seeks to create the (ideal) reading community to which the writing aspires."[58]

Johnson stresses the particularity of each "reading community" and warns against extrapolating lightly from the elite to other cultural levels.[59] Yet, with appropriate caution, we can apply some of his insights to Mark and his audience.[60]

As a first step, it is useful to consider not simply the literary implications of writing a *bios*, but also its social and cultural ramifications. To write a biography of a philosopher or a religious figure was to immortalize his memory, to create a literary monument to his life and teaching. Rather than reducing Mark's work to a "memory aid," a depository of earlier tradition, or even a natural evolution from an earlier oral period, we should understand his actions as an attempt to produce an authoritative, written document.[61] His work, we can assume, was both an attempt to keep alive the memory of a figure with whom he was personally intensely invested, and also a bid to legitimize a very specific view of that figure. Our author would have been aware that there were those who held different assessments of Jesus, both in the wider world and perhaps within other early Christian groups, but his work constructs what he sees as the "right" portrait, the account that for him best captures the life and significance of the figure at the heart of his faith.[62] Moreover, by linking Jesus firmly to the story of Israel (through quoting prophetic texts), and by articulating a shared future hope (through Jesus's eschatological sayings), Mark's work aims to create a firm basis for Christian identity in the past, present, and future.

Other writers had similarly used biography to present their own view of important men, often in response to alternative positions. Philo, for example, in his *Life of Moses*, was very much aware of detractors (*Life of Moses* 1.2–3) but wrote both to extol the virtues of Moses and to commend him to non-Jews. Cornelius Nepos turned the political neutrality of his friend Atticus—presumably a cause for concern in some circles—into a virtue. And Tacitus, acutely conscious of those who were quick to criticize Agricola's promotion under Domitian, wrote not only to memorialize his father-in-law's memory but also to defend his reputation. It is hard

58. Johnson, "Constructing," 329.

59. Johnson, "Towards," 624–25.

60. For attempts to apply Johnson's work to Christian texts, see especially Kloppenborg, "Literate Media"; Keith, "Early Christian Book Culture"; L. W. Hurtado, "Manuscripts and the Sociology of Early Christian Reading," in Hill and Kruger, *Early Text*, 49–62.

61. So also Keith, "Early Christian," 31, 37–38.

62. So also J. M. Smith, *Why Βίος? On the Relationship between Gospel Genre and Implied Audience* (London: T&T Clark/Bloomsbury, 2015), 41–43.

not to see vested interests in both Lucian's defense of the memory of his teacher, Demonax, and Porphyry's account of his own master, the Platonic philosopher Plotinus.[63] And Philostratus is quite clear in his attempt to defend Apollonius from the charge of engaging in magical practices (an allegation that seems to have been promoted by the earlier composition of Moeragenes).[64] Much more is at stake in all of these works than simply penning a pleasing account of a life. Crucially at issue is the attempt to establish a normative way for that life to be remembered, positioning oneself and one's own circle as the appropriate "gatekeepers" of that memory, and thereby legitimating one's own way of life.[65]

Johnson's work reminds us of the social dimensions of all of this. Mark and the other biographers just mentioned were well aware of detractors and yet were also conscious of speaking for a group, a circle of like-minded individuals. Mark sets up a contrast between insiders and outsiders, those on the side of God and those on the side of humanity (8:33), and constructs an ideal reader/hearer who has "ears to hear" the deeper meaning of the story (4:9, 23). In a similar manner, Cornelius Nepos sets up an antithesis between perceptive and imperceptive readers in his prologue. While scholars have traditionally interpreted his reference to the "many readers" who will regard his writing as "trivial and unworthy" because of his inclusion of Greek customs as a sign that he wrote for a largely uncultured audience, Jeffrey Beneker argues instead that Nepos employs a clever literary device to set up two different types of readers—the "many," who are ignorant of Greek literature and customs, and by inference those who are well read and sophisticated enough to appreciate his work. Beneker identifies this as a literary trope: "the dedicatee wise enough to see past the superficial elements of a literary work and to appreciate its form or content on a deeper level."[66] Rather than criticize those who do not appreciate Greek ways, however, the work encourages all readers, whether familiar with Greek customs or not, to join the ranks of the more sophisticated reader, in effect to become insiders.

The notion of comprehending insiders would have been enhanced still further by the whole process of ancient book production. Once he had completed a first

63. On Porphyry's *Life of Plotinus*, see M. J. Edwards, "A Portrait of Plotinus," *ClQ* 43 (1993): 480–90.

64. See Philostratus, *Life of Apollonius of Tyana* 1.2–3; on the work of Moeragenes, see also Origen, *Against Celsus* 6.41.

65. So also Smith, *Why Βίος?*, 146.

66. J. Beneker, "Nepos' Biographical Method in the Lives of Foreign Generals," *CJ* 105 (2009): 112. The relevant passage is from the preface, 1–4; similar sentiments occur later in the work, 1.1 (on Pelopidas), 4.5–6 (on Timotheus), and 8.1 (on Agesilaus).

draft of his manuscript (whether written by hand or dictated to a secretary),[67] our author would have presented his work to a small circle of trusted friends and associates. Within a Christian circle, these are likely to have been church leaders and elders, perhaps teachers and missionaries, at all events people who had been in the faith for some time and whose opinions our author trusted. The group would offer suggestions and advice, not only on matters of grammar and syntax (if any had that degree of learning), but presumably on content and structure too. Once these suggestions were attended to and the author was happy with the revised version, the work was ready for a wider audience. Copies would be made and sent out to friends, patrons, and a broader circle of would-be readers.[68]

It is overwhelmingly likely that Mark expected his work to be read out at Christian gatherings. Even if his circle included some people of status and affluence who might be able to read the *bios* privately,[69] a large proportion of Christ followers were unable to read and could only have access to the work through recitation. Rather than using professional lectors (who were frequently employed by the elite),[70] it is more likely that the *bios* was read out by a member of the group. Paul certainly seems to have expected his letters to be read out to the churches to which they are addressed,[71] and in the second century Justin Martyr mentions reading the gospels

67. Paul of course used a secretary, and dictation was common (so R. J. Starr, "Reading Aloud: Lectores and Roman Reading," *CJ* 86 [1990–91]: 337; also N. Horsfall, "Rome without Spectacles," *G&R* 42 [1995]: 49–56, who notes the usefulness of dictation to those with failing eyesight). Although aware that it was "now so fashionable," Quintilian objects to dictation on the grounds that it leaves no time for measured reflection, and also because a slow secretary can cause problems (*Institutes of Oratory* 10.3.18–20); for information on writing oneself (at least among the elite), see M. McDonnell, "Writing, Copying and Autograph Manuscripts in Ancient Rome," *ClQ* 46 (1996): 469–91. Exactly how Mark wrote his work cannot now be recovered.

68. On ancient book production, see G. Downing, "Word Processing in the Ancient World: The Social Production and Performance of Q," *JSNT* 64 (1996): 29–48; McDonnell, "Writing," 486; Johnson, "Towards," 615–18; Gamble, "Book Trade," 28–29.

69. These people might have a slave read to them or they might read the text themselves, either out loud or silently (on the latter, which is no longer seen as unusual in antiquity, see B. M. W. Knox, "Silent Reading in Antiquity," *GRBS* 9 [1968]: 421–35; F. D. Gilliard, "More Silent Reading in Antiquity: *Non Omne Verbum Sonabat*," *JBL* 112 [1993]: 689–96; Johnson, "Towards," 594–600; also H. N. Parker, "Books and Reading Latin Poetry," in Johnson and Parker, *Ancient Literacies*, 186–30, esp. 196–98).

70. See Kloppenborg, "Literate Media," 42–43; Pliny names a couple of his lectors at *Letters* 8.1 and 5.19.3. On lectors generally, see Starr, "Reading Aloud."

71. See 1 Thess 5:27; this is the assumption of the author of Col 4:16 (the author of Rev 1:3 also expects his work to be read aloud).

in Christian assemblies. We should not, however, think of passive listeners; our ancient evidence suggests that recitations were anything but quiet affairs. Members of the group might question the reader as he—or she[72]—proceeded, and there would presumably be plenty of opportunity for discussion and vigorous questioning at the end. As Johnson notes, such active interrogation displays a confidence that the text in question has a depth of meaning that repays the group's efforts at interpretation and discussion.[73] Nor should we too quickly label this as "cultic" reading, at least in the earliest period, before Mark's work attained a revered status. Commenting on the time of Justin, John Kloppenborg argues that the combination of some kind of a meal (the Eucharist) along with the recitation of certain texts suggests a deliberate aping of elite practices.[74] But there is nothing in principle to stop us imagining a similar social setting several decades earlier, with at least some early Christian congregations modeling themselves either on elite practices or philosophical schools. Thus, like the examples offered by Johnson, Mark's circle would have formed a "reading community," defining and validating itself through Mark's *bios* and perhaps other texts deemed important and authoritative by the group (portions of the Jewish Scriptures, for example).[75]

If Mark's references to persecution are to be taken seriously, as a clear hint that his readers have experienced harassment and perhaps even suffering (as I think that they should), then this would only strengthen the need for a text like Mark's. At its most basic level, a community that sees itself as marginalized and persecuted by

72. Women were sometimes educated by a grammarian (see Cribiore, *Gymnastics*, 74–101), and female lectors were known in the ancient world (see Starr, "Reading Aloud," 339n13 for epigraphic references). Paul's letter to the Romans was presumably read out by Phoebe (Rom 16:1–2). Presumably any Christ follower with the requisite skill in reading could be called upon to recite the text.

73. Johnson, *Readers*, 202.

74. Kloppenborg, "Literate Media," 42–43. Commenting on early martyr texts, C. R. Moss similarly argues that we should not assume too quickly that this material belongs only to a liturgical context; *The Other Christs: Imitating Jesus in Ancient Christian Ideologies of Martyrdom* (New York: Oxford University Press, 2010), 8–18.

75. On early Christian reading of the Scriptures, see 1 Tim 4:13, and slightly later Justin Martyr, *Apology* 1.67; this obviously parallels Jewish synagogue practice—see Luke 4:16–21; Acts 13:15; 15:21; 17:10–11. Given the expense of producing large scrolls, however, it seems to me unlikely that any early Christian congregation would have owned more than a couple of them—at most—and it is perhaps more likely that they relied on collections of excerpts. On the expense of biblical texts, see R. S. Bagnall, *Early Christian Books in Egypt* (Princeton: Princeton University Press, 2009), 21. For the likelihood that even synagogues did not always have a full set of Torah scrolls, see C. Hezser, "Torah versus Homer," 14.

outsiders is likely to invest considerable time and energy into defining itself and articulating its shared values and commitments. Members of the circle would have acted as "gatekeepers" for what the text meant and how it should be interpreted, just as the text itself exerted a defining influence on their own practice and beliefs. Indeed, biography seems to have been particularly well suited to the process of group formation, with its stress on the person of a revered teacher or influential figure and its offer of his life as a model to others. Thus Mark's *bios* would have played an important role in binding the group together and validating its beliefs, becoming, as Chris Keith notes, "emblematic" of their identity as Christ followers.[76]

But how widely dispersed were these Christian readers? Scholars in the past have tended to imagine that the evangelists wrote for specific, self-contained "communities," located in specific geographical localities and exhibiting distinctive outlooks and concerns. In *The Gospels for All Christians* (1998), however, Richard Bauckham and a number of other contributors challenged this assumption, arguing instead that the gospels were written for a much wider, more open readership. Central to Bauckham's argument is the insistence that biographies were not written for small, closed groups, but typically—as literary works—expected to reach a broader, indefinite audience. This claim has been challenged to some extent by Justin Smith who distinguished between "focused" and "open" biographies, where the former category did have a distinguishable audience in mind.[77] Clearly the literary landscape was highly variegated and we cannot appeal to genre alone to determine the scope of an audience, yet Bauckham's point is well made. Undoubtedly Mark drew his inspiration and motivation from the church (or churches) with which he had most contact, and yet an author who has invested time and energy in a literary work, particularly one such as a biography, which might be expected to have a broad popular

76. Keith, "Early Christian," 28.

77. Smith, *Why Bíoç?*, 44–61; also 132–69. Rather more strident critiques can be found in P. Esler, "Community and Gospel in Early Christianity: A Response to Richard Bauckham's *Gospels for All Christians*," *SJT* 51 (1998): 249–53; D. Sim, "The Gospels for all Christians?," *JSNT* 84 (2001): 3–27; M. Mitchell, "Patristic Counter-Evidence to the Claim That 'The Gospels Were Written for All Christians,'" *NTS* 51 (2005): 36–79; J. Marcus, *Mark 1–8: A New Translation with Introduction and Commentary* (New York: Doubleday, 2000), 25–28; and H. N. Roskam, *The Purpose of the Gospel of Mark* (Leiden: Brill, 2004), 17–22. R. Last similarly resists Bauckham's proposal, arguing that literature produced within both Greco-Roman and Jewish associations was always "communal" and directed solely toward the group's own preservation: "Communities That Write: Christ-Groups, Associations, and Gospel Communities," *NTS* 58 (2012): 173–98. The difficulty is that the texts that Last produces are largely inscriptions or works such as *Jubilees*, which are very different in genre (and presumably function) to the gospels—a point Last seems to concede himself (178).

appeal, might well have hoped to reach a wide audience. As Richard Burridge notes, Mark presumably had a "target audience," composed not only of those within his own group but encompassing other like-minded Christian readers further afield.[78] Paul's letters are a useful analogy here. Although they were clearly inspired by one particular audience, even as he writes them the great apostle expects his letters to be disseminated to all the churches in each area (Gal 1:2; Rom 1:7), and later on the author of Colossians simply assumes that Paul intended his letters to be shared with even more distant Christian gatherings—an assumption that no doubt reflects the practice in his own late first-century context (Col 4:16). Although our evidence is sparse, this does seem to be what happened with Mark's *bios*. Within a couple of decades or so, the work was not only known but also used by three further biographers (Matthew, Luke, and John); of course, we do not know where any of these works were written, but it seems very unlikely that they were all penned in the same city.[79] And by the early second century, according to Papias, Mark's work had achieved some prominence within the churches of Asia Minor.[80] It is clear not only that early Christian groups exhibited an interest in texts, but that they also seem to have devised efficient means of producing and disseminating them. Presumably works became known by word of mouth and Christian congregations used whatever contacts they had at their disposal to acquire a copy.[81] Tore Janson highlights the practice in Flavian times of sending accompanying letters out with books, a

78. See R. A. Burridge, "About People, by People, for People: Gospel Genre and Audiences," in Bauckham, *The Gospels for All Christians*, 113–45. In support of Bauckham's thesis, see the collection of essays edited by E. W. Klink, *The Audience of the Gospels: The Origin and Function of the Gospels in Early Christianity* (London: T&T Clark, 2010). M. Bird is rather too sweeping in his dismissal of any link between Mark and a specific (we might say "originating" or "inspiring") community; "The Markan Community, Myth or Maze? Bauckham's 'The Gospel for All Christians' Revisited," *JTS* 57 (2006): 474–86.

79. For some rather tentative comments relating to Mark's geographical location, see the introduction to this volume, p. 9.

80. Eusebius, *Ecclesiastical History* 3.39.15.

81. As Gamble notes, Christian literature was probably not of any great interest to the commercial book trade, requiring early Christ followers to work out their own ways of disseminating their texts; "Book Trade," 31. On the economics of book production, see Bagnall, *Early Christian*, 50–69. Johnson provides a fascinating discussion of close-knit scholarly circles in and around Oxyrhynchus in the second century CE who wrote regularly to friends and acquaintances asking them to bring them books, frequently on quite specific topics. While these are clearly members of an exclusive cultural elite, it is not a huge jump to imagine Christian communities likewise making use of networks across the empire to source a text like Mark; Johnson, *Readers*, 179–99. See also Cribiore, *Gymnastics*, 146.

practice that would have ensured to some extent that new audiences understood the work and its purpose.[82] Not only would many congregations have found Mark's work congenial and helpful, but the very process of sharing texts created a sense of belonging to a wider movement.

In summary, then, Mark wrote for Christian believers, articulating a particular view of their founding figure. Although doubtless inspired by his connection with one particular congregation, our author probably hoped that his work would prove useful for others as they struggled to define their own Christian identity within the Roman world. We shall now turn to the way our author has ordered and constructed his story, turning first of all to its structure.

Mark's Structure

In a little over twelve thousand words (roughly the length of one scroll),[83] Mark's account traces Jesus's ministry from its start on the banks of the Jordan to its violent end and miraculous postscript in Jerusalem. In common with other biographies, Jesus is the subject of nearly every verb and is the central actor in virtually all the narratives.[84] Only a few scenes do not include him: the account of the death of John the Baptist (6:14–29), the short scenes depicting the plots of the high priests and the treachery of Judas (14:1–2, 10–11), the flight of the naked young man (14:51–2), and the women at the tomb (16:1–8). Yet even here, Jesus remains the focus around whom the scenes revolve. John the Baptist's violent end, for example, points ahead to Jesus's own death and establishes "King" Herod as a ruthless if misguided opponent, who not only will find a parallel later on in Pilate but also provides a contrast to Jesus's own "kingship."[85] Even when Jesus is not physically present or even mentioned, then, he is still very much in the audience's mind.

Mark's work has a relatively clear structure. The basic concept is a geographical one, with Galilean material (located particularly around the Sea of Galilee) in the first half, followed by a travel narrative in the middle section (8:22–10:52), and concluding with material set in Jerusalem. The opening account of the beginning

---

82. T. Janson, *Latin Prose Prefaces: Studies in Literary Conventions* (Stockholm: Almqvist and Wiksell, 1964), 106–12. Janson draws his evidence from poetry but extrapolates from this to a general point about book culture more widely. A. Y. Collins similarly suggests that the earliest copyists transmitted information about the author, even if only by word of mouth; *Mark: A Commentary* (Minneapolis: Fortress, 2007), 129.

83. So Bagnall, *Early Christian*, 52; he counts 12,076 words.

84. So Burridge, *What Are the Gospels?*, 189–91.

85. See below, pp. 178–86.

of Jesus's ministry—his appearance at the River Jordan, his baptism by John, and his temptation in the wilderness (1:1–13)—gives the work a chronological air, as do the three final chapters, which tell of the hero's last hours, burial, and its aftermath (14:1–16:8). Elsewhere, however, our author takes a topical approach. In the first, fast-paced section, characterized by an excessive use of the word *euthus* (immediately) and Jesus's growing popularity with the crowds, Mark collects together a series of conflict stories (2:1–3:6), a group of parables (4:1–34), a section on miracles (4:35–5:43), and a cycle of gentile stories (7:1–8:10). The central section of the biography contains a number of geographical locations, giving the impression of movement and travel; terms like "following" and "on the way" are frequent;[86] and this whole portion is framed by stories of Jesus giving sight to the blind (8:22–26; 10:46–52). Material found here is all to do with Christian discipleship, and the section reads rather like a rule book for Christian readers (phrases such as "if anyone," *ei tis*, are common). Finally, the Jerusalem material at the end of the work once again features a couple of collections, this time a second series of conflict stories (11:27–12:37) and a body of apocalyptic material (13:1–37). The opening of this section with Jesus's triumphal entry, closely followed by the incident in the temple and the note that the "chief priests and scribes now sought a way to destroy him" (11:18), however, has already begun to impose a chronological narrative of cause and effect on the material, which will be developed more fully with the concluding chapters.[87]

Within Mark's narrative, the anecdote is supreme. The work is largely a patchwork of short episodes—stories, sayings, and dialogues. Most tend to be brief—a description of a short scene, a stand-alone saying, or a combination of both. Traditionally referred to as *pericopae* (from the Latin term for "paragraph"), the Markan anecdotes have enjoyed a long history of research over the last century, largely initiated by the form critics. The most comprehensive analysis was carried out by Rudolf Bultmann, who divided the narrative material into "miracle stories" and "historical stories and legends," and the sayings material into a range of "dominical sayings" and "apophthegms" (or short units ending in a saying of Jesus).[88] Later

---

86. The word *hodos* occurs at 8:27; 9:33, 34; and 10:32.

87. The precise structure of Mark's Gospel is difficult to pin down, no doubt because of Mark's penchant for intertwining his material (a point we shall come back to in Chapter 5); see J. Dewey, "Mark as Interwoven Tapestry: Forecasts and Echoes for a Listening Audience," *CBQ* 53 (1991): 221–36.

88. R. Bultmann, *History of the Synoptic Tradition*, trans. J. Marsh (Oxford: Blackwell, 1968). Prior to Bultmann, M. Dibelius identified three types of narrative within the gospels: isolated sayings of Jesus, tales or legends, and paradigms (or examples); see Dibelius, *From Tradition to Gospel*, trans. B. L. Woolf (London: Ivor Nicholson and Watson, 1934), 37–132.

form critics tended to follow Bultmann's detailed classification, though with some modifications—the term "apophthegm," for example, was generally replaced by "pronouncement story."[89] More recently, as we have seen, Mark's short vignettes and sayings have been shown to map closely onto the short literary units that formed the basis of Greco-Roman education: *chreiai, gnōmai, diēgēmata,* and *mythoi* (anecdotes, maxims, short narratives, and fables).[90] Almost everything in Mark can be broadly identified as one of these forms, or a combination of a couple of them. And if sometimes the distinction between the various forms is a little blurred, that is probably a reflection of the difference between learning exercises in the classroom and using them in practice. Most ancient authors use these short anecdotal narratives in a much more fluid manner than the highly classificatory systems presented by the ancient grammarians would suggest, and Mark's use of these forms is both adept and artistic.[91]

Anecdotes were popular not only within the education system but within Greco-Roman literature more generally. We saw in the last chapter that they frequently functioned as *exempla* in the work of moralists and historians.[92] But it was in the *bios* that the anecdote really came into its own. As Arnaldo Momigliano notes, its focus on a small word or deed perfectly exemplified biography's attention to character and the essence of an individual rather than the grander sweep of historical narrative.[93] But while modern biographers are slaves to chronology, the same was not true of their ancient counterparts. In a discussion of how to praise a man, Quintilian notes that sometimes it is best to follow the progress of a person's life and the order of his actions, at other times it is better to divide a life into examples of

89. This is generally credited to V. Taylor, *The Formation of the Gospel Tradition,* 2nd ed. (London: Macmillan, 1953); A. J. Hultgren coined the term "conflict stories"; *Jesus and His Adversaries: The Form and Function of the Conflict Stories in the Synoptic Tradition* (Minneapolis: Augsburg, 1979). For an excellent study of Mark's anecdotes, see Moeser, *Anecdote.*

90. See pp. 83–86 above. M. R. Hauge argues, with some plausibility, that the parables of Jesus should be seen as fables (*mythoi*); "Fabulous Narratives: The Storytelling Tradition in the Synoptic Gospels," in Hauge and Pitts, *Ancient Education,* 89–105.

91. Highly literate authors show a natural degree of fluidity when it comes to naming the units within their work, drawing on rather more general terms such as *aphorismoi, paradeigmata,* or *apophthegmata*; see Moeser, *Anecdote,* 52, 57–66, for fuller discussion of all these terms. Moeser's own analysis of Mark 8:27–10:45 demonstrates the blending of various forms within Mark's narrative; *Anecdote,* 188–242. See also Hock, who notes the fluidity of these terms outside the schoolroom; "Introduction," 1:26.

92. See above, pp. 46–48.

93. Momigliano, *Development,* 68–73. On the use of literary units and their arrangement in ancient *bioi* in general, see Burridge, *What Are the Gospels?,* 115–16, 135–38.

different virtues; which method to employ depends on the subject (*Institutes of Oratory* 3.7.15–16). A chronological approach suited the lives of statesmen or kings, so it is not surprising to find Cornelius Nepos adopting this order in his brief sketches *On Famous Generals* and his longer biography of his friend and literary patron Atticus. Quite probably inspired by Nepos, Plutarch also favors this approach in his extensive political biographies. A chronological focus was particularly associated with Roman *vitae*, where the *cursus honorum* lent a naturally sequential structure to a man's public life. Thus Tacitus adopts an annalistic approach to his *Agricola*, moving through the various stages of his father-in-law's life and interspersing various anecdotal examples as illustrations of the man's virtuous character, producing a work that, in Harold Mattingley's opinion, is "rather the portrait of a career than of a man."[94] Yet not even in accounts of the most noble Romans of all—the emperors—was a chronological arrangement the only way to proceed. Suetonius favored a topical or thematic structure in his *Lives of the Caesars*, only adopting a more chronological approach (rather like Mark) as he came to his subject's final days and demise. Suetonius's presentation doubtless owes much to his antiquarian interests, which naturally incline him toward thematic "classification" rather than a more sequential approach, but clearly there was nothing particularly strange in this way of ordering a man's life.[95]

Biographers of philosophers (who are largely within the Greek tradition) tend to be much more fluid in their organization, and often evince virtually no discernible structure. Probably the closest analogy to Mark is Lucian's *Demonax*, written in the late second century CE. The opening sections of the work contain a preface (*Demonax* 1–2) followed by an overview of the philosopher's family, education, and early years (3), leading to a fuller description of his character—his love of liberty and free speech, his independent and easygoing simple life, his calm and forgiving nature, and the esteem with which he was held in Athens (3–12). The majority of the book, however, is given over to a series of unconnected, brief anecdotes (largely *chreiai*), featuring Demonax's pointed and witty sayings and together illustrating the virtues highlighted in the opening sequence (13–62). Only at the end does the work adopt a chronological approach, telling how the philosopher, at nearly one hundred years of age and unable to take care of himself, abstained from food and

94. *Tacitus on Britain and Germany*, trans. H. Mattingley (Middlesex: Penguin, 1948), 13.

95. See Aune, "Genre," 32. On Tacitus's structure in his *Life of Augustus*, see D. Wardle, *Suetonius: Life of Augustus* (Oxford: Oxford University Press, 2014), 14–18. Wardle notes that Suetonius structures his work according to "species" or categories; within these groupings material is generally arranged chronologically or hierarchically (though there are also short stretches with no clear organization).

cheerily left his life, and how he received a magnificent funeral despite his instructions to the contrary (63–67). Clearly a relatively full account of Demonax's death was important in setting out his character; Lucian alluded to it early on (4), and the way in which the philosopher met his end is a perfect illustration of his disposition (compare 66 with 19, 20, and 35). Furthermore, it is clear that this section had to be described in a more sequential, chronological manner—this is by far the most natural way to recount the end of a life, and it would be almost impossible through *chreiai* alone. In his description of Demonax's "passion narrative," therefore, Lucian abandons his earlier tight sequence of *chreiai* in favor of a *diēgēsis* (or narrative), which incorporates greater detail than the earlier *chreiai*, including notes on the affection in which the philosopher was held, the matter of his burial, and so on. *Chreiai* are not entirely absent from these closing passages (Lucian includes two), but the structure of the narrative is noticeably different from what has gone before. "These are a very few things out of many which I might have mentioned," Lucian remarks at the end, "but they will suffice to give my readers a notion of the sort of man he was" (*Demonax* 67).[96]

Similarly, the *Lives of Eminent Philosophers* outlined by Diogenes Laertius, while exhibiting a certain similarity of structure from one to another, have no great interest in plotting events of individual lives against any kind of timeline. Like Lucian, Diogenes is far more interested in establishing his subjects' characters and way of life than in establishing a strict chronological framework. What gives the mass of *Lives* a degree of "structure" is their place in Diogenes Laertius's overall project, which presents the "life story" of philosophy itself.[97] Adopting a rather different approach, Philo structures his *Life of Moses* in two different ways. The first book (which describes Moses as a king) proceeds chronologically, while the second book (which treats his qualities as lawgiver, priest, and prophet) proceeds topically.

Returning to Mark, it is clear that there is nothing strange about his ordering of material, either the anecdotal microstructure or the blend of the chronological and the thematic that characterizes the broader structure of the work as a whole. Nor is the turn to a more sequential narrative in the last few chapters particularly unusual. In fact, Mark is rather more carefully composed than many biographies: his collections of anecdotes tend to be arranged topically, and often exhibit rather elaborate chiastic structures.[98]

In the early second century, however, Papias declared that Mark's work was

---

96. Harmon, LCL 14. See further N. Hopkinson, ed., *Lucian: A Selection* (Cambridge: Cambridge University Press, 2008); D. Clay, "Lucian of Samosata: Four Philosophical Lives" (Nigrinus, Demonax, Peregrinus, Alexander Pseudomantis), in *ANRW* II 36.5:3425–29.

97. See above, pp. 17, 53.

98. For an analysis of Mark 2:1–3:8, see Lund, *Chiasmus*, 303–4.

"not in order" (*ou taxei*), and the bishop's comments have tended to cast a shadow over Mark's literary efforts to the present day.[99] It is generally agreed that *taxis* here is a rhetorical term, referring to a judicious ordering of material so as to produce a rhetorically pleasing and readable work.[100] Unfortunately, the rhetoricians say very little about what constituted good style, leaving modern scholars to their own speculations.[101] A range of Markan shortcomings have been suggested: the work's abrupt beginning and ending, the apparent absence of information regarding Jesus's paternity (a point we shall consider in the next chapter), and a lack of balance such that certain scenes are recounted with extreme brevity (such as the temptation) while others contain what seem to be irrelevant details (such as the young man who runs away naked). In their present position within Eusebius's work, Papias's comments on Mark are juxtaposed with what he has to say concerning *Matthew*, and scholars commonly argue that Papias was comparing Mark unfavorably with the later gospel. Matthew's work quickly established itself as the more popular work, and the author notably improves Mark at precisely the points just listed, besides imposing a neat fivefold division on his work.[102]

However, we have to remember that what we have now is *Eusebius's* ordering of Papias's statements; there is no reason to assume that the two comments occurred in such close proximity in the (now lost) original. In fact, it is clear from Papias's explanatory comments that he is comparing Mark not with Matthew but with *John*. His explanation for Mark's lack of *taxis* is not that he lacks the proper rhetorical training but that "he had neither heard the Lord, nor had he followed him," but wrote down the *chreiai* as he remembered them. The point at issue is one of chronology: Papias's point is not to criticize Mark (far from it, he draws on typical rhetorical *topoi* to stress the diligence and care with which he went about his endeavors[103]) but to head off any awkward comparisons with *John*, whose order is often at variance with that of Mark (the far more frequent visits to Jerusalem, the

---

99. Preserved now in Eusebius, *Ecclesiastical History* 3.39.15.

100. For discussion, see F. H. Colson, "Τάξει in Papias (The Gospels and Rhetorical Schools)," *JTS* 14 (1912): 62–69; M. Black, "The Use of Rhetorical Terminology in Papias on Mark and Matthew," *JSNT* 37 (1989): 31–41.

101. Lucian has a brief note on *taxis* at *How to Write History* 48. A fuller account can be found at Dionysius, *On Thucydides* 10–12; the word here is *oikonomia*, which Dionysius divides into a discussion of *diairesis* (division), *taxis*, and *exergasia* (balance). As Colson notes, Papias seems to use *taxis* in a rather general manner, roughly corresponding to Dionysius's *oikonomia*, "Τάξει," 62–67.

102. So Colson, "Τάξει."

103. Papias's comments are paralleled in Josephus, *Jewish Antiquities* 1.17, and Plutarch, *Life of Lycurgus* 6.4; 13.2; 25.4.

location of the temple incident, the date of the crucifixion, and so on).[104] The author of the Fourth Gospel was of course believed to have been an apostle, so it was to be assumed that he had preserved the correct order while Mark had not. As we have seen, Mark's lack of chronology would not have struck an ancient audience as odd in any way; what motivated Papias was not a worry over Mark's rhetorical abilities, but an apologetic desire to reconcile two apparently contradictory biographies.

Before leaving our consideration of Mark's structure, two points merit further consideration. First, Mark's series of anecdotes results in what is generally referred to as an "episodic narrative." Although common in the ancient world, especially among biographies, this type of writing differs in a number of ways from the more continuous style of narrative with which we are more familiar today. Whitney Shiner notes a number of features common to this type of work.[105] As we have already seen, similar episodes are grouped together to form discrete sections, such as the conflict stories in 2:1–3:6, where the series of short stories gives the impression of sustained conflict between Jesus and the religious authorities over a variety of topics. Moreover, the rapid sequence gives the impression that the narrator is presenting what is typical, a selection of the kind of things that characterized Jesus's life—an impression reinforced by Mark's frequent summary statements (such as 1:32–34, 39, and 4:33–34). Varying the length of episodes creates variety and ensures the listeners' attention, while also highlighting certain themes; initial short anecdotes, for example, quickly establish Jesus as a healer, while the more detailed accounts of miracles in 4:35–8:10 slow the narrative down and enhance the impression of Jesus as one able to perform extraordinary deeds. The longer account of the Baptist's death, too, stands out from the surrounding narrative and introduces themes that will come to prominence later on in Jesus's own passion. Unlike a more continuous narrative, causation is not particularly strong in Mark's Gospel. It is clear that events move toward the fulfillment of a divine plan that is foretold at many points either by Scripture or Jesus himself (for example, the three passion predictions, 8:31; 9:31; 10:33–34, or the announcements of 14:18, 27–28, and 30). As

104. See A. Wright, "Τάξει in Papias," *JTS* 14 (1913): 298–300; M. Hengel, *Studies in the Gospel of Mark* (London: SCM, 1985), 48; R. Bauckham, *Jesus and the Eyewitnesses: The Gospels as Eyewitness Testimony*, 2nd ed. (Grand Rapids: Eerdmans, 2017), 217–21.

105. W. Shiner, "Creating Plot in Episodic Narratives," in *Ancient Fiction and Early Christian Narratives*, ed. R. F. Hock, J. B. Chance, and J. Perkins (Atlanta: Scholars, 1998), 155–76. See also C. Breytenbach, who also discusses Aristotle's views on episodic narratives in *Poetics* 9.11–13: "Das Markusevangelium als Episodische Erzählung," in *Der Erzähler des Evangeliums: Methodische Neuansätze in der Markusforschung*, ed. F. Hahn (Stuttgart: Verlag Katholisches Bibelwerk, 1985), 138–69.

Shiner notes, this overcomes the potential randomness of episodic narrative and lends the work an air of "unfolding destiny."[106]

Second, it is worth reflecting on the practical value of Mark's episodic narrative within a listening community. Drawing on a number of anecdotal "lives," Simon Goldhill notes the ease with which short, memorable stories can be excerpted from their literary home and retold as illustrations in any number of contexts. The anecdote is complete in itself, and it does not need an original context to make its point. Moreover, its brevity allows it to organize knowledge and values in a particular, packaged way; in Goldhill's terms, it "circulates a view of the world with striking efficiency."[107] In the same way that Greco-Roman education involved the memorization of anecdotes in order to instill certain values and attitudes into students, so Mark may have expected his work to function almost as a Christian equivalent. Perhaps he intended not only that the whole biography should be read out and responded to but also that individual units might be remembered and reflected upon by the assembled group. Repeated exposure to Mark's *bios* would mean that even those without letters were able to memorize their favorite stories, and to apply them—in whole or in part—to their daily activities. The work provides anecdotes that highlight Jesus's identity as Christ and Son of God, those that show his ready wit and skill at outmaneuvering opponents, and others that might prove useful in a variety of contemporary situations (fasting, Sabbath observance, payment of taxes, association with outcasts, the need for generous giving, and so on). Thus the individual anecdotes would function as a Christian *paideia*, offering examples drawn not from the lives of great and noble Romans, but from that of their founding figure. Intriguingly, this raises the possibility that the oral circulation of *pericopae* was the result of Mark's literary crafting of the tradition into bite-size anecdotes rather than a defining characteristic of a pre-Markan oral period. In quite the opposite manner to the assumptions of the form critics, then, it may be that these memorable anecdotes began to circulate not primarily because of their oral use in anonymous Christ-following communities, but quite specifically because of Mark's *written* text.

---

106. Shiner, "Creating Plot," 168. So also S. S. Elliott, "'Witless in Your Own Cause': Divine Plots and Fractured Characters in the Life of Aesop and the Gospel of Mark," *Religion and Theology* 12 (2005): esp. 408–9.

107. S. Goldhill, "The Anecdote: Exploring the Boundaries between Oral and Literate Performance in the Second Sophistic," in Johnson and Parker, *Ancient Literacies*, 101. Goldhill discusses Lucian's *Demonax*, Philostratus's *Lives of the Sophists*, and Xenophon's *Memorabilia*—all of which have similarities to Mark in terms of the episodic nature of their narratives.

This brings us quite neatly to a consideration of exactly what sources and traditions Mark had in front of him as he composed his account.

Pre-Markan Tradition

My interest in this book is in reading Mark's *bios* as a finished product rather than attempting to isolate pre-Markan sources and traditions (a quest I find largely hopeless). For the sake of clarity, however, it will be useful to consider the question of what Mark inherited in both oral and written form. First, though, we need to continue our examination of Markan *pericopae* in an attempt to see whether they do in fact embody "oral tradition"—as many New Testament scholars suppose.

A striking feature of Mark's *pericopae* is their lack of circumstantial details. Not only do they generally omit any chronological markers, but they often fail to tell us where an event took place or even who was there.[108] The form critics saw this as evidence of the oral nature of these stories, which had lost their specificity as they were passed down within the tradition.[109] Comparison with other *bioi*, however, readily explains this phenomenon.[110] First, as we have already seen, the *chreia* form tended toward a minimalist approach when it came to circumstantial detail. A glance at Lucian's *Demonax* is instructive here. Although the philosopher's pithy retorts are quoted directly, their settings are frequently vague: "another time," "one day out walking," "when someone asked him," and so on.[111] Even when the questioner is named, along with a precise situation, we are still not told where the exchange took place, when it occurred, or who else was there. Lucian knew Demonax well, he had studied under him for a long time (*Demonax* 1), and on one occasion he specifically notes that he was present, though this short scene contains no more detail than any of the others (59).[112] The decision not to include circumstantial detail, then, must be a specific choice, based on the particular literary demands of the *chreia* form, not an indication that such details had become lost in the tradition.

---

108. See L. Alexander, "What Is a Gospel?," in *The Cambridge Companion to the Gospels*, ed. S. Barton (Cambridge: Cambridge University Press, 2006), 17–21.

109. This is clearly articulated by D. E. Nineham, "Eye-Witness Testimony and the Gospel Tradition I," *JTS* 9 (1958): 13–25, and "Eye-Witness Testimony and the Gospel Tradition III," *JTS* 11 (1960): 253–64.

110. As noted already by T. F. Glasson, "The Place of the Anecdote: A Note on Form Criticism," *JTS* 32 (1981): 142–50.

111. See, for example, *Demonax* 17, 23, 26, and 62.

112. Similarly, Xenophon recounts an event at which he was present, but goes on to give no indication of the occasion, date, or place (*Memorabilia* 3.3).

Second, the anecdote's context specifically within a biography is also important here. As we saw in the last chapter, *bioi* presented their subjects as models to be emulated and tended to display their characters through rather stylized, representational scenes. What is of interest is the type of thing that the subject said and did rather than the specifics of the occasion. Thus the range of detail we would naturally associate with eyewitness accounts—temporal, geographic or spatial indicators, the inner feelings of participants, and other extraneous details—are all pared down to a minimum: the sole point of interest is what the scene tells us about the subject's character. Isocrates, for example, arranged his encomiastic biography in a broadly chronological manner, but within individual *chreia* rarely offers any temporal markers or allows us to see how events connect with one another. On the occasions where specific dates do occur, they tend to have a literary purpose. For example, the reference to "winter" in 2.313 functions less to date the event than to demonstrate that the aging king "defied the elements to do his duty to the state." Furthermore, a wealth of circumstantial detail would detract from the grand, heroic status (or otherwise) of the biography's subject; readers of *bioi* want to catch sight of the great individual without being drawn into mundane and commonplace details.[113]

It follows from this, of course, that any attempt to look to Mark for chronological[114] or geographical details,[115] not to mention other historical features connected with Jesus's ministry, is unlikely to provide satisfactory answers. But what of the perennial quest to uncover pre-Markan tradition? Are we on any safer ground here?

Studies of oral tradition have burgeoned over the last couple of decades, with scholars situating themselves along a spectrum in which those who imagine oral

113. Similar ideas are expressed by S. Halliwell (on Isocrates's *Evagoras*), "Traditional Greek Conceptions of Character," in Pelling, *Characterization and Individualism in Greek Literature*, 56–57.

114. Scholars commonly assume from Mark that Jesus's ministry lasted a short time, perhaps no longer than a year (see for example, E. P. Sanders, *The Historical Figure of Jesus* [London: Penguin, 1993], 13; also Hägg, *Art of Biography*, 162–63). In view of the foregoing discussion, such a reading cannot be inferred from the text.

115. Mark's knowledge of Palestinian geography is disputed. Some argue he knows it well; Roskam, for example, contends that while his knowledge of Judea and the Decapolis is minimal, our author is "well informed" regarding Galilean geography; *Purpose*, 97–100, 104–13. Others argue that he is hopelessly confused; H. C. Kee, for example, notes that in 5:1–20 Mark seems to think Gerasa is on the sea, whereas it is actually quite far inland, and Jesus takes what seem to be awkward routes in 7:31 and 11:1; *Community of the New Age: Studies in Mark's Gospel* (Philadelphia: Westminster, 1977), 101–5. Once we appreciate the episodic nature of the narrative, however, the difficulties pointed out by Kee become less serious.

tradition to have quickly assumed a set form and content occupy one end and those who insist on the fluidity of Jesus traditions at the other.[116] I do not doubt for a moment that Mark was heir to a large body of oral tradition and that this material played a vital part in the group's collective memory and emerging sense of identity. As a good biographer, Mark would have sought out eyewitnesses (if any were still alive) or at least tracked down those who might possess useful information.[117] It is not impossible that he had a connection with Peter at one time, as tradition maintains, a connection that would certainly have furnished him with a rich store of material.[118] He may also have possessed written sources: perhaps letters, collections of *testimonia*, and memoirs.[119] Compilations of *chreiai* were common in the ancient world (indeed Q may be such a collection of early Christian maxims and *chreiai*, though Mark does not seem to have known it).[120] No doubt like Lucian

116. For useful overviews, see Rodriguez, *Oral Tradition*, and E. Eve, *Behind the Gospels: Understanding the Oral Tradition* (London: SPCK, 2013).

117. On the historian and his research, see S. Bryskog, *Story as History—History as Story: The Gospel Tradition in the Context of Ancient Oral History* (Tübingen: Mohr Siebeck, 2000). On eyewitnesses specifically, see Bauckham, *Jesus and the Eyewitnesses*. I am less convinced, however, that such eyewitness testimony would have brought Mark into contact with the "historical Jesus"; see the study of J. Redman, "How Accurate Are Eyewitnesses? Bauckham and the Eyewitnesses in the Light of Psychological Research," *JBL* 129 (2010): 177–97, and (rather more positively) R. K. McIver, *Memory, Jesus, and the Synoptic Gospels* (Atlanta: SBL Press, 2011). By way of comparison, Josephus complains that his rival Justus of Tiberius waited twenty years to publish his account of the war, by which time the eyewitnesses were dead (*Life* 359–60); in contrast, he himself wrote quickly so that participants could endorse his work's veracity (*Life* 361–66). Mark wrote his account after twice the length of time that Josephus assumes for the disappearance of eyewitnesses.

118. So Papias in Eusebius, *Ecclesiastical History* 3.39.3–4. An alleged connection with Peter (whether real or otherwise) accounts for the survival of Mark's work, even when it was absorbed into the more popular book by Matthew, and also provides an explanation as to why Matthew and Luke use the earlier work in such a slavish and unusual way. However, we should be wary of inferring too much from any Petrine connection—Peter had likely been dead almost a decade when Mark wrote, and the literary endeavor is clearly Mark's own. For fuller discussion, see my article, "Was Peter behind Mark's Gospel?," in *Peter in Earliest Christianity*, ed. H. K. Bond and L. W. Hurtado (Grand Rapids: Eerdmans, 2015), 46–61.

119. So Gamble, *Books and Readers*, 26; *testimonia* have of course been found at Qumran, particularly 4QTestim.

120. See, for example, the comments of Plutarch, *On Controlling Anger* 457D–E; *How a Man May Become Aware of His Progress in Virtue* 78F, and Seneca, *Moral Epistles* 33.7–8. Diogenes Laertius also drew extensively on collections of *chreiai* as he wrote his *Lives*; see Hock, "Introduction," 1:8–9, for the many references. Scholars have spent much time and

(*Demonax* 67) and the author of the Fourth Gospel (John 21:25), our author had a wealth of material at his disposal and selected only what suited his purposes. Crucially, however, we need to reckon with the *literary nature* of the Markan *bios*, not only in the selection, shaping, and rewriting of anecdotes, but also in their placement within a wider literary narrative that exerted its own demands upon the material.[121] Isolating pre-Markan material from the finished biography strikes me as far more difficult than is often assumed.

A further point to consider is the possibility that Mark wanted to challenge his readers, to jolt them out of their complacency or to encourage a subtly new way of articulating their story. We need to be careful here: Mark and his intended audience presumably shared a broadly similar overarching Christian narrative and there were no doubt constraints and limitations beyond which his *bios* could not stray without alienating his audience altogether.[122] Yet within certain boundaries, our author may

---

energy isolating a range of hypothetical sources. These include a "Twelve" source, a series of conflict stories (1:40–3:6), a book of parables (4:1–34), a collection of miracles (7:32–7; 8:22–26; 10:46–52), a short apocalypse, perhaps dating from the Caligula crisis in the 40s CE (ch. 13), and a pre-Markan passion narrative (on which, see below). The fullest account of Mark's sources is the study by W. L. Knox, who further suggests that earlier sources lie behind Mark's account of the death of John the Baptist, the *corban* story of 7:1–23, the denunciation of the Pharisees in 12:37b–40, and perhaps elsewhere. See *The Sources of the Synoptic Gospels*, vol. 1, *St Mark* (Cambridge: Cambridge University Press, 1953), esp. the list on 150–51. See also E. Meyer, *Ursprung und Anfaenge des Christentums*, 3 vols. (Stuttgart: Magnus, 1921–23), 1:133–47 (for the "Twelve" source); B. W. Bacon, "The Prologue of Mark: A Study of Sources and Structure," *JBL* 26 (1907): 84–106; D. W. Riddle, "Mark 4.1–34: The Evolution of a Gospel Source," *JBL* 56 (1937): 77–90; and P. B. Lewis, "Indications of a Liturgical Source in the Gospel of Mark," *Encounter* 39 (1978): 385–94 (who finds a "boat source"). Some have detected Aramaic sources behind the gospel (for an overview, see J. H. Charlesworth, "Can One Recover Aramaic Sources behind Mark's Gospel?," *Review of Rabbinic Judaism* 5 [2002]: 249–58), or even Mark's use of the *Gospel of Thomas* (S. Davies, "Mark's Use of the *Gospel of Thomas*, Part One," *Neot* 30 [1996]: 307–34; S. Davies and K. Johnson, "Mark's Use of the *Gospel of Thomas*, Part Two," *Neot* 31 [1997]: 233–61).

121. For a similar view on our inability to reconstruct the "oral phase," see Henaut, *Oral Tradition*, and rather more cautiously, D. Aune, "Greco-Roman Biography," in Aune, *Greco-Roman Literature and the New Testament*, 123–24. Even if Mark did have a number of sources at his disposal, it is unlikely that he consulted more than one at any time; see the discussion of compositional methods in F. G. Downing, *Doing Things with Words in the First Christian Century* (Sheffield: Sheffield Academic, 2000), 152–73.

122. On early Christian identity, see the essays in A. Kirk and T. Thatcher, eds., *Memory, Tradition, and Text: Uses of the Past in Early Christianity* (Atlanta: SBL Press, 2005). For a suggestion that the author of John's Gospel may have similarly sought to challenge readers,

have deliberately contested the assumptions of his readers at certain points, or at least emphasized certain traditions as he downplayed others. It is difficult to imagine, for example, that the story of the empty tomb was generally recounted within Mark's congregation in quite the abrupt and enigmatic manner that we have it in Mark 16:1–8. Similarly, the frequent motif of private teaching delivered only to the Twelve may hint at stories and interpretations not previously known to the listening audience (4:10–20, 33–4; 7:17–23; 8:14–21; 9:28–50; 10:10.12; 13:1–37). But how are we to differentiate between what Mark inherited and what he composed himself? The more we see our author as a *creative biographer*, rather than simply a transmitter of existing traditions, the more hopeless the task of identifying pre-Markan material becomes.

All of this applies equally to Mark's account of Jesus's death. Although source criticism is generally out of favor in gospel scholarship, the "pre-Markan passion narrative" has proved remarkably resilient.[123] Some are confident enough even to assign it a genre—usually a variant on the "Suffering Righteous One" found in certain scriptural texts.[124] This "source" was first identified by the form critics on

---

see T. Thatcher, "Why John Wrote a Gospel: Memory and History in an Early Christian Community," in Kirk and Thatcher, *Memory, Tradition, and Text*, 79–97.

123. See, for example, L. Shenke, *Studien zur Passionsgeschichte des Markus: Tradition und Redaktion in Markus 14,1–42* (Wuerzburg: Echtr Verlag Katholishes Bibelwerk, 1971); D. Dormeyer, *Die Passion Jesu als Verhaltensmodell: Literarishe und theologische Analyse der Traditions und Redaktionsgeschichte der Markuspassion* (Muenster: Aschendorff, 1974); J. B. Green, *The Death of Jesus: Tradition and Interpretation in the Passion Narrative* (Tübingen: J. C. B. Mohr [Paul Siebeck], 1988); R. Pesch, *Das Markusevangelium. II. Teil. Kommentar zu Kap. 8,27–16,20* (Freiburg: Herder, 1977), 1–27; G. Theissen, *The Gospels in Context: Social and Political History in the Synoptic Tradition* (Edinburgh: T&T Clark, 1992), 166–99; A. Y. Collins, *The Beginnings of the Gospel: Probings of Mark in Context* (Minneapolis: Fortress, 1992), and "Genre of the Passion Narrative," *Studia Theologica—Nordic Journal of Theology* 47 (1993): 3–28. More recently still, see the commentaries of Collins, *Mark*, 620–39; Marcus, *Mark 8–16*, 2:925; R. H. Stein, *Mark* (Grand Rapids: Baker Academic, 2008), 627–28; and C. Focant, *The Gospel according to Mark: A Commentary*, trans. L. R. Keylock (Eugene, OR: Pickwick, 2012), 557–58—all of which still assume some kind of underlying source at this point.

124. The texts in question are Genesis (Joseph narrative); Psalms; Isaiah; Wis 2; 4; 5; Esther; and Dan 6. See G. W. E. Nicklesburg, "The Genre and Function of the Markan Passion Narrative," *HTR* (1980): 153–84; R. Watts, "The Psalms in Mark's Gospel," in *The Psalms in the New Testament*, ed. S. Moyise and M. J. J. Menken (London: T&T Clark, 2004), 25–45. Noting that Mark never refers to Jesus as *dikaios*, Collins argues that Mark's source had more in common with *exitus* literature; "Genre of the Passion Narrative."

the basis of its greater literary cohesion, more specific settings, and chronologi-cal structure.[125] We have already seen, however, that a chronological account of a person's death is common in ancient *bioi*, even when the rest of the work tended toward a more topical arrangement. In fact, there may be a very good reason for the change in composition here, derived not from the use of a source, but the form of the material itself. It is not easy to describe a person's death through *chreiai* and maxims alone, particularly when that person is the subject of the anecdotes. An author is almost compelled to change course, to offer a more coherent narrative (even if it still contains many anecdotes), and to introduce a stronger sense of cause and effect into the account. Lucian's *Demonax* and Suetonius's *Lives*, as we have seen, are paradigmatic of this approach. As a counterexample, the apparent lack of a connected passion narrative in Q may be simply a result of its form; whoever put together this document could not have added an account of Jesus's death without seriously disrupting its anecdotal and gnomic structure. Turning back to Mark, we should not be in the least surprised to find that the language and style throughout the final chapters of Mark are entirely consistent with that of the earlier parts of the gospel. This was noted by C. H. Turner as long ago as the 1920s in a series of detailed analyses of Mark's Greek syntax and vocabulary.[126] More recently, redac-tion and narrative critics have offered more sophisticated literary and theological explanations for what an earlier generation of scholars took to be "clumsy editing."[127]

125. See Dibelius, *From Tradition*, 43, 178–217, and Bultmann, *History of the Synoptic Tradition*, 262–84. The form critics actually differed quite substantially in their reconstruction of this source—for Dibelius, Mark had made only a few, easily identifiable alterations to an extremely primitive account dating to shortly after Jesus's death; Bultmann, however, detected a much more complex development, in which brief kerygmatic statements (similar to Mark 10:33–34 or 1 Cor 15:3b–5) were gradually expanded as the account was passed down. The two scholars also differed over the degree to which this early passion account reflected the Jewish Scriptures: for Dibelius, stories that had parallels in the Scriptures (especially Pss 22; 31; 69; and Isa 53) formed the backbone of the original narrative, which was put together to show that the shameful events were in accordance with God's will; for Bultmann, however, the primitive narrative was broadly historical, into which stories illustrating proofs from prophecy were inserted.

126. The original articles were published in various editions of *JTS* but are now conveniently gathered together in Turner and Elliott, *Language and Style*. Turner's own view was that Mark's material stemmed largely from Peter, though other material was interwoven into Peter's testimony. On Mark's rather unusual word order, see 126–30, along with J. K. Elliott's note in the same work, 144–45.

127. It is commonly argued, for example, that Mark's identification of Judas as "one of the Twelve" in 14:10 may be an attempt to underline the treachery of his betrayal by a close

And others have noted the presence of recurring patterns at several places within the gospel, patterns that strongly suggest authorial arrangement.[128] The failure of scholars to agree on either the exact length or the contents of any kind of "pre-Markan passion source" should have alerted us long ago to its fictitious nature.[129]

Once again, this does not mean that Mark did not know accounts of Jesus's death. On the contrary, I assume that our author was familiar with a range of interpretations of that event—some that saw Jesus's death as a martyrdom, others that cast him as a scapegoat, the Suffering Righteous One, or Isaiah's Servant of the Lord.[130] All of these were attempts to come to terms with Jesus's shameful death, to make sense of it against the history of Israel, and to construct a distinctively Christ-following story around it. The commemoration of the Eucharist would have ensured that one, or perhaps more, of these understandings were articulated over and again within Mark's Christian fellowship. Some of these interpretations may even have begun to circulate with a basic narrative framing: the stories of the Jewish martyrs and Roman *exitus* literature would readily have served as models for such

---

friend rather than an indication that he used a source that only now introduced the disciple. Along similar lines, F. Neirynck argued that the "double expressions" so prevalent in Mark are simply a feature of our author's style, rather than conflation of sources; *Duality in Mark: Contributions to the Study of the Markan Redaction* (Leuven: Leuven University Press, 1988).

128. So Beavis, *Mark's Audience*, 114–26. She lists the arrangements at 7:31–7; 8:22–26, 27–33; 14:53, 55–65; and 15:1–5, but others could be added to this inventory. See also the discussion of the parallel cycles of stories in 6:30–7:37//8:1–26 in R. M. Fowler, *Loaves and Fishes: The Function of the Feeding Stories in the Gospel of Mark* (Chico, CA: Scholars, 1981), 7–31. Fowler concludes that parallelism here is "the intentional handiwork of an author and not the chance preservation of variant traditions" (31). So also F. J. Matera, *The Kingship of Jesus: Composition and Theology in Mark 15* (Chico, CA: Scholars, 1982), 16.

129. See the analysis by M. L. Soards, "Appendix IX: The Question of a Pre-Markan Passion Narrative," in *The Death of the Messiah: From Gethsemane to the Grave; A Commentary on the Passion Narratives in the Four Gospels*, ed. R. E. Brown (New York: Doubleday, 1994), 1492–1524; also the conclusion of W. Telford, *Writing on the Gospel of Mark* (Dorchester: Deo, 2009), 710. A number of works have taken issue with the "pre-Markan passion narrative," though their efforts have largely gone unheeded; see, for example, W. H. Kelber, ed., *The Passion in Mark: Studies on Mark 14–16* (Philadelphia: Fortress, 1976), especially the introduction by J. R. Donahue (1–20) and the conclusion by Kelber (153–80). See also Matera, *Kingship of Jesus*, and more recently W. Arnal, "Major Episodes in the Biography of Jesus: An Assessment of the Historicity of the Narrative Tradition," *Toronto Journal of Theology* 13 (1997): esp. 209–15.

130. For a useful overview of early interpretations of Jesus's death, see A. J. Dewey, "The Locus for Death: Social Memory and the Passion Narratives," in Kirk and Thatcher, *Memory, Tradition, and Text*, 79–97.

short accounts. In general, however, I assume that Mark the thoughtful biographer has been as active in these final chapters as elsewhere in his gospel, creatively editing and arranging his material in an attempt to set the fluid and perhaps wide-ranging traditions concerning Jesus's death into a literary work. We shall look at Mark's account of Jesus's death in more detail in Chapter 6, where we will note his interest in matching Jesus's death to his teaching in an attempt to show that Jesus died in a manner entirely in keeping with his life.

One final point deserves consideration, though we may not be able to arrive at a clear answer: Was Mark the first to write a *bios* of Jesus? Mark's is clearly the earliest extant life of Jesus, though we cannot rule out the possibility that others had attempted such a work already. Writing in the 50s, the apostle Paul shows remarkably little interest in the events of Jesus's life. What preoccupied him was not the earthly Jesus but the risen Lord. When he cites sayings or traditions of "the Lord," it is invariably without any biographical connection (the account of the Lord's Supper in 1 Cor 11: 23–26 is something of an exception in this regard, with its brief connection to "the night he was handed over"). Clearly Paul's Christian narrative existed quite independently of specific stories about Jesus; the apostle obviously had a wealth of traditions, and these could be appealed to when necessary, but Paul gives no hint that he knows of (or needs) a connected and authoritative "life of Jesus." Equally striking in this early period is the fluidity that characterizes the Jesus tradition. Paul's letters give the impression that devotees of the new faith made little distinction between genuine and non-genuine tradition: some sayings undoubtedly went back to the earthly Jesus, but some may have come from else-where—Greco-Roman *topoi*, Jewish ethics, citations from Scripture, words of John the Baptist, early Christian prophets, and so on. The body of tradition that Paul appeals to is clearly free and not yet fixed; what was decisive for him was the idea that the teaching as a whole rested on the authority of the Lord.[131]

The question is, of course, how typical was Paul? Can we infer from his letters that the earliest Christians generally had little interest in the earthly life of their founding figure? The idea seems counterintuitive, though it is as well to underline the fact that there is no evidence for what scholars tend to call "synoptic-like" ma-terial in this earliest stage. We might reasonably surmise, however, that there was an interest in the earthly Jesus in at least some circles, and that anecdotes and sayings did spread around the earliest congregations (some based, at least originally, on eye-

---

131. See J. Schröter, "Jesus and the Canon: The Early Jesus Traditions in the Context of the Origins of the NT Canon," in Horsley, Draper, and Foley, *Performing the Gospel*, 104–22; also C. Jacobi, *Jesusüberlieferung bei Paulus? Analogien zwischen den echten Paulusbriefen und den synoptischen Evangelien* (Berlin: de Gruyter, 2015).

witness accounts, others perhaps inspired by Scripture or contemporary concerns), though without as yet a fixed framework. The Q document, perhaps roughly contemporary with Mark, is illustrative here. Although largely a list of *sayings*, Q does seem to be moving in the direction of biography: both the John the Baptist material and the temptation story are recounted early on (at what seems to be their correct chronological place), some sayings have a setting attached, and the death of Jesus is clearly *implied* (Luke/Q 11:49–51)—even if not directly narrated—along with his future return (Luke/Q 12:22).[132]

Mark's work takes things to a different level. In his account, stories and sayings are firmly historicized, pinned down to a specific point in the life of Jesus from which they were destined never to escape.[133] Of course, a certain flexibility continued, even after Mark had penned his biography. The later evangelists were quite happy to alter Mark's material, sometimes quite substantially, and the wealth of textual variants within these texts shows that later scribes continued to alter the earlier narrative in line with their theological ideas.[134] Mark's was, however, the first—or perhaps the most successful—attempt to create a biography around Jesus. His work secured certain stories and sayings as definitive "Jesus tradition," while perhaps also excluding others, and furnished Christian teaching with both a literary and historical framework. And, Mark firmly declares, this too is gospel, *euangelion* (1:1). Thus, as Detlev Dormeyer observes, the use of the term "gospel" here may be a deliberate attempt to broaden its meaning, now to include the life of Jesus from the baptism to his final days in Jerusalem, and to argue in effect

132. D. Dormeyer and H. Frankemölle identify Q as halfway between a sayings source and a biography; "Evangelium als literarische Gattung und als theologischer Begriff: Tendenzen und Aufgaben der Evangelienforschung im 20. Jahrhundert, mit einer Untersuchung des Markusevangeliums in seinem Verhältnis zur antiken Biographie," *ANRW* II 25.2, 1600–1601. G. Downing compares Q with Cynic lives, especially as they are recounted in Diogenes Laertius, in "Quite Like Q: A Genre for Q; The 'Lives' of the Cynic Philosophers," *Bib* 69 (1988): 196–215. Those who collected Jesus's sayings into Q, he argues, were aware of and instinctively used the model of a Cynic *Life*. J. Kloppenborg Verbin identifies three redactional layers to Q and labels the last of these (Q3) a "proto-bios"; *Excavating Q: The History and Setting of the Sayings Gospel* (Edinburgh: T&T Clark, 2000), 160–63. On the biographical features of Q, see Schröter, *Erinnerung*, 460, and Labahn, *Der Gekommene*, 72–73.

133. So also Schröter, "Jesus and the Canon," 104–22. Despite John's reordering of much of Mark, historical Jesus scholars still tend to prefer Mark's account.

134. See, for example, D. Parker, *The Living Text of the Gospels* (Cambridge: Cambridge University Press, 1997), and B. Ehrman, *The Orthodox Corruption of Scripture: The Effect of Early Christological Controversies on the Text of the New Testament* (Oxford: Oxford University Press, 1993; 2nd ed., 2011).

that a biographical account of Jesus's life and work should be part of Christian proclamation.[135]

So far in this chapter, we have considered a number of broad similarities between Mark's Gospel and other ancient biographies, particularly those of philosophers. One feature, however, would have struck Greco-Roman readers as rather unusual, and perhaps a little unsettling: the work's lack of an opening preface, along with its relatively muted authorial voice. We shall consider this in our concluding section.

Authorial Voice

Most Greco-Roman literature exhibits a strong authorial voice. This is immediately apparent in the opening preface and continues throughout the work. Historians in particular were given to long, often formulaic introductions, where they might declare the importance of their topic and their own impartiality and qualifications for the task, often rounding things off with a self-effacing note regarding their stylistic and literary abilities. Lucian pours scorn on histories that circulated without prefaces, likening them to bodies without heads (*How to Write History* 23). The great man's disdain, however, shows that it was not entirely unknown even for histories occasionally to appear in this manner.[136]

Prefaces to other types of literature tended to be less elaborate, though it was unusual for a work to circulate without some kind of opening words. Biographers tended to include a few introductory comments, usually relating to the significance of their subject and their reasons for writing. Xenophon was famously brief (such that Lucian assumes the headless horrors take their inspiration from him). The opening to his *Agesilaus* is concise, noting only the difficulty of the task before him and his determination to attempt it (*Agesilaus* 1); yet the personality of Xenophon,

135. D. Dormeyer, "Die Kompositionsmetapher 'Evangelium Jesu Christi, Des Sohnes Gottes' Mk 1.1. Ihre Theologische und Literarische Aufgabe in der Jesus-Biographie des Markus," *NTS* 33 (1987): 452–68. The fact that Mark can use the term "gospel" both in its more restricted "Pauline" use and also to refer to Jesus's wider teaching and ministry leads M. Hengel to suggest that his understanding of the term was still new and contested in some circles; *Studies in the Gospel of Mark* (London: SCM, 1985), 53. See also Schröter, "Jesus and the Canon," 111–13, and above, pp. 10–11.

136. On Greek prologues, see Janson, *Latin Prose Preface*, esp. 51–52, 96–100; Alexander, *Preface*; D. Earl, "Prologue-Form in Ancient Historiography," *ANRW* I 22:842–56; also K. Yamada, "The Preface to the Lukan Writings and Rhetorical Historiography," in *The Rhetorical Interpretation of Scripture*, ed. S. E. Porter and D. L. Stamps (Sheffield: Sheffield Academic, 1999), 154–72.

guiding his reader and offering his own views and opinions on the king's fine character, is apparent throughout the book. His fellow Athenian, Isocrates, includes a fairly lengthy preface in which he tells Nicocles that his purpose is to describe for posterity his father Evagoras's way of life, to ensure that his noble qualities are remembered, and to encourage people to take upon themselves the task of praising contemporary men—a task he has made particularly difficult for himself by attempting to write a prose eulogy (*Evagoras* 1–11). The authorial "I" is ever present, complaining at one point (presumably with a degree of false modesty) that he is already past his prime (*Evagoras* 73)!

The opening to Lucian's *Demonax* is brief, brisk, and businesslike. Our author claims to have met with two great men: one, Sostratus, was a man of "enormous physical prowess"; the other, Demonax, possessed a "highly philosophical mind." Noting that he has given an account of Sostratus elsewhere, and offering a few highlights of that man's career, Lucian declares that he will now turn his attention to Demonax, both to record his former teacher's memory and to provide a pattern for contemporary young men (*Demonax* 1–2). With this, he plunges straight into the biography. Throughout the work the authorial "I" is present, such as at *Demonax* 12, where Lucian declares that he will cite a few of his teacher's witty remarks, but not intrusively. Apart from the occasional aside (44, 54, 59), the *chreiai* continue with little intervention until the final concluding sentence in which Lucian appears once more (67).

Tacitus made use of his preface to complain about the recent political climate, to lament the fact that the writing of a great life needed any kind of justification, and to welcome the changed times under Trajan. Only briefly at the end does he mention that the purpose of the book is to honor his father-in-law (*Agricola* 1–3). Once again, the authorial "I" is frequent, sometimes with a personal reflection (4, 24), at other times with a justification for including certain material (10), and later with an account of the effect of Agricola's death on the family (43) and Tacitus's own quite moving sorrow that he was unable to be with him at the end (45). After hearing the work, the audience would no doubt feel that they knew Tacitus and understood something of his interests and concerns—or at least those aspects of his persona he chose to display.

One biographer who does not allow his authorial presence to intrude much within his work is Diogenes Laertius. His large compilation does not include a preface, and the audience is left with no indication as to what motivated him to undertake such an onerous task or why it takes the form that it does. Nor does he tell us anything about himself or his own philosophical convictions. As the work progresses, he includes his own short epigrams on particular philosophers, occasionally gives his own views on matters of philosophical history, or comments on the plausibility of information he has gleaned from his sources.[137] In general, though, he is an unobtrusive guide who eschews directly stepping into the limelight himself.

If Diogenes Laertius is unobtrusive, Mark is positively shadowy. His work opens with only the barest declaration of its scope (1:1) and no indication of the identity of its author or his qualifications for the task ahead of him. As the *bios* proceeds, however, it does exhibit a clear and consistent point of view.[138] Our author adopts the persona of an omniscient, third-person narrator, who knows the thoughts and motivations of all the characters. He frequently includes asides, all of which enhance the sense of a trustworthy guide: short explanatory comments (2:15; 3:10, 30; 5:42; 6:14; 16:4), clarifications of Jewish practice (7:3–4, 11b), translations of Aramaic (5:41; 14:36; 15:34), notes to underline the implications of Jesus's words (7:19b) or to urge the audience to appreciate a deeper significance (13:14).[139] The narrator is closely aligned with Jesus; readers see and know only what the narrator and/or Jesus tell them, encouraging a close identification between the audience and the hero of the story. Yet for all of this, the author's identity remains strangely elusive.

Scholars rarely discuss Mark's lack of a literary prologue, but those who do tend to offer the same answer: our author refrains from putting his authorial stamp on the material because the work is essentially not his own. In both shape and content it is largely composed of oral Jesus tradition, and Mark's contribution was simply to put it all together.[140] This explanation is of course deeply rooted in the form-critical view of gospel formation, a view that in my opinion is heavily flawed. Nor is it likely that Mark's reticence is simply because he sees his work as a communal activity.[141] As we have seen, all ancient book production had a communal dimension, but this does not usually detract from the clear sense that most works had "authors." Whether reliable or not, Papias and other early church fathers remembered (or simply assumed) that an *individual* stood behind the text, not a community.

---

137. W. James, "Diogenes Laertius, Biographer of Philosophers," in *Ordering Knowledge in the Roman Empire*, ed. J. König and T. Whitmarsh (Cambridge: Cambridge University Press, 2007), 138.

138. See N. R. Petersen, "Point of View in Mark's Narrative," *Semeia* 12 (1978): 97–121.

139. On Mark's asides, see Fowler, *Loaves and Fishes*, 160–64.

140. Hurtado, "Greco-Roman Textuality," 101. In a similar vein, R. A. Guelich suggests that the writer did not identify himself because the gospel was not his own but God's; *Mark 1–8.26* (Dallas: Word, 1989), xxvi.

141. This has recently been argued by Last, "Communities That Write," 196.

More plausibly, Oda Wischmeyer suggests that Mark took his cue from the Jewish Scriptures. The sacred Jewish texts similarly narrate events from the standpoint of an omniscient narrator without allowing an authorial voice ever to intervene.[142] Openings are often abrupt, with little more than a vague time reference (so Gen 1:1; Ruth 1:1; Ezra 1:1; Esth 1:1), or a note of someone's death (so Josh 1:1; Judg 1:1; 2 Sam 1:1; 2 Kgs 1:1). Prophetic texts give the name of the prophet, often with a note of his father, hometown, and perhaps a date (so Neh 1:1; Isa 1:1; Jer 1:1–3; Hos 1:1), and short stories briefly introduce their central characters (Job 1:1; Tob 1:1–2). Perhaps the closest opening to Mark's is that of Proverbs, which boldly announces, "The proverbs of Solomon, Son of David, King of Israel" (1:1), and then proceeds straight into a collection of sayings. Two Hellenistic texts do include a preface, Ecclesiasticus (written by the author's grandson and translator) and 2 Macc 2:19–32 (an abridgement of the earlier work by Jason of Cyrene), though the highly philosophical first-person treatise known as 4 Maccabees does not (unless we take 1:1–6 to function in this capacity). Thus, despite a couple of examples to the contrary, the overwhelming Septuagintal tradition would tend to be against prefaces and the interruption into the text of a strong authorial "I." As we have seen, Mark adopts the biographical form, but draws his language and themes not from the Greek literary tradition, but from the Jewish texts with which he was familiar. In this context, we should perhaps not be surprised to find him eschewing the stronger authorial "I" of his pagan contemporaries in favor of the much more muted authorial presence of the LXX.[143]

142. See O. Wischmeyer, "Forming Identity through Literature: The Impact of Mark for the Building of Christ-Believing Communities in the Second Half of the First Century CE," in *Mark and Matthew I, Comparative Readings: Understanding the Earliest Gospels in Their First-Century Setting*, ed. E.-M. Becker and A. Runesson (Tübingen: Mohr Siebeck, 2011), 366; also Alexander, *Preface*, 14–15.

143. Both Philo and Josephus include prefaces and an authorial presence, even when outlining the life of Moses (so Philo) or retelling biblical narrative (so Josephus). The educational background of these two authors puts them in the highest layers of elite *literati*, and both are keen fully to embrace Greco-Roman literary forms in all their aspects. It is presumably also Luke's higher educational level that leads him to include a prologue in his rewritten version of Mark, however brief (Luke 1:1). On the latter, see Alexander, *Preface*, who identified the Lukan prologues with the "scientific" rather than the historiographic tradition; in contrast, Yamada argues that Luke's preface fits within the parameters of historiography, "Preface," as does S. Adams, "Luke's Preface and Its Relationship to Greek Historiography: A Response to Loveday Alexander," *JGRChJ* 3 (2006): 177–91. None of these scholars considers prefaces to biographical works in any depth.

One further point is also worth considering in this regard. As more and more honors were in the domain of the emperor and his family, it became increasingly difficult for Roman aristocrats to achieve *fama* or *dignitas*. Literature, however, offered a new avenue, and many texts show what aristocratic Romans hoped to gain from their literary endeavors. A common trope among elite Romans was that writing was a means to immortality; while the body would inevitably die, one's thoughts and ideas could be preserved for posterity through the written word. Pliny the Younger is almost obsessive about this, urging Octavius Rufus to publish his works with the following words: "Bear in mind that you are bound by man's mortality, but that this one memorial of yourself can set you free: everything else is fragile and fleeting like man himself, who dies and is no more" (*Letters* 2.10.4).[144] In the world of aristocratic male competition, the literary prologue was a means of drawing attention to oneself, of achieving glory and renown, and ultimately of ensuring that one's name was remembered.[145] We might well imagine that a similar quest for reputation and immortality motivated the literary endeavors of aspiring authors lower down the social or educational pecking order. As we shall see in the following chapters, however, Mark's story has very definite—and subversive—views on glory and honor. His hero instructs his followers not to be like the gentiles lording it over others; he will deny himself to the point of behaving like a servant and will die a shameful death on a cross. Only once will he openly reveal his true identity, and then it will lead not to worldly reputation and esteem, but to his condemnation (14:62). It is hard to imagine the author of such a text seeking to set himself up as a literary figure amid a circle of adulatory friends and admirers. If Mark knew of the self-promoting literary prefaces common in his day, it is hardly surprising that he looked elsewhere for his opening.

Mark may have had his reasons for opening as he did, but readers would have found his lack of authorial comments somewhat odd, particularly if they were used to pagan literature. The abrupt opening to the biography, however, already showed in a very clear way that this was to be no conventional "life."

In the next chapter, we shall begin to read Mark's work as an ancient biography. My intention here is not to attempt to shoehorn the narrative into a predetermined biographical script; we have already seen that biography as a genre is much too variable for any such attempt to be meaningful. Rather, I am interested in how

---

144. Radice, LCL 55. See also 1.3.4–5; 5.5, 5.8.7, 5.21; 6.16; 7.4.10; 9.14, 27; the references are from Johnson, *Readers and Reading Cultures*, 61–62.

145. On the *vir magnus* and his circle of friends and companions, see Johnson, *Readers and Reading Cultures*, 202–3.

the account conforms to the broad expectations of the genre, and in what ways it differs. What would have struck readers who approached it as a biography as commonplace, and what as strange? And how should we explain some of Mark's deviations from general expectations? The focus of this chapter will be squarely upon the life and ministry of the central character, Jesus. An analysis of other characters will be the topic of Chapter 5, while an examination of Jesus's death is reserved until Chapter 6.

CHAPTER 4

A Life of Jesus

Since the ancient biographers gave prominence to character portrayal for blame or praise, the recent interest of narrative critics in . . .
character portraits is certainly not out of place. However, they have
looked to modern literary theorists for insight into the evangelists'
methods of characterization and have failed to note that some of
the techniques used by modern writers were unknown in antiquity.

—Graham Stanton[1]

Aristotle was of the opinion that "actions are signs of character."[2] With these
words, the ancient polymath articulated the deeply established assumption
in antiquity that the best way to appreciate character was not by deferring to the
judgment of an authoritative narrator but simply by observing a person's words and
deeds. Thus, while some of the more eulogistic biographies might list a man's virtues
before going on to illustrate them,[3] the majority of *bioi* simply supplied a variety of
anecdotes or maxims, and allowed their readers to form their own opinions.[4] This
style is often referred to as "indirect characterization," or "showing" rather than
"telling." The great master here was Plutarch, who eschewed heavy-handed character

---

1. G. Stanton, "Matthew: βίβλιος, εὐαγγέλιον, βίος?," in *The Four Gospels, 1992: Festschrift
for Frans Neirynck*, ed. F. van Segbroeck with C. M. Tuckett, G. Van Belle, and J. Verheyden
(Leuven: Leuven University Press, 1992), 1200.

2. Aristotle, *Rhetoric* 1.9.33; also 1367b.

3. For example, Xenophon first lists Agesilaus's virtues (*Agesilaus* 3–8), then provides examples to illustrate each one. Nepos's Epaminondas tends to follow this pattern too (*Lives* 15),
and to a lesser extent the second book of Philo's *Life of Moses*.

4. See Xenophon, *Agesilaus* 1.6; *Memorabilia* 1.1.20, 3.1; Isocrates, *Evagoras* 76. See further,
R. Burridge, *What Are the Gospels? A Comparison with Graeco-Roman Biography*, 2nd ed.
(Grand Rapids: Eerdmans, 2004), 172.

descriptions in favor of a series of vignettes, inviting his readers to contemplate the complexities of life and to come to their own judgment.[5]

Rather curiously to us, perhaps, there was no expectation that a biographer should include among his anecdotes what a historian might regard as the "main events" of a life. Once again, Plutarch is instructive. He famously declared himself uninterested in "the most illustrious deeds," being convinced rather that it was in life's trivialities that "the signs of the soul" were most clearly revealed:

> For it is not histories that I am writing but Lives; and in the most illustrious deeds there is not always a manifestation of virtue or vice, nay, a slight thing like a phrase of a jest often makes a greater revelation of character than battles where thousands fall, or the greatest armaments, or sieges of cities. Accordingly, just as painters get the likenesses in their portraits from the face and the expression of the eyes, wherein the character shows itself, but make very little account of the other parts of the body, so I must be permitted to devote myself rather to the signs of the souls in men, and by means of these to portray the life of each, leaving to others the description of their great contests. (*Alexander* 1.2–3)[6]

Rightly, Plutarch saw that the way into a person's true character (the "soul," *psychē*) is through what might sometimes appear to be inconsequential events, relationships with others, or chance remarks among friends. Not only does this differentiate biography from history or annals, but it remains even today a widely used way to expose a person's character and way of life: recalling the time when "X did Y" is still effective in exposing a person's "soul."

Mark's biography uses exactly this method of characterization. While our author

5. See the discussion on Plutarch's technique in T. Duff, *Plutarch's Lives: Exploring Virtue and Vice* (Oxford: Oxford University Press, 1999), 9.

6. Perrin, LCL 99. As Burridge notes in *What Are the Gospels?*, 62, Plutarch is not really interested in genre theory here; more likely he is indirectly apologizing for not having enough space to cover all of the ground on Antony (see also *Pompey* 8.6–7 and *Nicias* 1.5). It should be noted that Latin biography was rather different in this regard: perhaps because of the strong tradition of the *cursus honorum*, Latin *vitae* do tend to cover all the main events of the subject's life, particularly his public deeds and achievements; see T. Hägg, *The Art of Biography in Antiquity* (Cambridge: Cambridge University Press, 2012), 192, 236, who cites Augustus's *Res Gestae* and Nepos's *Eminent Commanders of Foreign Nations*. To some extent, the accumulation of public deeds *was* what constituted character to a Roman. Nepos worries that if he gives a full account of Pelopidas's actions he may seem to be relating a history rather than a life, but if he only touches on his hero's principal exploits his readers may not realize what a great man he was (*Pelopidas* 16.1).

is quite clear on the matter of Jesus's identity (a point we shall return to in a moment), his characterization of Jesus is generally indirect. The audience is encouraged to piece together a portrait of Jesus through his speech and actions, by considering the way in which he treats supplicators, opponents, and friends, and through what other characters say about him (for good or ill). Occasionally the author grants us access to Jesus's inner feelings and emotions, but there are few details.[7] His preferred method of characterization is to present a series of anecdotes and to allow his audience to reach their own conclusions.[8] Indeed, verbs of seeing are frequent in this gospel, highlighting the sense that Jesus's deeds are brought into the open and held up to public scrutiny. All of this gives a vivid sense of an audience not merely hearing stories, but *watching* the protagonist as events unfold.

Furthermore, Mark does not always feel compelled to stick to what we might think are the "main events" of Jesus's ministry. He frequently juxtaposes important matters with more intimate, private scenes. For example, the hugely significant gathering of the chief priests to plot Jesus's arrest is immediately followed by a domestic scene in which Jesus is anointed by a woman (14:1–9); it is perhaps only our familiarity with this sequence of events that stops us seeing just how oddly the second scene fits with the first. Similarly, the cursing of the fig tree (11:12–14, 20–21) seems at first glance to be an odd and inconsequential story, particularly in its present location, flanking the far more significant incident in the temple (which for Mark leads directly to Jesus's death, 11:18). If Mark's *bios* is a blend of the important and the seemingly trivial, however, it would hardly have surprised an ancient reader used to finding a subject's "soul" in any or all of these stories.

As noted already, Mark is particularly concerned with the question of Jesus's identity. Modern scholars tend to differentiate between identity and character, and

7. He is angry and upset by the Pharisees' hardness of heart (3:5), feels love toward the rich man (10:21), and is visibly shaken in Gethsemane (14:32–42); on the latter, see below, p. 232. Mark more commonly gives us the feelings of *other* characters, particularly toward Jesus; the reasons for this will be explored in the next chapter.

8. On Mark's method of characterization, see E. Best, "Mark's Narrative Technique," *JSNT* 37 (1989): 43–58; M. A. Tolbert, "How the Gospel of Mark Builds Character," *Int* 47 (1993): 347–57; and Chris W. Skinner and Matthew R. Hauge, eds., *Character Studies and the Gospel of Mark* (London: Bloomsbury, 2014). Attempts to read Mark's Jesus specifically as the central character of a *bios* include V. Robbins, *Jesus the Teacher: A Socio-Rhetorical Interpretation of Mark* (Philadelphia: Fortress, 1984); R. Burridge, *Four Gospels, One Jesus? A Symbolic Reading*, 2nd ed. (Grand Rapids: Eerdmans, 2005), 35–65, and Burridge, *Imitating Jesus: An Inclusive Approach to New Testament Ethics* (Grand Rapids: Eerdmans, 2007), 159–85; K. Keefer, *The New Testament as Literature: A Very Short Introduction* (Oxford: Oxford University Press, 2008), 23–29; and Hägg, *Art of Biography*, 181.

to assume that Mark has little interest in the latter.[9] To an ancient mind, however, the two were intimately connected. A biography of a praiseworthy king showed him behaving in a regal manner, exhibiting the range of virtues commonly associated with kingship such as piety, justice, mastery of his passions, or courage. Similarly, an effective general should display leadership, bravery, self-restraint, and patriotism. It is clear from Theophrastus's *On Character* that certain characteristics or patterns of behavior were expected of certain "types" of person—the flatterer, the boor, the garrulous man, and so on. An example of this way of thinking from Mark's Gospel is the "character" of Judas. Introduced as the one who betrayed Jesus (3:19), Judas proceeds to go about his appointed task; no reasons are given for his treachery—indeed none are needed—he simply acts in the manner expected of a "betrayer." Identity is thus firmly bound up with character and behavior, and the two are not easily pried apart. As we shall see in the course of this chapter, Mark's characterization of Jesus adds not only to a fuller understanding of the hero's identity (what it means to be the Son of God) but also provides a solid way of life for followers to imitate.

Jesus is, of course, the central character for Mark, but, as Stephen Moore observes, we need to guard against assuming too quickly that he is being presented as a "round" character by our own modern standards.[10] What Mark presents us with is a Jesus who displays a set of virtues that we are invited to admire and to emulate. What he does not do is to open up Jesus's inner life to public scrutiny: we are not encouraged to see any development in Jesus, to observe conflicting emotions, or still less to work out what "makes him tick." Such interests are a result of the huge success of the modern novel with its intense preoccupation with individuality and inner character.[11] As we saw in Chapter 2, however, these interests were far from the minds of ancient authors, particularly biographers, whose primary interest was in displaying certain virtues that the would-be disciple was encouraged to emulate. With this in mind, we shall work through Mark's Gospel, section by section, highlighting Jesus's distinctive character and way of life.

9. So D. E. Aune, "Greco-Roman Biography," in *Greco-Roman Literature and the New Testament*, ed. D. E. Aune (Atlanta: Scholars, 1988), 124.

10. S. D. Moore, "Why There Are No Humans or Animals in the Gospel of Mark," in *Mark as Story: Retrospect and Prospect*, ed. K. R. Iverson and C. W. Skinner (Atlanta: SBL Press, 2011), 83–86. Moore is arguing here against the approach initiated by D. M. Rhoads and D. Michie in their groundbreaking *Mark as Story: An Introduction to the Narrative of a Gospel* (Philadelphia: Fortress, 1982); 3rd ed., ed. D. M. Rhoads, J. Dewey, and D. Michie (Minneapolis: Fortress, 2012).

11. See above, pp. 51–56.

Mark's Opening Section (1:1–15)

One of the classic arguments brought against identifying Mark as an ancient *bios* is the work's apparent lack of interest in Jesus's early years.[12] Ancient biographies would typically start with a note of their subject's ancestry (his *genos*) and nobility of descent (*eugeneia*), characteristically recording a person's home city, parents, and any unusual phenomena at birth.[13] Unlike a modern biography, however, this was not from a sense that family and childhood experiences played an important part in shaping the adult person. Rather, as we saw in Chapter 2, it was assumed that part of a man's character was innate, drawn from his family background and circumstances. Certain families and geographical locations were believed to exhibit rather stereotypical characteristics (for good or ill), and nobility of birth was assumed to equate to a certain nobility of spirit, providing a solid groundwork upon which other aspects of character might build.[14] Even when no details were given, it was important to state that the family was illustrious; Philo, for example, while refraining from naming Moses's parents, assures his readers that they were the best in their generation.[15]

Where childhood stories were included, their purpose was solely to allow the youth to display the great qualities that would later distinguish the man. The great tactician would characteristically show a precocious ability on the battlefield from an early age, or the budding politician might show a flair for statesmanship far beyond his years.[16] In the case of philosophers or teachers, it was important to stress the ed-

12. This was one of K. L. Schmidt's objections; see above, pp. 20–21.

13. See J. H. Neyrey, "Josephus' *Vita* and the Encomium: A Native Model of Personality," *JSJ* 25 (1994): 177–206, and M. W. Martin, "Progymnasmatic Topic Lists: A Composition Template for Luke and Other Bioi?," *NTS* 54 (2008): 18–41.

14. For a helpful discussion, see S. Haliwell, "Traditional Greek Conceptions of Character," in *Characterization and Individualism in Greek Literature*, ed. C. B. R. Pelling (Oxford: Clarendon, 1990), 32–59.

15. Perhaps, as L. H. Feldman notes, Philo's intention was to focus everything on Moses himself: *Philo's Portrayal of Moses in the Context of Ancient Judaism* (Notre Dame: University of Notre Dame Press, 2007), 16–17. Philo further notes that Moses was the seventh generation from Abraham, and that Pharaoh's purpose in killing the babies was not to stop the Israelites becoming too numerous (as the account in Exodus suggests) but to prevent the birth of Moses. Similarly, C. Nepos does not include the names of Militiades's parents, and simply assures his readers that they were eminent (*Lives of Eminent Commanders, Militiades* 1).

16. In the preface to 3.1 of his *Memorable Doings and Sayings*, Valerius Maximus says that stories of early childhood display the "natural temper of a spirit destined in course of time to attain the highest pinnacles of glory" (Shackleton Bailey, LCL 492). He goes on to give

ucation (*paideia*) that the boy had received, perhaps a note of his illustrious teachers, and, of course, his precocious gift for learning. Luke's Gospel reflects this convention, where our one canonical story of Jesus's childhood depicts him as a skilled interpreter of the Law and points forward to the wisdom of the grown man (Luke 2:41-51). Later on, some of the noncanonical gospels take this even further, providing us with all kinds of stories of the boy Jesus who already knew himself to be God (the *Infancy Gospel of Thomas* is a good example here). What, then, are we to make of Mark's abrupt opening, beginning as it does with Jesus's appearance at the River Jordan?

It should be acknowledged from the start that an absence of family and childhood details is not entirely unknown in ancient *bioi*. Xenophon's *Memorabilia*, for example, does not refer to Socrates's descent or childhood, and his family is mentioned only once (*Memorabilia* 2.2). Lucian of Samosata notes that his hero Demonax's innate natural qualities had already manifested themselves in his youth (*Demonax* 3), though he provides no stories to serve as examples. Similarly, Diogenes Laertius often gives little more than the father's name and the city of origin, and he has few childhood stories to tell, even of his most illustrious philosophers.[17] And the highly fictional *Life of Aesop* says nothing of the hero's ancestors, birth, or upbringing; when we first meet Aesop, he is an ugly slave with a speech impediment.[18]

What links several of the characters mentioned in the last paragraph is the sense that dwelling on the subject's family and childhood would not be particularly edifying. Ancient authors were quite well aware that praiseworthy men did not always have an impressive background, and this might be especially the case with philosophers. Aristotle offered a number of strategies for concealing a less than ideal family background, most of which tended to stress that it was the man himself rather than his ancestors who should be praised.[19] Valerius Maximus, a near contemporary of Mark, expresses a similar sentiment:

several examples, of both politicians and generals. See further C. B. R. Pelling, "Childhood and Personality in Greek Biography," in Pelling, *Characterization and Individualism*, 213-44.

17. C. Nepos also tends not to provide many childhood stories; in his description of the Athenian general Alcibiades (who was taught by Socrates) he says that he is passing quickly over such things so that he can get to matters of "a higher and better nature"; *Alcibiades* 7.2.

18. Lucian's *The Passing of Peregrinus* also contains no account of birth or childhood (perhaps as a reflection of Lucian's disdain); nor does the anonymous *Secundus the Silent Philosopher* (though this is, in many ways, a highly unusual *bios*).

19. Pseudo-Aristotle, *Rhetoric to Alexander* 1440b.30-1441a.14. Plato is similarly said to have insisted that the greatest form of nobility is that which comes from a man himself rather than his ancestors (Diogenes Laertius, *Lives of Eminent Philosophers* 3.88-89).

So Virtue's access is not fastidious. She suffers lively dispositions stirred to action to enter her presence and gives them a draught of herself that is not generous or grudging from discrimination of persons. Equally available to all, she assesses the desire you bring, not your station, and in the taking in of her good things she leaves the weight for you yourself to determine, so that you carry away with you just so much as you can bring your mind to sustain. So it happens on the one hand that persons born in humble circumstances rise to the highest dignity and on the other that offshoots of the noblest family trees fall back into some disgrace and turn the light they received from their ancestors to darkness.[20]

In fact, Valerius Maximus devoted a whole chapter to "those born in a humble situation who became illustrious." These included Tullus Hostilius (Rome's third legendary king), who was born in a country cottage and looked after livestock as a young man; Gaius Terrentius Varro (consul 216 BCE), who was the son of a butcher; and Cato the Censor, whose family were farmers in Tusculum.[21]

In his *progymnasmata*, Theon offers ways in which an orator might turn humble origins to one's advantage. If the subject cannot boast good birth or other advantages, he suggests, a writer might note that he was not brought low by misfortune, made unjust by poverty, nor servile in want. It might even be to a man's credit that he became illustrious despite coming from a small city. He continues, "It is also praiseworthy if someone from a humble home becomes great, as did Socrates, the son of the midwife Phaenarete and the stone carver Sophroniscus. It is also worth admiring a workman or someone from the lower class who makes something good of himself, as they say Simon the leather worker and Leontiun the courtesan became philosophers. For virtue shines brightest in misfortunes."[22] This might have been a sensible way forward for Mark. Although other early Christian writers claimed Davidic descent for Jesus, with all the messianic associations that it conferred, this

20. Valerius Maximus, *Memorable Doings and Sayings* 3.3.ext.7 (Shackleton Bailey, LCL 492).

21. Valerius Maximus, *Memorable Doings and Sayings* 3.4. Other men on the list are King Tarquin, King Servius Tullius, and Marcus Perperna (consul 130 BCE); the foreign examples are Socrates, Euripides (the Athenian playwright), and Demosthenes (the Athenian orator). The next set of anecdotes treats "those who degenerated from famous parents," of whom Valerius comments, "I have to tell of those who degenerated from their splendour, noble monsters steeped in the foulest filth of sloth and rascality" (3.5, preface; Shackleton Bailey, LCL 492).

22. G. A. Kennedy, *Progymnasmata: Greek Textbooks of Prose composition and Rhetoric* (Atlanta: SBL Press, 2003), 52. The Greek word translated "stoneworker" here is *hermogly-phos*, which J. Butts translates as "sculptor," "The Progymnasmata of Theon: A New Text with Translation and Commentary" (PhD diss., Claremont Graduate School, 1987), 475.

was clearly not a genealogy that held any great interest for Mark.[23] He did, however, know something of Jesus's background: that his mother's name was Mary, that he was a carpenter, that the family came from Nazareth, and even the names of his brothers (Mark 6:1–6). Whatever social status we assign to a village *tektōn*, Jesus's origins were comparatively humble and would have displayed no great promise of nobility of spirit or character to an ancient audience. Similarly, in the absence of any concrete information, the evangelist might have assumed that Jesus received very little education, and certainly nothing that would be impressive by Roman standards.[24] Because his hero lacked any great pedigree or education, Mark might have made a virtue out of Jesus's insignificant birth, presenting him as standing in the line of Socrates, as a great man despite his humble origins. Yet he does not go down this path, choosing to keep most of his information relating to Jesus's family until more than a third of the way through his work.

In fact, Mark claims a very different ancestry for his hero: his father is none other than God himself. The scene in Mark 1:9–11 is generally regarded as an account of Jesus's baptism, but this is only part of the story. Mark generally has little interest in baptism, and the ritual serves only as the setting for a much more crucial element within the narrative—the voice of God that declares Jesus to be his beloved son in whom he is well pleased (1:11). Irrespective of whether the term "Son of God" (*huios theos*) is original to the work's opening sentence,[25] the identification here of Jesus as God's Son forms the climax to these opening verses. Whether Mark regarded Jesus as God's Son *prior* to this event, so that the heavenly voice simply endorsed what was already the case, is unclear. More likely, the torn heavens and descent of the Holy Spirit imply some kind of change to his status: that the God of Israel has entered the human realm, infused Jesus with his Spirit, and adopted him as his Son.

The concept of divine sonship was readily understandable to both Jews and

23. Blind Bartimaeus twice refers to Jesus as "Son of David" in 10:47–48 but drops the title (in favor of *rabbouni*) once he is in Jesus's presence; "Son of David" is conspicuously absent from Mark's triumphal entry (11:1–10), and the exchange in 12:35–37 seems deliberately to distance Jesus from the Son of David awaited by the scribes. As P. J. Achtemeier notes, there seems to be a "growing denial of Jesus as Son of David rather than a growing affirmation of that fact"; *Jesus in the Miracle Tradition* (Eugene, OR: Cascade, 2008), 153. Attempts to give greater prominence to Mark's use of the title seem to me to be misplaced.

24. Writing in the second century, Celsus was probably not the first to ridicule Jesus's humble origins; he mocked his upbringing in a Jewish village, characterized his mother as a poor spinner woman, and claimed that he had hired himself out in Egypt as a workman because of his poverty (*Against Celsus* 1.27–29, 38; 6.34).

25. See discussion in A. Y. Collins, *Mark: A Commentary* (Minneapolis: Fortress, 2007), 130.

Romans. For Jews, it could be used in a relatively commonplace manner: God was frequently seen as a father figure and all Jews thought of themselves as "sons of God" by virtue of God's election and covenant, though the influence of Hellenistic philosophy meant that by Mark's day the term tended to be used in a more individual sense of a person who lived a virtuous life (as it is used in Wis 2:16–18).[26] Mark's juxtaposition of sonship with *christos* (1:1), however, along with his clear allusion to a royal psalm in 1:11, suggests that the title is deliberately used to evoke the Jewish *king*, who was frequently identified as God's Son.[27] For Jewish readers, then, Mark's scene casts Jesus as a royal figure, standing in a uniquely filial relationship with God, and chosen for a specific task.

Roman readers (both Jews and gentiles) were familiar with the idea that great men might be descended from gods or heroes, though often the divine connections tended to stretch back to a mythic past. Thus Isocrates traced Evagoras's ancestry back to Zeus, a heritage that ensured his divine protection (*Evagoras* 13–18, 25); other sons of Zeus included Diogenes the Cynic[28] and Apollonius of Tyana (Philostratus, *Life of Apollonius of Tyana* 1.3). Xenophon linked Agesilaus with Heracles (*Agesilaus* 1), Pythagoras claimed to have been Hermes's son in a different life, Plato was fathered by Apollo, and Empedocles was said to be descended from Asclepius.[29] Closer to Mark's day, Julius Caesar traced his lineage to Aeneas and the goddess Venus, while Augustus associated himself with Apollo.[30] To those who did not believe such tales, Plutarch asks whether the Roman state could have achieved its present power if it had not been of divine origin (*Romulus* 8). Furthermore, most Roman emperors were declared divine (*divus*) on their deaths, leading to the prac-

---

26. A further use of "sons of God" in the Jewish Scriptures, though one probably not intended by Mark, is to denote heavenly beings, for example those in Gen 6:1–4, or Job 1:6. On the fatherhood of God, see M. R. D'Angelo, "Abba and Father: Imperial Theology in the Contexts of Jesus and the Gospels," in *The Historical Jesus in Context*, ed. A.-J. Levine, D. C. Allison, and J. D. Crossan (Princeton: Princeton University Press, 2006), 64–78.

27. See also Ps 89:26–27 and 2 Sam 7:14. The quotation in 1:11 seems to combine elements from Ps 2:7 and either Isa 42:1 or Gen 22. On the meaning of "Son of God" to Jews, see A. Y. Collins, "Mark and His Readers: The Son of God among Jews," *HTR* 92 (1999): 393–408; see also her *Mark*, 135.

28. According to Diogenes Laertius, *Lives* 6.2.77.

29. On the last three, see Diogenes Laertius, *Lives* 8.1.4 (Pythagoras); 3.1–2, 43 (Plato); and 8.2.61 (Empedocles). Porphyry claims Pythagoras was the offspring of Apollo (*Life of Pythagoras* 2). See Collins, "Mark and His Readers." Jewish legends, too, told of the impregnation of humans by angels, for example 1 Enoch 6–7; Testament of Solomon 5:8.

30. On Aeneas, see Homer, *Iliad* 2.819–22; 5.247–8. For Julius Caesar, see Suetonius, *The Divine Julius* 6; for Augustus, see Suetonius, *The Divine Augustus* 70, 94.

tice of referring to the living emperor as *divi filius*, or son of his deified predecessor. The title underscored the source of the son's power (through the divine father) and thus the legitimacy of his claim to rule.[31] Interestingly, several of the Julio-Claudian emperors owed their position not to biology but to *adoption*, a common practice among the elite to ensure succession and inheritance.[32] The abundance of coins, inscriptions, edicts, and temples, not to mention honorific games and festivals, ensured that imperial titles were well known throughout the empire.[33]

Standing at the beginning of Mark's account, then, the voice of God declares Jesus's striking and unexpected paternity. How precisely his life will map onto those of other divine sons—both Jewish and Roman—remains to be seen, but if Michael Peppard is right to see the dove as a deliberate counter-symbol to the militaristic imperial eagle, readers might already suspect that this particular Son of God will rule "not in the spirit of the bellicose eagle, but in the spirit of the pure, gentle, peaceful and even sacrificial dove."[34]

31. In the Greek-speaking east, where the imperial cult flourished, the emperor was commonly referred to as *theou huios*. Even in Rome, however, recent studies have shown that emperors received divine honors during their lifetimes; Augustus in particular constructed his "divine aura"—indeed, his very name designated him as "more than human" (for a discussion of the name Augustus, see Dio Cassius, *Roman History* 53.16.8). On the terminology used of Roman emperors, see S. R. F. Price, "Gods and Emperors: The Greek Language of the Roman Imperial Cult," *JHS* 104 (1984): 79–95. More recently, see I. Gradel, *Emperor Worship and Roman Religion* (Oxford: Oxford University Press, 2002), and K. Galinsky, "Continuity and Change: Religion in the Augustan Semi-Century," in *A Companion to Roman Religion*, ed. J. Rüpke (Oxford: Blackwell, 2007), 71–82. On the boundary between the human and divine, see D. S. Levene, "Defining the Divine in Rome," *TAPA* 142 (2012): 41–81.

32. Emperors tended to adopt more potential heirs than they needed, so Augustus adopted both Tiberius and Agrippa Julius Caesar and forced Tiberius to adopt his nephew Germanicus. For a full and persuasive discussion of this theme, see M. Peppard, *The Son of God in the Roman World: Divine Sonship in Its Social and Political Context* (Oxford: Oxford University Press, 2011). On adoption more generally, see H. Lindsay, *Adoption in the Roman World* (Cambridge: Cambridge University Press, 2009); also R. B. Lewis, *Paul's "Spirit of Adoption" in Its Roman Imperial Context* (London: T&T Clark, 2016), 44–56.

33. That Mark intends his readers to draw connections between Jesus's sonship and that of the imperial rulers will become clear toward the end of his work, most notably in the crucifixion narrative of ch. 15; see below, pp. 237–41.

34. M. Peppard, "The Eagle and the Dove: Roman Imperial Sonship and the Baptism of Jesus (Mark 1.9–11)," *NTS* 56 (2010): 431–51. The presence of the dove has led to much scholarly speculation. Birds were often used to designate the arrival or departure of gods, particularly in Homer (see E. P. Dixon, "Descending Spirit and Descending Gods: A 'Greek' Interpretation of the Spirit's 'Descent as a Dove' in Mark 1:10," *JBL* 128 [2009]: 759–80)

One final aspect of Jesus's new paternity is also worth noting. While an adoptee would come under the *potestas* of a new father and acquire a new set of family connections, the flip side was the loss of one's former name, paternity, and family. Jesus's adoption by the God of Israel would mean that he was no longer to be regarded as the son of his birth father. This may explain the surprising absence of any mention of Jesus's biological father in Mark: he has been comprehensively replaced by a new, heavenly father.[35] Although named in the Nazareth synagogue, Jesus's birth family is conspicuously absent from the whole account of his return to his hometown (6:1–6). And earlier, in 3:31–35, the Markan Jesus distances himself from his biological family, declaring that his true family are those who do the will of God. It is generally assumed that Jesus detaches himself from his "real" family for theological and pastoral reasons, that Mark writes to encourage faith in an audience pulled apart across family lines by their adherence to the gospel. There may well be some truth to this, but it may also be worth considering whether the relativizing of Jesus's biological family is also partly an inevitable side effect of his divine adoption.

---

and may well have seemed like a good image to Mark to represent the arrival of God's spirit. Quite possibly the dove functions as some sort of omen. Suetonius, for example, says that Vespasian's family was of "obscure descent" and boasted "no ancestral honors" (*Vespasian* 1.1), so he is careful to devote a whole chapter to prodigies associated with the start of his reign (5). The early reign of Tiberius is similarly accompanied by omens (*Tiberius* 14). As U. Riemer notes, the "upstart" Vespasian needed divine legitimation for his rule (as Augustus did earlier), and Tiberius needed his own succession ratified, the hereditary nature of the *princeps* not yet being fully established; U. Riemer, "Miracle Stories and Their Narrative Intent in the Context of the Ruler Cult of Classical Antiquity," in *Wonders Never Cease: The Purpose of Narrating Miracle Stories in the New Testament and Its Religious Environment*, ed. M. Labahn and B. J. Lietaert Peerbolte (London: T&T Clark, 2006), 39–40. Noting the connections between 1:9–11 and Jesus's death, L. E. Vaage links the dove here (*peristera*) and the bird flying into the heavens that often accompanies accounts of noble deaths (see Lucian, *The Passing of Peregrinus*). While the adoption scene is clearly invoked as Jesus expires (see below, p. 245), I do not see clear links with Jesus's death quite as early as this; the dove, it seems to me, is simply the visible manifestation of the Holy Spirit's descent. See L. E. Vaage, "Bird-Watching at the Baptism of Jesus: Early Christian Mythmaking in Mark 1:9–11," in *Reimagining Christian Origins: A Colloquium Honoring Burton L. Mack*, ed. E. A. Castelli and H. Taussig (Valley Forge, PA: Trinity Press International, 1996), 280–94.

35. Both Matthew and Luke, apparently independently, give Jesus's father's name as Joseph, suggesting that his name was well known. Neither of these later evangelists, however, present the baptism scene as an adoption; they both, in very different ways, show that Jesus became the "Son of God" at his conception.

It is at this point that Jesus receives the Holy Spirit. Mark does not simply say that the Spirit rested upon him (as translations of 1:10 often suggest),[36] but states much more graphically that the Spirit entered *into* him (*eis auton*). God's Spirit is well known from the Jewish Scriptures as an indication of the divine presence in a range of specially appointed figures, including kings, prophets (particularly Elijah and Elisha), and future messianic leaders.[37] Clearly for Mark Jesus emerges from his baptism as the Spirit-filled Son.[38]

Far from explaining away a humble ancestry, then, Mark has given his hero the most prestigious background possible. His old family ties are exchanged for an opening scene in which he is chosen by God to be his Son. What this means for Jesus, and indeed all those who would follow him, becomes clearer as the *bios* unfolds.

Following his baptism and divine adoption, the Markan Jesus is immediately driven into the wilderness for forty days, where he is tempted by Satan (1:12–13). This is a strange little passage, made only more curious by the fact that Mark does not say what these temptations involved (unlike the parallel passage in Q), or even whether Jesus prevailed over Satan.

Those who detect a highly apocalyptic strand running through the gospel attach a great deal of importance to this scene. For them, Satan is the ultimate enemy who makes his presence felt early in the narrative.[39] Still others argue that Satan is defeated here, with subsequent exorcisms serving as a "mopping up" exercise.[40] But neither of these two assumptions are by any means clear from the text itself.

First, while we cannot know exactly what the term *Satanas* conjured up in the minds of Mark's audience, Satan's role in the narrative is not particularly striking. His most important scene is within the dialogue of 3:22–27, where he is equated with Beelzebul, the prince of demons, and metaphorically linked with a householder who must first be bound if his house is to be plundered. Here he is clearly

36. See, for example, the RSV.

37. Of the many texts, see Num 24:2 (Balaam); 2 Kgs 2:9–15 (Elijah and Elisha); and Isa 11:2; 42:1; 61:1 (messianic leaders).

38. It is not uncommon in biographies of the poets for an encounter with a divine figure to lead to the bestowal of great gifts; Collins notes that both Aesop and the lyric poet Archilochus were transformed by encounters with the Muses (*Mark*, 147).

39. See, for example, H. C. Kee, *Community of the New Age: Studies in Mark's Gospel* (Philadelphia: Westminster, 1977), 64–76, who argues for a dualistic system in which demons are personifications of evil. See also E. Shively, "Characterizing the Non-human: Satan in the Gospel of Mark," in Skinner and Hauge, *Character Studies and the Gospel of Mark*, 127–51.

40. So, for example, Rhoads, Dewey, and Michie, *Mark as Story*, 83.

an evil power, stronger and more difficult to subdue than the unclean spirits that feature commonly in Mark's account. The remaining two uses, however, are much more muted. In 4:15 he opposes the work of Jesus, ensuring that his word comes to nothing, and in 8:33 Peter is referred to as Satan in a passage where the Markan Jesus seems to be drawing on the older scriptural usage of Satan as a stumbling block (as, for example, in Job 1–2). The explanatory comment here might well apply to other passages: "Satan" is whatever prompts people to act according to human desires rather than those of God.[41]

Second, there is no hint in Mark's short narrative that Satan *is* in fact defeated. Satan's role here is simply to tempt Jesus (*peirazō*), nothing more. Certainly the unclean spirits later in the narrative know nothing of his defeat; their grip on human beings continues unabated, with the dreadful scene of the man possessed by a legion of demons standing as a terrible example of human misery and despair (5:1–20). There is no doubt that Satan is a force to be reckoned with for Mark, and it is clear that Satan's demons need to be stamped out, but the fight is an ongoing one and it is not at all evident that our author thought that it had already been won, either in this early narrative or even at the cross. Satan is still an active force for Mark, against which followers have to be vigilant. A better contender for his eventual defeat is the *parousia*, when the stars will fall from above, the powers in heaven will be shaken, and the elect will be gathered from the four winds (13:24–27). But that is all far in the future, or at least well beyond Mark's narrative time.

Rather than focus on Satan here, we would do better to give our full attention to Jesus. We are told that the Spirit drove him into the wilderness, using the same verb used to denote Jesus's own exorcisms of unclean beings (*ekballō*; 1:34; 3:22; 7:26).[42] While it would be too much to describe Jesus as "resistant," the strong verb leaves an image of a hero who may not be too clear initially about what it means to be the Spirit-filled Son of God, or the course his life is about to take. In order to understand the main thrust of this scene, it needs to be read with the verses that immediately follow: after the arrest of John, we are told, Jesus appears openly proclaiming the kingdom of God with confidence and clarity (1:14–15). Jesus has been forced into the wilderness only to emerge with a newly found mission and authority. The stress throughout this short section of Mark's narrative is not so much on the temptations offered by the (silent) Satan, still less on the angels and

---

41. So also T.-S. B. Liew, "Tyranny, Boundary and Might: Colonial Mimicry in Mark's Gospel," *JSNT* 73 (1999): 21.

42. Mark's Spirit is described simply as *to pneuma* with no explanatory adjective, though it is clear from the previous scene that this is the Spirit of God and that Jesus is ultimately thrust into the deserted place by God himself.

wild beasts,[43] but rather on Jesus's time in the wilderness and subsequent acceptance of his divinely appointed task.

The motif of the hero testing his vocation was a common *topos* of ancient biography. The most famous example is the "Choice of Heracles," recounted by Socrates in Xenophon's *Memorabilia* (2.1.21) on the basis of a tale told by Prodicus, a philosopher of the fifth century BCE. According to the story, Heracles, on the verge of manhood, went to a quiet place to decide whether to pursue the path of virtue or of vice. As he pondered the matter, two goddesses appeared: Kakia, the coquettish goddess of vice, and Aretē, the beautiful but plainly dressed goddess of virtue. Both tried to persuade the young hero to follow their path, the short and easy way of *kakia*, or the long and difficult way to *aretē*. The same story was told by Philostratus in his *Life of Apollonius of Tyana* (6.10), and it was a favorite of the Cynic-Stoic tradition, in which it functioned almost as a metaphor for the idea that it was better to face hardships on the path to virtue than to choose the easy way of vice.[44] The "wilderness" frequently functions as a place of testing, and stories of ascetic experiences in secluded places are common in *bioi*.[45] Josephus, for example, records his three-year training as a young man with Bannus in the wilderness (*Life* 8–27).

Mark's brief account here, then, is best understood in the light of the traditional *topos* of the youth who withdraws to a quiet place to contemplate the path his life is to take. His audience would have taken the short scene as an initial trial: Will Jesus respond to Satan or resist his temptations and prove himself worthy of his divine adoption?[46] It is clear from 1:14–15 that he chooses the latter path. Filled

43. The role of the wild beasts here is not clear. F. G. Downing draws comparisons between the Markan Jesus and Romulus, noting that wild beasts play a role in the early story of both; *Doing Things with Words in the First Christian Century* (Sheffield: Sheffield Academic, 2000), 138.

44. See Guthrie, *A History of Greek Philosophy*, 3:277–78, 366–67; H. J. Rose, "Herakles and the Gospels," *ARW* 34 (1937): 42–60; Haliwell, "Traditional," 32–33. C. Gill, "The Question of Character Development: Plutarch and Tacitus," *ClQ* 33 (1983): 469–87, notes that the conception of youth as an unstable period in which a young man could be drawn toward either virtue or vice was a Roman cliché. (Mark gives no indication of Jesus's age — a point I shall return to below — but the implication is that, like an adolescent, he has entered a new stage in his life.) On the critical nature of youth, see E. Eyben, "The Beginning and End of Youth in Roman Antiquity," *Paedagogica Historica* 29 (1993): 247–85.

45. See Martin, "Progymnasmata," 37, who also cites Philostratus, *Life of Apollonius of Tyana* 1.8.

46. See M. A. Powell, *What Is Narrative Criticism?* (Minneapolis: Fortress, 1990), 75–76, and J. L. Resseguie, *Narrative Criticism of the New Testament: An Introduction* (Grand Rapids: Baker Academic, 2005), 96, both of whom similarly stress the theme of trial or testing here.

with God's Spirit, he possesses powerful resources for good against whatever evil Satan can throw at him. Jesus will of course be tempted once more in Gethsemane, on the eve of his death (14:36), but for now his resolve seems strong.

Jesus in Galilee (1:16–8:21)

What strikes the hearer as we enter the first main section of the biography is the energy with which Jesus goes about his mission, "immediately" moving from one situation to another. He is quite at home in the public sphere, taking to the road and surrounding himself with male followers (1:16–20; 2:14; 3:13–19). He renounces his hometown of Nazareth in favor of an itinerant lifestyle, centered on the fishing villages around the Sea of Galilee. Indeed, his one visit home is met with resistance and suspicion, leading Jesus to remark that "a prophet is not without honor, except in his own country, and among his own kin, and in his own house" (6:1–6). Clearly Jesus's divine adoption entails a break with all that has gone before.

Miracles

The first half of the gospel is dominated by stories of mighty deeds.[47] One anecdote after another establishes Jesus as a powerful exorcist and healer, one who can rally crowds and inspire amazement in all he does (1:27–8; 2:12; 5:42; etc.). As the narrative proceeds, we learn that he can control the forces of nature (4:35–41; 6:45–52), raise the dead (5:21–24, 35–43), and provide food for vast numbers of people (6:30–44; 8:1–10).

Those familiar with the Jewish Scriptures would have heard echoes of the great men of Israel's past: Moses, who healed people bitten by snakes through a bronze serpent (Num 21:4–7); Elijah, who raised a widow's son from the dead (1 Kgs 17:17–24); and Elisha, who similarly raised a dead child (2 Kgs 4:18–37) and who could both cure leprosy and inflict it on others (2 Kgs 5:1–27). Acting in the power

---

47. Mark includes eighteen miracle stories—four exorcisms, nine healings, two feedings, two rescues at sea, and one prophetic sign—along with a number of summaries; e.g., 1:32–34, 39; 3:7–12; 6:53–56. All but two of these (9:14–29; 11:12–14) occur in the first half of the gospel (the second granting of sight to a blind man, 10:46–52, forms an *inclusio* with the first in 8:22–26, and the two stories together frame Jesus's teaching in the central section of the gospel). On miracles in Mark, see F. J. Matera, "'He Saved Others; He Cannot Save Himself': A Literary-Critical Perspective on the Markan Miracles," *Int* 47 (1993): 15–26; several of the essays in Achtemeier, *Jesus in the Miracle Tradition*; and E. Eve, *The Healer from Nazareth: Jesus's Miracles in Historical Context* (London: SPCK, 2009), esp. 92–117.

of God, each of these men was able to provide food for the hungry, and each (along with Joshua) was able to part the sea.[48] David and Solomon, too, were widely associated with exorcisms (Josephus, *Jewish Antiquities* 6.166–69; 8.44–45); and by the first century, Honi (Onias) the Circle Drawer and Hanina ben Dosa had gained a reputation for amazing feats.[49] Other hearers would be put in mind of Asclepius, the greatest of all healing deities, whose shrine at Epidaurus contained inscriptions thanking the God for curing the blind and the lame, and even raising the dead.[50] Tales circulated about Apollonius of Tyana, who was credited with healing the blind, the lame, and the paralyzed, driving out evil spirits, enabling a woman to give birth successfully, and raising a young bride from the dead.[51] Kings and emperors, too, were reputed (at least in their own propaganda) to have supra-human abilities: Plutarch records Pyrrhus's ability to heal (*Pyrrhus* 3.4); Philo credited Augustus with calming storms and healing pestilence (*Embassy to Gaius* 144–45); and, in a bid to demonstrate his sovereignty over the sea, Gaius rode over the Bay of Baiae (albeit along a bridge made of ships).[52] Even as Mark wrote, stories were circulating about Vespasian in Alexandria, telling how he gave sight to a blind man

48. Feedings: Moses (Exod 16:1–18), Elijah (1 Kgs 17:8–16), Elisha (2 Kgs 4:42–44). Parting the sea: Moses (Exod 14:15–29), Joshua (Josh 3:1–16), Elijah (2 Kgs 2:6–8), Elisha (2 Kgs 2:13–15).

49. Onias is referred to by Josephus, *Jewish Antiquities* 14.22–24; see also J. D. Crossan, *The Historical Jesus: The Life of a Mediterranean Jewish Peasant* (San Francisco: HarperSanFrancisco, 1991), 142–58, for discussion of rabbinic texts associated with these two figures.

50. For a selection of relevant texts, see W. Cotter, *Miracles in Greco-Roman Antiquity* (Oxford: Routledge, 1999), 15–30; also J. den Boeft, "Asclepius' Healings Made Known," in Labahn and Lietaert Peerbolte, *Wonders Never Cease*, 20–31.

51. Admittedly, Philostratus only compiled his biography of Apollonius in the third century CE, but there is no reason to doubt that stories of his miracles stretch back to earlier times (whether or not Philostratus was dependent on an earlier biography by Apollonius's disciple Damis). Philostratus's desire to distance his subject from the charge of magic would presumably lead to his downplaying the miraculous side of the tradition. For texts, see Cotter, *Miracles*, 43–45, 83–89; on the existence of traditions well before Philostratus wrote, see E. Koskenniemi, "The Function of the Miracle Stories in Philostratus's *Vita Apollonii Tyanensis*," in Labahn and Lietaert Peerbolte, *Wonders Never Cease*, 78–80.

52. Suetonius, *Gaius Caligula* 4.19.2–3; Josephus, *Jewish Antiquities* 19.16; the escapade seems to have been an attempt to rival that of Xerxes across the Hellespont.

and restored the use of another's hand.[53] And Martial and other poets told how nature itself recognized the divinity of the Flavian emperors.[54]

Biographers made good use of such extraordinary tales. On a general level, they were hugely entertaining. The insertion of miraculous stories into even quite serious histories had a long pedigree, stretching back to Herodotus and continuing through the works of sober authors such as Julius Caesar and Josephus until it became a particularly popular feature in the second century CE.[55] Adding an extraordinary story here and there—the presence of unicorns in Gaul (so Caesar) or a plant with amazing abilities to exorcise demons (so Josephus)[56]—lent wonder to an account, along with a sense of entering a far-off, exotic world. Incorporating extraordinary stories, however, might also have a much more serious goal. Suetonius, for example, included the story of Vespasian's miraculous healings in Alexandria to lend the emperor authority (*auctoritas*) and majesty (*maiestas*)—qualities he claims that the emperor lacked before this clear sign not only of divine approval but also of his own godly status (*Vespasian* 7.2).[57] Philostratus was prepared to tell tales of Apollonius's amazing exploits, despite the risk of fueling charges that he was a magician, to show

---

53. The relevant texts are: Tacitus, *Histories* 4.81–82; Suetonius, *Vespasian* 7.2 (who says that the second man was lame); Dio Cassius, *Roman History* 65.8 (who adds that the Nile also overflowed its banks in his honor). The healings must have occurred around 69/70 as Vespasian made his move on the imperial throne. Noting that Jesus spat (*ptuō*) in the man's eyes in Mark 8:22–25, E. Eve makes an intriguing link to Vespasian's healing of the blind man, which is also said to have involved spittle, arguing that Mark deliberately modeled his account on the Alexandrian story; "Spit in Your Eye: The Blind Man of Bethsaida and the Blind Man of Alexandria," *NTS* 54 (2008): 1–17. T. S. Luke warns against assigning too early a date for the Vespasianic story, arguing that links between the new dynasty and the Alexandrian god Serapis would have found a more congenial environment in the reign of Titus, and even more so that of Domitian, rather than Vespasian (who was anxious to distance himself from the philhellenic Nero); "A Healing Touch for Emperor: Vespasian's Wonders in Domitianic Rome," *G&R* 57 (2010): 77–106. Josephus's silence on the matter, however, to which Luke appeals, may simply be due to his attempt to situate the Jewish God (rather than Serapis) at the center of political affairs. Thus the story (in some form or other) might well have been current in Mark's day.

54. See, for example, Martial, *Book of Spectacles* 17; 30.1–4; *Epigrams* 1.6; 8.21; for fuller discussion, see Riemer, "Miracle Stories," 33–38.

55. See Koskenniemi, "Function," 73–74.

56. Julius Caesar, *Gallic War* 6.26–28 (on unicorns) and Josephus, *Jewish War* 7.180–86 (on the plant).

57. As Riemer notes, Tacitus is more skeptical, though even he notes the presence still of eyewitnesses (*Histories* 4.81.1–2).

that, in the end, the philosopher stands above the tyrant.[58] And Diogenes Laertius recounted stories of Pythagoras and his disciple Empedocles being able to still storms, predict earthquakes, and cure the sick so as to demonstrate their complete understanding of the secrets of nature.[59]

Returning to Mark, we should not rule out the entertainment value of Jesus's miraculous deeds. It is easy to imagine a first-century audience wide-eyed at their hero's abilities, taking careful note so as to pass on the tales to their friends. Yet for Mark, as for other biographers, the purpose of the miracles was much more serious. At a very basic level, the miracles establish Jesus's cosmic authority: empowered by the Holy Spirit, Jesus's amazing deeds mark him out not only as a man who enjoys God's favor but also as a powerful force to be reckoned with. At times his powers are equal to those of the Jewish God, particularly the two times that he stills storms.[60] The significance of the miracles, however, goes still further. Coupled with his proclamation that the "kingdom of God" is at hand (1:15), Jesus's great deeds show God's kingly rule mightily breaking into people's lives, restoring what was broken, excluded, or despised. No doubt Mark had the messianic hopes of Isa 35:5–6 in mind: the glorious age when the blind would see, the deaf hear, the lame leap, and the dumb sing.[61] The feeding miracles, too, give a taste of the messianic banquet to come, a magnificent future feast to which Jew and gentile alike will be invited.[62] And yet, despite their illustration of both Jesus's power and the imminence of the kingdom, it is important to note that miracles for Mark are not in themselves adequate grounds for discipleship. As Paul Achtemeier notes, the first disciples in Mark are called *before* he has performed any great deeds; and, as we shall soon see, discipleship for Mark is not about following a wonder worker but being ready to follow Jesus to the end.[63]

58. Koskenniemi, "Function," 76.

59. For texts, see Cotter, *Miracles*, 37–39, 143–45.

60. See Pss 29:3; 89:8–9; 107:23–20; Neh 1:4; Hab 3:15; Jonah 1:4–7; Testament of Naphtali 6:1–10 (the latter dates to the second century CE); see also Isa 43:1–10, which has several points of contact with the sea stories. On Jesus's "divinity" in Mark, see n. 123 on p. 155 below.

61. Although Mark does not quote or allude to this passage directly, his appreciation of Isaiah is well documented. See, for example, R. E. Watts, *Isaiah's New Exodus and Mark* (Tübingen: Mohr Siebeck, 1997); M. D. Hooker, "Isaiah in Mark's Gospel," in *Isaiah in the New Testament*, ed. S. Moyise and M. J. J. Menken (London: T&T Clark, 2005), 35–49.

62. This seems to be the significance of the two narratives: the first is an invitation to Jews (6:35–44), the second to gentiles (8:1–10). On the theme of the messianic banquet, see Isa 25:6–8; 34:5–7; Zech 9:15, and discussion in D. E. Smith, "Messianic Banquet," *ABD* 4:788–91.

63. Here Mark is strikingly different from Luke, for whom miracles *are* a legitimate basis for discipleship. For discussion, see Achtemeier, *Jesus*, 159–62.

Jesus's miracles do, however, disclose something of his character. In a perceptive study, Wendy Cotter points out that many of those who petition Jesus for healing or exorcism (either for themselves or others) are "bold, brash, outrageous" and even "rude."[64] The leper who approaches him in 1:40–45, for example, would inspire fear and disgust in the audience, and a horror at his insistent appeal to Jesus; the friends of the paralyzed man willfully destroy another's property to push their charge to the front of the line (2:1–12); and Bartimaeus, reduced by his blindness to begging, would have aroused revulsion in an audience, all the more so by his raucous pestering. Ordinarily, each of these petitioners should earn a rebuke, a stern warning to know their place and to keep to it. Yet in each case, Jesus sees through their reprehensible actions to the utter desperation and distress that prompts them, and their unshakeable belief that he can help. Even when Jesus is initially unwilling to intervene, as seems to be the case with the story of the Syro-Phoenician mother (8:24–30), he is willing to listen to a supplicator and to change his mind.[65] Jesus's decision to help these people demonstrates not only his self-control (*sōphrosynē*) in the face of overbearing, persistent, and even aggressive behavior, but also his *philanthrōpia*—his loving concern for others, his kindness and clemency. As Cotter points out, these were among the most highly praised qualities in a man, from Homer onward.[66]

The text highlights Jesus's concern for others in a number of episodes. He feels compassion toward the leper (1:41),[67] the epileptic boy (9:22), and the crowds who were "like sheep without a shepherd" (6:34; see also 8:2). He shows a fatherly kindness toward the sick, referring to the paralyzed man as "my son" (2:5) and the woman with a hemorrhage as "daughter" (5:34), and several times he thinks to feed people (5:43;

---

64. W. Cotter, *The Christ of the Miracle Stories: Portrait through Encounter* (Grand Rapids: Baker Academic, 2010). Cotter's main interest lies in the pre-Markan stories, but much of her discussion is equally applicable to the stories as they appear in Mark; as she notes, Matthew tones down the problematic nature of these stories far more than Mark appears to do (7–8). I would, however, be less confident in uncovering pre-Markan traditions than Cotter is; see my comments on pp. 106–15 above.

65. This would not necessarily have been seen as a fault. Cotter cites Dio Cassius's approval at Hadrian's readiness to accept correction from a commoner, *Roman History* 69.6.2 (*Christ*, 190–91).

66. Cotter, *Christ*, 9–13. On *philanthrōpia* specifically, see H. Martin, "The Concept of Philanthrōpia in Plutarch's Lives," *AJP* 82 (1961): 164–75.

67. There is a textual variant here: while most texts read the uncommon word *splanchnizomai* (pity/compassion), a minority read *orgizomai* (anger). For a robust defense of *splanchnizomai* here, see P. J. Williams, "An Examination of Ehrman's Case for *orgistheis* in Mark 1.41," *NovT* 54 (2012): 1–12.

6:30–44; 8:1–10). In the first boat story, his display of godlike powers over nature is not for his own self-aggrandizement but to calm his frightened followers (6:35–41).[68] Conversely, he can be moved to anger and grief by the lack of compassion he finds in others (3:5; see also 10:14). It is no surprise to find Mark's Jesus flaunting convention, openly eating with tax collectors and "sinners" (2:15–17) and disowning his natural family when they try to take him home (3:31–35). In all of this, Jesus's Spirit-filled self-confidence and courage allow him to challenge the customs of his day.[69]

Despite a very practical concern for others, there is something slightly "other-worldly" about Mark's Jesus. He has an uncanny ability to know what others are saying (2:8) and to know when a desperate woman touches his clothes (5:30–33). He speaks in slightly better Greek than those around him, occasionally using rather more "correct" or formal features drawn from classical Greek or, on occasion, from the prophetic literature of the LXX.[70] And he frequently needs to withdraw from the throng and to take himself to a quiet place, often to pray (1:35–37, 45; 3:7, 19b–20; 6:31–32, 46; 7:24). All of this contributes to the impression of someone who, though strong-minded and disciplined, retreats to the solitude of the wilderness to hear the voice of God anew.

Conflict

Jesus's great success, however, breeds resentment, and conflict begins to appear as early as the five anecdotes contained in 2:1–3:6. Variously described as "scribes," "Pharisees," and "Herodians," these opponents challenge both what he says and what he does. They take issue with his claim to forgive sins (2:1–10), with his eating companions (2:15–17), with the fact that he does not require his disciples to fast (2:18–20), and with his unwillingness to reprimand his disciples for plucking grain on the Sabbath (2:23–28). What is significant about these exchanges is that they are public, set in the agonistic world of male honor and debate. Jerome Neyrey underscores the "hostile and aggressive" nature of these *chreiai*, which anthropologists would assign to the game of "challenge and riposte," so ubiquitous in an

---

68. So Cotter, *Christ*, 206.

69. Valerius Maximus devotes a chapter to self-confidence (*fiducia sui*), noting that men of courage are frequently able to challenge custom; *Memorable Deeds and Sayings* 3.7.

70. So J. A. L. Lee, "Some Features of the Speech of Jesus in Mark's Gospel," *NovT* 27 (1985): 1–26, who cites, among other things, Jesus's use of *men* (found in 4:4; 9:12; 12:5; 14:1; and 14:8), *eu* (14:7), the optative, *ō* + vocative (9:19), and *ou mē* + subjunctive/future for a prohibition or strong denial (see discussion on 18–23). Perhaps unconsciously the author has given Jesus a manner of speaking more in keeping with his status.

ancient Mediterranean setting.[71] Jesus's opponents seek to shame him, to expose him as a blasphemer and a lawbreaker, and to hold him up to public ridicule and contempt.[72] But their attempts are thwarted: the Markan Jesus shows himself to be a master of the one-liner (2:10, 17, 19, 27–28; see also 5:39 and 6:4) and runs rings around his rivals, who never offer any response. Things come to a head in the fifth and final incident in this group. Set on a Sabbath, his opponents watch Jesus to see whether he will heal a man with a withered hand. Jesus himself takes the initiative, issuing them with a direct challenge: "Is it lawful on the Sabbath to do good or to do harm, to save life or to kill?" His adversaries have no answer to make, and they watch in silence as Jesus heals the man (3:1–6). An ancient audience would have appreciated the dynamics at work here: far from shaming Jesus, his opponents are themselves humiliated by his superior wit and understanding, exposed as indecisive, and ultimately dishonored. It is hardly a surprise that these local "worthies" want Jesus out of the way, or to find them plotting his death in 3:6.[73]

These controversy stories frame two sayings that stress the impossibility of grafting what is new onto what is old (2:21, 22). As the *bios* continues, it becomes clear that Jesus himself represents the "new cloth" or the "new wine."[74] But far from being a lawbreaker, as his opponents suppose, Jesus shows a deeper understanding of the meaning and purpose of the Law. The controversies allow Jesus once again to demonstrate his *philanthrōpia*, his kindness and compassion, over against his Markan opponents, whose strict legalism borders on the callous and coldhearted.[75] Jesus's superior understanding of the Law will be underlined again in the lengthy exchange that opens ch. 7. His rivals ask why Jesus's disciples do not wash their hands before meals; in response, Jesus accuses them of replacing God's Law with their own and quotes Scripture at them (Mark 7:6–10 reflects Isa 29:13; Exod 20:12; 21:17;

---

71. J. H. Neyrey, "Questions, *Chreiai*, and Challenges to Honor: The Interface of Rhetorical Culture in Mark's Gospel," *CBQ* 60 (1998): 657–81.

72. On mockery specifically, see D. Neufeld, *Mockery and Secretism in the Social World of Mark's Gospel* (London: Bloomsbury, 2014).

73. There are similarities here with the *Life of Aesop*, where the central character continually bests his opponents with his superior wit; see S. S. Elliott, "'Witless in Your Own Cause': Divine Plots and Fractured Characters in the Life of Aesop and the Gospel of Mark," *Religion and Theology* 12 (2005): 405–6.

74. On the chiastic structure here, see N. W. Lund, *Chiasmus in the New Testament: A Study in Formgeschichte* (Chapel Hill: University of North Carolina Press, 1942), 303–4.

75. Needless to say, I am referring to the Markan characterization of these opponents here, not the historical scribes and Pharisees; on the latter, see E. P. Sanders, *Judaism: Practice and Belief, 63 BCE–66 CE* (London: SCM, 1992), 380–451.

Deut 5:6; and Lev 20:9).[76] As was the case with the earlier clashes, the opponents have no response to make and simply disappear from the narrative.

Other, more isolated accounts of conflict follow the same pattern. Jesus's family hear he is "beside himself" (*existēmi*) and come to take him home, only to find Jesus disowning them (3:21, 31–35). Scribes from Jerusalem come to investigate, declaring that Jesus is himself possessed and that he exorcises through the power of Beelzebul. Their higher status ("from Jerusalem") raises the stakes; these men are more highly regarded and so have more to lose as a result of public humiliation.[77] Yet, once again, Jesus easily dismisses their judgment, not only exposing their argument's lack of logic but also warning that they may themselves be guilty of an "eternal sin" (3:22–30). Jesus barely interacts with Pharisees in search of a "sign from heaven" (8:11–13), and later trumps their literal understanding of the Law of divorce (Deut 24:1–4) with his own, superior perception of the relationship between men and women (10:2–9, drawing on Gen 1:27; 5:2; and 2:24).

Jesus's words and actions, then, are constantly tested in public, and all are shown to be true and worthy. While it is nearly always the slighted rivals who challenge him, Jesus is ready to take the initiative himself on occasion and always has the last word. He speaks with boldness and authority and is clearly superior to the Galilean religious leaders in wit, argument, and knowledge of the Law. Within these opening chapters, Mark has cast Jesus as an honorable, even elite male—as befits God's chosen son. He exhibits the manly virtues of *philanthrōpia* (humanity) and *sōphrosynē* (self-control, moderation). Of course, Mark does not name these virtues—he prefers to express himself though the language of the Septuagint—but it is clear that so far he presents a Jesus who exhibits qualities that Roman readers would find attractive.

Identity

A further theme that is introduced in this first section is the question of *identity*. As we have seen already, the audience is informed right from the beginning that Jesus is the Christ (1:1), and the opening section further designates him as God's Son (1:9–11). For Mark, the two titles seem to be almost interchangeable, with "Son of God" functioning as a clarification of *christos*. Jesus will be declared God's Son in three pivotal scenes throughout the gospel: to Jesus alone at his baptism (1:9–11), to

---

76. On the relation between Jesus's authority and that of the Jewish Scriptures, see Liew, "Tyranny," 13–16.

77. Neyrey, "Jesus, Gender," 65.

his closest followers at the transfiguration (9:2–8), and finally to a wider audience by a Roman centurion at his death (15:36–39).

While the audience has the benefit of the prologue, however, characters within the narrative do not know what to make of Jesus. Whether it is those gathered in the Capernaum synagogue, the shocked scribes, awestruck disciples, resentful townspeople, or even Herod, the questions are always the same: Who is this? And where does he get his authority (1:27; 2:7; 6:2, 14)? Human characters offer a range of possible identities for Jesus: most common in direct speech is teacher (*didaskalos*),[78] and less frequently rabbi[79] or lord (*kyrios*).[80] There is speculation that he may be a prophet, perhaps like Elijah (6:15; 8:28) or John the Baptist returned from the dead (6:14, 16; 8:28), or maybe he is possessed by Beelzebul, the prince of demons (3:22, 30). Only unclean spirits are capable of recognizing Jesus for who he truly is—the Holy One of God (1:24–25), Son of God (1:34; 3:11–12), or Son of the Most High (5:7).

Jesus, however, prefers less exalted ways to refer to himself. He likens himself to a physician (2:17), a bridegroom (2:20), and a prophet (6:4).[81] And while he once refers to himself as Lord (11:3)[82] and once as teacher (14:14), his preferred title is the more enigmatic Son of Man (*ho huios tou anthrōpou*).[83] Most scholarly discussion of this phrase has centered on historical questions: Did Jesus really use this term? If so, what did he mean by it?[84] For our purposes, however, historical questions are of only limited value. Given its use in Q, it seems overwhelmingly likely to me that Jesus did use the term to refer to himself and that Mark inherited the expression

78. Mark 4:38; 5:38; 9:17, 38; 10:17, 20, 35; 12:14, 19, 32; and 13:1.

79. Mark 9:5; 10:51; 11:21; and 14:45.

80. Mark 7:28.

81. Implicitly too, perhaps, a shepherd (*poimēn*, 6:34).

82. Jesus uses the term in 5:19, where he tells the man who has been possessed by a legion of demons to go home and tell people "how much the Lord has done for you." The man takes the designation to mean Jesus himself (as 5:20 makes clear), though in its context it is more likely to refer to God.

83. Mark 2:10, 27–28; 8:31, 38; 9:9, 31; 10:33, 45; 13:26; 14:21, 41, and 62. I recognize the sexist nature of the common translation of this phrase, but Son of Humanity/Humankind is not particularly elegant.

84. For good overviews of the topic, see A. Y. Collins, "The Origin of the Designation of Jesus as 'Son of Man,'" *HTR* 80 (1987): 391–407; D. R. Burkett, *The Son of Man Debate: A History and Evaluation* (Cambridge: Cambridge University Press, 1999); M. Müller, *The Expression "Son of Man" and the Development of Christology: A History of Interpretation* (Sheffield: Equinox, 2008); and L. W. Hurtado and P. W. Owen, eds., *Who Is This Son of Man? The Latest Scholarship on a Puzzling Expression of the Historical Jesus* (London: T&T Clark, 2010).

from tradition (presumably now translated rather awkwardly into Greek). Of more interest to the present study, however, are the following questions: Why does Mark retain it, even making it Jesus's primary self-designation?[85] And why do no other characters use it of him?

As is well known, the rather odd term occurs 166 times in the LXX, both in the singular and the plural (the former without the article), where it consistently refers to "a human being" or "people" in general.[86] By far the most extensive use of the term is in Ezekiel, where God refers to the prophet as "Son of Man" (using the vocative, *huie anthrōpe*), a usage that seems to stress his humility and unworthiness. The Markan Jesus's use of the definite article with the phrase is odd and seems to lend a particularity to the term: "this specific Son of Man," "*this* human being." Noting this, an earlier generation of scholars imagined that "the Son of Man" was the title of an eschatological figure, perhaps based on Dan 7, where "one like a Son of Man" plays a role at an apocalyptic end time. Nowadays, this view is rightly out of favor—there is simply no evidence for the use of "Son of Man" as a title in Second Temple Judaism.[87] More importantly, the suggestion misses the crucial fact that *its use on Jesus's lips is not to exalt himself but quite the opposite.*[88] The Markan Jesus continually shuns lofty titles and the acclaim of others. Although he is quite capable of making authoritative claims about himself—to be able to forgive sins (2:10), to be sovereign over the Sabbath (2:28), and to assert that it will be loyalty to *him* that determines a person's standing at

85. Matthew and Luke do sometimes alter it; for example, Matthew (who has a particular fondness for the term, using it some thirty times) sometimes adds it where Mark does not have it (e.g., Matt 16:13; cf. Mark 8:27; Luke 9:18), and sometimes removes it altogether (e.g., Matt 16:21; cf. Mark 8:31). Given the fluidity of these traditions, even among literary documents, there is no reason to imagine that Mark included the phrase *solely* because it was in his tradition.

86. It is clearly a known expression in Aramaic and Hebrew, but it is only found in Greek texts that have been translated from those languages. On its use in Aramaic, see A. L. Lukaszewski, "Issues Concerning the Aramaic behind ὁ υἱὸς τοῦ ἀνθρώπου: A Critical Review of Scholarship," in Hurtado and Owen, *Who Is This Son of Man?*, 1–27.

87. Besides Dan 7:13, the phrase also occurs in the *Similitudes of Enoch* (1 Enoch) 48:10, 52:4; and 4 Ezra 13. Both apocalyptic texts are developments of Daniel in which the "Son of Man" becomes a more exalted figure, but there is no evidence for a widespread expectation of such a divine mediator within first-century Jewish circles. See R. Leivestad, "Exit the Apocalyptic Son of Man," *NTS* (1972): 243–67, and L. W. Hurtado, "Fashions, Fallacies and Future Prospects in New Testament Studies," *JSNT* 36 (2014): esp. 307–13.

88. So also D. R. A. Hare, *The Son of Man Tradition* (Minneapolis: Fortress, 1990), 189–90.

the *parousia* (8:38)—he chooses to present himself as nothing but a human being. The definite article lends the term a greater specificity—it is clearly *Jesus* who is in view, not any other human, or "people" in general—but the meaning of the phrase is still grounded in its ordinariness, its lack of pretension, and its façade of modesty.[89] Both Jesus's vocation and place in God's evolving eschatological drama are cloaked by an unassuming diffidence to public acclaim. For Mark, the connection with Daniel's heavenly "Son of Man" was presumably an advantage: the phrase could encapsulate Jesus's self-deprecation and yet at the same time hint at his future glory (as 8:38; 13.26; 14:62 make clear).

Given this highly literary use of the term, it would clearly be inappropriate for other characters to refer to Jesus as "Son of Man." The term is perfectly understandable to them, they know that Jesus is referring to himself, but their experience of him so far is one of wonder and admiration. Naturally enough, they seek to pin more exalted titles on him: John the Baptist, Elijah, or one of the prophets (8:28). A strikingly similar feature occurs in Philostratus's *Life of Apollonius of Tyana*. Impressed by his great powers, the people of Asbama say that the philosopher is "a son of Zeus"; he, however, claims to be only the "son of Apollonius" (*Life of Apollonius of Tyana* 6).[90]

The element of modesty and restraint implicit within Jesus's use of "Son of Man" is worth exploring in a little more depth. Such moderation (*metriotēs*, or *moderatio* in Latin) was a widely recognized virtue at the time Mark wrote. Valerius Maximus declared that it was "the most salutary part of the soul" and devoted considerable space to it.[91] It was moderation that made people curb any tendency toward arrogance, to resist the impulse to claim positions and titles too quickly (however well deserved), to refuse honors offered by others, and to curb an overzealous ambition

---

89. Hare suggests that the *historical* Jesus used it in such a way, and that the phrase functioned as a modest self-reference when alluding to the prophetic task he shared with John (*Son of Man*, 257–82). My suggestion is that the *Markan* Jesus uses it this way (I am far less sure of our ability to reconstruct the way in which the historical Jesus used it). Hurtado helpfully points out that linguistically the phrase functions to "refer" rather than to "characterize," so that it is the rest of the sentence that clarifies its meaning ("Summary and Concluding Observations," in Hurtado and Owen, *Who Is This Son of Man?*, 166–67); this is certainly true, though I would see more meaning within the reference itself than Hurtado does, particularly given its strong scriptural resonances.

90. Similarly, in *Life of Apollonius of Tyana* 4.31, Apollonius does not encourage people to pay him honors because he fears it will arouse envy (*hos mē phthonoito*). "Envy," of course, will also appear in Mark at 15:10.

91. Valerius Maximus, *Memorable Deeds and Sayings* 4.1; the quotation is from the preface; Shackleton Bailey, LCL 492.

or even righteous anger. Its use in the early imperial period, however, may have evoked rather more specific cultural associations. After the settlement of 27 BCE, Augustus was well known for his refusal to accept anything that smacked of despotic rule; he presented himself as scrupulously attached to the old republican ways and anxious to turn down anything that conferred on him exceptional powers (this is known as *recusatio imperii*).[92] In his *Res Gestae*, the *princeps* carefully prefaced his accomplishments with a list of offices and honors *not* accepted; as Kirk Freudenburg notes, the point of this elaborate performance was to categorize his government as one of restraint, and "to set respectable Roman limits around his highly contradictory person."[93] This was to be a practice followed by Augustus's successors, all of whom in various ways sought to combine supreme powers with an elaborate display of restraint and denial.[94] Refusal, in Andrew Wallace-Hadrill's words, "was a ritual performed throughout the reign of each emperor, in an astonishing variety of contexts. Not to be a king, nor to be a god incarnate was not enough. Each title was worth turning down or abstaining from: consul, *Pater Patriae*, the praenomen *Imperatoris*—all except the modest power of *tribunicia potestas* that veiled the reality. The emperor's victory was perpetual; and the fact best advertised by refusing triumphs."[95]

In a similar vein, Tiberius frequently forbade the use of language that implied his superiority (Suetonius, *Tiberius* 27–31), and Augustus on occasion preferred a homespun toga over more ostentatious robes (Suetonius, *The Divine Augustus* 5, 40, 73).[96] Of course, not all emperors showed the same degree of moderation in this regard, and a Gaius or a Nero might easily fall into despotic display, but we should be wary of understanding this pose as merely a sham or charade: the refusal of honors showed a genuine respect for the senate and citizen body, an adherence to the old republican divisions of society, and an acknowledgment that the emperor's power stemmed ultimately not only from the gods but from the people themselves.[97]

Needless to say, there are a number of differences between imperial refusals

---

92. A. Wallace-Hadrill, "*Civilis Princeps*: Between Citizen and King," *JRS* 72 (1982): 32–48; K. Freudenburg, "*Recusatio* as Political Theatre: Horace's Letter to Augustus," *JRS* 104 (2014): 105–32.

93. Freudenberg, "Recusatio," 111.

94. Wallace-Hadrill, "*Civilis Princeps*," 36.

95. Wallace-Hadrill, "*Civilis Princeps*," 37.

96. Wallace-Hadrill, "*Civilis Princeps*," 38–39. Later on, Suetonius would see Julius Caesar's adoption of the titles "Emperor" and "Father of the Fatherland" as evidence of a lack of restraint (*moderatio*), so justifying his assassination; *The Divine Julius* 76.

97. See the discussion in Wallace-Hadrill, "*Civilis Princeps*," esp. 45–48.

and what we find in Mark. In the latter, no one aside from demons is specifically offering Jesus titles, nor does he refuse them (though the question of Jesus's identity and appropriate ways to capture it are never far from events). It is not my intention to suggest that Mark has deliberately modeled his portrait of Jesus here on the emperor; the point is rather that Mark wrote in a cultural environment where moderation and restraint were praiseworthy virtues in a man of the highest standing. Furthermore, like emperors and men of note, Jesus's power and status actually have nothing to do with which titles he chooses to accept. The audience know that he is Christ and Son of God and that he has extraordinary powers, even if he prefers to present himself more moderately as the Son of Man. Crucially, too, the humility already displayed here by Jesus will come to the fore in the teaching of 8:27–10:45 (as we shall see below).

Similar motifs, I suggest, are at work in the Markan theme of "secrecy." Since William Wrede drew attention to this feature in 1901, the so-called messianic secret has attracted intense scholarly scrutiny.[98] It is used by the Markan Jesus in three main contexts: first, to silence the unclean spirits who always know exactly who he is; second, in association with healings, where Jesus (somewhat ineffectually) commands those cured not to tell others what he has done (e.g., 1:44; 5:43); and third, to stop the disciples proclaiming his identity (8:30; 9:9). As the traditional name suggests, the secrecy motif is generally thought to revolve around Jesus's *messianic identity*. Most modern interpreters argue that Mark wants to redefine the term "Christ" so that it incorporates the idea of suffering, hence Jesus's messianic status has to be concealed until his death, at which point the Roman centurion can proclaim his divine Sonship to the world (15:39). It is certainly the case that, for Mark, Jesus's messianic status is integrally linked with his death: Jesus is clearly a messiah who dies. The difficulty, however, lies in imagining that this was news to any of Mark's readers. The "traditional" interpretation only really makes sense in a (Jewish) context where people hold a triumphalist understanding of the Messiah

---

98. Wrede argued that the very first Christians identified Jesus with the Messiah only at the resurrection, but later on they came to believe that his earthly life had also been messianic. The secrecy motif in Mark is the coming together of these two (pre-Markan) strands of interpretation: Jesus's public life was indeed messianic, but the (unhistorical) secrecy motif allows this to be made public only at the resurrection (see 9:9); W. Wrede, *The Messianic Secret*, trans. J. C. G. Grieg (Cambridge: Clarke, 1971; German orig., 1901). For more recent discussion, see the collection of essays in C. M. Tuckett, ed., *The Messianic Secret* (Philadelphia: Fortress, 1983); H. Räisänen, *The Messianic Secret in Mark's Gospel* (Edinburgh: T&T Clark, 1990); Watson, *Honor*; and Neufeld, *Mockery*.

that needs to be significantly modified in order to encompass a dying Savior.[99] But we have already seen that most of Mark's audience are likely to have been familiar with the Christian story already, and that at least some are from the gentile world. This latter group presumably only became familiar with the term "messiah" at the same time that they heard of Jesus's death and resurrection, and they would have had no need for the title to be reconfigured. More significantly, perhaps, Mark's work does not suggest that the term "messiah" was in any need of clarification; if it had been, the more obvious route would have been to include a short saying from Jesus (along the lines of 12:35–40 perhaps).

Recently, a number of scholars have started to interpret Mark's "secrecy" passages in terms of the ancient categories of honor and shame. For some, the concealment goes back to Jesus himself, representing a defense strategy to avoid the envy and hostility that his great powers would inevitably have aroused among his opponents.[100] This is perfectly possible, but it does not tell us why Mark has retained the motif and why it is so dominant in his work. A plausible answer to this, in my view, has been supplied by David Watson in his monograph *Honor among Christians*. Watson situates Jesus within an ancient culture that prized public affirmation and honor, as it applied to both oneself and one's family. An important way to acquire honor, he notes, was through beneficence, the granting of goods or services to others who would then spread word of their patron's generosity.[101] Through his healings and exorcisms, Jesus confers gifts of exceptional value on people, benefactions that ordinarily would bring him fame and honor. By enjoining those healed to silence, however, Jesus not only makes no demands on them (in that they are freed from the obligation of praising him) but also attempts to avoid the honor that is due to him. Similarly, demons ascribe honor to Jesus through their grand titles; Jesus's efforts to silence them are again attempts to avoid honor and perhaps this time not to be beholden to them.[102] And the silencing of the disciples is once more an attempt to play down the immense honor in which he would be held if his true

---

99. Even this needs to be significantly modified nowadays; see the excellent treatment by M. V. Novenson, *A Grammar of Messianism: An Ancient Jewish Political Idiom and Its Users* (New York: Oxford University Press, 2017).

100. See, for example, J. J. Pilch, "Secrecy in the Gospel of Mark," *PACE* 21 (1992): 150–53, and "Secrecy in the Mediterranean World: An Anthropological Perspective," *BTB* 24 (1994): 51–57.

101. Watson himself is careful to identify Jesus as a "broker" rather than a "patron" as he mediates divine power (*Honor*, 46–47), though I doubt that Mark's Christology is quite as careful as this implies.

102. Watson, *Honor*, 56–61.

status were too openly discussed. Quite often, of course, Jesus's efforts are ignored: people *do* tell and his fame spreads far and wide (e.g., 6:14, 32–33, 55; 7:24). Jesus is clearly worthy of the utmost honor, yet, crucially, Mark makes it clear that this is not something that he seeks. How this fits not only with the character of Jesus but with the way of discipleship more generally will again become apparent in the teaching of 8:27–10:45.

Thus both the "secrecy" motif and Jesus's use of "Son of Man" language have much in common. Jesus continually exercises moderation and restraint, refusing to put himself in the limelight and to accept the honor that he is due. Of course, on one level this is a shrewd move by Mark: those who do not grasp at honor are in fact the most honorable.[103] Yet characters within the narrative, and even the narrator himself, continually refocus attention back to Jesus.[104] The recognitions by the impure spirits keep more exalted titles in mind, even as Jesus silences them and presents himself as nothing but a lowly human; and people continually divulge his "secret," even as Jesus charges them not to. Only at the end will Jesus accept the titles offered to him—"Christ, Son of the Blessed" (14:61–62) and to some extent "King" (15:2)—though now they will lead not to glory and honor, but to death.

Throughout this first major section of his work, then, Mark has presented Jesus as an elite male, as befits the Son of God.[105] As we have seen, he displays a range of virtues—compassion, self-control, restraint, moderation, and modesty. He scorns a life of luxury, speaks boldly to the religious leaders, and impresses the crowds with

103. Watson, *Honor*, 53, who notes Apollonius of Tyana's refusal loudly to broadcast his deeds (Philostratus, *Life of Apollonius of Tyana* 8.15).

104. From a literary perspective, E. S. Malbon draws attention to the tension between what the Markan narrator says of Jesus (that he is the "Christ," the "Son of God" who is able to perform godlike feats and inspire amazement in all who meet him) and what Jesus says of himself (that he is the "Son of Man" and that others should keep his identity and mighty works to themselves). She rightly observes that "a Jesus who talks like the narrator could hardly be a Jesus who 'came not to be served but to serve' (10:45), but a Jesus who affirms only what the Markan Jesus says could hardly bear the full weight of the gospel of 'Jesus Christ, the Son of God' (1:1)"; "History, Theology, Story: Re-contextualizing Mark's 'Messianic Secret' as Characterization," in Skinner and Hauge, *Character Studies*, 53.

105. On masculinity, particularly in connection with elite males, see the essays in S. D. Moore and J. C. Anderson, eds., *New Testament Masculinities* (Atlanta: SBL Press, 2003), and B. E. Wilson, *Unmanly Men: Refigurations of Masculinity in Luke-Acts* (Oxford: Oxford University Press, 2015), 39–75. There were of course competing views of "masculinity" in the ancient world (as we shall see in Chapter 6), but the virtues listed here would have been accepted by most.

his authority. He is a defender of women and a generous benefactor who provides his people with food, heath, and restored relations. The only traditional "manly" virtue that is conspicuously absent here is skill on the battlefield;[106] this would not of course be expected in a philosopher, though as Warren Carter points out, Jesus's triumph over the demonic "legion" that inhabits the man in the Gerasene graveyard may suggest that Jesus could have had glory here too, had he wanted it (5:1–20).[107] Mark's purpose in these opening chapters was presumably to present an admirable Jesus, one who could hold his head high among the great men of the Greco-Roman world. If Jesus chooses to stress a quite different set of "slave-like virtues" for those willing to enter the kingdom of God, it is not because he has a lowly disposition but because he makes a conscious choice to present himself in a different manner. An articulation of the virtues and way of life associated with God's kingdom is presented in the central section of the gospel.

Teaching on Discipleship (8:22–10:52)

Despite the epithet "teacher," Mark's Jesus has so far engaged in very little teaching.[108] The first part of the gospel includes only three relatively short blocks of instruction: the parables (4:1–34), the discussion of purity (7:1–23), and the enigmatic warning relating to the "leaven" of the Pharisees and Herod (8:11–21). Each of these passages begins in public but quickly relocates to a more private setting ("when he was alone," 4:10; "when he had entered the house," 7:17; or "in the boat," 8:13), where Jesus attempts to instruct his disciples in "the secret of the kingdom of God" (4:11).[109] As archetypal "insiders," the disciples withdraw with their master

---

106. On the close connection between manliness and war, see T.-S. B. Liew, "Re-Markable Masculinities," in Moore and Anderson, *New Testament Masculinities*, 96–97.

107. W. Carter, "Cross-Gendered Romans and Mark's Jesus: Legion Enters the Pigs (Mark 5:1–20)," *JBL* 134 (2015): 139–55.

108. Only one-fifth of Mark's Gospel is devoted to Jesus's words, suggesting, as Hägg notes, that Mark was more interested in what he did and how he appeared to those immediately around him than in what he said. Put otherwise, Jesus for Mark was an example of a way of life rather than the mouthpiece of a doctrine (*Art of Biography*, 161). Presumably this also lies behind Mark's decision to cast his work as a biography rather than as a sayings gospel.

109. P. Sellew has noted the similarities in structure exhibited by 4:1–20; 8:14–21; 7:1–23; 9:14–29; and 10:1–12 (all of which are teaching blocks); "Composition of Didactic Scenes in Mark's Gospel," *JBL* 108 (1989): 613–34. However, I would be less certain than Sellew that any of these represented pre-Markan arrangements; I think it more likely that Mark himself was responsible for the similar patterns.

to a quieter space, where they will hear his teaching and discuss its meaning.[110] So far they have learned that following him will be hard, and that although there are several routes to failure, some of those who receive the message will respond exponentially and the growth of the kingdom of God will be abundant (4:1–32). They know too that what matters is not the upholding of purity laws, but right behavior (7:1–23). And, perhaps hardest of all, they have been urged to respond to Jesus's mission with understanding (8:11–21). Now, in the central section of the biography, the Markan Jesus will turn his attention to teaching once again, this time outlining the challenging demands of discipleship.

The coherence of this middle section of Mark's work has long been recognized by scholars. It is framed by stories of the restoration of sight to blind men (indeed, the only such healings in Mark; 8:22–26; 10:46–52). The little phrase "on the way" (*en tē hodō*) echoes throughout the various sections (8:27; 9:33, 34; 10:17, 32), and underscores the idea of discipleship, which is such a prominent theme throughout these chapters.[111] And the whole section is structured around Jesus's three passion predictions, each of which is followed by resistance from his disciples and the need for further instruction (8:31; 9:31; 10:33–34). The predictions grow in specificity each time, as do the details of the disciples' misunderstandings: we are told only that Peter "rebukes" Jesus in 8:32; the discussion of the disciples over greatness is given in reported speech in 9:34; and the misunderstanding of the sons of Zebedee is given more dramatically in vivid, direct speech in 10:35–40.[112] All of this gives the impression of a tightly worked set of chapters whose contents will be pivotal to the developing biography.

Once again, the primary recipients of Jesus's teaching in these chapters are the disciples. All of Jesus's most important teaching, including crucially the three passion predictions, is given to them alone either on the journey (8:27–33; 9:30–50; 10:23–31, 32–45), down a mountain (9:9–13), or in a house (10:13–16). These are Jesus's closest followers, an inner group who have been privy to all of his instruction and who are generally comfortable asking him questions and seeking clarification. Yet the message is not only for them. Mark occasionally introduces a wider group into these chapters: crowds appear in 8:34–9:1 and 10:1–9, and a rich man runs up

---

110. On male private space where nonrelated males gather to enjoy the company of others or to discuss ideas, see Neyrey, "Jesus, Gender," 49.

111. In the LXX, the "ways of the Lord" (*hodos*) refers to following the demands of God: see Exod 32:8; Deut 5:33; Jer 7:33; see also Mark 1:1. "The Way" is frequently used in Acts as a term for believers: 9:2; 18:25; 19:9, 23; 22:4; 24:14, 22.

112. A. D. Kaminouchi, *"But It Is Not So among You": Echoes of Power in Mark 10.32–45* (London: T&T Clark, 2003), 68–70.

to Jesus in 10:17–22. If the teaching is given first and foremost to the Twelve, it is clearly intended for all who would follow Jesus.

The section starts with Jesus seizing the initiative and asking his disciples who they think he is. Acting as spokesman for the group, Peter declares Jesus to be the Christ (8:27–30). This is the first time in the gospel that human characters have understood anything of Jesus's identity, but it is not yet the full picture. Directly before this incident, Mark includes an unusual two-stage healing of a blind man at Bethsaida. In response to Jesus's first attempt at a cure, the blind man sees partially (men look like trees to his damaged eyes); it is only when Jesus tries again and the man looks intently that he sees clearly (8:22–26). Mark has juxtaposed this story with Peter's recognition scene for a good reason. While the disciples have reached an important level of understanding, it is only a first step. Peter has understood something important, but he does not yet see plainly. For that, a more somber note needs to be introduced into the narrative, and Jesus plainly tells his disciples that he will die (8:31). It is clear that Peter (and presumably the other disciples too) have not yet realized this (8:31–33). But worse is to come. Summoning a large crowd, Jesus explains that discipleship means following him, even to death. His opening words sum up the teaching of this entire middle section: "If any want to become my followers, let them deny themselves and take up their cross and follow me. For those who want to save their life will lose it, and those who lose their life for my sake, and for the sake of the gospel, will save it" (8:34–35).

From now on, the Markan Jesus outlines the theory of discipleship in a number of sections that read like a rule book for believers ("If anyone . . . , whoever . . . ," etc.).[113] As he makes his way to Jerusalem, the themes of self-sacrifice and willingness to serve become stronger, even as Jesus's predictions of his impending death become ever clearer. Followers are to give up everything, not only riches (10:17–22),[114] but homes and families too (10:23–30). "Many that are first will be last, and the last first," Jesus declares (10:31), urging his followers to reject the way in which power is exercised in their surrounding culture, and to understand that true greatness can only be found in putting oneself last and acting as a slave (*doulos*): "You know that among the Gentiles those whom they recognize as their rulers lord it over them, and their great ones are tyrants over them. But it is not so among you; but whoever wishes to become great among you must be your servant, and whoever wishes to

113. On this section, see M. D. Hooker, *Not Ashamed of the Gospel: New Testament Interpretations of the Death of Christ* (Grand Rapids: Eerdmans, 1994), 47–67; Kaminouchi, *But It Is Not So*, 9–17.

114. The word in 10:22 it *ktēma*, which denotes "anything gotten"—property, possessions, or any kind of goods.

be first among you must be slave of all. For the Son of Man came not to be served but to serve" (10:42–45).

It is often pointed out that the concept of a "servant king" has antecedents in both the Jewish and Greco-Roman traditions.[115] Although the Markan Jesus highlights the practice of gentile *leaders* in 10:42, his teaching here is not primarily concerned with kingship.[116] Rather it refers to relations among believers more generally, and in particular the kind of behavior that distinguishes followers of Christ from others. In a striking rejection of contemporary society, the Markan Jesus makes it clear that members of the Christ-following community are not to be concerned with self-aggrandizing and courting the esteem of others. Instead, true discipleship is characterized by service to others for the good of the community. As David Watson observes, believers are called on to reject the honor codes so prevalent in the world around them and to embrace a new understanding of honor, one based on service, suffering, and debasement.[117]

This countercultural teaching is not simply a blueprint for others but forms the basis for how Jesus will conduct his own life. We have already noted his consistent rejection of grand titles and acclaim, even if other characters in the narrative continually put him at the center. As the gospel progresses, Jesus will give up everything, put himself last, and take up his cross. It is clearly the crucifixion, emblematic as it was of shame and degradation, that turns the ancient honor system on its head. For Mark, Christian discipleship involves seeing honor and virtue in what the contemporary world shunned as ignoble and contemptuous.[118] Like the *Life of Aesop*,

115. See M. Weinfeld, "The King as the Servant of the People," *JJS* 33 (1982): 189–94; D. Seeley, "Rulership and Service in Mark 10:41–5," *NovT* 35 (1993): 234–50; and O. Wischmeyer, "Herrschen als Dienen—Mk 10,41–45," *ZNW* 90 (1999): 28–44. See Deut 17:23; 1 Kgs 12:7; Plato, *Republic* 5.463B; 7.540B; *Laws* 6.762E; Xenophon, *Memorabilia* 3.2.3; Aelian, *Various Histories* 2.20; Seneca, *On Clemency* 8.1; *Letter of Aristeas* 101, 188–265; Philo, *Special Laws* 4.165–66; Josephus, *Jewish War* 4.616 (on Vespasian); and Dio Chrysostom, *On Kingship* 3.53. On the tension, especially in Greek thought, between the pretensions of kingship and the need to be accessible and attentive to one's subjects, see Wallace-Hadrill, "*Civilis Princeps*," 32–35.

116. Wischmeyer, "Herrschen." Kingship, insofar as it relates to *Jesus*, will of course appear later in the gospel, and there the relation between monarchy and service will be relevant.

117. Watson, *Honor*, 80, citing Plato, who declared that to be a ruler rather than a servant was proper to a man (*Gorgias* 492b), and Seneca, who argued that servitude crushes the spirit (*On Anger* 2.21.3).

118. Mark does not seem to be entirely novel in this regard; the apostle Paul expresses himself in a similar manner in 1 Cor 9:19–23, where he talks of making himself a slave to all; see D. B. Martin, *Slavery as Salvation*, 86–116.

whose protagonist is an ugly yet wily slave, Mark's *bios* undermines traditional ideas of who deserves honor and urges its audience to share in a radically different view of the world.[119]

Linked to this renunciation of worldly honor is a disdain for wealth and luxury. This has already been apparent from Jesus's itinerant lifestyle and dependence on the generosity of others, but it is spelled out in Jesus's interaction with the rich man in 10:17-22 and the discussion that follows it in 10:23-31. Although such teaching ran counter to general cultural expectations, it was fairly common in the teaching of philosophers. Socrates, for example, is said to have disdained wealth and luxury (Plato, *Apology* 23C, 30A–B, 31C, 36D), a feature Lucian is quick to assign to Demonax (*Demonax* 4, 5, 8, 63). Philostratus credits Apollonius with an indifference to money (*Life of Apollonius of Tyana* 1.13, 21; 2.25; 4.45), and Diogenes Laertius notes a similar attitude among a number of his philosophers.[120] Philo, too, claims that Moses lived in frugal contentment and had no time for luxury.[121] Those who seek the kingdom of God and who would follow Jesus are similarly called on to relinquish their confidence in worldly possessions, and to put their trust in the way of Jesus alone.

As a counterpart to Jesus's increasing emphasis on slave-like behavior, Mark includes a scene in which Jesus's heavenly glory is displayed before a small group of disciples (9:2–8). The mountaintop revelation exhibits strong Jewish motifs, playing in particular with the Sinai story of Exod 24 and Elijah's "still small voice" in 1 Kgs 19. However, as Candida Moss points out, the passage also has similarities with the commonplace "divine epiphany" scene in Greek myth, where the central character is similarly transfigured (usually involving some kind of illumination), inspiring fear and worship among onlookers.[122] The heavenly voice once again declares Jesus to be his "beloved Son," this time with the command to "Listen to him" (*akouete autou*,

---

119. See Watson, *Honor*, 130–36; on the *Life of Aesop* more generally, see above, pp. 72–73.

120. Diogenes Laertius notes that Plato did not charge fees, while Speusippus did (*Lives* 4.1.2); that Xenocrates refused to accept gifts of money (4.2); and that, despite being very wealthy, Anesilaus cared little for money (4.6.38).

121. *Life of Moses* 1.29. Josephus, however, tends to emphasize the wealth of Moses, perhaps reacting against charges that Jews were a nation of beggars; Feldman, *Studies*, 547.

122. C. Moss, "The Transfiguration: An Exercise in Markan Accommodation," *BibInt* 12 (2004): 69–89. For a thorough discussion of the culturally determined character of epiphanies, see G. Petridou, *Divine Epiphany in Greek Literature and Culture* (Oxford: Oxford University Press, 2015). Interestingly, Petridou notes that witnessing epiphanies often raises the status of the recipients and identifies them as favored by the gods, despite the terror that often accompanies them (334). Is this perhaps an aspect of the disciples' "characterization" that has been insufficiently attended to?

9:7). Despite Jesus's teaching on self-denial, the scene provides a dramatic reminder of his identity—the one who will take up his cross and make himself a slave of all is indeed the Spirit-filled, divine Son of God.[123]

Jerusalem (11:1–13:44)

With ch. 11, Jesus arrives in Jerusalem. He enters in royal manner, sending two of his disciples ahead to conscript a colt, and rides into the city to the acclamation of the crowds (11:1–10). The scene underscores Jesus's great popularity and the hopes that he inspires in the Passover pilgrims who recognize him as "one who comes in the name of the Lord" (11:9). It also sets up the theme of jealousy (*phthonos*), which will later play a pivotal role in the trial scenes (see especially 15:10). We shall see later on that Mark casts Jesus in the common trope of the philosopher put to death because he aroused the rulers' envy. Here the festival crowd show their enthusiastic support for Jesus, a support that will continue until his arrest (11:17; 12:12; 14:2).

The following day, Jesus returns to Jerusalem and causes a disturbance in the temple (11:15–19). The meaning of this scene is clarified by the story of the fig tree that frames it: like the fig tree that has not borne fruit, the temple will be destroyed (11:12–14, 20–25). With this anecdote, Mark introduces a new set of opponents— the "chief priests and scribes" (11:18). This will be the group that eventually engineers Jesus's arrest, though initially their plans are thwarted because of their fear of the crowd (11:18).

As in Galilee, Jesus again engages his opponents in verbal conflict, and once

---

123. Scholars continue to discuss whether Mark thinks that Jesus was "divine." Part of the problem is that we tend to understand this in monotheistic terms, with clear-cut divisions as to who was and who was not a "god." Mark seems to me far less clear on the matter, and presumably not nearly as bothered by it as modern scholars. His Jesus is certainly touched by divinity in some ways, though the God of Israel is clearly a separate (and remarkably transcendent) character in the narrative. See the useful study by M. E. Boring, "Markan Christology: God-language for Jesus?," *NTS* 45 (1999): 451–71. On the now deeply unfashionable *theios anēr* label, he notes, "the issue is whether the Hellenistic world was familiar with a figure filled with supernatural power manifest in divine wisdom and/or miraculous deeds, a figure who was more than merely human but less than a fully fledged god. This general religious type does seem to have been common enough" (458). This seems to me to be an eminently sensible judgment, and one that applies to the subjects of several biographies (within a Jewish context, we might think of Philo's Moses, who is specifically said to be divine—*Life of Moses* 1.6, 27; 2.51, 291). On God in Mark, see J. R. Donahue, "A Neglected Factor in the Theology of Mark," *JBL* 101 (1982): 563–94.

again he easily beats them in an impressive display of ready wit and oral dexterity. In 11:27 it is his rivals—"chief priests, scribes, and elders"—who open hostilities by questioning his authority. Jesus gets the better of them, reducing them to admitting that they did not know from where John the Baptist derived his authority. Jesus openly tells a parable against them, foretelling their own destruction, but is saved from arrest by their fear of the crowds (12:12). Once again, they try to trap him, sending some Pharisees and Herodians to ask him about taxes, but again Jesus gets the better of them (12:13–17). Next, Sadducees ask him about the resurrection, and are told that they know nothing about either the Scriptures or the power of God (12:18–27). Finally, a wise scribe asks him which is the greatest commandment and is commended for his response. After that, we are told, no one dared to ask anything more (12:34). As Benny Liew observes, Jesus and the authorities swap roles over the course of these anecdotes: although they start on the offensive, the shamed authorities are quickly reduced to silence, and we will not hear of them again until they plot Jesus's death in 14:1. Jesus, however, grows in honor so that when he issues his own challenge in 12:35–37, asking how the scribes can say that the Christ is the son of David, no one rises to the bait and his question is left unanswered.[124]

The themes of self-denial that characterized the central section of the gospel are briefly reprised in Jerusalem. Jesus warns his disciples to beware the honor-seeking scribes, who like the best seats in the synagogues and places of honor at feasts (12:38–40), and commends instead a poor widow for her extravagant giving to the temple (12:41–44). But now Jesus's teaching takes a new turn. With ch. 13, he begins to speak of future things, dissolving the time between his own day and that of Mark's audience.[125] If they were not aware of the application of the *bios* to their own situation before, it is made abundantly clear now. This chapter foregrounds a theme that has been implicit all along: that Jesus's followers must be prepared to imitate their master, even if it means losing their lives.

Imitation of Jesus

As we noted in Chapter 2, there was always a certain tension in an ancient biography between outlining the life of a unique, historically determined individual and yet at the same time offering that life as a paradigm for others to follow. For Mark, Jesus

---

124. Liew, "Re-Mark-able," 104–7. On Mark's view of Davidic messiahship, see above, pp. 127–28.

125. On the similarity between Mark 13 and the "farewell dialogue" in Jewish and Greco-Roman literature, see Robbins, *Jesus the Teacher*, 173–79.

is the unique Son, chosen by the Deity and filled with his Spirit, and yet, as Tomas Hägg observes, he "becomes an example through his way of life."[126] Although the verb "to imitate" (*mimeomai*) does not appear in Mark's work, the call to "follow me" (*akolouthein*) is frequent (1:17; 8:34; 10:21 [10:28, 52]).[127] Perhaps its resonance with the Jewish idea of "walking with (or "in the ways of") God" commended this expression to Mark.[128] Would-be disciples are called to "follow" Jesus, to learn from his example, and to model their lives on his.

The sense of following Jesus is woven into the very structure of the *bios*. We have already noted Mark's rather abrupt opening at the banks of the Jordan, where the Baptist declares that he has baptized (*ebaptisa*) with water while Jesus will baptize (*baptisei*) with the Holy Spirit (1:8). Yet we do not actually see Jesus baptizing, and baptism itself plays no further role in the work. This all looks odd until we understand that the reference to future baptism here relates not to the baptism of characters in the story, but of Mark's Christian believers who have themselves been baptized in the name of Jesus. Everything we know about baptism in the early church suggests that it involved water and the gift of the

126. Hägg, *Art of Biography*, 161. See also the discussions in R. A. Burridge, *Imitating Jesus: An Inclusive Approach to New Testament Ethics* (Grand Rapids: Eerdmans, 2007), 159–85; M. A. Tolbert, *Sowing the Gospel: Mark's World in Literary-Historical Perspective* (Minneapolis: Fortress, 1989), 133–35; D. Capes, "Imitatio Christi and the Gospel Genre," *BTBR* 13 (2003): 3; Hurtado, "Following Jesus"; F. J. Matera, *New Testament Ethics: The Legacies of Jesus and Paul* (Louisville: Westminster John Knox, 1996), esp. 31–34; and R. Hays, *The Moral Vision of the New Testament: Community, Cross, New Creation* (London: T&T Clark, 1996), 73–92. The idea of imitating Christ is found in many other NT texts: e.g., 1 Thess 1:6; 1 Cor 11:1; 2 Cor 10:1; Phil 2:5; Eph 4:32; 5:1–2; and 1 Pet 2:21–3; for examples of imitation of Christ in the patristic era, see Capes, "Imitatio Christi," 16–19, and C. R. Moss, *The Other Christs: Imitating Jesus in Ancient Christian Ideologies of Martyrdom* (New York: Oxford University Press, 2010).

127. For a useful discussion of *mimēsis* (albeit in relation to Paul), see E. A. Castelli, *Imitating Paul: A Discourse of Power* (Louisville: Westminster John Knox, 1991), esp. 59–87. Contrary to H. D. Betz, I see no reason to distinguish between "following" (which he sees as Palestinian-Jewish in origin) and "imitation" (which he sees as a Hellenistic concept); *Nachfolge und Nachahmung Jesu Christi im Neuen Testament* (Tübingen: Mohr Siebeck, 1967), 3. Mark may use scriptural language, but the call is clearly to *mimēsis*. See also Moss, *The Other Christs*, 21–23, 28, who similarly sees imitation and discipleship as virtually indistinguishable.

128. See, for example, Gen 5:22 (Enoch); 6:9 (Noah); 24:40 (Abraham); and the command in Deut 5:33. For a useful discussion, see K. Grobel, "He That Cometh After Me," *JBL* 60 (1941): 397–401.

Spirit (1 Cor 16:11; Acts 2:38). Jesus's baptism scene, then, which as we have seen provides only the setting for the declaration of his divine paternity, would remind Mark's believing audience of their own baptism, the place where their own Christian journey began.[129] Interestingly, a similar feature characterizes Christian art of a slightly later period where it is often difficult to tell whether the scene represents the baptism of Jesus or that of a believer.[130] Quite possibly both are deliberately intended: for early Christian artists, as for Mark, the baptism of believers is an imitation of that of Jesus.

At the other end of the gospel, Mark's ending is also abrupt. The narrative breaks off just as the women have been told by the heavenly messenger that Jesus has been raised and are told to take the good news to Peter and the disciples (16:6). The frightened women, however, are too awestruck to do anything but run away without delivering their message (16:8). Once again, this strange scene makes most sense when seen as a direct address to Mark's listeners.[131] Like the women, they know the story of the empty tomb, but they are afraid and uncertain how to respond. The challenge Mark issues to them is to continue to believe and to follow, whatever the personal cost, and to see that their own lives are now part of the continuation of the story.[132] Mark's truncated story line, then, maps perfectly onto the Christian life of believers. It begins where the story begins for all of them—with baptism—and it ends at the point where many in Mark's church found themselves—knowing the story, but too paralyzed by fear, uncertainty, and the threat of persecution openly to proclaim the word. The gospel was presumably written to strengthen these people, to provide the life of Jesus as a model for a truly Christian life, and to equip them for continuing mission in the world.

One further structural pattern encourages links between the life of Jesus and believers, again involving John the Baptist. John plays only a cameo role in Mark, but he functions as the decisive first step in a threefold pattern. John comes first, preaches, and is handed over (1:7, 14); later on, we are told of his execution and

---

129. So also Collins, *Mark*, 147.

130. See R. M. Jensen, *Living Water: Images, Symbols, and Settings of Early Christian Baptism* (Leiden: Brill, 2011), 26–29.

131. Hays notes that Mark likes to end units with questions or exhortations that address the audience directly, e.g., 8:21; 13:37; similarly here, the lack of closure calls the listener to active response (*Moral Vision*, 90).

132. Hurtado suggests that the absence of resurrection appearances reinforces Mark's concern to focus on Jesus as the sole model for discipleship. Elsewhere in the NT, resurrection appearances serve to certify witnesses as authoritative figures (for example, 1 Cor 9:1; 15:3–11 or Matt 28:16–20), but in Mark the unique significance of Jesus is preserved until the end; "Following Jesus," 26–27.

burial (6:17–20).[133] Next comes Jesus, who also preaches (1:14) and is handed over (9:31; 10:33; 14:10); he, too, is executed and buried (15:21–47). Finally, Jesus's disciples and followers will themselves preach (3:14; 13:10) and be handed over to councils, beaten in synagogues, and bear testimony before governors and kings (13:9–13).[134] The verbs *kēryssō* and *paradidōmi* link each of the participants in this sequence. So too does the theme of slave-like behavior: the Baptist demeans himself, expressing his utter unworthiness in comparison to the "mightier one" (1:7); Jesus too, as the Son of Man, is rejected and killed (8:31); and followers are called on to become slaves of all (10:44).[135] The fate of disciples, of course, lies beyond narrative time, but Jesus's words in ch. 13 connect the hearers' present circumstances to the life—and death—of Jesus.

What, then, are followers of Jesus to emulate? As we have seen, the first part of the gospel presents a Jesus who exhibits a number of virtuous qualities. Followers clearly did not have Jesus's great powers, but they could emulate his compassion for the sick and demon-possessed. They might renounce a life of wealth and luxury, and like their master adopt a modest demeanor. And while they might not have his ability in debate, his example might give them courage as they faced opponents. With the central section, however, Jesus's teaching becomes much harder: followers are called on to deny themselves, even to take up their cross (8:34). As the story proceeds, Jesus will do just that: despite his Spirit-possession and extraordinary powers, he will allow himself to be arrested, becoming progressively passive as the narrative unfolds through his trials and lonely death. The theory of discipleship articulated in 8:27–10:45 becomes reality in a life lived to its very end according to the arduous and all-encompassing demands of the gospel.

But to what extent is Mark's audience to take this literally? We have already seen that biographies of great men could hardly expect readers to follow their heroes in all respects: the idea was not that admirers attempted to engage in the same battles

---

133. John was presumably still well known in Mark's day as a significant messianic figure in his own right (as he was still a figure to be reckoned with by Josephus at the end of the century); this perhaps necessitated the *synkrisis* of 1:7–8 and Mark's insistence that Jesus is utterly superior to his predecessor—John might baptize with water, but Jesus will baptize with the Holy Spirit.

134. See J. B. Hood, "Evangelicals and the Imitation of the Cross: Peter Bold on Mark 13 as a Test Case," *EQ* 81 (2009): 116–25: "The cross is Jesus's destiny; for Mark, it is also the destiny, the pattern, and the expectation for all who would follow him" (119).

135. On John the Baptist as a *slave* messenger here, see R. F. Hock, "Social Experience and the Beginning of the Gospel of Mark," in *Reimagining Christian Origins: A Colloquium Honoring Burton L. Mack*, ed. E. A. Castelli and H. Taussig (Valley Forge, PA: Trinity Press International, 1996), 311–26.

or political activities, but rather that the audience distilled the *qualities exhibited by their heroes in these situations* and emulated them.[136] As Teresa Morgan observes, Plutarch was not inviting readers to emulate his subjects by marching on Rome or founding a city, but to derive timeless virtues from his accounts; readers needed adaptable ideals rather than specific programs for action.[137] In a similar way, we might understand Mark's talk of taking up one's cross in a metaphorical manner, as clearly in Luke, who alters the saying so that it refers to taking up one's cross *daily* (*kath hēmeran*; 9:23). The implication would then be (as presumably it is for Luke) that listeners' lives are full of smaller instances of self-denial, that their posture should be one of continually eschewing worldly wealth and honor, putting others first, abandoning family and anything that stands in the way of following Jesus. Mark has certainly been understood in this way, by biblical scholars and ethicists alike.[138]

Two features, however, suggest that Mark intends his audience to take Jesus's instructions literally. First, the following material in 8:35–37 clearly refers to physical life and death, suggesting that the same is in view here. Second are the references to persecution that haunt several of the episodes contained within the gospel.[139] The interpretation of the parable of the sower lists persecution as one reason for the failure of the seed (4:17). Later on, Jesus promises Peter and the others that they will receive back one hundredfold all that they have given up, along with *persecutions* (10:30). And James and John are told that they will drink from Jesus's "cup" (10:39), a reference most take to the brothers' own martyrdoms. With ch. 13 the references become stronger, now specifically relating to a time beyond the narrative: wars, earthquakes, and famines will occur (13:7–8), and believers will find themselves on trial (13:9–10). Although the Markan Jesus promises that the Holy Spirit will guide them, he warns too that families will be torn apart and that they will be hated by all for their faith (13:11–31a). Whoever endures to the end, though, will be saved

136. See above, pp. 48–49.

137. T. Morgan, "Not the Whole Story? Moralizing Biography and *Imitatio Christi*," in *Fame and Infamy: Essays for Christopher Pelling on Characterization in Greek and Roman Biography*, ed. R. Ash, J. Mossman, and F. B. Titchener (Oxford: Oxford University Press, 2015), 353–66.

138. R. H. Gundry, for example, is quite clear that taking up one's cross does not mean following Jesus to crucifixion but rather "means no more than exposing oneself to shame and ridicule by following him wherever he goes"; *Mark: A Commentary on His Apology for the Cross* (Grand Rapids: Eerdmans, 1993), 435. See also J. Jeremias, *New Testament Theology* (London: SCM, 1971), 1:242.

139. On persecution, see above, p. 9. For a literal interpretation here, see—among others—Collins, *Mark*, 408; Hays, *Moral Vision*, 80; and Hurtado, "Following Jesus," 12.

(13:13b). We shall see in Chapter 6 that much of Mark's passion narrative speaks to these circumstances, reassuring listeners that everything they have suffered was not only foreseen by Jesus but endured by him too. Mark's work presumably needs to be read in much the same way as accounts of the death of Socrates, Cato, or Roman *exitus* literature more generally. On one level they contain powerful stories of the ultimate sacrifice, accounts of virtue and honor that might appeal to a broad range of readers and inspire lofty virtues of steadfastness, courage, and endurance in everyday life. But for those unfortunate enough to find themselves facing persecution, they provided blueprints of noble deaths that readers might emulate, quite literally, in their own sufferings.

In my view, the Markan Jesus's direction to take up one's cross is not simply metaphorical; it seems likely that our author knew of some who had already died for their faith and envisaged the very real likelihood that others may be required to follow the same path. The work makes it clear that disciples must live as he lived and be prepared to die as he died. As Morna Hooker notes, "They must be willing to share his pain, his shame, his weakness, his death."[140] Thus Mark presents not only Jesus's way of life but also his death as a pattern for true discipleship. We shall return to the topic of Jesus's death in Chapter 6, but I would like to finish this chapter with a consideration of something that, at first sight, appears to be an odd omission in a first-century biography.

Jesus's Appearance

One curious feature of Mark's biography is that he never provides a physical description of his subject.[141] Even at the transfiguration scene, where Jesus's displays his heavenly glory, we are told only that he was "transfigured" (*metamorphoō*) before his inner group of disciples: his *clothes* become brilliantly white, but nothing specific is said of his face or body (9:2–3).[142] Such reticence was not entirely

140. Hooker, *Not Ashamed*, 51; so also Moss, *The Other Christs*, 30–31, and P. Middleton, "Suffering and the Creation of Christian Identity in the Gospel of Mark," in *T&T Clark Handbook to Social Identity in the New Testament*, ed. J. B. Tucker and C. A. Baker (London: Bloomsbury, 2014), 173–89.

141. Noted by J. Fitzgerald, "The Ancient Lives of Aristotle and the Modern Debate about the Genre of the Gospels," *Restoration Quarterly* (1994): 211; also Hägg, *Art of Biography*, 185.

142. So also Luke 9:29; Matthew adds that his face shone like the sun (Matt 17:2), though that hardly counts as a physical description. Interestingly, the only description of Jesus's appearance in the NT is of the risen Christ in Revelation; no author says anything about his physical appearance—a feature that was to lead to much speculation later

unknown in ancient *bioi*: Xenophon, for example, does not describe his patron Agesilaus, though his personal association with the man would have made it very easy for him to do so;[143] Diogenes Laertius does not generally offer descriptions of his philosophers; and Josephus gives no account of his (undoubtedly handsome) appearance in his autobiographical *Life*. This, however, was unusual: most biographers included some comment on the subject's appearance, often toward the beginning of the work. Cornelius Nepos (who by no means always supplied a description) tells us that Alcibiades was the "most handsome of men" (7.1), that Iphicrates was a man "large of mind and body" (11.3), and that Eumenes was "tall and handsome" (18.11).

Such descriptions were not offered merely to satisfy idle curiosity, or even to provide a mental image to accompany the subject's words and deeds. There was a long-held association in Greek thought between physical appearance and character, hence the expression *kalos kagathos*—"the beautiful and the good." Thus there is nothing strange to find Plato declaring that the ideal ruler should be very good looking (*Republic* 7.535A). Conversely, ugliness was associated with low social status and dubious morals—in the *Life of Aesop*, the subject's ugliness marks him out from the opening paragraph as an antihero. In fact, "physiognomics"—"the systematic diagnosis of a man's character from his bodily features"[144]—attained quasi-scientific status from Aristotle onward, and was a favorite topic in the writings of both philosophers (particularly in the Stoic and Epicurean traditions) and medics (who associated outward appearance with theories of the humors). Certain facial or bodily features were associated with specific characteristics: short necks, for example, were indicative of craftiness, while large, strong bodies were a sign of courage and soft hair suggested effeminacy.[145] Eyes were often thought to be a window into the soul, whether bright, keen, blazing, or godlike.[146] In general, though, physical balance and harmony were the best indicators of a worthy man.

---

on. For a fascinating discussion, see J. E. Taylor, *What Did Jesus Look Like?* (London: Bloomsbury, 2018).

143. Agesilaus is described by Cornelius Nepos in less than flattering terms; *Agesilaus* 17.8: short of stature, lame, unattractive, and liable to inspire contempt among those who met him for the first time. Even those who knew him, Nepos suggests, found it hard to admire him.

144. A. M. Armstrong, "The Methods of the Greek Physiognomists," *G&R* 5 (1958): 52. See also E. C. Evans, "Physiognomics in the Ancient World," *TAPA* 59 (1969): 1–101.

145. See Evans, "Physiognomics," who stresses that these connections were not rigid but might change over time or according to an author's particular philosophical outlook (see, for example, the discussion of Seneca, 33).

146. Eyes were a favorite of Homeric description; see, for example, Agmemnon's Zeus-like eyes (*Iliad* 2.478–79) or Odysseus's blazing eyes (*Odyssey* 6.131–32).

Given their interest in character (*ēthos*), it is no surprise to find biographers describing their subjects' physical appearance, and often drawing on the standard physiognomic theories of their day. Some are brief, little more than a passing comment (as with the examples from Cornelius Nepos noted above). Often, though, biographers give what Elizabeth Evans refers to as a more "photographic" or "iconistic" description.[147] Tacitus and Plutarch offer portraits of their subjects, but Suetonius's detailed descriptions of his emperors are justly the most celebrated.[148] Of the divine Augustus he has this to say:

> He was unusually handsome and exceedingly graceful at all periods of his life, though he cared nothing for personal adornment.... His expression, whether in conversation or when he was silent, was so calm and mild, that one of the leading men of the Gallic provinces admitted to his countrymen that it had softened his heart.... He had clear, bright eyes, in which he liked to have it thought that there was a kind of divine power, and it greatly pleased him, whenever he looked keenly at anyone, if he let his face fall as if before the radiance of the sun; but in his old age he could not see very well with his left eye. His teeth were wide apart, small, and ill-kept; his hair was slightly curly and inclining to golden; his eyebrows met. His ears were of moderate size, and his nose projected a little at the top and then bent slightly inward. His complexion was between dark and fair. He was short of stature (although Julius Marathus, his freedman and keeper of his records, says that he was five feet and nine inches in height), but this was concealed by the fine proportion and symmetry of his figure, and was noticeable only by comparison with some taller person standing beside him.[149]

With the exception of his relatively short stature (which was perhaps well known), the rest of Augustus's description points toward the highest possible character—even the monobrow was considered a sign of kingly nobility, often associated with Heracles.[150] Conversely, Suetonius's portrait of Caligula, with his "nat-

---

147. Evans, "Physiognomics," 6.

148. For the use of physiognomics in the work of historians and biographers, see specifically Evans, "Physiognomics," 46–58; she lists some of Plutarch's descriptions, 57n131. Tacitus describes his father-in-law right at the end of the biography (*Agricola* 44).

149. Suetonius, *The Divine Augustus* 79; Rolfe, LCL 31.

150. Paul is also said to be small in the *Acts of Paul and Thecla* 3; smallness is seen positively by Archilochus and also has its advantages for the author of Pseudo-Aristotle, *Physiognomonica* 811a36–38; for discussion, see A. J. Malherbe, "A Physical Description of Paul," *HTR* 97 (1986): 170–75. On eyebrows that meet in the center, see Philostratus, *On Heroes* 33.39, and

urally forbidding and ugly face," his extreme paleness, thick neck and legs, "broad and grim" forehead, and thin hair points in no uncertain terms to the emperor's madness and depravity.[151]

Compared with most biographies, then, Mark's reluctance to describe Jesus is noteworthy. That this reticence has nothing to do with his Jewish background is clear from the fact that the Jewish Scriptures themselves frequently describe protagonists. Saul, for example, is the tallest and most handsome man in Israel (1 Sam 9:2); David is handsome and ruddy with beautiful eyes (1 Sam 16:12); and Eli is blind, old, and heavy (1 Sam 4:15–18). It appears almost mandatory for a biblical hero or heroine to be attractive, an attribute shared by Sarah (Gen 12:11–15), Joseph (Gen 39:6), Esther (Esth 2:7), Moses (Exod 2:2), and others. Even when God instructs Samuel to ignore appearances in the selection of Saul's successor (1 Sam 16:7), he still manages to choose a handsome man. At a slightly later period, both Josephus and Philo know the cultural resonances of physical beauty in a leader and show no reluctance to describe the appearance of their subjects. Philo refers to Moses's exceptional physical development and beauty;[152] similarly Josephus notes his extraordinary size as a baby and his "divine beauty," which amazed all who saw him (*Jewish Antiquities* 2.224, 231–32; and 3.83).[153] Clearly, then, Jewish writers shared the widespread view that physical beauty was a sign of both virtue and divine favor. At the very least, we might have expected Mark to mention in passing that Jesus was beautiful (*kalos*).

Perhaps Mark's lack of a physical description of Jesus is simply due to what Tomas Hägg calls his "ascetic narrative style," a style in which any kind of specific personality trait or description is relatively rare.[154] Nevertheless, one *effect* of having no

Clement of Alexandria, *Protreptricus* 2.30 (relating to Heracles). *Literary* portraiture was not unconnected to the great interest in *visual* portraiture in the Roman period: a distinguished Roman frequently decorated his home with statues and images of his distinguished ancestors, and cities were expected to honor their great men with statues; see M. J. Edwards, "A Portrait of Plotinus," *ClQ* 43 (1993): esp. 481–82.

151. Suetonius, *Gaius Caligula* 50; for a similar description, see Seneca, *On the Firmness of the Wise Person* 18.1 (cited by Evans, "Physiognomics," 29).

152. There seems to have been a tradition of Moses's beauty; see Feldman, *Philo's*, 56–57.

153. As Feldman suggests, Josephus may have stressed Moses's beauty in an effort to refute the charge that Moses had leprosy; *Josephus' Interpretation*, 384–86.

154. The phrase is from Hägg, *Art of Biography*, 185. Taylor suggests that the gospel writers say nothing about Jesus's appearance because he was simply plain, ordinary, and unkempt; *What Did Jesus Look Like?* This may well have been true on a historical level, but Mark could easily have slipped in a few complimentary adjectives had he wanted to (beauty, then as now, was in the eye of the beholder).

clear and distinctive portrait of Jesus is to heighten his paradigmatic character. Put differently, the fewer specific personal idiosyncrasies Jesus displays, the more easily he becomes a figure to imitate. It is worth reflecting on a number of other, related omissions in the Markan portrait: Jesus's lack of age, social status, and even gender.

On first reading, it is easy to miss the fact that Mark's Jesus is ageless. We are used to Luke's note that Jesus was "about thirty years of age" when he began his ministry (Luke 3:23), not to mention centuries of Christian art and decades of films that reinforce this image. But Mark does not tell us when he was born, how old he was at the start of his ministry, or his age at death.[155] The *impression* is of a man in the prime of life—young enough to cope with a demanding itinerary, yet mature enough to speak with wisdom.[156] Mark's lack of any reference to time or date (other than locating Jesus's execution during the governorship of Pilate) lends the figure of Jesus a timeless air; he might be anything from late teens to early sixties. Similarly, Jesus's social status is curiously indeterminate: although a carpenter and a friend of fishermen and tax collectors, he speaks to religious authorities as equals and dies as a would-be king (15:26). And although we have seen that Jesus displays a range of manly virtues, there is something rather sexless about him: we never hear of a wife or have the slightest indication that Jesus behaves as a virile male.[157] Whether or not all of this is deliberate, the effect of this lack of specificity is to enhance the mimetic aspects of Jesus's character. Mark's Jesus can easily be appropriated by a variety of believers, irrespective of age, gender, or social standing.

It is also possible that the "blandness" that we have detected here may be an inevitable feature of founding figures in general. Mark Toher notes that, unlike Sulla, Julius Caesar, and later emperors, there is a surprising lack of solid characterization of Augustus in the literary sources. While Suetonius and others provide a good sense of the carefully constructed persona of a "conservative

155. In his *Life of Plotinus*, Porphyry similarly says little of his master's time and place of birth; what details are given appear in chapter 3, following the description of his death. As Edwards notes, however, the lack of interest in such "bodily" details is congruent with his Platonic philosophy—an outlook that the author of Mark would not have shared; "Portrait," 480.

156. Luke's note may go back to the historical memories of eyewitnesses who put him at around this age; alternatively, it may simply be a supposition based on Mark.

157. The display of some manly virtues would not be a bar to women's imitation—manliness, while rare in women, was applauded. See R. Darling Young, "The 'Woman with the Soul of Abraham': Traditions about the Mother of the Maccabean Martyrs," in *"Women Like This": New Perspectives on Jewish Women in the Graeco-Roman World*, ed. A.-J. Levine (Atlanta: Scholars, 1991), 67–81.

Roman of simple tastes," little of his real personality appears.[158] Perhaps it is in the nature of founding figures that attention tends to be drawn to their new ideas and teaching, to what distinguishes them from those who went before, rather than their more specific character traits. And the more those founding figures serve as a model for others, the less idiosyncratic they will be. If Mark did know what Jesus looked like, he clearly did not think that it was of any relevance to his audience.

By extending the "gospel" to include Jesus's life and ministry, Mark perhaps hoped to encourage his audience to recommit their lives not to a set of theological ideas but specifically to the *person* of Jesus. The biographical format allows Mark's hearers to experience Jesus as a "real" person: they are able to see his actions, hear his teaching, and enter into a renewed relationship with the founder of their faith. As they experienced Mark's text, the audience would become clearer in their sense of what it meant to be Christ followers, in their shared beliefs and values, the behaviors that categorized their group, and the way of life they were called upon to emulate. They would see that true commitment to Jesus Christ might well require a complete break with their past lives and associations, and that they would be required to join a new "family" of believers under the Fatherhood of God. Most importantly, though, commitment to Christ meant modeling their lives on that of Jesus, adopting his values and behavior, and being prepared to follow him, even to death.

For Mark, then, Jesus is not only the content of Christian proclamation but also the model of Christian discipleship. But where does that leave other characters in Mark's *bios*? What role do the disciples play? And what of opponents or minor characters? We shall consider them in the next chapter.

158. M. Toher, "Characterizing Augustus," in *Fame and Infamy: Essays for Christopher Pelling on Characterization in Greek and Roman Biography*, ed. R. Ash, J. Mossman, and F. B. Titchener (Oxford: Oxford University Press, 2015), 226–53. Toher also cites George Washington as another "colourless founding father."

CHAPTER 5

Other Characters

> The spotlight effect—the total concentration on one person that biography exacts—throws all the peripheral characters into shadow. These secondary characters may be more significant in historical terms, but they can only be partially accounted for in so far as they impinge on the subject's life. The result is distortion.
>
> —Victoria Glendinning[1]

The previous chapter explored the way in which Mark's *bios* shines its light with hardly a waver upon the person and character of Jesus. He dominates virtually every episode, he is the subject of nearly every verb, and his distinctive character and way of life are held up to the audience as a model to emulate. But what does this total concentration on Jesus do to peripheral characters? Are they left with any meaningful role and function within the work? And what, specifically, are we to make of the disciples? If Jesus himself is the paradigm for Christian followers, what function is left for them?

The popularity of narrative criticism has led to a surge of interest in "characterization" in the gospels, though as we shall see in this chapter a first-century audience may not have reacted to Markan characters in quite the same way that modern readers do. I shall start the analysis with "walk-on" parts, progressing to what appear to be more substantial characters (King Herod, the high priest, and Pilate), before turning to the Twelve and so-called minor characters (Blind Bartimaeus, the anointing woman, Joseph of Arimathea, and others). Along the way, I shall reflect on how supporting characters are depicted in other biographies, introduce the rhetorical technique of *synkrisis* (or comparison), and look at the occasional use of secondary characters as *exempla*. As we move through the various actors in the *bios*, we shall see that very few of them are of any interest to our author in their

---

1. V. Glendinning, "Lies and Silences," in *The Troubled Face of Biography*, ed. E. Homberger and J. Charmley (London: Macmillan, 1988), 60.

own right; the purpose of virtually every actor (or group) is primarily to enhance a particular quality exhibited by Jesus.

Peripheral Characters

The vast majority of Mark's extensive cast list is taken up with walk-on parts.[2] Actors emerge with a petition or a query and have their moment in the limelight before they disappear and are never heard of again. All the observations regarding ancient characters made in previous chapters are equally if not more valid for minor, supporting ones: these figures do not show any depth or development—in fact, many of them barely display any identifiable character traits at all. The sole purpose of actors such as Peter's mother-in-law (1:29–31), the man with the withered hand (3:1–6), or the five thousand men in the wilderness (6:33–44) is to set up a situation in which Jesus can display his miraculous powers, generous benefactions, or authoritative teaching. Indeed, these "characters" might be said to be little more than an extension of the "setting."

Although slightly more developed, most of Jesus's opponents fall into the same category. Those in Galilee appear in various combinations of "Pharisees," "scribes," "Herodians," or "scribes from Jerusalem." In the holy city they are joined by "Sadducees" and "chief priests, elders and scribes."[3] Whether in Galilee or Jerusalem, however, these "stock" opponents gather around Jesus in public spaces and behave in a stereotypical manner: they are quick to take offense, to criticize, and to challenge. Yet, as we saw in the last chapter, they are no match for Jesus: our hero easily defeats them in debate, emerging with his honor enhanced and silencing his critics. Of all these groups, the "scribes" receive the most attention. Their teaching lacks authority (1:22), proving to be either misguided (12:35–37) or lacking in awareness (9:11–13), and, despite their lack of humanity, they delight in public honor and esteem (12:38–40). They form

2. This group is variously known as "walk-ons" (so Seymour Chatman, *Story and Discourse: Narrative Structure in Fiction and Film* [Ithaca, NY: Cornell University Press, 1978], 138–39) or "stock" characters (Northrop Frye, *Anatomy of Criticism: Four Essays* [Princeton: Princeton University Press, 1973], 39–43, 171–77). For their use in gospel narrative, see D. Rhoads, J. Dewey, and D. Michie, *Mark as Story: An Introduction to the Narrative of a Gospel*, 3rd ed. (Minneapolis: Fortress, 2012), 117–36.

3. An earlier generation of scholars took the different groupings as indicative of Mark's sources; see M. J. Cook, *Mark's Treatment of the Jewish Leaders* (Leiden: Brill, 1978), who detected the presence of three written sources. For more contemporary studies, see E. S. Malbon, "The Jewish Leaders in the Gospel of Mark: A Literary Study of Marcan Characterization," *JBL* 108 (1989): 259–81; M. A. Powell, *What Is Narrative Criticism?* (Minneapolis: Fortress, 1990), 58–67; and Rhoads, Dewey, and Michie, *Mark as Story*, 123–30.

a negative foil against which the one good scribe stands out clearly (12:38–34). The good scribe warns against complacency and shows that the picture can sometimes be more complicated: along with Jairus and Joseph of Arimathea, other religious "outsiders," interest in Jesus can come from the most unlikely of places.

If religious leaders can occasionally be drawn to Jesus, his family show that those expected to be "insiders" are sometimes no better than opponents. Jesus's family appear early on in the *bios*, where they attempt to save their reputation by taking the "crazy" Jesus back home (3:21). Jesus, however, ignores them, turning their entreaties into an opportunity to redefine his "true" family in terms of faith rather than biology (3:31–35). Like the opponents (with whom they are closely connected in 3:19b–35), Jesus's family are on the side of humans rather than God (8:33). This one-dimensional portrait suggests that Mark has no interest in Jesus's family as *real-life people*, and questions of whether he had any reliable historical traditions here are probably beside the point. Instead, Mark's scene powerfully illustrates Jesus's severed ties with his family (a break he will require of those who follow him: 1:16–20; 10:28–30) and the emergence of the new kinship group forming around Jesus in anticipation of God's kingdom.[4]

At times, however, certain Markan characters have a degree of color that enables them to stand out from others. Our author provides a detailed description of the pitiful existence of the possessed man in the land of the Gerasenes—his continual self-harming among the tombs, his almost superhuman ("legionary") strength in overcoming all attempts to constrain him, and his rush to worship Jesus on sight (5:2–6). We are privy to the inner thoughts of the wretched woman with the flow of blood (5:25–28), the clever response of the Syro-Phoenician mother (7:27–29), and the sorrow of the rich man (10:17–22). Each one of these reflects Mark's skill as a writer and his ability to craft a vivid scene with the minimum of words. The Markan Jesus moves in a world consisting not only of stereotypical opponents and impressionable crowds but also of actors displaying real human concerns—utter dislocation from society, desperation, motherly courage and persistence, or an attachment to money. It is easy to imagine Mark's listeners having their favorites among this group, retelling their stories at home or to interested outsiders. Yet, despite the vividness of these characters, they too are far from being "real" individuals.[5] What characterization they achieve is revealed simply through their encounter with Jesus; they appear to have distinguishable traits, but in reality they display entirely pre-

---

4. See my earlier comments on Jesus's adoption on pp. 128–31 above.

5. Whether any are *historical* people is, of course, a different matter. For discussion of pre-Markan tradition, see pp. 106–15.

dictable and typical responses to him (usually expressed in terms of their "faith").[6] More broadly, as we saw in the last chapter, they allow Mark to highlight Jesus's concern for the distressed and his benevolence toward petitioners.

A notable feature of many of the cast noted so far is that they are imprisoned within their own *pericopae*. None of Jesus's supplicators ever strays from one *chreia* to another; all are contained within their own vignette. This is, of course, what we would expect in an episodic narrative: the character who links all of the episodes together is Jesus, and he will appear in almost every scene.[7] Once supporting actors have served their purpose within an individual story they can be forgotten. Even those who appear to cross episodic boundaries, however, such as opponents or Jesus's family, show little development from one scene to another. A good example of this is the series of controversies in 2:1–3:6. Each episode is distinct and self-contained, with no overlap with what precedes or follows. Mark is clearly not interested in providing a psychologically realistic account of growing antagonism toward Jesus. What gives the scenes this impression, however, is the skillful ordering of *pericopae*. In the first one, the scribes keep their misgivings to themselves, and it is only Jesus's knowledge of what is in their hearts that brings their objections into the open (2:1–12). The final scene, in contrast, heightens the tension: in this exchange, Jesus issues a direct challenge and his opponents are silenced and thereby shamed; small wonder, then, that they go out and plot his death with the Herodians (3:6). It is the repetition of similar scenes here, rather than an overarching plot, that would indicate to a listening audience that Jesus is now in grave danger.[8]

Similar dynamics are at work with Jesus's family. We have already noted their first appearance in 3:20–21, 31–35, where they come to take him home and are roundly ignored—even snubbed—by Jesus. Later on, when Jesus returns to his hometown of Nazareth, the family members are listed by name but not one of them appears, giving the impression that it is now their turn to abandon him (6:1–6). There is no attempt to provide any kind of "characterization" here, either within

6. For a useful discussion of these characters, see D. McCracken, "Character in the Boundary: Bakhtin's Interdividuality in Biblical Narratives," *Semeia* 63 (1993): esp. 32–33. On minor characters in the Hebrew Scriptures, see U. Simon, "Minor Characters in Biblical Narrative," *JSOT* 46 (1990): 11–19; and in Greek novels, see A. Billault, "Characterization in the Ancient Novel," in *The Novel in the Ancient World*, ed. G. L. Schmeling (Leiden: Brill, 1996), 115–29.

7. See the discussion in W. Shiner, "Creating Plot in Episodic Narratives," in *Ancient Fiction and Early Christian Narrative*, ed. R. F. Hock, J. B. Chance, and J. Perkins (Atlanta: Scholars, 1998), esp. 175–76, and above, pp. 104–5.

8. As we saw in Chapter 3, episodic narratives tend to have little interest in causation, particularly when the prime mover is in the divine realm; see above, pp. 104–5.

the two *chreiai* or between them; even if Mary and her sons are named, the family remains a shadowy presence. It is only the careful arrangement of anecdotes that allows the audience to appreciate Jesus's loss of their support.

One character who manages to appear in a number of episodes is John the Baptist. In certain respects, John occupies a relatively minor role for Mark: he appears in the prologue, where he is described in the manner of a wilderness prophet,[9] baptizes Jesus (1:1–11), and is almost immediately arrested (1:14). Yet, despite his early exit, the Baptist continues to haunt the biography in a number of places: Herod hears rumors that Jesus is John raised from the dead (6:14–16), a scene that leads into an account of the Baptist's death (6:17–29); after the transfiguration, Jesus and his disciples discuss the return of Elijah in a manner that recalls the Baptist (9:11–13); and in Jerusalem, Jesus turns a question regarding his own authority into one about the Baptist—a question his opponents are not willing to answer (11:27–33). Once again, there is no "characterization" of the Baptist, but by bringing him back into later episodes, the Markan author allows his audience to see not only that John heralded Jesus's arrival but also that the contours of his own life and death will form a blueprint for that of his more illustrious successor. The text never says this plainly—Jesus's words in 9:12–13 are as close as it gets—but Mark's skillful arrangement of anecdotes and placing of references to the Baptist at key points in the work allow his audience to infer a deeper level of meaning.

Markan Intercalations—A Form of *Synkrisis*?

All of this brings us to a peculiarity of Mark's Gospel: the author's so-called sandwich constructions, or intercalations.[10] This is where the author starts a story, pauses it to tell another one, and then resumes and completes the original account (what we might call an A–B–A structure). Six "classic" passages display this arrangement—Mark 3:20–35; 5:21–43; 6:7–32; 11:12–25; 14:1–11; and 14:53–72, though

9. Some of Mark's audience might already see a link here with Elijah; see 2 Kgs 1:8 (for Elijah's dress), and 2 Kgs 17–22 more generally.

10. E. von Dobschütz is usually credited with being the first to recognize this distinctive structure; see his "Zur Erzählerkunst des Markus," *ZNW* 27 (1928): 193–98. More recently, see F. Neirynck, *Duality in Mark: Contributions to the Study of the Markan Redaction* (Leuven: Leuven University Press, 1988), 133; J. R. Edwards, "Markan Sandwiches: The Significance of Interpolations in Markan Narratives," *NovT* 31 (1989): 193–216; G. van Oyen, "Intercalation and Irony in the Gospel of Mark," in *The Four Gospels, 1992*, ed. F. van Segbroeck, C. M. Tuckett, G. van Belle, and J. Verheyden (Leuven: Leuven University Press, 1992), 949–74; T. Shepherd, "The Narrative Function of Markan Intercalation," *NTS* 41 (1995): 522–40; and S. G. Brown, "Mark 11: 1–12:12: A Triple Intercalation?," *CBQ* (2002): 78–89.

some would add further episodes to this list,[11] and others suggest a "double" or even "triple" sandwich in certain places, giving a much more complicated structure.[12] In each of these cases, Mark has brought together two (or more) completely independent stories and inserted one into another so that the meaning of one spills over into the second. Much has been written about this distinctively Markan technique, though without any clear agreement on how exactly it works: Is the "meaning" to be found in the framing narrative, or the central one?[13] Is there always a chronological progression between the two stories, or do they sometimes occur concurrently (as appears to be the case in 14:53–72)? Perhaps we should not seek to pin things down too rigidly. The point is that Mark has deliberately brought together two distinct narratives, their juxtaposition encourages the audience to look for comparisons and contrasts, and in so doing to appreciate greater complexities of meaning than might otherwise be thought present, both in connection with the characters and the situations in which they find themselves. So, for example, if there were any doubts about the faithless intentions of Jesus's family in 3:21, they are dispelled by the scene's intercalation with the arrival of the Jerusalem scribes and their allegation that Jesus is possessed by Beelzebul (3:22–30). Thus the double scene shows that even people who should be "insiders" (Jesus's family) can easily find themselves aligned with the harshest of opponents.

Not all of Mark's intercalations disclose their meanings easily. Take for example the stories of Jairus's daughter and the woman with the hemorrhage (5:22–43). At first the comparison seems to be between Jairus and the woman. He is a named male, an authoritative ruler of the synagogue who approaches Jesus with a quiet assurance that his request will at least be heard. She is an unnamed female, poor and unclean, hiding her petition in a desperate touch, not of Jesus himself but of his garments. Yet both in the end will be rewarded for their faith, irrespective of their status or the manner of their request. As we conclude the story of Jairus's daughter, however, the contrast settles on the two recipients of Jesus's healing, and new themes begin to emerge. Listeners are encouraged to forge links between the two female characters:

11. Neirynck, for example, would include 15:6–32 (*Duality*, 133), and Edwards adds three more—4:1–20; 14:17–31; and 15:40–16:8 ("Markan Sandwiches").

12. For double structures in 14:1–31, see D. E. Nineham, *The Gospel of Saint Mark* (Harmondsworth: Penguin, 1963), 298, 398; E. Best, *The Temptation and the Passion: The Markan Soteriology* (Cambridge: Cambridge University Press, 1990), 91; and Donahue, *Are You the Christ?*, 59. For possible triple structures, see Brown, "Mark 11:1–12:12."

13. Edwards ("Markan Sandwiches") argues that the middle story nearly always provides the key to the theological purpose of the intercalation; Shepherd ("Narrative Function") argues that illumination goes both ways.

both are "daughters" (5:23, 34) and both are linked by the number twelve (5:25, 42). By healing her flow of blood, Jesus has taken away the woman's uncleanness and restored her to society; similarly, he takes away the uncleanness and finality of death, reuniting the young girl with her family. Both healings display Jesus's great powers, and both provide a glimpse of the kingdom of God as it breaks into human life. Moreover, both, in their own ways, point beyond the text to the lives of believers, who hope to be not only brought into the kingdom but also raised again to new life (the Greek word *egeirō*, used for the raising of Jairus's daughter in 5:41, will be used again of Jesus's own resurrection in 16:6). By bringing the two stories together, Mark has opened up a world of comparisons and meanings that would not have been possible if each story was read on its own. In other words, the intercalation is significantly more than the sum of its two parts.

Scholars have put forward a number of literary precedents for Mark's intercalation,[14] but the most likely background is the common rhetorical technique of *synkrisis*, or comparison. *Synkrisis* was developed particularly for use in oratory, but it could also be used to good effect in written works. It was particularly suited to the praise or blame of a person, and so was commonly found in both *encomium* and invective.[15]

In his *Rhetoric*, Aristotle discusses the technique of *auxēsis* (exaggeration or amplification) as a way of praising a person. A good strategy, he maintains, is to compare the subject favorably with others. Eminent men are best, "for it affords ground for amplification and is noble, if he can be proved better than men of worth." But comparison (*synkrinein*) with ordinary people is still useful, "since superiority is thought to indicate virtue."[16] Closer to Mark's own time, Quintilian discussed

---

14. Edwards, for example, discounts parallels in Homer on the grounds that Mark wants to make *theological* points (those in Homer are to add suspense); he finds better parallels in the Hebrew Bible, such as Hosea's prophecy in the midst of the story of his unfaithful wife (Hos 2), Nathan's prophecy in the midst of the David-Bathsheba story (2 Sam 11:12–25), or even the death of Absalom in 2 Sam 18:9–15 ("Markan Sandwiches," 199–203). However, as Edwards himself admits, in all of these cases the central element is an intentional commentary on the flanking story; in Mark it is a completely new story and it is left to the audience to make the connections.

15. Useful discussions of *synkrisis* include F. Focke, "Synkrisis," *Hermes* 58 (1923): 327–68; C. Forbes, "Comparison, Self-Praise and Irony: Paul's Boasting and the Conventions of Hellenistic Rhetoric," *NTS* 32 (1986): esp. 2–8; M. W. Martin, "Philo's Use of Syncrisis: An Examination of Philonic Composition in the Light of the Progymnasmata," *Perspectives in Religious Studies* 30 (2003): 271–97, and "Progymnasmatic Topic Lists: A Composition Template for Luke and Other Bioi?," *NTS* 54 (2008): 18–41.

16. See Aristotle, *Rhetoric* 1368a; similar sentiments are echoed in Pseudo-Aristotle, *Rhetoric to Alexander* 1440b.15; 1441a.28–33.

the place of comparison (*comparationis*) in the exercises of *encomia* and invective: the point, he says, is to ask which of two men is the better and which the worse. At issue is not simply the possession of virtues and vices, but their degree (*Institutes of Oratory* 2.4.21). While some rhetoricians, such as Theon, advised comparing only similar people ("where we are in doubt which should be preferred"), others, such as Hermogenes and Apthonius, were happy to extend *synkrisis* to include the contrast of dissimilar people.[17] A range of topics might be considered worthy of comparison, and the rhetoricians provide lists of suitable themes: a man's city, family, nurture, deeds, and so on. While a more formal comparison might include a number of these topics, an author might choose to scatter a number of briefer comparisons throughout his work.[18] In short, whether used to compare or contrast, and whether lengthy or brief, *synkrisis* provided a useful, and widely understood, foil to highlight the qualities of the protagonist.

Synkrisis is commonly found in the work of historians, particularly those with a strong interest in the moral character of protagonists. Thus Theopompus was fond of comparing the reaction of two historical figures to similar circumstances, and Josephus offered a comparison of Agrippa I and Herod (*Jewish Antiquities* 19.328–31).[19] *Synkrisis* is also found in the Hebrew Scriptures to some extent, featuring for example in certain passages within the Wisdom of Solomon (such as ch. 10).[20] Within a narrative text, Orpah's readiness to return home contrasts with Ruth's determination to remain with her mother-in-law (Ruth 1:6–18), just as the reluctance of Ruth's next of kin to take her in highlights the praiseworthy character of Boaz (Ruth 4:1–12). Neither Orpah nor Ruth's next of kin is essential to the plot; their purpose is simply to highlight the positive character traits of the main protagonists.[21]

17. On Theon: G. A. Kennedy, *Progymnasmata: Greek Textbooks of Prose Composition and Rhetoric* (Atlanta: SBL Press, 2003), 53; On Hermogenes: Kennedy, *Progymnasmata*, 83–84 (part of this section is lacking in the Greek original but is found in Priscian's Latin version). On Aphthonius: Kennedy, *Progymnasmata*, 113–15.

18. For more detail on the topic lists, see Martin, "Progymnasmatic." Clearly, only topics that suited the writer's purpose would be highlighted (so Theon, *Progymnasmata* 111; Nicolaus, *Progymnasmata* 51, 61).

19. On the use of *synkrisis* in historians, see Focke, "Synkrisis," 348–51. On Josephus, see L. H. Feldman, "Parallel Lives of Two Lawgivers: Josephus' Moses and Plutarch's Lycurgus," in *Flavius Josephus and Flavian Rome*, ed. J. Edmondson, S. Mason, and J. Rives (Oxford: Oxford University Press, 2005), 209–42.

20. See the study by A. T. Glicksman, *Wisdom of Solomon 10: A Jewish Hellenistic Reinterpretation of Early Israelite History through Sapiential Lenses* (Berlin: de Gruyter, 2011).

21. Simon, "Minor," 16–18.

It was in the work of biographers, however, that *synkrisis* really came into its own. It is used to good effect by Isocrates, who praised Evagoras by comparing him favorably with the great King Cyrus of Persia. While Cyrus conquered the Medes with a Persian army, a "deed which many a Greek or a barbarian could easily do," Evagoras accomplished most of his exploits through the "strength of his own mind and body." And while it remains unclear whether Cyrus could have endured the dangers faced by our hero, "it is obvious to all from the deeds of Evagoras that the latter would have readily attempted the exploits of Cyrus." Consequently, Isocrates concludes, "if any should wish to judge, not of the greatness of their successes, but of the essential merit of each, they would justly award greater praise to Evagoras than even to Cyrus" (*Evagoras* 37–39).[22] The point, of course, was that Cyrus was widely revered—to compare Evagoras favorably with him was high praise indeed.

In his *Life of Moses*, Philo compares his hero with a number of great figures from other nations: teachers from Greece and Egypt, he says, were unable to teach the boy anything (1.21), and Moses's laws were the best in the world, easily surpassing anything that had ever been put together either by Greeks or barbarians (2.12).[23] Similarly, Josephus compares himself with his rival, Justus of Tiberius (*Life* 336–37), a comparison that (unsurprisingly) demonstrates his own superiority as both a historian and a leader.[24] Luke develops a detailed *synkrisis* between Jesus and John the Baptist in the first two chapters of his *bios*, a comparison that clearly shows the superiority of Jesus over his predecessor.[25] And Philostratus made particularly good use of *synkrisis* within his lengthy account of Apollonius of Tyana. Not only is the protagonist continually contrasted with others (for example, Pythagoras [*Life of Apollonius of Tyana* 1.1–2] or Heraclitus [1.9]), but our author is also fond of contrasting rulers, depending on their attitude to philosophy in general and Apollonius in particular—thus the simplicity of the Indian king's palace is compared favorably with the pompous splendor of Babylon (2.25), and Vespasian and Titus (who both consulted Apollonius on good government) are frequently contrasted with Nero

22. Van Hook, LCL 373.

23. As Martin notes, the purpose of these comparisons is presumably to demonstrate the superiority not only of Moses but of the Jews themselves; "Progymnasmatic," 32–34.

24. Martin, "Progymnasmatic," 35.

25. Martin, "Progymnasmatic," 38–40. *Synkrisis* also features strongly in Hebrews; see M. W. Martin and J. A. Whitlark, "The Encomiastic Topics of Syncrisis as the Key to the Structure and Argument of Hebrews," *NTS* 57 (2011): 415–39. On the identification of *synkrisis* in the New Testament by the church fathers, and for a discussion of their hermeneutical methods, see D. J. Sheerin, "Rhetorical and Hermeneutic *Synkrisis* in Patristic Typology," in *Nova et Vetera: Patristic Studies in Honor of Thomas Patrick Halton*, ed. J. Petruccione (Washington, DC: Catholic University of America Press, 1998), 22–30.

and Domitian (both of whom opposed Apollonius; 4.35; 5.27–32; 6.29–33). In 7.1–3, Philostratus runs through a list of philosophers who stood up to tyrants; all were the best of their kind, he notes, though none could have stood up to Domitian in the manner of Apollonius (7.1–3).[26] Thus the portrait of Apollonius that Philostratus develops emerges to a large extent through contrasts.

The real master of the technique, however, was Plutarch. His *Parallel Lives* exhibits a highly unusual structure, composed of a series of paired biographies (one Greek, one Roman), each sharing a common prologue and closing comparison (or *synkrisis*). As Christopher Pelling notes, the introduction to each pair tends to highlight the similarities between the protagonists while the rather formulaic *synkrisis* draws out their differences.[27] But the "spirit of *synkrisis*" operates at a much more sophisticated level within the lives themselves, so that the hero's character is clarified through a succession of comparisons with others.[28] A particularly elaborate example is Fabius Maximus, the embodiment of strategic caution, who is brought into contact successively with five less circumspect commanders.[29] Less directly, the contrast between Cleopatra and Octavia (who represents the world of Roman values and duty) says something about Antony, the man who must decide between them.[30] Often the first life establishes the "norm" from which the second is a variation (as in the case of Antony and Demetrius), but the important thing is that the two lives are read together as a complete book, not as individual biographies.[31] The structure cries out for comparison, so that readers are encouraged to reflect on the two lives, and ultimately the moral questions that they raise.[32] Plutarch reflects on his method in another work:

26. For a similar assessment, see W. T. Shiner, *Follow Me! Disciples in Markan Rhetoric* (Atlanta: Scholars, 1995), 132–35. Philostratus also pauses to compare the trade of Ethiopia with that of Greece (*Life of Apollonius of Tyana* 6.2) and the wisdom of India with that of Egypt (6.7).

27. C. B. R. Pelling, *Plutarch: Life of Antony* (Cambridge: Cambridge University Press, 1988), 13–14. Useful discussions of Plutarch and his method in the *Lives* can also be found in D. A. Russell, "On Reading Plutarch's Lives," *G&R* 13 (1966): 139–54, and *Plutarch* (London: Duckworth, 1973); also T. Duff, *Plutarch's Lives: Exploring Virtue and Vice* (Oxford: Oxford University Press, 1999).

28. Russell, "On Reading," 150. He sees the technique at work in microcosm in Plutarch's many *men . . . de* sentences; "On Reading," 151.

29. Russell, "On Reading," 150.

30. Pelling, *Plutarch*, 13–14.

31. Duff, *Plutarch's Lives*, 10.

32. Duff, *Plutarch's Lives*, 10.

> It is not possible to learn better the similarity and the difference between the
> virtues of men and women from any other source than by putting lives beside
> lives and actions beside actions, like great works of art, and considering whether
> the magnificence of Semiramis has the same character as that of Sesostris or the
> intelligence of Tanaquil the same as that of Servius the King. (*On the Virtue of
> Women* 243)

Other writers were rather more subtle in their use of *synkrisis*. Brian McGing
has drawn attention to the important role *synkrisis* plays in Tacitus's *Agricola*. In
order to praise his subject, Tacitus continually juxtaposes him with other characters;
he "does not 'compare' him with men of similar virtue and achievement, but rather
'contrasts' him with his inferiors," contrasts that highlight his military prowess, his
bravery, and resistance to corruption.[33] At times historical information is skewed
quite drastically to achieve Tacitus's literary points—for example, the clear and
highly unlikely implication that all previous governors of Britain had been ineffec-
tual.[34] At a much deeper level is an implied contrast between Agricola's obedience,
restraint, and moderation, and Domitian's secrecy, scheming, and hatred.[35] Tacitus was keenly aware of the kind of criticism that men who had prospered under
Domitian's tyrannical reign might face (a group that included not only Agricola but
Tacitus himself). The work as a whole addresses the question of how a responsible
and virtuous citizen should serve a state ruled by a tyrant. Unlike members of the
Stoic opposition, who unrealistically opposed tyranny and suffered empty glory
through their ostentatious deaths, Agricola was practical, wise, and restrained. He
may have suffered at the hands of Domitian in the end (Tacitus is a little hazy at
this point), but he died having "made a substantial contribution to Rome."[36] The
use of *synkrisis* allows Tacitus not only to present Agricola as a moral example to
others but also to contrast him favorably with his contemporaries.

An interesting feature of the *Agricola* is that the protagonist, though never far
from the narrator's mind, is not always one of the two parties being compared.
So, for example, Tacitus compares the Britons favorably with the Gauls so as to
provide Agricola with worthy opponents (11.2–4). The Britons are also compared
to the Stoic opposition. Both groups had been deprived of their liberty, and both
were willing to go to their deaths rather than compromise (a position that contrasts

33. B. C. McGing, "Synkrisis in Tacitus' *Agricola*," *Hermathena* 132 (1982): 15.

34. McGing, "Synkrisis," 16–17. For historical difficulties in Tacitus's portrait, see Mc-
Ging, "Synkrisis," 19–20.

35. McGing, "Synkrisis," 21.

36. McGing, "Synkrisis," 22.

with Agricola's obedience and restraint). "Both Britons and Stoics, then, represent a code of conduct which is admirably, but wastefully, courageous. Both help to reinforce the value of Agricola's way of life, which is courageous *and* useful, and to cast it in a clearer light."[37] Tacitus's use of *synkrisis*, then, is wide-ranging. On a fairly straightforward level, it is used to heighten Agricola's praiseworthy qualities, but at a deeper level it is used to make political comparisons, defending the behavior of Agricola and men like him in the face of possible detractors.

Mark does not offer any *formal* comparisons of people and situations—indeed, as we saw in Chapter 3, it seems highly unlikely that he had the kind of rhetorical training that would enable him to do so. But frequent exposure to literature that made use of *synkrisis* might easily have encouraged him to bring characters together in ways that enhanced certain virtues. Exposure to Greco-Roman sculptural friezes, which characteristically featured a series of panels depicting different scenes, might also have shown Mark the importance of the placement of episodes (it is interesting that in the passage quoted above Plutarch also makes a connection between *synkrisis* and art). In whatever way the technique came to him, the result for Mark is a rich tapestry of stories that allows a greater depth and sophistication to the story he tells. Most comparisons are, of course, with Jesus, where the portrait of others serves to highlight his superior qualities, but occasionally other characters are contrasted in their response to him. I shall illustrate this with two rather lengthier examples— first Herod, and then the high priest and Pilate.

"King Herod"

The sheer length and detail of this short story, or *diēgēsis*, suggests that it has some importance for Mark (6:14–29). At first glance, however, it appears to have little to contribute to the emerging character of Jesus: outside the introductory verses (6:14–16), our hero does not make an appearance, nor do his disciples or even the usual opponents. Instead, we have a very different cast list: King Herod, his wife Herodias, a dancing daughter, and an array of Galilean celebrities. The only familiar character is John the Baptist, and it is with his death that the account is, at least superficially, concerned.[38]

---

37. McGing, "Synkrisis," 22–23.

38. Along with most scholars, I assume that the story of the banquet and the dancing girl are fictitious; if the story existed in a pre-Markan form (as is quite possible), I assume that Mark has adapted it for his own purposes. Useful studies of this passage include: R. Fowler, *Loaves and Fishes: The Function of the Feeding Stories in the Gospel of Mark* (Chico, CA: Scholars, 1981), 119–32; A. Stock, *Call to Discipleship: A Literary Study of Mark's Gospel*

Many commentators have assumed that the vignette has little connection with its immediate Markan setting.[39] It fills in the space between the sending out of the disciples and their return, and it is presented as a flashback, apparently completing the story of the Baptist who, when we last heard of him, had been arrested (1:14).[40] More broadly, however, the story seems to invite links between John's death and that of Jesus later on. Several words are used only here and in the account of Jesus's passion: the quest for an "opportune time," *eukairos/eukairōs* (6:21; 14:11); to swear, *omnuō* (6:23; 14:71); to grieve, *perilypos* (6:26; 14:34); to seize, *krateō* (6:17; 12:12; 14:1, 44, 46, 49); to bind, *deō* (6:17; 15:1); to kill, *apokteinō* (6:19; 8:31; 9:31; 10:34; 14:1); and in both cases the corpse, *ptōma*, is placed in a tomb (6:29; 15:45–46).[41] All of this suggests that John is cast as a prototype, his violent end prefiguring that

---

(Wilmington, DE: Michael Glazier, 1982), 191–99; J. Delorme, "John the Baptist's Head— The Word Perverted," *Semeia* 81 (1998): 115–29; C. Focant, "La tête du prophète sur un plat, ou, L'anti-repas d'alliance (Mc 6.14–29)," *NTS* 46 (2001): 334–53; A. Smith, "Tyranny Exposed: Mark's Typological Characterization of Herod Antipas (Mark 6:14–29)," *BibInt* 14 (2006): 259–93; J. A. Glancy, "Unveiling Masculinity: The Construction of Gender in Mark 6:17–29," *BibInt* 2 (1994): 34–50; R. S. Kraemer, "Implicating Herodias and Her Daughter in the Death of John the Baptizer: A (Christian) Theological Strategy?," *JBL* 125 (2006): 321–49; R. A. Culpepper, "Mark 6:17–29 in Its Narrative Context: Kingdoms in Conflict," in *Mark as Story: Retrospect and Prospect*, ed. K. R. Iverson and C. W. Skinner (Atlanta: SBL Press, 2011), 145–63; and G. D. Miller, "An Intercalation Revisited: Christology, Discipleship and Dramatic Irony in Mark 6.6b–30," *JSNT* 35 (2012): 176–95.

39. So, for example, M. D. Hooker, who assumes that Mark fitted the two stories together "clumsily"; *A Commentary on the Gospel according to St Mark* (London: A&C Black, 1995), 158; also R. Pesch, *Das Markusevangelium*, vol. 1, *Einleitung und Kommentar zu Kap. 1, 1–8, 26* (Freiburg: Herder, 1976), 344; and D. E. Nineham, *The Gospel of Saint Mark* (Harmondsworth: Penguin, 1963), 172.

40. Interestingly, as Focant notes, there are no details regarding when John was arrested, how long he was in custody, or the date of his execution; "La tête," 341. All of this suggests that supplying historical information is not Mark's main point here. On the differences between Mark's account and that of Josephus in *Jewish Antiquities* 18.116–19, see Focant, "La tête," 336–40, and especially Kraemer, "Implicating," 325–40.

41. Some have seen further connections between the character of Herod here and Pilate in 15:1–15. In this reading, the Roman governor is also impressed by Jesus (15:5; the word here is *thaumazō*, amazed); he seizes on the Passover custom demanded by the people to rid himself of an awkward case only for it to backfire and to find himself forced to crucify Jesus. See Fowler, *Loaves*, 123–24; M. McVann, "The 'Passion' of John the Baptist and Jesus before Pilate: Mark's Warnings about Kings and Governors," *BTB* 38 (2008): 152–57; Smith, "Tyranny," 282–83; and Miller, "Intercalation," 179. Although there are undoubtedly connections between the two characters, Herod is primarily contrasted with *Jesus*, as we shall see below.

of Jesus.[42] If so, the account functions in a similar manner to the Markan prologue (1:1–15), in that it alerts the audience to information that is not yet known to other characters: in this case, the fact that Jesus's mission will involve his death. Just as the prologue spelled out Jesus's identity clearly for the audience, creating a sense of "knowing insiders" who watch other characters stumbling toward realization, so here the flashback to a different world allows the audience prior knowledge of events not yet made clear to characters within the drama.[43]

Despite all of this, however, the scene cannot really be said to be the Baptist's "passion." Not only is there no mention of his suffering, but he is not the main character—he does not even appear on the stage until the end, when his head appears on a platter, passed from one actor to another, and his disciples bury what remains of his corpse (6:28–29).[44] The main character in the scene is quite clearly Herod: the account begins with his anxious reflections on Jesus's identity and his acknowledgment of guilt in the matter of John's death (6:16); he is mentioned more than any other character; and the tension in the scene revolves around *his* decisions. Although women are also present, they are part of his household and their activities reflect on him.[45]

Two features are key to understanding the passage. First is the short discussion in 6:14–16 that revolves around Jesus's identity.[46] Some say he is John the Baptist raised

42. The account may even point to the latter's resurrection: although is it clearly not true for Mark that *John* has been raised, this is the first time that resurrection has been mentioned in the text and may be designed to point forward to the one character who will be raised from the dead. Kraemer suggests that the story was made up in order to respond to "early Christian anxieties and contestations about the relationship between Jesus and John," and that the account is designed to "refute not simply the suggestion that John the Baptist has been resurrected but more precisely the possibility that Jesus is John raised from the dead by telling a narrative in which the body of John is desecrated in a manner that makes it impossible to resurrect it, at least physically, by severing the head from the body"; "Implicating," 341. It is not impossible that the story served such a purpose at an early stage, but as we have it now in Mark, the contrast between Jesus and King Herod seems more marked than that between Jesus and the Baptist.

43. So also Focant, "La tête," 343.

44. So also J. Marcus, *Mark 1–8: A New Translation with Introduction and Commentary* (New York: Doubleday, 2000), 403–4.

45. While I agree with Focant that John is not the central character, I would disagree with his claim that the main characters are Herod and his wife ("La tête," 338); as we shall see, Herodias for Mark is simply an extension of her husband.

46. So also Fowler, *Loaves*, 120, and Miller, "Intercalation," 177. The three options will reappear at 8:28, just before Peter makes his important confession at Caesarea Philippi.

from the dead, others that he is Elijah, and still others that he is one of the "prophets of old." Herod favors the first of these options, and the rest of the section is presented as a flashback, introduced by the word *gar*, outlining the sordid events leading up to the Baptist's death.[47] The audience of course knows that none of the options raised is adequate, but they ensure that questions of Jesus's identity continue to hover about the text.

Second is the identification of the Jewish ruler as "King Herod." Commentators are quick to point out that this particular Herod was not a king, and that his official title was tetrarch (literally ruler of a fourth of a kingdom).[48] The fact that the term "king" (*basileus*) is used so extensively in this passage, however—it occurs five times (6:14, 22, 25, 26, 27) along with a reference to Herod's kingdom, *basileia* (6:23)—suggests that Mark has used the title quite deliberately. The only other character in the *bios* to be referred to as "king" is of course Jesus, and the title will come into some prominence in ch. 15 (where it is found at 15:2, 9, 12, 18, 26, and 32).[49] "King" might not be the title Jesus would choose for himself (as 15:2 will demonstrate), but it certainly captures something of the Son's true status. Given the use of the title both here and in ch. 15, then, we should not be surprised to find the beginning of a contrast between two very different ways of exercising kingship. In Gabriella Gelardini's terms, the scene is a contest for a royal title.[50]

Some of Mark's audience might remember this particular Herod. Known in his earlier years as Antipas, he grew up in Rome and expected to inherit the whole of his father's kingdom—that is, before a change of will and various representations to Augustus left him with only a meager share. Ironically, it was precisely his attempt to become king that led to his banishment by Gaius in 39 CE.[51] Others might simply assume that Mark is talking about Herod the Great, the most famous Jewish monarch; or they may have confused him with King Agrippa II, a friend of Vespasian, whose sister Berenice's affair with Titus in Rome was causing a stir even as Mark

47. Mark's favorite historic presents are replaced in this scene by verbs in the aorist and imperfect, underlining the sense of events now past.

48. See Josephus, *Jewish War* 2.93–95, 167–68, 183; *Jewish Antiquities* 17.317–20; 18.27, 136, 252.

49. The only other time that the title is used in Mark is at 13:9, where it refers to the unspecified kingly rulers before whom disciples will stand trial.

50. G. Gelardini, "The Contest for a Royal Title: Herod versus Jesus in the *Gospel according to Mark* (6,14–29; 15,6–15)," *ASE* 28 (2011): 93–106. As she notes, the name "Herod" also implies a heroic or even semi-divine descent (95).

51. He was confirmed as tetrarch of Galilee and Peraea in 6 CE, and again in 14 CE, when Tiberius came to power (*Jewish War* 2.167–68); see also Strabo, *Geography* 16.2.46. The title appears on his coins, along with the name "Herod."

wrote.[52] At all events, the figure of "King Herod" here clearly represents an ostentatious Hellenistic ruler. The story is set in his royal court, a place of dynastic marriage and political intrigue, characterized by decadence, opulence, and excess. The scene takes place at the ruler's birthday feast attended by "courtiers and officers and the leading men of Galilee," during which—scandalously—a young princess dances.[53] In contrast to the surrounding scenes, the audience is suddenly transported into an erotic setting, typified by a destructive male gaze and the capricious exercise of power.

Central to the scene is the trope of the evil ruler who persecutes the righteous man of God. The Hebrew Scriptures furnish many examples: the Egyptian Pharaoh (Exod 1:15–22; 5:1–23), Joash's persecution of Zechariah (2 Chr 24:20–44), the persecutors of Daniel and his friends (Dan 3:12–20), Darius (Dan 6:10–18), and of course Antiochus Epiphanes (Dan 11:29–45 and 2 Macc 5:11–9:29).[54] Josephus draws on this trope, too, as demonstrated by his portrait of Antiochus Epiphanes (*Jewish Antiquities* 12.246–359), as later will Matthew in his depiction of Herod the Great (Matt 2:1–18) and Luke in his portrait of Agrippa I (Acts 12:20–23). As Abraham Smith notes, however, "tyrant" types were equally common in the Greco-Roman world, featuring as stock characters not only on the stage but in school exercises and political invective as well.[55] Such types were commonly contrasted with the philosopher. In the Greek world the prime examples were Hiero and Simonides, or Dionysius I of Syracuse and Plato.[56] For Romans, the trope was epitomized in the encounters between Nero and Seneca, or other Stoic martyrs,[57] and is frequently found within the biographical tradition (as we saw earlier, the motif is put to good use by Philostratus in his *Life of Apollonius of Tyana* 7.1–3). Clearly, then, Mark is

52. Berenice had been close to Titus since at least 69 CE. D. C. Braund suggests that animosity toward the Jewish queen in Rome explains both why she kept away from the city until 75 and Titus's dismissal of her on his accession in 79; "Berenice in Rome," *Historia* 33 (1984): 120–23.

53. Xenophon describes a similar toxic mix of feasting and death in a banquet held by Cyrus the Persian that was accompanied by ritual dancing, an orchestra, and the cutting of the throats of sacrificial victims; *Cyropaedia* 7.7. Livy, Cicero, and Seneca all tell the story of Lucius Quinctus Flaminius's expulsion from the senate in 184 BCE for beheading a condemned man at a dinner party at the request of a courtesan; for further details, see Kraemer, "Implicating," 337. Like the other authors listed here, Mark plays on his audience's love of the exotic, aristocrats behaving badly, and their sense of moral righteousness.

54. Culpepper provides a useful table of scriptural parallels; "Mark 6:17–29," 148–49.

55. Smith, "Tyranny," 263–70.

56. On Hiero and Simonides, see Xenophon, *Hiero* 1.1–2; on Dionysius, see Pseudo-Plato, *Epistles* 2.231a–b; also Plutarch, *Dionysius* 4.3–4.

57. Tacitus, *Annals* 15.34–35, 60–64; Dio Cassius, *Roman History* 66.12.

drawing on a well-known literary *topos* in his account of the encounter between John and the tyrant Herod.

The prominence of women within this narrative has frequently been noted. "Good" women for Mark are in need of help and healing (1:29–31; 5:24b–34) or display extravagant devotion (12:41–44; 14:3–9). Herodias and the (unnamed) daughter, however, are portrayed very differently. These are women out of control, who do not know their place.[58] To an ancient mind, women were always a potential source of disruption, and Mark's hearers would know that when the behavior of royal women is prominent it is a sure sign that male power is being discussed. Josephus uses this trope to good advantage in his *Jewish War*. Female characters come to prominence in this lengthy work only in one place—at the court of Herod the Great—and the Jewish historian spends what seems like an inordinate amount of space describing both the seething mass of rivalries and resentment that characterizes court life and the paranoia of a king who has lost all sense of moderation or self-control. The outrageous female characters allow Josephus to present a portrait of a ruler whose household is out of control, who is dominated by women and his passions, and who is therefore completely unfit to rule.[59]

58. For a useful critique of much patriarchal interpretation, which seems to take delight in the "scheming" women and the supposed sensual nature of the dance (an element Mark certainly does not dwell on), see Glancy, "Unveiling," 43–50. See also T.-S. B. Liew, "Re-Mark-able Masculinities: Jesus, the Son of Man, and the (Sad) Sum of Manhood," in *New Testament Masculinities*, ed. S. D. Moore and J. C. Anderson (Atlanta: SBL Press, 2003), 93–135; Kraemer, "Implicating," 346–47; and B. Baert, "The Dancing Daughter and the Head of John the Baptist (Mark 6:14–29) Revisited: An Interdisciplinary Approach," *Louvain Studies* 38 (2014): 5–29.

59. See H. K. Bond, "Josephus on Herod's Domestic Intrigue in the *Jewish War*," *JSJ* 43 (2012): 295–314. Interestingly, Josephus also casts aspersions on Antipas by suggesting that he was ruled by his wife; *Jewish Antiquities* 18.240–55. Scholars have frequently noted connections between Mark's portrait of Herodias and Jezebel, who of course schemed to be rid of Elijah (1 Kgs 19:1–3); see D. M. Hoffeditz and G. E. Yates, "*Femme Fatale* Redux: Intertextual Connection to the Elijah/Jezebel Narratives in Mark 6:14–29," *BBR* 15 (2005): 199–221; S. A. Cummins, "Integrated Scripture, Embedded Empire: The Ironic Interplay of 'King' Herod, John and Jesus in Mark 6.1–44," in *Biblical Interpretation in Early Christian Gospels*, vol. 1, *The Gospel of Mark*, ed. T. R. Hatina (London: T&T Clark, 2006), 31–48; and Culpepper, "Mark 6:17–29," 149–50. Others have highlighted the links with Esther: see, for example, R. Aus, *Water into Wine and the Beheading of John the Baptist: Early Jewish-Christian Interpretation of Esther 1 in John 2:1–11 and Mark 6:17–29* (Atlanta: Scholars, 1988), 41–66. And still others have explored the link between banquets, women, and death more broadly in the Jewish Scriptures: see for example N. Duran, "Having Men

Similar tropes are at play in Mark. While women might appear to gain some prominence here, their purpose is simply to say something about "King Herod." And the portrait is not a complimentary one. It is Herodias who acts in stereotypically "male" ways in this scene: she has the political acumen to see the damage that the Baptist's charges can bring to the royal couple and seeks her revenge (6:17–19). When the opportunity presents itself, she seizes her chance and demands an outcome that she knows will both trouble her husband and undermine his authority. Herod, in contrast, displays a range of emotions: he is fearful, indecisive, and lacks the strength of his convictions. He is caught up in the excesses of his birthday party, makes an utter fool of himself, and realizes too late that he is trapped by his own rash promise. He would rather save face before his courtiers than protect a man he knows to be "righteous and holy" (6:26) and exposes himself as weak, vulnerable, and finally compromised. The scene is one of utter chaos: Herod is able to control neither his own household nor the violent and conflicting emotions within himself; he is more interested in preserving the honor in which he is held by his retainers than in doing what is right. To a first-century audience, the story had a clear meaning: "King" Herod is unmanly and unfit to rule.[60] The Baptist might have lost his head in this scene, but in reality it is Herod who is unmanned, rendered impotent, and symbolically castrated.[61]

But what does all of this have to do with Jesus? We noted in the last chapter that Mark presents Jesus as an elite male, even one with royal and imperial connections: he bests opponents, bestows benefactions on petitioners, and conducts himself with restraint and modesty. In the episode that frames the Herod story, Jesus confers his authority on his disciples and sends them out to preach, heal, and cast out demons (6:6b–13); not only do they carry out his bidding, but everything turns out just as Jesus said it would (6:30).[62] Although the word "kingdom" is not used here, it is clear that the disciples are extending God's kingdom, offering it to all who will accept. And although Jesus is not described as a "king," it is clear that he acts in the authoritative way of a monarch, sending others to do his will and to further his goals.[63] The contrast between Jesus and "King Herod" could hardly be clearer. Like

---

for Dinner: Deadly Banquets and Biblical Women," *BTB* 35 (2005): 117–24. While Mark may have drawn vocabulary and themes from all these stories, however, his account is not fundamentally "dependent" on any of them.

60. So also Miller, "Intercalation," 182–83.

61. Glancy, "Unveiling," 47; also Liew, "Re-Mark-able," 123.

62. The Markan intercalation is an unusual one here, with almost all of the material in the first section (6:6b–13), leaving only the disciples' return for the completing segment (6:30).

63. So also Fowler, *Loaves*, 120. The verb *proskaleō* (to summon) stresses Jesus's authority (so R. H. Gundry, *Mark: A Commentary on His Apology for the Cross* [Grand Rapids:

other gentile (appointed) rulers, Herod lords it over his subjects (10:42), yet he is ultimately weak and unmanly; his is a kingdom where violence prospers and the voices of the righteous are silenced. Jesus, however, behaves regally; while Herod sends out executioners, Jesus sends out his followers to heal and to save, and to establish a very different kind of kingdom. Jesus is not outdone by womanly tricks (though he does listen to the Syro-Phoenician woman),[64] nor is he swayed by the outrageous requests of friends (10:35–40). Throughout the entire *bios* he remains firm and resolute in the path God has set out for him. Mark's listeners could be in no doubt as to who is the real kingly figure.

Further contrasts to Herod's murderous banquet are supplied by the story of the feeding of the five thousand, which Mark situates immediately after the return of the Twelve (6:31–44). Here, Jesus is the host, determining the seating arrangements, sourcing and blessing the food, while the disciples once again act as his helpers, distributing food to his guests. The scene evokes a number of scriptural images: the manna in the wilderness, Elisha's provision of food in 2 Kgs 4:38–44, and the banquet of the messianic age.[65] But there are other connotations too. As David Sick points out, Mark's use of the word *symposion* (6:39) and the reference to people "reclining" (*anaklinō, anapiptō*, 6:39–40) suggest a public banquet where those gathered recline on the lush green grass. The fish, he argues, were probably dried or smoked, and were widely eaten as condiments; together with the bread they constituted the "standard menu in classical dining."[66] What Mark describes, then, is a huge, lavish feast in which five thousand are fed until satisfied. The portrait of Jesus that emerges from this is one of a great benefactor, a wealthy euergetist who feeds his people. And although extended only to men, there is no sense of social stratification in this banquet—attendees are presumably from all walks of

---

Eerdmans, 1993], 300–301), and in classical Greek the word *apostolos* (6:30) can be used of those engaged in a military or naval expedition (so Hooker, *Commentary*, 162). Both shades of meaning tend to enhance the portrait of Jesus as a counter King to Herod here. Gundry objects to this reading on the grounds that "Jesus's kingship" does not appear in the *pericope* (*Mark*, 311); he is technically correct, but as I hope to have demonstrated in the last chapter, Mark endows his Jesus with elite, even kingly/imperial virtues long before this scene.

64. The woman with the hemorrhage does not manage to trick Jesus; 5:24–34.

65. Promised in a number of scriptural texts, including Isa 25:6; Pss 23:5; 63:5; Exod 24:11; Deut 16:15; Neh 8:10–12; and Zech 14:16.

66. D. H. Sick, "The Symposium of the 5,000," *JTS* 66 (2015): 11. John changes Mark's *ichthus* to *opsarion*, the diminutive of *opson* (relish); John 6:9, 11; see also John 21:9–13, where the menu consists not of the *ichthues* just caught by the disciples, but *opsarion* smoked by Jesus; Sick, "Symposium," 9. As Sick notes, the lack of wine in Mark 6 is puzzling; he assumes its presence (11–13).

life, and there are no obvious divisions according to class or age, as was common at contemporary banquets.[67] Herod's feast, in contrast, is open only to the great and the good, events take on a macabre tone, and the only "food" on offer is the head of a prophet on a platter. Once again, the juxtaposition of stories contrasts the two men to Jesus's advantage.[68]

It is clear, then, that Mark has introduced "King Herod" as a foil to Jesus. While the story recounts the Baptist's death and points forward to that of Jesus, deeper contrasts are at play, ones that present "King" Jesus and his kingdom in a completely different manner from that of "King Herod" and his realm. As Geoffrey Miller notes, "Jesus is a magnanimous king who has come to serve and to bring life to others";[69] Herod in contrast is a petty tyrant whose weakness and desire for honor bring only death.

The High Priest/Pilate

Mark's trial scenes form a carefully structured unit, with the Roman trial (15:1–20) paralleling the earlier Jewish proceedings (14:53–72).[70] In both trials, the questions revolve around two themes. In the Jewish trial, Jesus is first accused by many false witnesses who are unable to agree with one another in their testimony against him. Finally, some stand up and accuse him of threatening not only to destroy the temple but also to build another in three days "not made with hands" (*acheiropoiēton*). Yet even this is inconclusive, and Jesus resolutely remains silent (14:60–61a). In response, the high priest introduces a new theme, now questioning Jesus specifically regarding his identity: "Are you the Christ, the Son of the Blessed?" Jesus's answer is clear and forthright: "I am; and you will see the Son of Man seated at the right

---

67. Mark is clear that there were five thousand *men* (*andres*; contrast Matt 14:21 and Luke 9:13–14). It is *possible* that Mark has deliberately removed women from this account; if so, he may want to show that Christian gatherings (i.e., the Eucharist) are places where women know their place, unlike the unruly *symposia* caricatured in the story of Herod. Such a reading, however, is far from clear. On Hellenistic public *symposia*, see Sick, "Symposium," 19–25.

68. Focant also sees Herod's banquet as a parody of the Last Supper; "La tête," 352–53.

69. Miller, "Intercalation," 183–84.

70. For fuller discussion of these passages, including the many historical questions they raise, see my earlier studies in *Pontius Pilate in History and Interpretation* (Cambridge: Cambridge University Press, 1998), 94–119, 194–202, and *Caiaphas: Friend of Rome and Judge of Jesus?* (Louisville: Westminster John Knox, 2004), 98–108. On the deliberate Markan parallelism between the trials, see also F. J. Matera, *The Kingship of Jesus: Composition and Theology in Mark 15* (Chico, CA: Scholars, 1982), 7–8, 99.

hand of Power, and coming with the clouds of heaven" (14:62). This is blasphemy, the high priest declares, and all the council (*pantes*; 14:64) condemn him to death.

The trial before Pilate is briefer at this point, and while it similarly revolves around two sets of charges, they are reversed. Pilate begins with the question of Jesus's identity: "Are you the King of the Jews?" Again, Jesus chooses to answer this, though his response is far more guarded than before the high priest: *su legeis*, he says, perhaps implying "The words are yours, not mine" (15:2).[71] Jesus is a "king" (a theme I shall explore more fully in the next chapter), but not in any sense that the Roman prefect would understand.[72] The chief priests now accuse him of "many things" (*polla*), but Jesus, as earlier, refuses to engage with their charges and remains silent (15:5a).

Both trials end with mockery and abuse of the prisoner, each appropriate to the charge brought against Jesus. Following the Jewish trial, it is apparently members of the council who spit on him, cover his face, strike him, and call on him to "prophesy," while unspecified guards (*hupēretai*) beat him (14:65). In the fuller account that follows the Roman proceedings, Jesus is taken inside the *praetorium* by Roman soldiers who, after scourging him (15:15), subject him to an undignified mockery of what they see as his kingly pretensions, dressing him in imperial purple, crowning him, and paying him mock homage (15:16–20).

Finally, in both scenes Jesus is contrasted with another character.[73] In the Jewish trial, it is Peter who, alone of the disciples, has followed Jesus to the high priest's house and now stands warming himself by the fire (14:54). As Jesus is tried before the high priest, a maid (*paidiskē*) notices Peter and accuses him of having been with the Nazarene. Peter denies it and moves away from the light of the fire, only to be challenged twice more by the maid and other bystanders. Now Peter's denials become more intense: he calls down a curse on himself and swears "I do not know this man of whom you speak" (14:71). We shall come back to the portrayal of Peter later on in this chapter, but it is clear that Mark's hearers are presented with two ways to behave if called upon to answer for their faith: that of Jesus, who calmly declares his identity even before the most powerful religious leader, and that of Peter, who

---

71. J. Schwiebert may be correct to read Jesus's words here as a counterquestion, along the lines of his response to opponents in 11:27–33 and 12:13–17. "Do you say it?" would throw the charge back at Pilate; "Jesus's Question to Pilate in Mark 15:2," *JBL* 136 (2017): 937–47.

72. See further, pp. 237–41 below.

73. See A. Borrell, *The Good News of Peter's Denial: A Narrative and Rhetorical Reading of Mark 14:54, 66–72* (Atlanta: Scholars, 1998), esp. 61, who notes the "common basic design" between Peter's denial and the Barabbas scene in the Roman trial, including the threefold questioning, and even linguistic links.

desperately attempts to distance himself from the charge of being a follower of Jesus, even before a lowly serving maid. Should they find themselves called upon to face trial and persecution, to stand before governors and kings (as 13:9–11 predicts), it is clear which model Mark's hearers are to follow.

In the course of the Roman tribunal, the contrast is with Barabbas. Suddenly we are told that a crowd appears, asking Pilate to honor his usual custom and to release a prisoner of their choosing (15:6, 8). Mark sets up the element of choice from the beginning, noting that there was a man named Barabbas among those in prison who had committed murder in the insurrection (15:7).[74] In response to Pilate's offer to release the "King of the Jews," the once-friendly crowd, stirred up by the chief priests, shouts instead for Barabbas, a choice they maintain until their wish is granted (15:9–15). The persistent use of the title "king" in this scene heightens what is at stake in the choice between the two men: Will the Jewish crowd choose Jesus as their king and leader, or an insurrectionary, tainted with rebellion and murder? Read in the aftermath of the disastrous war of 66–70 CE, when Jews really did put their trust in political aspirants and armed rebellion, the drama of Mark's scene is not hard to appreciate. The true "king," all along, was none other than Jesus.

Above and beyond these contrasts is yet another, that between the high priest and Pilate. As usual in his strongly episodal narrative, Mark provides no connecting link between the two trials. We have already seen that the Jewish court condemns Jesus to death, with no suggestion that their verdict is anything but final (14:64). In 15:1, however, the whole council holds another consultation before binding Jesus and handing him over to Pilate, at which point the proceedings against Jesus start all over again. Whatever historical reasons necessitated a double hearing,[75] Mark's presentation gives each trial equal weight and invites comparisons not only between the two courts but more specifically between the two judges. Of all Markan characters, the high priest is perhaps the most shadowy. He is presumably part of the high/chief priestly group (*hoi archiereis*) who plot against Jesus in 11:18 and 14:1-2, and who later accuse Jesus before Pilate (15:3), stir up the crowd (15:11), and mock Jesus on the cross (15:31). It is only in the Jewish trial, however, that an independent "high priest" emerges (now referred to by the singular *ho archiereus*), who challenges Jesus, secures the death penalty, and once again disappears into the chief priestly group. Not only is the high priest not named, but he exhibits no in-

74. The Greek here is ambiguous: Is Barabbas also a murderer? Or simply in prison with murderers?

75. On the right of Jewish courts to execute, see J. S. McLaren, *Power and Politics in Palestine: The Jews and the Governing of Their Land, 100 BC–70 AD* (Sheffield: JSOT Press, 1991).

dependent character traits whatsoever. We might well suspect that Mark has drawn attention to this figure solely to provide a focal point for the contrast with Pilate. And the depiction of the high priest, however roughly sketched, is not a flattering one. He, along with his associates, convenes the council with the specific purpose of putting Jesus to death (14:55), but even so, the resulting kangaroo court has difficulty in making charges stick (14:56–59). Later, we find out—from a reliable witness—that the Jewish authorities are motivated by envy (15:10, a charge already implicit in 12:12 and 14:1–2). Only when he takes matters into his own hands and secures Jesus's "confession" from his own lips does the high priest finally succeed in his ungodly design.

In many respects, Pilate is the mirror opposite of the high priest. While the chief pontiff is referred to not by name but only by office, Pilate is referred to by name but not by office. No mention is made of his position as *praefectus* of Judea or to his imperial duties; his official status is as lightly sketched as possible. Similarly, while the high priest's one concern is to have Jesus put to death, Pilate seems in no hurry to condemn him; and while the high priest directs others toward a verdict (14:64), in Pilate's court it is the fickle Jewish crowd that, like the mob at a gladiatorial contest, pronounces in favor of crucifixion (15:13–15). I have argued elsewhere that Pilate is not to be read as a friendly, or even weak, character here.[76] He is quite aware of what is going on (15:10), and his repeated use of the title "king" seems more calculated to rile the people than genuinely to secure Jesus's release. Yet Mark's characterization of the prefect shows that, despite Jesus's *crucifixion*, the prime movers in his death were not the Roman authorities but hostile Jewish priestly leaders. Like John the Baptist earlier, Jesus is put to death by a fatal combination of murderous hatred (Herodias, the chief priests) and tyrannical rulers (Herod, Pilate) who delegate their authority and, in the end, vital questions over life and death to others (the dancing daughter, the crowd).[77]

The "characters" of both the high priest and Pilate, then, are sketched only insofar as they contribute to Mark's developing portrait of Jesus. They allow our author to explore questions of responsibility for Jesus's execution and reinforce the links between the Baptist, Jesus, and the fate of at least some of his followers (13:9–11). But what of the largest group of secondary characters, the disciples? What is their role in the Markan biography?

---

76. See Bond, *Pontius Pilate*, 103–16.

77. Useful explorations of the contrasts between the deaths of John and Jesus can be found in McVann, "The 'Passion,'" and A. Simmonds, "Mark's and Matthew's *Sub Rosa* Message in the Scene of Pilate and the Crowd," *JBL* 131 (2012): 733–54.

The Twelve

No group of Markan characters has aroused such close scholarly scrutiny as Jesus's disciples. Variously designated as "his/the disciples" (*hoi mathētai autou*), "those around him" (*hoi peri auton*), or "those who followed him" (*hoi akolouthountes*), the Markan Jesus is surrounded by what seem to be fluctuating groups of people. My interest in what follows, however, is the group identified as "the Twelve" (*hoi dōdeka*), Jesus's closest companions who accompany him throughout his ministry. What immediately strikes the modern reader about this group is their ambiguous role: in some scenes they drop their nets and follow Jesus without a second's pause (1:16–20) or successfully act as Jesus's deputies (6:7–13, 30), while in others they seem incapable of understanding Jesus's ministry (6:52; 8:32–3; 9:33–35; 10:35–41) and finally desert him (14:50).[78] This apparently complex portrayal of the disciples has been explained in various ways, but William Telford has helpfully identified two major lines of interpretation: the *polemical* view and the *pastoral* view.[79]

The *polemical* view puts great stress on what appear to be the disciples' negative traits: their lack of understanding, their fear and cowardice, their desire for personal glory, and their desertion of their master at the end (particularly the betrayal and denial by members of their group). This view rose to prominence with the work of the redaction critics in the 1960s and is most commonly associated with J. B. Tyson and Theodore Weeden.[80] Both regarded Mark's work as a polemical document that

78. For a useful overview of the disciples in Mark, see C. C. Black, *The Disciples according to Mark: Markan Redaction in Current Debate*, 2nd ed. (Grand Rapids: Eerdmans, 2012), 36–45.

79. These groups are from W. Telford, *The Theology of the Gospel of Mark* (Cambridge: Cambridge University Press, 1999), 131–37. In line with his particular interest in redaction, Black divides scholars into three "types," depending on how closely they assume Mark kept to his tradition; *Disciples*, 45–64. For the present purposes, the polemical/pastoral division appears most useful.

80. J. B. Tyson, "The Blindness of the Disciples in Mark," *JBL* 80 (1961): 261–68; T. J. Weeden, "The Heresy That Necessitated Mark's Gospel," *ZNW* 59 (1968): 145–58. See also J. Schreiber, "Die Christologie des Markusevangeliums," *ZThK* 58 (1961): 154–83; and W. H. Kelber, "Mark 14, 32–42: Gethsemane, Passion Christology and Discipleship Failure," *ZNW* 63 (1972): 166–87. J. D. Crossan would extend the polemic to cover the Jerusalem church, hence the negative portrayal of Jesus's family; "Mark and the Relatives of Jesus," *NovT* 15 (1973): 81–113. A more modern variant of this view comes from P. Middleton, "Suffering and the Creation of Christian Identity in the Gospel of Mark," in *T&T Clark Handbook to Social Identity in the New Testament*, ed. J. B. Tucker and C. A. Baker (London: Bloomsbury, 2014), 173–89. Taking a particularly harsh line toward the Twelve, Middleton argues not

aimed to combat an erroneous Christology within his own community. The two differing sides in the dispute are dramatized by the disciples on one hand (who hold the erroneous Christology) and Jesus on the other (who of course represents the correct, Markan view). Precisely what this Christology entailed, however, is not entirely clear. According to Tyson, Mark was attacking the Christology of the primitive Jerusalem church that overstressed Jesus's royal (Davidic) messiahship, while for Weeden the disciples represent a Hellenistic view of Jesus that denied the importance of the passion in favor of a triumphalist view of Jesus as a miracle-working divine man (*theios anēr*). In whatever way we delineate the erroneous Christology, however, Mark's response was the same: to stress the redemptive significance of Jesus's suffering and death.

The fundamental problem with this approach is that Mark's work does not appear to be primarily polemical. It was certainly possible for a *bios* to offer a distinctive view of a revered teacher, perhaps as an alternative to other accounts, but there is nothing to indicate that this was the case in the present work.[81] The fact that the *bios* was quickly referred to as a "gospel"—as good news—suggests that it was generally received as a more constructive work of encouragement and support.[82] More significantly, as David Daube points out, a teacher was held to be responsible for the behavior of his students; the close bond between master and disciple meant that criticizing his followers ran the very real risk of attacking Jesus himself.[83] And finally, the "polemic view" sits awkwardly with the many positive depictions of the

---

that they stand for a particular "heretical" group but that the Twelve themselves have lost all authority for Mark; thus Christian identity, he maintains, is constructed by Mark in *opposition* to the Twelve.

81. On the use of *bioi* to present a distinctive account of a teacher, see above, pp. 49–51.

82. E. Best, "The Role of the Disciples in Mark," *NTS* 23 (1976/77): 378. This does not of course mean that there are no polemic passages within the work; we saw in Chapter 3 that Mark may well have wanted to challenge certain assumptions and beliefs within his congregation (though working out what these may have been is no easy matter). There is, however, a world of difference between offering a new way to understand a hero within the shared assumptions of a supportive group and one that deliberately confronts and opposes strongly held prevailing assumptions.

83. D. Daube, "Responsibility of Master and Disciple in the Gospels," *NTS* 19 (1972/73): 1–15; so also E. Best, "Role of the Disciples," 395; and A. D. Kaminouchi, *"But It Is Not So among You": Echoes of Power in Mark 10.32–45* (London: T&T Clark, 2003), 34. Hence, for example, Xenophon attempted to clear Socrates of the charge of corrupting the youth of Athens by arguing that the unruly Alcibiades had always been corrupt and that Socrates had merely failed to teach him morality.

disciples throughout the *bios*, and the fact that, despite setbacks, their intimate relationship with Jesus extends beyond the end of the work (14:27–8; 16:7).

The second, *pastoral* way of interpreting the Twelve is much more common today and is particularly advocated by those adopting a more literary perspective.[84] Rather than stress the failings of the disciples, this approach pays greater attention to the ambiguities and complexities within Mark's presentation. A pioneer here was Robert Tannehill in an essay published in 1977.[85] Tannehill notes that the (Christian) readers of Mark would doubtless identify with characters in the narrative who responded most positively to Jesus, that is, the disciples. Mark was aware of this and "composed his story . . . in order to speak indirectly to the reader through the disciples' story."[86] Thus the disciples start off well but very soon begin to reveal the inadequacy of their response: they are in conflict with Jesus over important issues and in the end are revealed as "disastrous failures," utterly unable to take up the cross and follow their master. The reader is shocked by this and wants to distance him- or herself, but still retains something of the initial identification. The resulting tension forces the reader to examine his or her own response to Jesus, and to choose a different path from that of the disciples.[87]

Since the publication of Tannehill's essay, there have been a flood of treatments of Mark's disciples, most of them fine-tuning and developing his initial points. David Rhoads, Joanna Dewey, and Donald Michie, for example, see the disciples as "round characters," who struggle to follow Jesus but who are hampered by their own lack of understanding, their preoccupation with status, and their competitive natures. Despite all their failings, though, the "story guides the reader to judge the disciples but not to reject them."[88] Similarly, Elizabeth Struthers Malbon sees them as "fallible followers," sympathetic characters who want to do the right thing but who ultimately fail.[89] Some scholars combine a literary approach with a historical one,

---

84. A number of redactional approaches also belong to this category, most importantly, D. Hawkin, "The Incomprehension of the Disciples in the Markan Redaction," *JBL* 91 (1972): 491–500; C. Focant, "L'incomprehension des Disciples dans le deuxieme Egangile," *Revue Biblique* 82 (1975): 161–68; and E. Best, "The Role of the Disciples in Mark," *NTS* 23 (1976/77): 377–401.

85. R. C. Tannehill, "The Disciples in Mark: The Function of a Narrative Role," in *The Interpretation of Mark*, ed. W. R. Telford, 2nd ed. (Edinburgh: T&T Clark, 1995).

86. Tannehill, "Disciples in Mark," 175.

87. Tannehill, "Disciples in Mark," 190.

88. Rhoads, Dewey, and Michie, *Mark as Story*, 123–30.

89. E. S. Malbon, "Fallible Followers: Women and Men in the Gospel of Mark," *Semeia* 28 (1983): 29–48, and "'Reflected Christology': An Aspect of Narrative 'Christology' in the Gospel of Mark," *Perspectives in Religious Studies* 26 (1999): 127–45. Along similar lines,

noting the references to persecution that feature so heavily in the gospel, and argue that the disciples give the audience encouragement in the face of discrimination and extreme suffering. If even the first disciples could fail, Mark's hearers should not be too downhearted by their own failure.[90]

These readings show a deep appreciation for the ambiguities of the account, and certainly offer a way for modern readers to make sense of what seem to be conflicting character traits. But is this really the way that Mark's *first-century audience* would have understood the role of the disciples? Two points need to be underscored here. First, as we have already seen (pp. 51–56 above), characters in biographies tended to be drawn as "types" rather than as moral agents with distinctive personalities and individual human frailties. Authors expected a certain level of "identification" with the protagonist, in that audiences were encouraged to distill the hero's virtues and to apply them to their own lives, but it would be unusual to focus the same level of attention onto the supporting cast. Except for where secondary characters functioned as occasional *exempla* (a topic we shall come back to below), other actors in a *bios* are there simply to provide a background for the hero.[91]

Second, as we have already seen, Mark's work, like many *bioi*, is a patchwork of small anecdotes; these are certainly arranged in an artful form, but there is little

---

see J. Hanson, "The Disciples in Mark's Gospel: Beyond the Pastoral/Polemical Debate," *Horizons in Biblical Theology* 20 (1998): 128–55.

90. For example, B. M. F. van Iersel, "Failed Followers in Mark: Mark 13:12 as a Key for the Identification of the Intended Readers," *CBQ* 58 (1996): 244–63, drawing on the argument of T. Radcliffe, "'The Coming of the Son of Man': Mark's Gospel and the Subversion of the Apocalyptic Image," in *Language, Meaning and God: Essays in Honour of Herbert McCabe, OP*, ed. B. Davies (London: Chapman, 1989), 15–36. See also L. W. Hurtado, "Following Jesus in the Gospel of Mark—and Beyond," in *Patterns of Discipleship in the New Testament*, ed. R. N. Longenecker (Grand Rapids: Eerdmans, 1996), esp. 17–25. Less plausibly, in my view, some have suggested Mark modeled his disciples on characters from the Scriptures: for example, S. Freyne sees links with the "elect" of Daniel ("The Disciples in Mark and the *maskilim* in Daniel: A Comparison," *JSNT* 16 [1982]: 7–23) while R. Strelan appeals to the Watchers of Gen. 6:1 ("The Fallen Watchers and the Disciples in Mark," *JSP* 20 [1999]: 73–92).

91. M. A. Tolbert recognizes the typological nature of Markan characters. She takes the four different responses found in the parable of the sower to be representative of various characters within the text, with the disciples illustrating the "seed on rocky ground" (Peter himself is linked to a "rock" in 3:16)—they accept the word with joy, but quickly fall away in the face of persecution; "How the Gospel of Mark Builds Character," *Int* 47 (1993): 347–57. Ingenious as this theory is, it seems to me to cast the disciples in too harsh a light.

sense of coherence, development, or even consistency among secondary characters. With only a few exceptions, Mark's disciples tend to act as a group rather than as individuals; we are told nothing of their inner lives, hopes, or motivations.[92] They appear long enough to make a certain point in a particular scene and then disappear again, giving an overall effect of fracture and fragmentation. What drives the narrative is not the actions and decisions of characters, but the inexorable divinely willed movement toward Jerusalem and the cross. The storyline has already been determined before the *bios* even starts; as Scott Elliott observes, "characters enter a plot that is already in play before their arrival and that continues once they are gone."[93]

Two examples will illustrate these points. First, the disciples' entirely successful mission in 6:7-13, 30, seems oddly discordant with their incomprehension elsewhere, particularly as it will manifest itself in their very next appearance at the feeding of the multitude (6:31-44). This has encouraged scholars to scrutinize the brief report of their success in 6:30 and to detect an underlying irony that will in fact pave the way for their later failure. Thus Francis Moloney points out that they "announce" their achievements to Jesus as if they are masters of the situation, reporting everything that *they* have done and taught without acknowledging that their success is due entirely to Jesus. What seemed like a simple and positive report is now turned into a scene replete with "early signs of failure."[94] But this is surely an oversubtle interpretation of an excessively brief report (only sixteen words in Greek). There is nothing in Mark's account to suggest failure; the Twelve behave as model apostles here (and, as already noted, Mark casts them as envoys of the kingdom as part of the elaborate contrast between Jesus and King Herod). It is only when we try to impose a psychologically coherent portrait of the disciples and to make sense of their actions across *pericopae* that such a strategy seems necessary.

92. Peter is the only disciple whose words are ever reported: 8:29, 32; 9:5, 38 (here with John); 10:28; 11:21. On Peter, see below, pp. 206-9.

93. S. S. Elliott, "'Witless in Your Own Cause': Divine Plots and Fractured Characters in the Life of Aesop and the Gospel of Mark," *Religion and Theology* 12 (2005): 408; Elliott notes a similar fragmentation in the *Life of Aesop*. See also the helpful discussions of P. Merenlahti and R. Hakola, "Reconceiving Narrative Criticism," in *Characterization in the Gospel: Reconceiving Narrative Criticism*, ed. D. Rhoads and K. Syreeni (Sheffield: Sheffield Academic, 1999), 13-48, here 13-33; Shiner, *Follow Me!*, 3-8; and O. Lehtipuu, "Characterization and Persuasion: The Rich Man and the Poor Man in Luke 16.19-31," in Rhoads and Syreeni, *Characterization*, 80.

94. F. J. Moloney, "Mark 6:6b-30: Mission, the Baptist, and Failure," *CBQ* 63 (2001): esp. 660-61; and also Miller, "Intercalation," 189-91. In a similar vein, Fowler takes the disciples' peevish response in 6:36-38 to indicate that they *had* taken bread and money with them on their missionary journey, despite Jesus's command not to; *Loaves*, 117-18.

The second illustration concerns Peter. When we left him at Caesarea Philippi, Peter had been sternly reprimanded by Jesus, who not only referred to him as "Satan" but also accused him of being on the side of humans rather than God (8:33). His next appearance, however, is at the transfiguration scene, where he appears as one of Jesus's closest confidants, as if the embarrassing scene at Caesarea Philippi six days earlier had never taken place (9:2–8). What are we to make of this? Are we to assume that he and Jesus have talked things through? That the rebuke was less serious than it initially appeared? Or—as I have urged above—that Mark has no interest in creating a coherent characterization, either for Peter or for any other supporting actor?

None of this is to belittle Mark's literary achievement. If the form critics emphasized the gospel's episodic design too much—to the extent that individual *pericopae* appeared random and disconnected—narrative critics have tended to impose too much coherence on the text. Most modern narrative-critical discussions of the Twelve tend to assume that Mark writes "a single, unified story," in which the plot, settings, and characterization are all entirely coherent and consistent.[95] Where there are awkward jumps, or "narratorial slumbers,"[96] of the kind just identified, they appeal to the reader's imagination to fill the gaps.[97] The danger here is that modern readers expect to find coherent characters and are liable to fill the gaps in ways that achieve this (as illustrated above). Mark's text achieves its unity, however, in a very different way: what links all the episodes for our author is the central character, Jesus. The primary purpose of the *bios* is to highlight *his* qualities, to encourage others to imitate *him*, and to join the company of those who gather in his name. Mark's focus on Jesus is so all-pervading that other characters exist only to bring Jesus's *ēthos* and virtues into greater clarity. As Whitney Shiner rightly observes, "*Characters in Mark's Gospel serve primarily to further the portrayal of Jesus.*"[98]

95. See, for example, Rhoads, Dewey, and Michie, *Mark as Story*, 1–5; the quotation is from Tannehill, "Disciples in Mark," 171.

96. The phrase is from Syreeni, "Peter as Character," 149; Syreeni is talking about Matthew here, but the point is also true for Mark.

97. As Shiner wryly observes, "When the flat disciples of the individual episodes are strung together "as pearls on a string," they can be seen as multisided, but it may only be our modern penchant for complexity of characterization that we have discovered" (p. 12). This is a strategy shared, of course, with reader-response approaches; on the connections between the two approaches, see J. L. Resseguie, *Narrative Criticism of the New Testament: An Introduction* (Grand Rapids: Baker Academic, 2005), 30–33. On different concepts of "unity" in antiquity, see Merenlahti and Hakola, "Reconceiving," 31–33, a point conceded by Rhoads in "Narrative Criticism," 268.

98. Shiner, *Follow Me!*, 8 (italics original), also 13, 29 (and throughout his excellent book).

All of this means that it was not only inappropriate but also unnecessary for an ancient audience to look to the Twelve as examples of discipleship: as we saw in the last chapter, *Jesus himself performs that role*. While noting Jesus's exemplary portrait in Mark, however, scholars are often reluctant to accept the full implications of this.[99] The idea that Jesus himself should act as a model seems counterintuitive to modern readers. Mark Allan Powell's discussion of the Matthean Jesus is a good illustration of this. Powell notes that the modern reader's identification with Jesus will be "idealistic" in that "he represents the perfect model for what the implied reader would like to be." And to some extent this identification is encouraged by the text itself (especially in passages such as Matt 18:15–20; 25:31–45; 28:20). In other respects, however, "empathy with Jesus is severely limited," as "the character of Jesus is defined by a number of traits that the implied reader could never own": Jesus is saving (1:21), "authoritative" (23:8, 10), and "eternally present" (18:20; 28:20) "in ways to which the implied reader could never aspire." On this basis, Powell concludes that Matthew's readers will look to the disciples, rather than Jesus, as models for their own journeys.[100] Similar things could, of course, be said about the Markan Jesus: the text both encourages followers to imitate him (as we saw earlier) and yet also presents him as one who can forgive sins (2:5–12), raise the dead (5:35–43), and walk on water (6:45–51). The significant point here, however, as we saw in Chapter 4, is that imitation of the heroes of biographies does not mean following every detail of their lives, but rather seeing their character and modeling one's life on that. Thus Mark's readers are no more called upon to walk on water than readers of Plutarch's generals are to engage in battle, or readers

---

For similar points, see also Best, "Role of the Disciples," 399, and Best, "Mark's Narrative Technique," *JSNT* 37 (1989): esp. 51–53; R. A. Burridge, *Four Gospels, One Jesus? A Symbolic Reading*, 2nd ed. (Grand Rapids: Eerdmans, 2005), 46–49, and Burridge, *Imitating Jesus: An Inclusive Approach to New Testament Ethics* (Grand Rapids: Eerdmans, 2007), 163 and 182; Hurtado, "Following," 25–27; Borrell, *Good News*, 23; Lehtipuu, "Characterization," 73–105; and B. Witherington, *The Gospel of Mark: A Socio-Rhetorical Commentary* (Grand Rapids: Eerdmans, 2001), 3.

99. Tannehill notes that Jesus represents the positive alternative to the failure of the disciples, but seems reluctant to cast Jesus as a role model; "Disciples in Mark," 179–80; see also his "The Gospel of Mark as Narrative Christology," *Semeia* 16 (1979): 57–95. Similarly, J. F. Williams notes that Jesus repeatedly presents himself as the true paradigm for his followers in 8:27–10:45, noting the absence of any other exemplary characters here (so as not to detract from Jesus), but he does not appreciate that Jesus's paradigmatic qualities extend throughout the gospel, and prefers to look to "minor characters" as examples of discipleship; "Discipleship and Minor Characters in Mark's Gospel," *Bibliotheca Sacra* 153 (1996): 332–43.

100. Powell, *What Is Narrative Criticism?*, 56.

of Philostratus's *Life of Apollonius of Tyana* are to acquire miraculous powers. It is taken for granted that the hero is far superior than any who might come after him; what is important is that readers take away the character and way of life of the hero, and model themselves on that.[101]

The central role occupied by Jesus gives Mark much greater freedom with "the Twelve." They are not required to be "perfect" followers; they appear only in order to highlight something of the teaching and work of Jesus. In the following pages, I shall argue that the Markan disciples perform three main roles: (1) they aid Mark's presentation of Jesus as an exemplary and authoritative teacher who gathers a circle of followers (in this case by acting as praiseworthy followers); (2) they allow Jesus to expand on his teaching, particularly as it becomes increasingly difficult (in this case by their questions and misunderstanding); and (3) they allow Mark to highlight Jesus's courageous and lonely death (through their cowardice, and by providing counterexamples). We shall look at each of these in turn, but first it is worth asking one very basic question: What did Mark's audience know about the disciples above and beyond his *bios*?

Most narrative-critical discussions of Mark's disciples tend to confine themselves to the "story-world" created by the gospel itself. As Rhoads and Michie note, "Mark's narrative contains a closed and self-sufficient world with its own integrity, its own imaginative past and future, its own sets of values, and its own universe of meanings."[102] While a certain amount of historical information is deemed essential (as we might need to know something of Victorian England's gender, class, or clerical codes fully to appreciate Trollope's *Chronicles of Barsetshire*), events outside the text are deemed inadmissible.[103] This is largely due to narrative criticism's indebtedness to studies of modern novels where characters and events are (largely) fictional. But of course Mark's work is not a novel: as we saw in Chapter 2, biography deals, however creatively, with people and events that have counterparts in the real world. Moreover, the work was written for people who already knew the basic contours of the Christian story, and quite likely much else (hence Mark has no need to introduce John the Baptist or Pilate).[104] Thus Mark's portrait of the dis-

---

101. Our own, post-Chalcedonian position may also make it more difficult for modern audiences fully to consider imitating Jesus. Mark does not operate in a world where the lines between the human and the divine are quite so starkly drawn. See above, p. 155.

102. Rhoads and Michie, *Mark as Story*, 4; similar views are expressed in the 3rd ed. (with Dewey), 4–5.

103. So Rhoads, "Narrative Criticism: Practices and Prospects," 268; Powell, *What Is Narrative Criticism?*, 20; Resseguie, *Narrative Criticism*, 29–30, 33.

104. See above, pp. 54–55.

ciples could never be the sum total of all that his audience knows about them. The Markan disciples occupy a space alongside other, widely known traditions about these men—just as Mark's portraits of Pilate, King Herod, or John the Baptist were inevitably colored by whatever prior knowledge the audience brought to those texts. It is unlikely that listeners differentiated between the Markan disciples and whatever they knew of them outside the *bios*.[105]

But what exactly did early Christ-following audiences know about the disciples? From Paul's letters we can infer that most Christian groups knew that Jesus had twelve disciples and also that the figure of Peter was particularly well known.[106] Paul takes it for granted that Christ followers in both Galatia and Corinth know of Peter, and, despite their theological differences (Gal 2:11–14), the apostle always speaks of him highly and considers it necessary to spend time with him before he embarks on his own endeavors (Gal 1:18). He assumes that his audience knows of Peter's missionary activity (1 Cor 9:5; Gal 2:7–8), that they are aware of the tradition that Jesus appeared to him first (1 Cor 15:5), and it was surely no surprise for them to learn that Peter was regarded as a "pillar" of the Jerusalem church (Gal 2:9).[107] All of this was presumably equally well known to Mark's audience (wherever they were situated)[108] and is indirectly confirmed by a number

105. For similar arguments, see J. R. Donahue, "Windows and Mirrors: The Setting of Mark's Gospel," *CBQ* 57 (1995): esp. 4–8; Merenlahti and Hakola, "Reconceiving Narrative Criticism," 34–48; so also K. Syreeni, "Peter as Character and Symbol in the Gospel of Matthew," 106–52, who argues for an intermediate, symbolic world between the historical and the narrative.

106. Jesus's brother James occupies an ambiguous role in Paul: see Gal 1:19, 2:1–10, 12; 1 Cor 15:7. Curiously, apart from a brief mention in 6:3, James is absent from Mark. James's known adherence to the Law would presumably have led to his low standing among Mark's largely gentile, nonobservant audience. On James, see the essays in *The Brother of Jesus: James the Just and His Mission*, ed. B. Chilton and J. Neusner (Louisville: Westminster John Knox, 2001).

107. In both Galatians and 1 Corinthians, Paul refers to Peter by his Aramaic name, Cephas. See M. Williams, "From Shimon to Petros—Petrine Nomenclature in the Light of Contemporary Onomastic Practices," in *Peter in Early Christianity*, ed. H. K. Bond and L. W. Hurtado (Grand Rapids: Eerdmans, 2015), 30–45.

108. If Mark is to be located in Rome, then at least some of Mark's listeners may have had a personal connection with Peter. See my essay, "Was Peter behind Mark's Gospel?," in Bond and Hurtado, *Peter in Early Christianity*, 46–61. See also M. N. A. Bockmuehl, who outlines what "living memory" of Peter might have still been alive in Rome prior to Mark's work: *Simon Peter in Scripture and Memory: The New Testament Apostle in the Early Church* (Grand Rapids: Baker Academic, 2012), 141–50.

of hints within the work itself. The first time that we meet Peter (or Simon as he is at this point), Jesus promises to make him and his brother Andrew "fishers of people" (1:17). Unusually, this is a promise that is not clearly fulfilled within the *bios*, a feature that strongly suggests that Mark is relying on the audience's knowledge of Peter's *later* activities. Thus, as Whitney Shiner notes, this introduction to the disciples grounds Mark's whole discussion of them in the post-Easter story.[109] Despite their failures, the work points forward to their future restoration in the post-resurrection age (14:28; 16:7). Similarly, the future warnings contained in ch. 13 and the prediction of the fate of James and John (10:35–40) make no sense unless they are understood against the background of future faithfulness beyond the time of Jesus.[110] All of this tends to support Ernest Best's view that our author wrote for people who knew the subsequent history of the disciples and who were predisposed to treat them with respect and honor.[111]

We need to tread carefully here: just because the disciples have counterparts in the real world does not mean that they are any less Markan creations. They are still "paper people," cut by our author to fit the needs of his literary product.[112] What the audience's positive disposition toward them means, however, is that they were unlikely to have understood the disciples' misunderstandings and failures as criticisms. They may have been surprised and perhaps troubled by their difficulties, but this would be firmly embedded in a context of admiration and perhaps even reverence for Jesus's first followers. What the disciples' failures illustrate is just how difficult even the celebrated leaders of the movement found it to understand Jesus at first, especially before the resurrection.

With all of this in mind, then, we shall look at the three main ways in which the Twelve contribute to Mark's emerging portrait of Jesus.

---

109. Shiner, *Follow Me!*, 186. It is the resurrection, more so than the cross, that marks the turning point for Mark; see 9:9–10 in particular and fuller discussion in Watson, *Honor among Christians*, 74–83.

110. So also Hurtado, "Following," 23.

111. Best, "Role of the Disciples," 400; see also C. E. B. Cranfield, who argues that the relentlessness with which Mark underscores Peter's failure is most easily understood on the assumption that he had died a martyr's death by the time Mark wrote: "Mark's frankness, which earlier would have seemed malicious, would after Peter's martyrdom be welcomed as underlining the encouragement it afforded to weak disciples"; *The Gospel according to Saint Mark* (Cambridge: Cambridge University Press, 1959), 8. If there was a connection between Mark and Peter, or even Mark and Rome (a city where Peter was well known), this would only strengthen the comments made in this paragraph; see above, pp. 9, 108.

112. The term is from Elliott, "Witless," 401.

Jesus: An Exemplary and Authoritative Teacher
Who Gathers a Circle of Followers

Jesus's first act after the opening prologue is to gather a community of disciples around him. He takes the initiative, calls his own followers, and is instantly obeyed. Strikingly, Mark offers no reasons why some are called and others are not. Previous behavior does not seem to be important, and Jesus is quite happy to extend his calling to those generally regarded as disreputable, such as the tax collector Levi (2:14). When a would-be disciple comes to Jesus on his own initiative in 10:17–27, he is turned away. Following Jesus is an unexpected gift (4:11), an act of grace freely given by Jesus and requiring only a positive response.[113]

Jesus's disciples openly accompany him as he travels around Galilee, look for him when he takes himself away to a lonely place (1:36), and share his scandalous table fellowship (2:15–17).[114] It is not until 3:13–19, however, that Jesus "creates" the Twelve, choosing certain men to be his special companions.[115] Not only are they appointed to be with him, to preach, and to have authority over demons, but they are also called by name, beginning with Peter and ending with Judas. The renaming of disciples by their teachers was not uncommon (there are several examples in Diogenes Laertius's *Lives*),[116] and the reference to Judas's betrayal here is presumably intended to reassure the audience that Jesus knew, even at this early stage, what was in Judas's heart. In 6:7–13, 30, the Twelve are sent out in pairs on a successful mission, proving themselves eminently able to act as "apostles," to heal the sick, and to cast out demons. As the narrative progresses, it becomes abundantly clear that these twelve men have a close personal attachment to Jesus; they have made a clean break with the past, giving up their families and the comforts and securities of home in exchange for life with an itinerant preacher (10:28).

What is striking about this relationship is its intimacy. This is not simply a teacher-pupil relationship in which the teacher passes on a certain body of

113. E. S. Johnson, "Mark 10:46–52: Blind Bartimaeus," *CBQ* 40 (1978): 202; Shiner, *Follow Me!*, 246.

114. As Hurtado notes, Mark's use of plural verbs underlines the close connection between Jesus and his followers; Hurtado, "Following," 18 (drawing here on the work of C. H. Turner).

115. Mark uses the verb *poieō* here which gives a sense of "created" rather than simply "appointed"; so also Hanson, "Disciples," 138.

116. Aristotle, for example, renamed Tyrtamus Theophrastus on account of his graceful style (*Lives of Eminent Philosophers* 5.38); and Chrisippus got his name (which means "horse-hidden") from the philosopher Carneades because his statue in the Ceramicus was hidden by that of a horse (7.179).

teaching to students who pay for the privilege, or who join for a short time only—like the pupils of the Sophists, or Josephus and his teacher Bannus.[117] As Hans Weder observes, "the disciple is not there merely to learn from the teacher but to share his whole life with him without reservation."[118] Once again, the crucial idea here is one of imitation: the disciples devote their lives to Jesus, learning not only from his teaching, but from the way in which he conducts his life. There are similarities here with the relationship between Socrates and his "companions" (*hetairoi*),[119] or the tightly knit religious circles that gathered around Pythagoras, Epictetus, or Apollonius of Tyana.[120] Similar, too, is the sense that while a disciple is called to become like his master, he can never take his place. For Mark, all that the disciple can ever achieve comes ultimately from Jesus (as 6:7–13 makes plain).[121]

The close relationship between Jesus and the disciples is assumed by other characters in the biography. Jesus's opponents bring their criticisms of the Twelve to Jesus himself, and he is quick to defend their behavior (2:18–22, 23–28).[122] Conversely, the scribes of the Pharisees fully expect the disciples to be able to justify their

117. See K. Rengstorf, "μαθητης," *TDNT* 4:420; on Josephus's three years with his teacher Bannus, see his *Life* 11–12.

118. H. Weder, "Disciple, Discipleship," *ABD* 2:207–10 (trans. D. Martin).

119. See the useful discussion in Rengstorf, "μαθητης," esp. 415–26 (on *mathētēs* in the Greek world). Socrates rejected the teacher/*mathētēs* model, on the grounds that it smacked too much of the relationship between the Sophists and their students—he did not accept payment and offered something more than instruction. The basis of his relationship to those gathered about him was his own person, so he preferred the image of companions (see Plato, *Theaetetus* 150d; Xenophon, *Memorabilia* 1.4.19; 1.7.5). According to Diogenes Laertius, Socrates told Xenophon to "follow me and learn" when the latter was unable to tell Socrates where men in Athens went to become good and honorable (*Lives of Eminent Philosophers* 2.48). Nothing like this exists in either the Hebrew Scriptures or the later rabbinic schools (the word *mathētēs* is not found in the LXX); the relations between Elijah and Elisha and between Jeremiah and Baruch are more of master and assistant (Rengstorf, "μαθητης," 426–31).

120. On the markedly religious dimension here, in which disciples formed closely knit circles that venerated their leader and that were able to survive his death, see Rengstorf, "μαθητης," 421–23 (with references). Lucian seems to be mocking this type of close-knit religious community when he talks of the disciples of Peregrinus possibly erecting a sanctuary to him on the place where he set fire to himself; *The Passing of Peregrinus* 28, 30, 29, 41.

121. So also Weder, "Disciple," 208.

122. As Daube notes, Jesus does not seem at all surprised to be questioned about his disciples' behavior; "Responsibility," 4.

master's scandalous eating arrangements (2:15–17). In these public scenes there is no gap between the teacher and his followers.

In all of these episodes, the Twelve symbolize the model community constructed around Jesus. They are the precursors of the "family of faith" in Mark's own day (3:31–35), and their actions in 6:7–13, 30, anticipate those of Christian missionaries beyond the time of Jesus. But at their most fundamental level, they contribute to a portrait of Jesus as an authoritative teacher at the center of a tightly knit group, whose call is instantly obeyed, who knows his disciples intimately, and who inspires devotion.

Jesus: Teacher of Difficult Truths

If the Twelve serve as model disciples in public, they take on a rather different role in private. Here they act as questioners, drawing Jesus out on certain topics, and allowing him to develop his teaching in more depth. So, for example, they ask Jesus about the parable of the sower, a query that allows him to continue his instruction throughout most of ch. 4.[123] Their question about purity allows Jesus to expand upon his theme in 7:14–23; it is at the disciples' prompting that Jesus explains his teaching on divorce in clearer terms in 10:10–12; and the wonder of a small inner group at the size of the temple ashlars allows Jesus to teach about future events in 13:3–37.[124] At other times it is the disciples' misunderstanding that prompts Jesus to explain more fully, specifically the extension of God's promises to the gentiles (8:14–21),[125] the necessity for Jesus's death (8:32–33), or the nature of true greatness (9:33–37; 10:35–45).

It is important to recognize that the questions and misunderstandings of the Twelve do not in any way threaten their status as privileged insiders. Their inability to grasp Jesus's teaching, particularly the new honor code that Jesus seeks to establish, would be equally difficult for Mark's contemporary listeners to understand, entrenched as they also were in the prevailing cultural norms. The questions of the Twelve are only those that any ancient listener might have had. As Shiner observes,

---

123. Although the parable is explained in 4:10–20, the teaching actually extends until 4:32.

124. Within the Twelve, Mark identifies a smaller group composed of Peter, James, and John and sometimes Andrew (5:37–43; 9:2–8; 13:3–37; 14:33–42). This group is privy not only to certain events (such as the raising of Jairus's daughter and the transfiguration) but also to special teaching (e.g., 9:9, and here in ch. 13).

125. J. B. Gibson argues, persuasively in my view, that this is the meaning here, rather than a general lack of faith on the disciples' part; "The Rebuke of the Disciples in Mark 8:14–21," *JSNT* 27 (1986): 31–47.

"In their lack of comprehension, the disciples represent the general human condition rather than a perverse reaction of an especially corrupt group."[126] What their lack of comprehension does is to highlight both the complexities of Jesus's teaching and its countercultural and difficult nature. In effect, the disciples' questions and misinterpretations give Mark's audience permission to contemplate the demands that following Jesus involves, and to afford Mark space to explain them in greater depth. Far from characterizing the disciples as chronically lacking in understanding, then, what we have here is a literary device that allows Mark to offer further instruction to his listening audience.[127]

All of this was common in the *bioi* of philosophers. In a detailed comparison of Mark with Xenophon's *Memorabilia*, Vernon Robbins highlights the way in which Socrates's companion-disciples learn through asking questions. As he notes, occasional failures, false starts, and corrections are all expected aspects of this particular relationship and do not carry the moral weight that would accompany such features in the Hebrew Bible.[128] In his *Life of Plotinus*, Porphyry often notes his own lack of understanding (10.31, 35–39), a narrative device that emphasizes the difficulty of comprehending Plotinus's philosophy (clearly Porphyry remains a faithful follower, even to the extent of making his master's works available to a wider public).[129] Similarly, opposition to the master's death is a common feature of biographical narrative: we need only think of the distress Socrates's impending death causes to his companions (*Phaedo* 116a, 117c–e) or consider Lucian's highly cynical presentation of the distress caused to his disciples by Peregrinus's intention to set fire to himself (*The Passing of Peregrinus* 33).[130] Readers would hardly be surprised, then, by Peter's resistance to his master's impending death in 8:32. More striking still are the similarities between Peter and Damis in Philostratus's account of Apollonius of Tyana. Damis is Apollonius's first and most cherished disciple, yet he is frequently portrayed as lacking understanding (*Life of Apollonius*

126. Shiner, *Follow Me!*, 251.

127. So also Best, "Disciples in Mark," 399; and Telford, *Theology*, 131–32, who notes, "In addressing his disciples in private, the Markan Jesus is in actuality addressing the church, for whom the Gospel was written and expanding on the tradition in the light of the community's contemporary needs" (132). There are similarities here to the character of Dr. Watson in A. Conan Doyle's Sherlock Holmes novels, whose lack of perspicuity allows the great detective to describe the steps by which he solves his cases in some depth.

128. Robbins, *Jesus the Teacher*, 125–69; see also Best, "Role," 384.

129. G. Miles, "'I, Porphyry': The Narrator of the *Vita Plotini*," in *Open Access Australasian Society for Classical Studies Proceedings, 2–5 February 2010* (Perth: University of Western Australia, 2010), 3–4.

130. Shiner, *Follow Me!*, 256–57, 271–73.

of Tyana 1.21–22; 2.22; 7.37) or fearful (6.25; 7.31), and is commonly reprimanded by Apollonius (7.26).[131] Damis's failings provide a foil to his master, and underscore Apollonius's fidelity to his philosophical teachings all the more.[132]

A common motif in Jewish apocalyptic texts may also be relevant here. John Markley identifies what he calls "human imperception in the face of divinely revealed mysteries" in works such as Daniel, 1 Enoch, 4 Ezra, 2 Baruch, and others.[133] In these texts, angelic mediators frequently respond with puzzlement or surprise at the human seer's inability to grasp what is being revealed to him. The purpose of this response, however, is not to denigrate the seer (who is often explicitly said to be exceptionally righteous) but to "identify the limits of the seer's unaided human comprehension."[134] The motif heightens the heavenly quality of what is revealed, making it clear that the teaching comes not from the seer's own intellect, but directly from God. Although apocalypse is a very different genre from biography, Mark's work does have apocalyptic touches (most notably in ch. 13) and it may be that our author has drawn on both genres in his depiction of the disciples at this point. What Jesus reveals are heavenly "secrets" (4:11), which even his closest followers find almost impossible to grasp.

Overall, then, the disciples' persistent questioning and misunderstanding would not have been seen by an ancient audience as an indication of "failure" but as part of the expected interaction between a religious teacher and his students. Mark's Gospel certainly includes a large number of episodes featuring questions and misunderstandings, but the primary purpose of this is to highlight the difficulty of Jesus's teaching and perhaps too its quality as divine revelation rather than the obtuseness of his inner circle.[135] The confusion of the Twelve allows Jesus's teaching to stand out all the more clearly, highlighting just how much he asks of followers, and how much it will cost him to walk that path himself.

131. Also noted by Best, "Disciples in Mark," 395–96. C. H. Dodd finds a similar lack of understanding in Hermetic literature; *Historical Tradition in the Fourth Gospel* (Cambridge: Cambridge University Press, 1963), 319–21.

132. So also Shiner, *Follow Me!*, 132–35.

133. J. R. Markley, "Reassessing Peter's Imperception in Synoptic Tradition," in Bond and Hurtado, *Peter in Early Christianity*, 101. See also his full-length study, *Peter—Apocalyptic Seer* (Tübingen: Mohr Siebeck, 2013), esp. 41–114.

134. Markley, "Reassessing," 101.

135. J. Dewey rightly notes that the "negative" portrayal of disciples was probably taken far less seriously by a first-century listening audience than by modern ones accustomed to printed texts; "Mark as Interwoven Tapestry: Forecasts and Echoes for a Listening Audience," *CBQ* 53 (1991): 235–36.

Jesus: A Courageous and Lonely Death

Once Jesus arrives in Jerusalem (11:1–11), the disciples no longer seem confused. Their "failure" in this final section seems to be one of nerve. They have accepted that Jesus must die, but Peter, followed by the others, thinks that he can stand firm (14:29–31). Jesus, however, knows better and predicts that one of them will betray him, Peter will deny him, and all will fall away (14:26–31). As the narrative progresses, each of these predictions comes true.

Yet once again we should be wary of judging the Twelve too harshly here. They fall away at the end because they *must*—their desertion in 14:26–28 was foreseen by God in Scripture (Zech 13:7) and is all part of a larger divine purpose. We shall see in the next chapter that the Markan Jesus goes to the cross alone, quite simply because he is the only one able to do so. Only he can endure to the bitter end, only he is able to face the terrifying power of evil, and only he will be raised again by God.[136] At this stage in the narrative, no one else—not Peter, nor the rest of the Twelve, nor any other person—could follow his lead. The focus throughout is on Jesus, the perfect example of a life of discipleship. As earlier, the disciples act as foils to Jesus: just as earlier their self-importance and competition for status showed his humility, now their weakness and cowardice throw the strength and courage of Jesus into sharp relief.[137] What the desertion of the disciples at this point does, then, is to put Jesus in the spotlight, to enhance his dignity and resolve in the face of death, and to underline his utter obedience to the will of God. Once Jesus has been raised from the dead, others can follow in his path, and the *bios* clearly sees a role here for the Twelve. An appearance to them in Galilee is plainly predicted by Jesus in 14:28, and a second promise of such an event forms the central element in the message of the angelic young man at the tomb (16:7). Despite the disciples' absence from his painful and lonely death, then, Mark clearly sees a later role for the Twelve. They will be reinstated—and this time they will be able to follow their master, even to death (as 10:35–40 and 13:9–13 make clear).

As earlier, the use of the disciples as a foil for their master has parallels within other *bioi*. Socrates's grief-stricken friends throw their master's calm resolve and refusal to save his life into relief (Plato, *Phaedo* 115e, 117d–e). And Philostratus's *Life of Apollonius of Tyana* frequently contrasts the hero's courage with his followers' numerous failures; when Apollonius first travels to Rome under Nero, only eight

---

136. Tolbert, "How the Gospel of Mark," 356.
137. Best, "Disciples in Mark," 399.

of his thirty-four companions stand by him (4.37), and Damis's constant fear frequently highlights the philosopher's bold resolve (7.13–15, 31, 38, 41).[138]

Within this section of his work, Mark pays particular attention to the behavior of two disciples, presenting them to his audience as negative *exempla*: first Judas, then Peter.[139] We have already noted the prevalence of *exempla* in the Greco-Roman educational system, along with their widespread use within both history and biography.[140] These short vignettes generally highlighted one character trait (courage, loyalty, kindness, and so on), and could be both positive and negative, highlighting either paradigms of behavior to emulate or warnings of what to avoid. *Exempla* are common both in Jewish literature with a Hellenistic coloring (for example, Ben Sira's casting of Solomon as the model sage; 47:13–18) and in early Christian writings (for example, Heb 11; James 2:21–26; or Acts 4:34–5:11). While Roman authors tended to draw on acknowledged "villains" for negative examples, however, Jewish writers seem to have been much more willing to exploit the failings of even the greatest of heroes.[141]

Both Judas and Peter provide negative examples, depicting the type of behavior Mark's audience should avoid. Judas takes on the role of "betrayer," a disloyal follower who colludes with his master's enemies in engineering his arrest (14:10–11). Many details that modern readers would like to know (particularly the reasons for his actions) go untold: Mark's interest here is rigidly confined to the act of betrayal itself. The only extraneous detail our author allows himself is the reminder that Judas was "one of the twelve" (14:10), a note that increases the sense of tragedy in the scene. Judas shows that even the closest follower can be a betrayer: if Judas could act in this way, so could anyone—all are potential Judases.[142] The Markan Jesus has already warned that family members (presumably Christian believers) will be divided, and that one will deliver another over to death (13:22), a passage that may well suggest that many in Mark's audience have had experience of betrayal themselves.[143]

138. Once again, this is also noted by Shiner, *Follow Me!*, 132–35.

139. Shiner, *Follow Me!*, 16.

140. See above, pp. 46–47.

141. Best, "Disciples in Mark," 396, who cites the use of King David by Jewish writers.

142. Stock, *Call to Discipleship*, 194–95.

143. Van Iersel, "Failed Followers," 256. If Mark is to be located in Rome (see above, pp. 8–9), there is a strong link here to contemporary events. Tacitus notes that during the Neronian persecution many martyrs were convicted on the evidence of others (*Annals* 15.44); although writing fifty years or so later, there is no strong reason to doubt his testimony here. See C. P. Jones, "The Historicity of the Neronian Persecution: A Response to Brent Shaw," *NTS* 63 (2017): 146–52.

If so, Judas's example takes on a very real and sinister coloring and acts as a warning to any who might be tempted to betray fellow believers in Mark's own day.[144]

Peter's denial functions in a similar manner. Of all the disciples, Peter receives the most attention in Mark's *bios*: he is the first to be called, he stands at the head of the Twelve, and he is the first to be renamed. Even within Jesus's inner group, Peter always takes precedence (1:29; 5:37; 9:2; 13:3; 14:33) and typically acts as a spokesman for the Twelve (1:36; 8:29; 9:5–6; 10:28; 11:21; 14:29–31).[145] He follows Jesus longer than any other disciple, but his desertion is also highlighted more than that of anyone else: Jesus predicts his denial (14:30–31)—it is recounted at some length (14:66–72) and even includes a reference to the earlier prophecy (14:72). All of this gives the impression of a characteristically Markan triple repetition, presumably underlying the shocking completeness of Peter's denial.[146] Yet for all of this narrative attention, Peter does not become a "rounded" character.[147] The focus in the high priest's courtyard is entirely on the act of denial itself, as Peter's threefold

144. Drawing on the later criticisms of Celsus (Origen, *Against Celsus* 2.12, 18) and the "criterion of embarrassment," scholars usually suppose that Judas's betrayal belongs to pre-Markan tradition. There is, however, no prior evidence for this. As Fowler notes, references to *paradosis* in Paul do not necessarily indicate betrayal by a disciple: 1 Cor 11:23 may simply refer to Jesus's arrest; Rom 4:25 and 8:32 seem to indicate Jesus's handing over by God; while Gal 2:20 suggests that Jesus delivered himself up. Furthermore, Paul shows no knowledge of Judas losing his privileged place—in 1 Cor 15:5 the risen Jesus appears to the *Twelve* (*Loaves*, 136, 224n81). A. Y. Collins similarly raises the possibility that the Judas story was invented "as an incident in keeping with Jesus's apparent abandonment by all" ("From Noble Death to Crucified Messiah," *NTS* 40 [1994]: 492). If these scholars are correct, then Mark may have deliberately crafted the Judas story as an *exemplum* to warn of the dangers of betrayal, and perhaps also to form a pair along with the Peter story.

145. For useful overviews, see Black, *Disciples*, 37–45; E. Best, "Peter in the Gospel according to Mark," *CBQ* 40 (1978): 547–58; T. E. Boomershine, "Peter's Denial as Polemic or Confession: The Implications of Media Criticism for Biblical Hermeneutics," *Semeia* 39 (1987): 47–68; and P. Merenlahti, "Characters in the Making: Individuality and Ideology in the Gospels," in Rhoads and Syreeni, *Characterization*, 49–72; and R. Whitaker, "Rebuke or Recall? Rethinking the Role of Peter in Mark's Gospel," *CBQ* 75 (2013): 666–82. T. Wiarda argues for a greater level of "individualization" for Peter than is presented here, particularly in the denial episode; "Peter as Peter in the Gospel of Mark," *NTS* 45 (1999): 19–37. On Peter more generally, see M. Hengel, *Saint Peter: The Underestimated Apostle* (Grand Rapids: Eerdmans, 2010), and Bockmuehl, *Peter*.

146. For a thorough and perceptive analysis of this scene, see Borrell, *Good News*.

147. So also Syreeni, who asks, "Does the narrative really encourage the reader to take an interest in Peter's character or "personality," or does it rather make the reader look for a symbolic meaning?" ("Peter as Character," 145).

renunciation becomes ever more desperate and reprehensible. Like Judas, Peter finds himself in a situation warned of by Jesus (13:9–11), but he caves in under pressure. Once again, members of Mark's audience may have had firsthand experience of such "trials," or knew of those who had.[148] At all events, this last episode in which a disciple appears in the work stands as a grim warning of how hard following Jesus can be and of the trials that await even the most devoted follower. Peter, then, like Judas, stands here for a particular type of behavior—an example of what to avoid.

In many respects, Judas and Peter act as counterparts to one another: while Judas's crime is that he identified Jesus, Peter's is that he claims not to know him.[149] But our author treats the two men differently. Judas is the recipient of a special woe: "it would be better for that man if he had not been born," Jesus says in 14:21. Despite being "ashamed of the Son of Man" (8:28), however, Peter is offered a second chance by the angelic young man at the tomb, who specifically directs the women to take the message of a future reunion with Jesus to Peter (16:7).[150] What seems to make the difference are Peter's tears (14:72). While elite Romans tended to see remorse as a sure sign of servility, the Jewish tradition, along with certain philosophers, prized remorse along with its more positive aspect, repentance.[151] This, of course,

148. Writing in the early second century, Pliny the Younger informs the emperor Trajan that he asks suspected Christians in Bithynia Pontus three times whether they are Christians. He says that he has not been present at trials of Christians before, and so is not entirely sure how they are to be conducted (*Letters* 10.96). As Jones points out, however, this suggests that he knew such trials had taken place at an earlier period, presumably during the Neronian persecution in Rome ("Historicity," 152). See also Middleton, "Suffering," 185, and Whitaker, "Rebuke or Recall?," 678–82.

149. So van Iersel, "Failed Followers," 260.

150. Perhaps for Mark denial is not so reprehensible as betrayal; the denier can always stand firm a second time. If so, Mark would be rather more lenient than the author of Heb 6:4–6, who suggests that there is no return for the person who commits apostasy. Best argues that nothing excludes Judas from the reference to "disciples" in 16:7 ("Role," 387); this is true, though the lack of a specific mention of him here, along with the condemnation in 14:21, does seem to exclude Judas.

151. For a detailed study, see L. Fulkerson, *No Regrets: Remorse in Classical Antiquity* (Oxford: Oxford University Press, 2013), esp. 1–22. As she notes, remorse in general tended to be associated with those of low status—women, children, or slaves. Aristotle believed that shame at shortcomings could help a person to improve, while Plato saw tears in particular as a recognition of one's faults, and therefore the first step toward overcoming them. See Aristotle, *Nicomachean Ethics* 1128b10–12, 15–21; and R. Baumgarten, "Dangerous Tears? Platonic Provocations and Aristotelian Answers," in *Tears in the Graeco-Roman World*, ed. T. Fögen (Berlin: de Gruyter, 2009), 85–104.

is exactly what Jesus calls for in his very first public declaration (1:14–15). What saves Peter, then, is that, unlike Judas, he repents, and so is called to start again in Galilee (14:28; 16:7).

It is only in these two *exempla*, I suggest, that Mark shows any particular interest in the disciples, and even here our author is not at all interested in painting them as real human beings but rather in using them to exemplify certain types of behavior he wishes his audience to avoid. Elsewhere, as I have argued, Mark uses the Twelve to develop his portrait of Jesus. They have ambiguous and sometimes conflicting traits simply because they are used in differing ways throughout the narrative.[152] Toward the beginning of the *bios*, the Twelve contribute to a portrait of Jesus as an authoritative teacher at the center of a group of devoted followers. In the central section, Mark's focus is on Jesus as a teacher of difficult and countercultural ideas; here the questions and incomprehension of the Twelve represent the "ordinary" response to Jesus's message and allow the Markan Jesus to explain things in greater depth. In the final section, the disciples' fear and cowardice acts as a foil to Jesus's single-minded acceptance of his death. Peter's potentially disastrous denial contrasts starkly with Jesus's own fulsome acceptance of his identity before the high priest, and Mark's audience could be in no doubt as to which model to follow.

"Minor Characters"

A group that has come to some prominence in recent discussion consists of the so-called minor characters. In his programmatic essay of 1977, to which I have already alluded, Robert Tannehill argued that in place of the utter failure displayed by the Twelve, Mark introduces a range of minor characters who provide a brief glimpse of how true disciples should respond. These characters emerge toward the end of the book (as the Twelve become ever more incapable of understanding) and are usually thought to include Blind Bartimaeus (10:46–52), the anointing woman (14:3–9), Simon of Cyrene (15:21), and Joseph of Arimathea (15:42–46), though some would also include the Roman centurion at the cross (15:39) and the women at the tomb (15:40–1; 16:1–8).[153] According to this view, the purpose of these characters is to act as *replacements* for the disgraced disciples, to step in and perform

---

152. So also Lehtipuu, "Characterization and Persuasion," 80.

153. Tannehill, "Disciples," 190. See also J. R. Donahue, "A Neglected Factor in the Theology of Mark," *JBL* 101 (1982): 582–86; Rhoads and Michie, *Mark as Story*, 129–35 (where they are referred to as the "little people"); Tolbert, "How the Gospel," 355; and Middleton, "Suffering," 187. Williams counts twenty-two characters in Mark who step out of the crowd and encounter Jesus in some way; he sees various stages of progression, with minor characters

roles that the disciples have failed to fill (anointing Jesus, proclaiming his name at his death, burying him, and so on). Their role is summed up succinctly by Bas van Iersel: "Without exception they are people who act in the right way where Jesus's supporters fail. Do not they rather than the disciples play the role readers of the book might wish to imitate?"[154]

Attractive as this reading of Mark's *bios* may be, it is clearly closely linked with a view of the disciples that sees them as "failures"—a view I have sought to dispute in the previous section of this chapter. There seem to me to be two further flaws. First, as we have already seen, the model Mark's readers are called upon to emulate is that of Jesus himself, not the Twelve. As we move into the passion narrative, Mark shows that discipleship requires total commitment, and whether it is their lack of readiness in Gethsemane, their flight at the arrest, or Peter's denial in the high priest's courtyard, the primary function of the failure of the Twelve is to highlight *Jesus's* unwavering resolution and obedience to God's will.[155] Once his apparently shameful death has been vindicated through the resurrection, others can be called upon to follow Jesus's example, but before that he must act alone. The disappearance of the Twelve, then, does not create a "gap" in discipleship that needs to be filled by a series of minor characters. Quite the opposite: the departure of the Twelve focuses the audience's attention all the more on the horror of Jesus's lonely death—a sequence made even more real and pressing by the knowledge that they might themselves be called upon to imitate it (8:34–38).

The second major problem with interpreting characters in this way is that it fails to take Mark's view of discipleship seriously enough. Following Jesus, for our author, is fundamentally about living one's life in a self-negating way and following Jesus—if necessary—even to a shameful death. Belief in miracles is not an adequate ground for discipleship for Mark (the first disciples are called *before* Jesus performs any miracles at all; 1:16–20), nor is faith alone. What counts for Mark is a person's readiness for martyrdom. As Paul Middleton observes, "The invitation found in Mark 8:34–8 represents the final and decisive test of one's status as a follower of Jesus."[156] None of the "minor characters" is ever tested in the way that the Twelve

---

acting as examples of what it means to follow Jesus and accept his teaching, particularly in 10:46–16:7 ("Discipleship").

154. B. van Iersel, *Reading Mark* (Edinburgh: T&T Clark, 1989), 188. Van Iersel does, however, stop short at describing these people as "disciples" (188, 201).

155. So also R. A. Burridge, "Reading the Gospels as Biography," in *The Limits of Ancient Biography*, ed. B. McGing and J. Mossman (Swansea: Classical Press of Wales, 2006), esp. 34–35.

156. Middleton, "Suffering," 176.

are: they are not called upon to understand what it means to be "last of all," nor do we know how long their enthusiasm for Jesus lasted (none of them outlives their episode). As Mark himself makes clear, discipleship can take many forms, from those who quickly fall away to those whose faith is strong (4:13–20). Where these particular actors might fit into that spectrum is far from clear.[157]

Furthermore, it is by no means obvious that all these characters belong together in anything approaching a "group." In fact, the closer we look at them, the more substantial differences begin to emerge between them.[158] Several of these characters act as *exempla* in a similar manner to Judas in 14:10–11 and Peter in 14:54, 66–72. What they exemplify, however, is not "discipleship" in general, but specific traits required of those who would follow Jesus. It may be helpful to look at each of them in turn.

Blind Bartimaeus (10:46–52)

We have already noted the significance of the two healings of blind people that frame the important body of Jesus's teaching in 8:22–10:45. Clearly Mark wants to show that heeding Jesus's message will lead to spiritual "sight." But what of Bartimaeus himself? He certainly follows Jesus, but is this enough to cast him in the role of a disciple?[159]

157. This is also noted by Rhoads and Michie, who suggest that the women's failure at the end is due to being asked more than they expected; *Mark as Story*, 134; see Shiner, *Follow Me!*, 19.

158. So also E. S. Malbon who notes that both the Twelve and other characters display successes and fallibilities; Mark, she says, has a twofold message for the reader—"anyone can be a follower, no one finds it easy"; "'Fallible Followers': Women and Men in the Gospel of Mark," *Semeia* 28 (1983): 29.

159. Johnson regards him as a "prototype of the true disciple" who provides a "model for the Christian who needs to know what it means to see and be saved"; "Mark 10:46–52," 201. It is interesting that Bartimaeus is named, a feature that has led R. Bauckham to argue that he was a known follower (indeed the eyewitness ultimately responsible for this story); "The Eyewitnesses in the Gospel of Mark," *SEÅ* 74 (2009): 19–39. Names, however, seem to be more random than this. In an analysis of named characters in Greek novels, A. Billault notes that in *Daphnis and Chloe* almost all the characters are named, while in the *Aithiopika* this amounts to only around 25 percent; moreover, unnamed characters are not necessarily less crucial for plot development than named ones. Following a tradition going back to Homer, Xenophon of Ephesus often gives ironical names to his characters (as perhaps Mark has done here). See A. Billault, "Characterization in the Ancient Novel," in *The Novel in the Ancient World*, ed. G. L. Schmeling (Leiden: Brill, 1996), 123–24.

Bartimaeus is the only named recipient of a healing miracle, and Mark translates his name for the audience as "Son of Timaeus." There may well be a link here between this "Son of Honor" who sits and begs in abject poverty and Jesus's teaching about discipleship in the preceding chapters. What is surprising about the story, however, is the subordinate role taken by the healing (especially in comparison with the earlier cure of the blind man at Bethsaida in 8:22–26).[160] Instead, our author pays greater attention to Bartimaeus himself. What is important is not so much his knowledge of Jesus—he is the only character in the gospel to hail him as "Son of David," but for Mark this is at best an inadequate identification, and in any case, he drops the title when he speaks to Jesus directly, now favoring "rabbouni" (10:51).[161] Rather, as Paul Achtemeier notes, what Bartimaeus displays is *persistence*: he ignores the rebukes of those around him and continues his attempts to catch Jesus's attention until he is rewarded with his greatest desire (10:51). Drawing on accounts of beggars from the first-century Mediterranean world, Wendy Cotter sees Bartimaeus here as a recognizable "type": he is presented as "the usual loud and raucous, flattering and pestering beggar."[162] Readers would expect Jesus to have nothing to do with him (an expectation shared initially by the bystanders in the story). Nor does Bartimaeus allow social niceties to stand in his way: he does not stop to make sure he is fully clothed, but casts off his *himation* (outer garment) in his haste to get to Jesus.[163] Of course, the story says a great deal about Jesus: his compassion, his ability to disregard social and cultural norms, and his ability to grant a person's deepest needs. But Bartimaeus functions as a brief *exemplum*. Like the woman with the hemorrhage (5:25–34) or the Syro-Phoenician mother (7:25–30), Bartimaeus is an example of persistent faith. Such persistence, Mark assures his readers, will have its rewards.

Anointing Woman (14:3–9)

The story of an unnamed woman who anoints Jesus is the middle scene of a classic Markan intercalation, which opens with the plots of the chief priests and scribes

160. So P. J. Achtemeier, *Jesus in the Miracle Tradition* (Eugene, OR: Cascade, 2008), 146–47; noting the similarity between this and the call of Peter in Luke 5:1–11, he goes on to suggest that the story was originally an account of how Bartimaeus became a disciple of Jesus (148–51).

161. So Cotter, *Christ*, 48–51.

162. Cotter, *Christ*, 62–68, esp. 64.

163. See Cotter, *Christ*, 69–71, for a full discussion of the significance of the *himation* here.

against Jesus in 14:1–2. From the intrigue of the council chamber we move to the intimate, private setting of a meal in Bethany, at the house of Simon the leper. While Jesus is eating, a woman appears with a bottle of extremely expensive aromatic oil, which she breaks and pours on his head. Certain bystanders (*tines*) become angry and ask why the oil was not sold and the money given to the poor. Jesus, however, silences them, claiming that she has done a "good deed" (*kalon ergon*),[164] even anointing his body for burial (14:6–8). Immediately following Jesus's extravagant commendation of the woman, however, is the completion of the earlier story in which Judas goes to the chief priests to hand him over (14:10–11).

The most striking feature of this scene is the contrast between the woman and Judas. As Elizabeth Struthers Malbon notes, we are presented with "the unnamed woman, who gives up money for Jesus and enters the house to honor him (14:3–9), and Judas, the man who gives up Jesus for money and leaves the house to betray him (14:1–11)."[165] As so often in Mark, insiders—even "one of the Twelve"—cannot always be depended on, while devotion can come from unexpected places.[166] We should not, however, read more into this scene than the text allows. Despite frequent claims to the contrary, there is no indication that the woman is "anointing" Jesus here in the sense of recognizing his messianic identity. As Adela Collins points out, such anointings in the Septuagint, whether of kings or high priests, use olive oil (*elaion*), not the aromatic oil used here (*myron*).[167] Nor is there any indication

164. The same phrase appears in Xenophon's rendering of Prodicus's account of Heracles's decision between Virtue and Vice; *Memorabilia* 2.1.31.

165. Malbon, "Fallible Followers," 40. See also J. R. Edwards, "Markan Sandwiches," 208–9; L. Hurtado, *Mark*, 229–30; Collins, *Mark*, 641; Marcus, *Mark 8–16*, 937–43; and J. A. Kelhoffer, "A Tale of Two Markan Characterizations: The Exemplary Woman Who Anointed Jesus's Body for Burial (14:3–9) and the Silent Trio Who Fled the Empty Tomb (16:1–8)," in *Women and Gender in Ancient Religions*, ed. S. P. Ahearne-Kroll, P. A. Holloway, and J. A. Kelhoffer (Tübingen: Mohr Siebeck, 2010), 87–89.

166. Judas is consistently referred to in the passion narrative as "one of the Twelve," presumably to reflect the enormity of his betrayal; see also 14:18–21 and 43–45.

167. Collins, *Mark*, 142, who cites 1 Kgdms (LXX) 10:1; 16:13; and Lev 8:12 (the last relating to the anointing of the high priest Aaron). Those who see this as a messianic anointing include E. Schüssler Fiorenza, *In Memory of Her: A Feminist Theological Reconstruction of Christian Origins* (New York: Crossroad, 1983), xiii–xiv; H. Hearon, "The Story of 'the Woman Who Anointed Jesus' as Social Memory: A Methodological Proposal for the Study of Tradition as Memory," in *Memory, Tradition, and Text: Uses of the Past in Early Christianity*, ed. A. Kirk and T. Thatcher (Atlanta: SBL Press, 2005), 111; J. Dewey, "Women in the Gospel of Mark," *Word and World* 26 (2006): esp. 27; also T. Matilla, "Naming the Nameless: Gender and Discipleship in Matthew's Passion Narrative," in Rhoads and Syreeni,

that the woman herself understands her actions as an anointing for burial. It is *Jesus* who interprets them in this way, adding a new, somber note to the dinner party. It is difficult, therefore, to talk of her "discipleship" in any meaningful way. What the woman displays above all in this scene is an extravagance of giving. She completely drains a flask of expensive perfume worth around three hundred denarii, or almost a year's wages; she gives willingly and abundantly, lavishly anointing Jesus for a joyous feast with no thought for her own future needs.[168] In this she aligns herself with the poor widow of 12:41–44, who gives her "life" (*psychē*) and becomes a living embodiment of self-denying service (8:34, 35–37).[169] The fact that the woman is not named directs attention to her actions; like Bartimaeus earlier, she acts as an *exemplum*, illustrating one aspect of the behavior characteristic of those who would follow Jesus.

Simon of Cyrene (15:21)

Of all Mark's minor characters, none has received more praise for their discipleship than the man from Cyrene. His story occupies only one verse, where we are told that he carried Jesus's cross (or, more accurately, the crossbeam) to the place of crucifixion.[170] To many, he serves as a living enactment of Jesus's central demand that disciples deny themselves, take up their cross, and follow him (8:34). Brian Blount, for example, sees him as a paradigm of discipleship, declaring that he functions as

---

Characterization, 162–63 (Matilla's comments relate to the anointing woman in Matthew but can easily be extended to Mark).

168. On the practice of anointing a guest for a meal, see LXX Amos 6:6; Pss 22:5; and Isa 25:6–7; also Josephus, *Jewish Antiquities* 19.239. Collins notes the *myron* that flows down Aaron's head over his beard and onto his garment in LXX Ps 132 as a metaphor for plenty and prosperity (*Mark*, 642).

169. Lest the woman's gift be misconstrued, Mark adds a further element to the story through the angry outrage of certain bystanders. Although the tradition moved in the direction of interpreting these people as the Twelve (see John 12:4, and a number of commentators, e.g., Hurtado, *Mark*, 229, and Marcus, *Mark 8–16*, 940), there is no indication of this in Mark. The detractors are outraged that at the Passover feast, of all times, Jesus can condone such waste and ignore the needs of the poor. Jesus's response, however, makes it clear that, as in 2:18–22, he will not always be present. There will be plenty of time to give to the poor once Jesus has gone.

170. On the practice of carrying the crossbeam (*patibulum*) to the place of crucifixion, see R. E. Brown, *The Death of the Messiah: From Gethsemane to the Grave; A Commentary on the Passion Narratives in the Four Gospels* (New York: Doubleday, 1994), 913.

a "model worthy of imitation in the Markan community."[171] He takes the place of another Simon—Simon Peter—who has now deserted his master.[172]

Attractive as this view may be, there are a number of difficulties with it. Most striking is Mark's use of the word *angareuō*, to press into service (the same word is used in Matt 5:42, where it refers to conscription by Roman soldiers). Far from being a voluntary act, Simon here is *forced* to carry Jesus's cross—presumably against his will. Furthermore, there is no indication that Simon has "denied himself" in any way, nor that he later became a follower of Jesus.[173] Even the grammar of the scene conspires to belittle Simon's actions: although he is clearly the subject of the subjunctive verb here ("he carried," "he took up"), the central actors in the scene are the Roman guards, the unspecified "they" who have just mocked Jesus (15:15–20) and who will now take him to Golgotha, where they will offer him myrrhed wine, crucify him, and divide his clothing (15:22–24). Despite the wealth of detail that surrounds Simon, then, his story is all but engulfed by the executioners' march to Golgotha and their relentless desire to crucify their prisoner. Simon's act forms part of a catalog of deeds perpetrated by the soldiers on the now passive Jesus.

I have suggested elsewhere that the figure of Simon is part of the mockery that pervades this whole section of the narrative (a feature we will analyze in more detail in the following chapter).[174] He takes his place in a brutal burlesque of a kingly procession, which extends from Jesus's first appearance in the soldiers' barracks to his place of execution. More specifically, Simon is forced to act as a lictor, the attendant who went before a magistrate (whether the emperor or a lower official), holding the

171. B. K. Blount, "A Socio-Rhetorical Analysis of Simon of Cyrene: Mark 15.21 and Its Parallels," *Semeia* 64 (1993): 178. For similar interpretations, see also Marcus, *Mark 8–16*, 1048; Witherington, *Mark*, 394n145; K. E. Brower, "'We Are Able,' Cross-Bearing Discipleship and the Ways of the Lord in Mark," *Horizons in Biblical Theology* 29 (2007): 177–201.

172. So Myers, *Binding*, 385. Some argue that Simon of Cyrene was invented by Mark specifically to contrast with Peter; see S. Reinach, "Simon de Cyrène," in *Cultes, Mythes et Religions*, 5 vols. (Paris: Leroux, 1904–23), 4:181–88; also R. Funk and the Jesus Seminar, *The Acts of Jesus: The Search for the Authentic Deeds of Jesus* (San Francisco: HarperSanFrancisco, 1998), 154–55, 261, 360.

173. The mention of Simon's two sons, Alexander and Rufus, has suggested to some that the younger men were known to Mark's congregation, and that their father's act was included simply for historical reasons; so G. Theissen, *The Gospels in Context: Social and Political History in the Synoptic Tradition*, trans. L. M. Maloney (Edinburgh: T&T Clark, 1992), 166–99; and Brown, *Death*, 913–14.

174. H. K. Bond, "Paragon of Discipleship? Simon of Cyrene in the Markan Passion Narrative," in *Matthew and Mark across Perspectives*, ed. K. A. Bendoraitis and N. K. Gupta (London: T&T Clark/Bloomsbury, 2016), 18–35.

fasces over his left shoulder, the sign of the magistrate's *imperium*. The *fasces* were common symbols of power in the early imperial age and are frequently found on the funerary reliefs of city magistrates and priests of the imperial cult. Indeed, when the Alexandrian mob sought to make fun of King Agrippa I by dressing up a man called Carabas as a mock king (in a passage that has a number of similarities with the mockery by the soldiers in Mark), they placed two young men with rods (*hrabdoi*) on either side of him to act as attendants (Philo, *Flaccus* 38). Read in this way, the audience's attention is not on Simon, but on Jesus, the mock king who makes his way to the cross. Simon does not need to provide a model of discipleship—that role is still very much occupied by Jesus himself.

The Centurion (15:39)

As Jesus expires on the cross, a centurion who stands opposite him declares, "Truly this was the [or 'a'] Son of God." Traditionally these words have been seen as a "confession," a christological high point of the gospel. Adherents of the "messianic secret" motif interpret this as the grand denouement, the first time that Jesus is truly understood as the suffering messiah—and by a gentile at that.[175] More recently, however, doubts have been raised about this interpretation, with some arguing that the centurion's words are ambiguous at best,[176] and perhaps even sarcastic.[177] If so, the centurion, like other characters in the story, is taunting Jesus, with the full implications of his words understood by Mark's readers only on an ironic level.

In favor of a more positive reading, however, is the frequent use in both martyriological and biographical literature of the trope of the vindication of the pious

175. So V. Taylor, *The Gospel according to St Mark*, 2nd ed. (London: Macmillan, 1966), 597; Collins, *Mark*, 765–67; Marcus, *Mark 8–16*, 1059; Matera, *Kingship*, 145; H. L. Chronis, "The Torn Veil: Cultus and Christology in Mark 15:37–39," *JBL* 101 (1982): 97–114; and K. R. Iverson, "A Centurion's 'Confession': A Performance-Critical Analysis of Mark 15:39," *JBL* 130 (2011): 329–50. On the secrecy motif, see above, pp. 147–49.

176. W. Shiner categorizes the centurion's remark as "ambiguous" in that he mistakes Jesus for "a divine or divinely inspired person on a Hellenistic model"; "The Ambiguous Pronouncement of the Centurion and the Shrouding of Meaning in Mark," *JSNT* 78 (2000): 4.

177. This reading seems to be gaining momentum in the scholarly literature; see D. H. Juel, *A Master of Surprise: Mark Interpreted* (Minneapolis: Fortress, 1994), 74; M. Goodacre, "Scripturalization in Mark's Crucifixion Narrative," in *The Trial and Death of Jesus: Essays on the Passion Narrative in Mark*, ed. G. van Oyen and T. Shepherd (Leuven: Peeters, 2006), 33–47; N. Eubank, "Dying with Power: Mark 15,39 from Ancient to Modern Interpretation," *Biblica* 95 (2014): 247–68. The latter provides a helpful analysis of this passage in other gospels (248–51) and early Christian texts and interpretation (251–53).

sufferer by a converted judge or executioner.[178] When he brings the poison to Socrates, for example, the prison officer says, "I have come to know in this time that you are the noblest and gentlest and the bravest of all the men that have ever come here," and bursts into tears (*Phaedo* 116c). Clearly we are to understand that even a hardened jailer cannot remain unaffected by the great philosopher's presence. In the Jewish Scriptures, King Nebuchadnezzar is astonished that Daniel and his companions can withstand the burning furnace and blesses their God (Dan 3:95–96 LXX). Similarly, when Apollonius makes what looks to be a last, fateful journey to confront Domitian in Rome, he is befriended by Aelian, one of the emperor's men, who realizes that Apollonius "was a man whom nothing could terrify or startle" (*Vita Apollonii* 7.21). And in Acts, the centurion Julius treats Paul well (Acts 27:3) and even saves his life (27:43), despite being charged with conveying him and other prisoners to Rome.[179]

In Mark's narrative, the centurion is part of the execution party, a man who has presumably witnessed many deaths in his years of service on the battlefield, in the arena, and on the cross. It is quite natural that Pilate should seek confirmation from him later on that Jesus is indeed dead (15:44–45). His declaration in 15:39, however, shows that, despite his shameful death, Jesus is indeed the possessor of divine power—a fact recognized even by a hostile Roman.[180] Unlike other bystanders, who cannot discern the meaning of events in front of them (15:35–36), the centurion has a flash of insight and testifies to Jesus's divine sonship at a moment in the narrative when the voice of God is conspicuously absent. The slightly unusual anarthrous phrase *huios theou* (lit. "a son of [a] God") may suggest that for Mark this is not a

178. See J. Pobee, who notes the presence of a number of motifs from martyrological literature in Mark 15; "The Cry of the Centurion—A Cry of Defeat," in *The Trial of Jesus*, ed. E. Bammel (London: SCM, 1970), 91–102; also Iverson, "Centurion's 'Confession,'" 345; and Shiner, "Ambiguous," 11–14, for parallels in Greco-Roman literature.

179. In a similar manner, Josephus has an Egyptian scribe with considerable skill in predicting the future foretell the birth of a child (i.e., Moses) who will surpass all others in virtue (*Jewish Antiquities* 2.205); as L. H. Feldman notes, the fact that the scribe is an outsider lends a certain gravitas to his prediction; *Josephus' Interpretation of the Bible* (Berkeley: University of California Press, 1998), 377. Outsiders are used to compliment Jews elsewhere in Josephus, to good effect—see *Jewish Antiquities* 2.263; 4.117; 8.165, 149; *Against Apion* 114–15 (Feldman, 558–59).

180. Historically, Pilate had only auxiliary troops, drawn largely from the pagan cities of Judea (see Bond, *Pontius Pilate*, 13–14); most likely, however, Mark simply intends the centurion to be seen as a Roman. See also Collins, *Mark*, 764 (with more on the role of centurions).

full Christian confession.[181] Like the unclean spirits who recognize Jesus as "the Son of God" (*ho huios tou theou*) in 3:11, the centurion makes his declaration without necessarily becoming a believer himself. Mark's readers, however, would understand the full implications of the phrase; harking back to Jesus's divine adoption in 1:11 and the foreshadowing of his heavenly glory in 9:2–8, Jesus was truly God's only, beloved Son.[182]

The Roman executioner, then, is profoundly affected by Jesus and sees him as a hero or a demigod, but he is not to be seen as a representative gentile follower, still less the first person fully to understand what "suffering messiahship" really means. The naming of the deceased at the moment of death was a common Roman custom; here, the centurion is the one to give voice to Jesus's true "name," in the manner of an epitaph.[183] The focus of attention, however, continues to be on Jesus as the audience awaits the explanation of the terrible omens that accompany his demise (15:33, 38).

Joseph of Arimathea

As the day wanes, Joseph of Arimathea asks Pilate for permission to bury the body. Joseph, we are told, is a respected member of the council who eagerly awaits God's kingdom (15:43). Joseph's attitude toward Jesus is ambiguous: his actions encourage us to imagine that he has a certain amount of sympathy for him,[184] though the fact that he is a member of the council (even if he is now described as a *bouleutēs* rather than a member of the *synedrion*) links him to those who earlier sought his death.[185] Joseph's overriding concern seems to be piety; he is anxious to bury the body before the approaching Sabbath so that the land should not be defiled (Deut 21:22–23). The need for courage (15:43) is probably due to the fact that Jesus has been executed on a charge of treason. The ensuing burial is hasty and perfunctory: there is no suggestion that the body is washed or anointed with aromatic spices or perfumed oil; Joseph simply buys a linen cloth to wrap up the corpse and lays it in

181. This may also be implied by the imperfect tense here; see Collins, *Mark*, 767. Contra Pobee, "The Cry," 101.

182. Collins may be right to see a play on the imperial title *divi filius* (*theou huios*) here; *Mark*, 767–68. See discussion above, pp. 128–30.

183. Burridge, *Four Gospels, One Jesus?*, 62.

184. On the "Christianization" of Joseph in tradition, see W. J. Lyons, *Joseph of Arimathea: A Study in Reception History* (Oxford: Oxford University Press, 2014).

185. As Marcus notes, if Joseph were a sympathizer, we would expect some cooperation between him and the women; *Mark 8–16*, 1074.

a tomb.[186] Like John the Baptist earlier, Jesus is buried; but while John is laid to rest by disciples (6:29),[187] Jesus is hastily interred by a stranger.

Women at the Tomb

Finally, the gospel ends with the three named women at the empty tomb.[188] Their main narrative role for Mark is to *see* a chain of events, stretching from Jesus's death, to the place of his burial, and finally the disappearance of his body.[189] Their familiarity with Jesus (15:40–41) puts them in an excellent position to vouch for these events: the same Jesus who preached in Galilee was crucified, buried, and has now been raised. Once they receive the angelic announcement in 16:6–7, however, their apologetic role is complete. Like the male disciples earlier, they run away in fear, stricken by terror at the enormity of what they have just witnessed. In a work with so many entreaties to silence (1:45; 5:43; and 7:36–37, for example), it is of course hugely ironic that the women fail to proclaim their message.[190] This, however, was presumably of no great concern to Mark—his biography has made known not only events at the tomb, but the whole life and significance of this Son of God. The work calls not only the disciples and Peter (16:7), but all Christ followers to ground themselves in "Galilee," and to start their life of commitment anew.

186. For the historical events behind this, see H. K. Bond, *The Historical Jesus: A Guide for the Perplexed* (London: Bloomsbury, 2012), 162–65. On the difficult chronology here (which probably did not particularly bother Mark), see H. K. Bond, "Dating the Death of Jesus: Memory and the Religious Imagination," *NTS* 59 (2013): 461–75.

187. The words *sōma* and *tithēmi* also occur here, encouraging hearers to make the link between the two men.

188. On the women here, see A. T. Lincoln, "The Promise and the Failure: Mark 16:7, 8," *JBL* 108 (1989): 283–300; while not minimizing the women's failure, Lincoln stresses v. 7 and the assurance that the women (and all disciples) are able to overcome failure. Also D. Catchpole, "The Fearful Silence of the Women at the Tomb: A Study of Markan Theology," *Journal of Theology for Southern Africa* 19 (1977): 3–10; L. W. Hurtado, "The Women, the Tomb, and the Climax of Mark," in *A Wandering Galilean: Essays in Honour of Sean Freyne*, ed. Z. Rodgers, M. Daly-Denton, and A. Fitzpatrick-McKinley (Leiden: Brill, 2009), 427–50; and Kelhoffer, "A Tale," 89–95.

189. Edwards regards the interlinking of the scenes with Joseph and the women as yet another Markan intercalation, though one of "less importance." The point for him would be that the women watch events, but Joseph *acts*; "Markan Sandwiches," 213.

190. Malbon, "Fallible Followers," 45.

Thus the so-called minor characters for Mark perform a range of different functions. Bartimaeus and the anointing woman act as *exempla*, heightening the need for persistence or giving one's all. Simon is conscripted into the soldiers' mockery, while the centurion performs the apologetic role of executioner-turned-proclaimer. Joseph's piety allows Jesus's body to be buried, and the three named women form a vital link between the cross and the empty tomb, before deserting Jesus as thoroughly as their male counterparts.

The foregoing analysis has shown that to focus discussion of discipleship on "the Twelve"—both their presence and absence—is a mistake.[191] In the course of the various episodes that make up Mark's work, a variety of characters may step forward and exemplify an aspect of discipleship (faith, persistence, generosity, humility, and so on), just as the Twelve appear to fail as much as they succeed. The one character who consistently exemplifies Christian discipleship for Mark is none other than Jesus himself. He makes the will of God known, not only through his teaching, but just as clearly through the way he lives his life.

Summary

This lengthy chapter has surveyed a wide range of secondary characters, from supporting "walk-ons" and opponents, to King Herod, Pilate, and the Twelve. Three features stand out.

First, with the possible exception of a handful of disciples, the overriding impression is that none of these characters holds any particular interest for Mark; all owe their place to what light they shed on Jesus. Some enable Jesus to perform his ministry, others conspire against him; some exemplify the values of the kingdom, and others throw the character of Jesus into relief (this is particularly true of the Twelve). There is no need for any of these characters to be drawn any more clearly: as we saw in the last chapter, Jesus embodies his own teaching in a way that makes him both teacher and example.

Second, this chapter has sought to demonstrate that Markan characterization is largely determined not by authorial directives or psychological gap-filling, but by the placement and juxtaposition of episodes. Through comparison and contrast, the Markan text reveals many more layers of meaning than the surface itself might initially suggest and encourages the audience to reflect more deeply on the complexities of the unfolding story.

Third, and finally, several Markan characters interrelate with real flesh-and-blood people, particularly those called to be part of Jesus's closest group of follow-

---

191. So also Donahue, "Neglected," 585.

ers. While this does not detract from their literary nature (they are still Markan creations), their actions cannot fully be understood without at least some attempt to imagine them against a wider background of early Christ-following traditions and assumptions.[192] In this, the identification of Mark's work as a *biography*, rather than a (largely fictitious) novel or short story, has a very specific hermeneutical application.

I am quite well aware that the reading strategies outlined here will not necessarily appeal to modern readers. Contemporary audiences are programmed to fill in gaps, to read psychologically, or to push against the grain. We are no longer comfortable with the prominence of "great men," and actively seek to retrieve the hidden stories of others—women, for example, or other marginalized characters. Few of us now want our literature to occupy itself with moral examples (there is a reason why Victorian *Lives* are no longer in vogue). Of course, once a text is cut free from its author—a rather messier process in the ancient world than today—and transposed into different cultural settings, it can be read in any way that a reader chooses, and we are entirely at liberty to make whatever sense of it as we please. My intention in this chapter is not to "shut down" other ways of reading, but simply to propose the likeliest way in which a first-century reader would have approached Mark's biography.

For Mark, there is a distinction between the time of Jesus and the post-Easter age, with the resurrection dividing the two. Only after Jesus has been raised from the dead can the full story be told (9:9), and Jesus's closest followers can realize their true potential as Christian missionaries and martyrs. In the time of Jesus, however, no one really understands what is going on, and Jesus himself must provide the example for others to follow. As we move into the passion narrative, Jesus's character and demeanor are first contrasted with those of others, particularly at Gethsemane and during his trials. Gradually, however, his followers all fall away until Jesus is left entirely alone to undergo his humiliating and painful death. In a sense, Jesus has to go to the cross alone—his death has a salvific importance that those of his followers will not have. But Jesus's death will also act as a model for others, those who come after him in the post-Easter age, and who will be called upon to suffer persecution for their faith. It is to these climactic events that we shall turn our attention in our final chapter.

192. It was perhaps in response to changing perceptions of the Twelve that led to a softening of Peter in particular by some of Mark's first interpreters (so Matt 16:17–20 and Luke 22:31–32).

CHAPTER 6

The Death of Jesus

The condition of human life is chiefly determined by its first and last days, because it is of the greatest importance under what auspices it is begun and with what end it is terminated; and therefore we judge that he only has been fortunate whose lot it has been to receive the light propitiously and to yield it back quietly.

—Valerius Maximus[1]

In Chapter 2 we saw that the manner of a man's death was extremely important in the ancient world, and that—for biographers in particular—the moment of transition between life and death was an especially clear window into a person's character.[2] This was all the more significant in the case of a philosopher or a teacher, where it was crucial that his end should be in keeping with his teaching, and that death was simply an extension of the principles by which he lived. A good death established his teaching as true and worthy of emulation. And the way in which he met his death—his fortitude, resilience, and the lessons he drew from it—mattered far more than what killed him.

Socrates's death in 399 BCE became the ultimate paradigm for the demise of a philosopher. Not only did he face his end with a courageous spirit—bidding farewell to his family and friends, washing his own body, and discussing philosophy to the last—but just as importantly his death emphasized the truth and consistency of his teaching. Throughout life, he had already distanced himself from the pursuits and distractions of the flesh. Showing no anguish, he faced his end with fearlessness and nobility, safe in the assurance that his soul would live on in a better world. As the numbness from the poison spread from his feet up through his body, he faded gently from life, the moment of death almost imperceptible as his soul was set free

---

1. Valerius Maximus, *Memorable Doings and Sayings* ("On Deaths Out of the Ordinary") 9.12 praef. Shackleton Bailey, LCL 493.

2. See above, pp. 56–66.

from its physical prison. He was released from life without violence because he had practically released himself already; death for him was simply one more step along the path he had already traveled, so that at the end there was nothing to constrain his eternal soul. As Christopher Gill notes, the calm tranquility of his passing is "the quietness of a ritual, the *kartharmos* or purification of the soul from the prison of the body."[3]

Yet, as we have already noted, this is hardly a credible portrayal of the effects of hemlock poisoning—which involved trembling, spasms, convulsions, vomiting, and finally organ failure. However the "historical Socrates" died, it was not like this. Clearly what mattered most was not the actual course of events, but *the way that the story was told*—the details, additions, or omissions that transformed even a hideous state execution into something noble and praiseworthy. The same death might be described in very different ways, depending on who was doing the telling. And, as we saw earlier, there was a general expectation that biographers might exert a certain amount of artistic license when it came to describing their subject's demise.[4] The fact that the deaths of certain philosophers attracted a number of quite different accounts suggests that final moments were often a contested issue, with rival groups of followers or opponents producing versions to suit their own estimation of the man and his message. We might guess, for example, that those who claimed that Empedocles heard a loud voice in the middle of the night and was taken up into heaven were followers of the philosopher. Those who maintained that he slipped into the sea and was drowned, or who stated that he fell from a carriage, broke his thigh, and died of an illness were rather less well disposed toward him. And no doubt the story that he threw himself into Etna's burning crater to confirm a report that he was a god (a ruse that failed when one of his distinctive bronze slippers was found) was put about by those who were downright hostile and contemptuous of him.[5]

It was vitally important, then, that Mark should give his hero a commendable

---

3. C. Gill, "The Death of Socrates," *ClQ* 23 (1973): 28. Socrates's death is recounted in Plato's *Phaedo*; for a useful introduction, see H. Tarrant, *Plato: The Last Days of Socrates* (London: Penguin, 2003), 99–115.

4. See above, pp. 65–66.

5. Diogenes Laertius notes a number of accounts of Empedocles's death (*Lives* 8.67–74); similarly, Philostratus records a number of accounts of Apollonius's end (*Life of Apollonius of Tyana* 8.29–30). This was a feature not confined to philosophers; Plutarch notes various reports of Scipio's death—some that he died naturally, others that he poisoned himself, and still others that claimed his enemies broke into his house at night and smothered him (*Romulus* 26.4). Arrian also notes a number of accounts of Alexander's death (*Anabasis* 7.25–27).

THE DEATH OF JESUS

exit, one that continued to demonstrate and reflect his earlier way of life and instruction. But how exactly was this to be done? In this final chapter, I shall unpack Mark's account of Jesus's death. Starting with the fact of crucifixion itself, we shall see how Mark emphasized Jesus's earlier teaching on self-denial and shame so that, paradoxically, a shameful exit formed the only fitting end to his biography. I shall also examine the way in which our author retains a sense that Jesus's death is salvific while also presenting it as a model for others to emulate. We begin, however, at the place where Mark undoubtedly also began: with an appreciation of the full horror of Jesus's humiliating death.

A Slave's Death

Crucifixion was the most shameful, brutal, and degrading form of capital punishment known to the ancient world, reserved for slaves, brigands, and any who set themselves up against imperial rule.[6] It was intended to be public, both to act as a deterrent to others and to provide spectacle, even entertainment, to onlookers.[7] It was a form of death in which the caprice and sadism of the executioners were allowed full reign, as they devised ever more gruesome ways to ridicule the condemned.[8] Stripped naked, the victim was humiliated and shamed as he suffered extreme agony, perhaps for several days, until, overcome by suffocation and exhaustion, the merciful end would come. The cross symbolized the complete destruction not only of the physical body but also of the person's identity. Usually the victim's body was left to rot or to be eaten by animals, and the remains were left unburied. So offensive was the cross that civilized people preferred not to talk about it, and

6. See M. Hengel, *Crucifixion in the Ancient World and the Folly of the Cross* (London: SCM, 1977); D. W. Chapman, *Perceptions of Crucifixion among Jews and Christians in the Ancient World* (Tübingen: Mohr Siebeck, 2008); J. G. Cook, *Crucifixion in the Mediterranean World* (Tübingen: Mohr Siebeck, 2014).

7. On ridicule and spectacle (and also on the sociological question of what made executions compelling to the crowd) see K. M. Coleman, "Fatale Charades: Roman Executions Staged as Mythological Enactments," *JRS* 80 (1990): 44–73.

8. For the association of the cross and mockery, see Josephus, *Jewish War* 5.51; Seneca, *Dialogue 6: On the Consolation to Marcia* 20.3; Philo, *On Flaccus* 73–85; and Suetonius, *Galba* 9.1. On parody more specifically, see J. Marcus, "Crucifixion as Parodic Exaltation," *JBL* 125 (2006): 73–78. For links between crucifixion and "gallows humor," see my article "'You'll Probably Get Away with Crucifixion': Laughing at the Cross in the *Life of Brian* and the Ancient World," in *Jesus and Brian*, ed. J. E. Taylor (London: T&T Clark/Bloomsbury, 2015), 113–26.

few Roman writers ever dwelled on any of the details.[9] Cicero described crucifixion as "the greatest punishment of slavery" (*Against Verres* 2.5), while Josephus labeled it "the most pitiable of deaths" (*Jewish War* 7.203).

Jesus's crucifixion would have come down to Mark as part of his inherited tradition and was presumably too well known to be omitted or lightly brushed aside. In any case, its salvific effect was a crucial part of Christian teaching, as Paul's letters make clear.[10] A work like Q, which was largely a series of sayings, might not need a coherent account of Jesus's demise (though even here it is clearly alluded to; Luke/Q 11:49–51).[11] A biography of Jesus, however, would need to face it head on. But how should it be done?

I have already noted my skepticism regarding a pre-Markan passion narrative. Despite its tenacity within scholarship, there seems to me to be very little evidence for it, and much that counts against Mark's dependence on some such hypothetical source.[12] This does not, of course, mean that Mark had no sources or traditions connected with Jesus's death before him. Quite the contrary—it seems to me that there were likely to be many accounts of Jesus's death in existence, several of them incorporating scriptural tradition into their interpretations. Already in the 50s, Paul could draw on a range of ideas surrounding the paschal lamb (1 Cor 5:7), the Servant of the Lord (Phil 2:5–11), the scapegoat, and even the curse of Deut 21:23 (Gal 3:13).[13] All of these were attempts to come to terms with Jesus's violent death, to make sense of it against the history of Israel, and to construct a distinctively

---

9. So Cicero, *For Rabirius* 16; more generally, see Hengel, *Crucifixion*, 37–38. For Jews, the victim brought a curse on the land; see P. W. Martens, "'Anyone Hung on a Tree Is under God's Curse' (Deuteronomy 21:23): Jesus's Crucifixion and Interreligious Exegetical Debate in Late Antiquity," *Ex Auditu* 26 (2010): 69–90.

10. On the cross in Paul, see J. D. G. Dunn, *The Theology of Paul the Apostle* (London: T&T Clark/Continuum, 1998), 207–33.

11. On Jesus's death in Q, see A. Kirk, "The Memory of Violence and the Death of Jesus in Q," in *Memory, Tradition, and Text: Uses of the Past in Early Christianity*, ed. A. Kirk and T. Thatcher (Atlanta: SBL Press, 2005), 191–206.

12. See pp. 110–13 above.

13. For fuller discussion, see M. Hengel, *The Atonement: A Study of the Origins of the Doctrine in the New Testament* (London: SCM, 1981), 64, 71–73; D. R. Schwartz, "Two Pauline Allusions to the Redemptive Mechanism of the Crucifixion," *JBL* 102 (1983): 259–68 (which includes discussion of the scapegoat ritual applied to Jesus); S. McKnight, "Jesus and His Death: Some Recent Scholarship," *CR:BS* 9 (2001): 185–228; J. D. G. Dunn, "When Did the Understanding of Jesus's Death as Atoning Sacrifice First Emerge?," in *Israel's God and Rebecca's Children: Christology and Community in Early Judaism and Christianity*, ed. D. Capes, A. D. DeConick, H. K. Bond, and T. Miller (Waco: Baylor University Press,

Christian story around it. The commemoration of the Eucharist would have ensured that one, or perhaps more, of these understandings were articulated over and
again within Mark's Christian fellowship. Some of these interpretations may even
have begun to circulate with a basic narrative framing: the stories of the Jewish
martyrs and Roman *exitus* literature would readily have served as models for such
short accounts.

In what follows, I shall assume that Mark had a range of traditions and anecdotes that informed his account, but that he was himself responsible for selecting
and crafting his material, sometimes quite substantially. I see Mark's account of
Jesus's death as a very specific reception of the Jesus tradition, one that harnessed
disparate sources and collective memories of Jesus and transposed them into the
expectations of a particular literary genre. Adapting material so that it fitted into
a biography, particularly a biography of a revered teacher, was by no means a me-
chanical undertaking. Traditions, anecdotes, and sayings had to be weighed, sifted,
and placed appropriately; connections needed to be made across various sections;
and the final product needed both to produce a pleasing effect and to speak to the
present needs of the anticipated audience.

Our familiarity with Mark's account of the crucifixion should not blind us to
the fact that our author had many other options before him. The cross itself was
a given, but almost all of the details could have been written up differently. Mark
could, for example, have recorded Jesus's death fairly briefly; instead, he seems to
dwell on it, to go out of his way to describe Jesus's last few moments at length,
producing the longest account of a crucifixion to have come down to us from antiquity.[14] It would have taken some skill, but even a crucifixion could—like hemlock
poisoning—have been redeemed. Jesus could have shown courage and calmness
throughout, blissfully giving up his spirit in the final moment, perhaps with the
voice of God commending his actions. More specifically, Jesus could have been
cast as an innocent martyr (rather in the manner that Luke would later adapt his
material),[15] with the hero displaying a noble spirit and a stoic indifference to death.

2007), 169–81; and A. J. Dewey, "The Locus for Death: Social Memory and the Passion
Narratives," in Kirk and Thatcher, *Memory, Tradition, and Text*, 119–28.

14. So also M. Goodacre, "Scripturalization in Mark's Crucifixion Narrative," in *The
Trial and Death of Jesus: Essays on the Passion Narrative in Mark*, ed. G. van Oyen and
T. Shepherd (Leuven: Peeters, 2006), 34. On the length of Mark's passion narrative, see
above, p. 32.

15. On Jesus's death in Luke, see J. S. Kloppenborg, "'Excitus clari viri': The Death of
Jesus in Luke," *TJT* 8 (1992): 106–20; G. Sterling, "Mors philosophi: The Death of Jesus in
Luke," *HTR* 94 (2001): 383–402; P. Scaer, *The Lukan Passion and the Praiseworthy Death*

But although Mark does include a handful of more "noble" features (which we shall come back to), this is not the dominant tone of his narrative. There is no getting away from the fact that Mark's account, particularly in the crucifixion scene, is the very opposite of a "good death": Jesus dies alone, in agonized torment, with no one to perform even the most basic rites. As Adela Collins puts it, Jesus's death in Mark is "anguished, human, and realistic."[16]

Rather than attempting to explain Mark's crucifixion against more traditionally "noble" categories, we would do better to look at the way in which he actually works with his material. One striking feature is that, despite its length, the narrative contains surprisingly little on Jesus's physical sufferings. He is beaten by Jewish council guards (14:65), flogged by Roman soldiers (15:15), and crucified (15:24, noted again in 15:25), but Mark does not dwell on any of this. There is no gory interest in torture, or praise of endurance such as we find in accounts of the Jewish martyrs or the Greek Anaxarchus. What Mark does emphasize, however, are the negative associations commonly linked to crucifixion: the victim's passivity, mockery, and abandonment. Each of these is worth exploring in more detail.

The Markan Jesus becomes increasingly passive as the scenes unfold. The once authoritative, combative Jesus who bested opponents with ease is gradually silenced by the narrative. He speaks boldly before the high priest (14:62), but manages only two words before Pilate (15:2), and after that says nothing until his agonized cry on the cross.[17] Nor does the omniscient narrator give us any further insight into his

---

(Sheffield: Sheffield Phoenix, 2005); K. Iverson, "The Present Tense of Performance: The Immediacy and Transformative Power in Luke's Passion," in *From Text to Performance: Narrative and Performance Criticisms in Dialogue and Debate*, ed. K. R. Iverson (Eugene, OR: Cascade, 2014), 131–57.

16. A. Y. Collins, "Mark's Interpretation of the Death of Jesus," *JBL* 128 (2009): 553–54.

17. The Roman trial scene may have struck Mark's audience as rather anticlimactic. They might well have expected Jesus to deliver a long speech before the Roman governor, perhaps protesting his piety and readiness to die (in the manner of Socrates, the Jewish martyr Eleazar, and countless others); so J. Taylor, "The Role of Rhetorical Elaboration in the Formation of Mark's Passion Narrative (Mark 14:43–16:8): An Enquiry," in *Greco-Roman Culture and the New Testament*, ed. D. E. Aune and F. E. Brent (Leiden: Brill, 2012), 16. Instead, Jesus answers only the question about kingship (and that in a slightly evasory manner) and remains silent in the face of the many charges brought by the chief priests (15:3–5). We might explain this in a number of ways. Perhaps, as J. H. Neyrey suggests, we should read Jesus's silence here in the context of honor and shame, so that Jesus's manner is a "silence of dismissal," a gesture of disdain toward both Pilate and his chief priestly accusers; "Questions, Chreiai, and Challenges to Honor: The Interface of Rhetoric and Culture in Mark's Gospel," *CBQ* 60 (1998): 657–81. As Neyrey notes, a reading which invokes honor/shame seems more

thoughts or feelings.[18] Others assert their power over Jesus's body: arresting him (14:43–50), beating him (14:65), binding him (15:1), scourging him (15:15), changing his clothes (15:16–20), and finally crucifying him (15:24). His lack of agency is emphasized by the verb *paradidōmi*, as he is passed from one authority to another (9:31; 10:33; 14:10–11, 18, 21, 41–42; 15:1, 10, 15). Like a slave, Jesus endures it all, disempowered, humiliated, shamed, violated—nothing less manly and honorable could be imagined.[19]

Perhaps even more striking is the element of mockery here. It begins already in Pilate's court. "Are you the King of the Jews?," the prefect asks (15:2), and the repeated use of this phrase, even toward a crowd that has clearly expressed its preference for the insurrectionary Barabbas, can only be read as a taunt.[20] Once Jesus

---

plausible than the common view that Jesus's silence is an allusion to the Suffering Servant of Isa 53:7. Or, with W. S. Campbell, we might see Jesus's silence here as a "legitimate defense tactic"; "Engagement, Disengagement and Obstruction: Jesus's Defense Strategies in Mark's Trial and Execution Scenes (14.53–64; 15.1–39)," *JSNT* 26 (2004): 283–300. Campbell cites both Apollonius's enforced brevity before Domitian (*Life of Apollonius of Tyana* 8.2) and the proceedings against Jesus ben Ananias (*Jewish War* 6.300–305). However, Philostratus feels the need to include a lengthy defense speech from Apollonius in his biography (even though it was not needed!), and Jesus ben Ananias's lack of defense was taken as a sign that he was a madman—neither, it seems to me, constitutes much of a "tactic." Or, we might note that lengthy speeches are not characteristic of the Markan Jesus; outside ch. 13, he rarely strings more than a few sayings together. Overall, though, I suspect that Jesus's silence before Pilate is largely due to his growing passivity and isolation within the narrative.

18. See R. C. Tannehill, "The Gospel of Mark as Narrative Christology," *Semeia* 16 (1979): 80–81. Although for very different reasons, Socrates also seems to become increasingly remote the closer he gets to death; Plato's style becomes more chastened, and he no longer describes moods and emotions in detail as the chill moves up the hero's body; see G. W. Most, "A Cock for Asclepius," *ClQ* 43 (1993): 97. S. S. Elliott also notes parallels with the *Life of Aesop*, which similarly depicts a character "swallowed up by the narrative plot that created him" (though Aesop's death is much less central to his *bios* than that of Jesus); "'Witless in Your Own Cause': Divine Plots and Fractured Characters in the Life of Aesop and the Gospel of Mark," *Religion and Theology* 12 (2005): 407.

19. On masculinity in the ancient world, see B. E. Wilson, *Unmanly Men: Refigurations of Masculinity in Luke-Acts* (Oxford: Oxford University Press, 2015), 39–75, and 190–242, on Jesus's crucifixion (Wilson is discussing the Lukan version, but her comments are even more pertinent with respect to Mark). See also T.-S. B. Liew, "Re-Mark-able Masculinities: Jesus, the Son of Man, and the (Sad) Sum of Manhood," in *New Testament Masculinities*, ed. S. D. Moore and J. C. Anderson (Atlanta: SBL Press, 2003), 93–135.

20. See my study, *Pontius Pilate in History and Interpretation* (Cambridge: Cambridge University Press, 1998), 99–119.

is passed into the hands of the Roman soldiers, the mockery becomes even more intense. Now he is dressed up in imperial purple and given a crown, while the soldiers salute him, strike and spit upon him, and kneel down in mock homage (15:16–20). Clearly they find the idea that such a man might be "King of the Jews" utterly ridiculous. Once they emerge from the *praetorium*, the soldiers commandeer Simon of Cyrene to carry Jesus's cross. While this is often seen as a gesture of goodwill on the part of the soldiers, there is no textual warrant for such a claim. Those who press Simon into service are exactly the same people who have just mocked Jesus and subjected him to abuse. It is better to understand their actions here, then, as a continuation of the mockery. Simon takes his place in the grim procession to Calvary, forced to carry the condemned man's crossbeam like a *lictor* with his *fasces* accompanying a magistrate.[21] Jesus's Roman executioners are unrelenting in their brutality, offering him wine mixed with myrrh not as an analgesic but as a further means of torture.[22] And, as a final insult, they attach the scornful title "King of the Jews" over his dying body. Even on the cross, the ridicule continues, now by a wider group of people: passersby, chief priests and scribes, and even those crucified with him (15:29–32).

Finally, the Markan scene is striking in its abandonment of Jesus. The teacher who only a few days previously attracted large and enthusiastic crowds at his entry to the city (11:9–10) is now rejected by everyone: first by Judas, "one of the Twelve" (14:10–11), then by the rest of the disciples (14:50), the naked young man (14:51),[23] Peter (14:66–72), and the crowd (15:6–15). On the cross, the Markan Jesus endures the depths of abandonment and degradation, articulated through the words of LXX Ps 21. The psalm plays an important role in the crucifixion scene and may well go back to an early stage of reflection on Jesus's death,[24] but within its present

---

21. See above, pp. 214–16.

22. On the basis of *b. Sanhedrin* 43a, this is commonly understood to be an analgesic (though the passage in question mentions frankincense, not myrrh). Once again, however, there is nothing in the text to suggest that the soldiers wish to extend any kind of mercy toward Jesus. On wine mixed with myrrh as a form of torture, see E. Koskenniemi, K. Nisula, and J. Toppari, "Wine Mixed with Myrrh (Mark 15:23) and *Crurifragium* (John 19:31–32): Two Details of the Passion Narratives," *JSNT* 27 (2005): 379–91. Jesus, of course, refuses to drink the wine (15:23).

23. On the flight of the naked young man as a contrast to Jesus's calm acceptance, see H. Fleddermann, "The Flight of a Naked Young Man (Mark 14:51–52)," *CBQ* 41 (1979): 412–18.

24. Allusions to LXX Ps 21 can be found at 15:24 (Ps 22:18); 15:29 (Ps 22:7); and most importantly in Jesus's cry in v. 34 (Ps 22:1). See further, S. P. Ahearne-Kroll, *The Psalms*

Markan context it expresses the hero's sense of utter desolation.[25] This comes out most strongly in Jesus's last audible cry: "My God, my God, why have you forsaken me?" (15:34). Much has been written on this verse, with a sizeable body of scholars arguing that Mark intends his audience to understand the cry in the light of the *ending* of the psalm, which seems to finish on an optimistic note. There is, however, nothing in the Markan text that would seem to warrant such a view, and Mark could not be sure that even a Jewish-Christian audience would be sufficiently familiar with the psalm to make the connection. Indeed, Stephen Aherne-Kroll has recently argued that the ending of Ps 22 (at least in the Greek version, LXX Ps 21) is not a new situation of thanksgiving, but continued pleading with God to intervene.[26] In the end, it is better to take Mark's text at face value here: his Jesus dies in utter desolation, abandoned not only by his erstwhile followers, but apparently by God himself.[27]

Last words were particularly important within the biographical tradition.[28] Socrates's command to offer a cock to Asclepius expressed his piety (despite his conviction for atheism), and was perhaps an ironic jest that he was now "cured" from physical existence; Lucian's Demonax died with wise and even humorous words on his lips; and Suetonius was always careful to record fitting last words for his emperors. Even a manly silence could be commendable, in the manner of both Pompey and Julius Caesar following the assassins' stabs (Plutarch, *Pompey* 79.1–4; Suetonius, *The Divine Julius* 82.2). In contrast to all of this, Jesus's cry of desolation signifies a bad death, a wretched and miserable exit, fully in keeping with his servile execution on a Roman cross.

In this vivid scene, Mark has turned conventional ideas of a death that is good and even noble upside down. He has gone out of his way to emphasize Jesus's pas-

---

of Lament in Mark's Passion: Jesus's Davidic Suffering (Cambridge: Cambridge University Press, 2007).

25. Useful discussions can be found in R. E. Brown, *The Death of the Messiah: From Gethsemane to the Grave; A Commentary on the Passion Narratives in the Four Gospels* (New York: Doubleday, 1994), 1455–65, and K. S. O'Brien, *Use of Scripture in the Markan Passion Narrative* (London: T&T Clark/Continuum, 2010), esp. 147–54.

26. S. P. Ahearne-Kroll, "Challenging the Divine: LXX Psalm 21 in the Passion Narrative of the Gospel of Mark," in van Oyen and Shepherd, *Trial and Death of Jesus*, 119–48.

27. So also M. D. Hooker, *Not Ashamed of the Gospel: New Testament Interpretations of the Death of Christ* (Grand Rapids: Eerdmans, 1994), 64. On the character of the Markan Jesus, particularly in the face of death, see D. Rhoads, J. Dewey, and D. Michie, *Mark as Story: An Introduction to the Narrative of a Gospel*, 3rd ed. (Minneapolis: Fortress, 2012), 111–15.

28. See the excellent paper by J. M. Smith, "Famous (or Not So Famous) Last Words" (paper given to the Markan Literary Sources Section, SBL Annual Meeting, Atlanta, 2016).

sivity, the mockery that he endured, and his abandonment and degradation. Even his burial, as Mark describes it, will be carried out by a stranger, and if not exactly shameful will be perfunctory and lacking in all but the most basic of provisions (15:42–46). In order to appreciate the full scope of what Mark is doing here, we need to turn back for a moment to the earlier parts of the biography, first to the opening chapters, and then to the major body of teaching in 8:22–10:52.

Setting Up an Ending

As we saw in Chapter 3, Mark began his biography with a portrait of Jesus that would be attractive to Jew and gentile alike. He is adopted by God as his Son (1:9–11) and quickly shows himself to be a force to be reckoned with. Thoroughly at home in the public sphere, he energetically travels throughout Galilee in the company of his male companions, outmaneuvering opponents wherever he goes. He is a powerful healer, one able to rally crowds and inspire amazement in all he does (1:27–8; 2:12; 5:42; and so on); a man who can provide food for thousands of people (6:30–44; 8:1–10), control the forces of nature (4:35–41; 6:45–52), and even raise the dead (5:21–24). Although worthy of high honor, he refuses titles and public esteem, modestly referring to himself only as the "Son of Man." We are presented in these opening chapters with an authoritative, self-controlled Jesus, offering benefactions to all who petition him and demonstrating many of the qualities prized by elite males.

Although he is referred to as "teacher," the main body of instruction is reserved for the central section of the biography, in 8:22–10:52. Here the Markan Jesus turns all worldly conceptions of honor on their head in favor of a deeply countercultural focus on what contemporary society would usually brand as shameful. Disciples are called on to deny themselves, to act as slaves or servants to one another, and to care nothing for status or prestige. They are asked to give up everything—not only riches (10:17–22) but also homes and families too (10:23–30), and possibly even their lives (8:34–38). True honor and greatness in the community that gathers around Jesus lie not in courting the esteem of others but in embracing a new understanding of honor based on ignominious service, suffering, and disgrace. Significantly, however, this is not only instruction given to others; rather, it is crucially the basis for Jesus's own way of life, and ultimately, his death (as 10:42–45 makes clear).[29]

<hr/>

29. On these central chapters, see especially A. D. Kaminouchi, *"But It Is Not So among You": Echoes of Power in Mark 10.32–45* (London: T&T Clark, 2003), and D. F. Watson, *Honor among Christians: The Cultural Key to the Messianic Secret* (Minneapolis: Fortress, 2010). See above, pp. 150–55.

As Mark moves toward the passion narrative, it becomes apparent that Jesus has a choice over his own death. Our author stresses Jesus's courage and fortitude as he makes his way to Jerusalem in obedience to the will of God, even though he knows how things will end (8:31–32; 9:30–32; 10:32–34). He enjoys a quiet last evening with his friends during which he calmly speaks of what is to come and sorrowfully predicts their desertion (14:17–25). The Gethsemane scene points in the same direction. Although commentators since Celsus have tended to stress Jesus's strong emotions here (Mark uses the verbs *ekthambeō* and *adēmoneō*, and draws on the language of Pss 42–43), the significance of the scene, as Origen pointed out, is surely to be found in Jesus's final words to the Father, "not what I want but what you want" (14:36).[30] The Markan Jesus submits to his cruel death in the full knowledge of what he is doing. When his "hour" arrives (14:41) he is ready, and he welcomes the arresting party with a quiet dignity (14:43–50).[31] Such foreknowledge and resolve find many parallels within the biographical tradition: Apollonius, for example, similarly knew when his end was upon him, as did Demonax, who took steps to speed it up.[32] Philo's Moses, too, strikingly prophesied not only his own death but also his subsequent ascension into heaven (*Life of Moses* 2.288–91). Clearly, then, the "good" philosopher knows when his end has come and does not shirk from embracing it.

Mark is quite clear that Jesus has done nothing to deserve death. He draws on the motif of the unjust ruler who acts against the hero out of "envy" (*phthonos*). This tradition was exemplified by Socrates where the state acted unjustly against a pious man (*Apology* 28a), but it is also found in numerous other *bioi* and martyr literature (as we saw in connection with "King Herod" and John the Baptist in Chapter 4). Julius Caesar awoke envy in his fellow citizens (Plutarch, *Caesar* 69); and many of Cornelius Nepos's generals met their deaths because of envious compatriots.[33] "Envy," of course, is a clever trope: it not only implies that any accusations

30. Origen, *Against Celsus* 2.24. M. D. Hooker argues it is unlikely that Jesus's followers would have invented a scene such as this one, and that the pull would have been toward crafting a calmer, more serene narrative; *A Commentary on the Gospel according to St Mark* (London: A&C Black, 1995), 346. In my view, it is difficult to know what the earliest Christians would have found useful, and Mark's note that the disciples were sleeping does not inspire too much faith in the historical accuracy of his account at this point! For a similar reading to the one taken here, see A. Y. Collins, "From Noble Death to Crucified Messiah," *NTS* 40 (1994): 481–503.

31. On the concept of the appointed "hour" or divine sign, see Droge and Tabor, *A Noble Death*, 31–35, 37, 41–42.

32. Philostratus, *Life of Apollonius of Tyana* 8.28; Lucian, *Demonax* 65.

33. The motif is widespread in the lives of Cornelius Nepos; see, for example, *Themistocles* 2.8; *Chabrias* 3; *Datames* 5; *Timoleon* 20.1; and *Hannibal* 23.3. The author of 1 Clement

are unfounded, but also raises the standing of the one envied.[34] It is important to note that Mark does not say that Jesus was *innocent*;[35] the charges are true—Jesus *is* the Christ, the Son of the Blessed (14.61), and, in a sense, he *is* a king (15:2, 26). The problem is that opponents cannot see it.

For Mark, then, Jesus's free choice to submit to the will of the Father, even though he has done nothing deserving death, is the ultimate expression of what it means to be a "slave of all." As David Rhoads, Joanna Dewey, and Donald Michie note, Jesus's "crucifixion is the ultimate consequence of a life of service and of his refusal to oppress others to save himself. And in this tragic execution—misunderstood, falsely accused, abandoned—he is least of all."[36]

It was surely with this end in sight that Mark composed his carefully integrated central chapters.[37] His artful composition shows that there is no mismatch between what Jesus teaches and his death; he remains true to his teaching to the very end. And, just as significantly, what he demands of others is no more than he is prepared to undergo himself. But what exactly does the death of Jesus achieve for Mark?

Significance

Mark's Gospel is notoriously difficult to pin down when it comes to the reasons for Jesus's death.[38] On a very general level, it is clearly God's will that Jesus should die: the impersonal *dei*, "must," is used at 8:31, implying divine necessity (see also 8:33; 10:32; and 14:36). Moreover, Jesus's death is clearly in accordance with the Scriptures: sometimes a specific passage is cited (12:1–12; 14:27), while at other

---

puts the deaths of Peter and Paul down to envy (5.2.5), though this was presumably inspired by the death of Jesus.

34. Although the term "envy" does not appear until 15:10, it is clearly what drives Jesus's Jerusalem opponents from the start (see 11:18 and 14:1–12).

35. For Luke, it is important to stress that Jesus was "righteous" (*dikaios*); see Luke 23:47.

36. Rhoads, Dewey, and Michie, *Mark as Story*, 111.

37. On the careful composition here, see N. Perrin, *What Is Redaction Criticism?* (Philadelphia: Fortress, 1970), 41–63.

38. There is an extensive literature on this topic. Besides the commentaries, useful discussions can be found in Hooker, *Not Ashamed*, 47–67; C. K. Barrett, "The Background of Mark 10.45," in *New Testament Essays: Studies in Honour of Thomas Walter Manson*, ed. A. J. B. Higgins (Manchester: Manchester University Press, 1959), 1–18; Kaminouchi, *"But It Is Not So among You"*; S. Dowd and E. S. Malbon, "The Significance of Jesus's Death in Mark: Narrative Context and Authorial Audience," *JBL* 125 (2006): 271–97; A. Y. Collins, "Mark's Interpretation of the Death of Jesus," *JBL* 128 (2009): 545–54; and C. Breytenbach, "Narrating the Death of Jesus in Mark," *ZNW* 105 (2014): 153–68.

times the Markan Jesus alludes to the Scriptures in general (9:12; 14:21, 49). Two passages, however, go further, though neither are as clear-cut as modern theologians would like them to be.

In 10:45 the Markan Jesus describes his death as a "ransom for many" (*lytron anti pollōn*). As is commonly noted, *lytron* is a technical term in the LXX designating money paid to free a slave or a captive.[39] The phrase in 10:45, then, suggests that Jesus's death is a substitution, that he dies in place of "the many." Exactly what people are ransomed *from*, however, is less clear: Is it from Satan? From sin?[40] From all the powers that enslave human beings?[41] Or even from coming tribulations?[42] Any, or even all, of

39. *Lytron* is used in the LXX in Lev 27:31 and Prov 13:8, while the plural (*lytra*) occurs in Lev 25:24, 51–52; Isa 45:13; Exod 21:29–30; 30:11–16; and Num 3:11–13; 35:31–4. For a full account, see A. Y. Collins, *Mark: A Commentary* (Minneapolis: Fortress, 2007), 499–504, who also draws on inscriptional evidence from Asia Minor. She detects ideas of expiation and propitiation in the term, suggesting sacrificial overtones. Similar themes can be found in Paul (see especially Rom 3:24–25) and also Rev 1:5b–6. The idea of vicarious atonement, that the self-sacrifice of a righteous individual had salvific consequences for others, is found in a number of Jewish texts; for example, 2 Macc 7:37–38; 4 Macc 1:11; 6:29; and 17:21–22; see M. de Jonge, "Jesus's Death for Others and the Deaths of the Maccabean Martyrs," in *Text and Testimony: Essays in Honour of A. F. J. Klijn*, ed. T. Baarda, A. Hilhorst, G. P. Luttikhuizen, and A. S. van der Woude (Kampen: Kok, 1988), 142–51; Droge and Tabor, *Noble Death*, 115; and J. Klawans, *Josephus and the Theologies of Ancient Judaism* (Oxford: Oxford University Press, 2013), 123. A similar sentiment can be found in Aristotle, *Nicomachean Ethics*, book 9, 8.9.1169a.

40. The idea that Jesus's death liberates people from *sin* is a popular one, particularly among those who see a link here with Isa 53; see C. H. Dodd, *According to the Scriptures: The Substructure of New Testament Theology* (London: Nisbet, 1952), 88–96; R. E. Watts, *Isaiah's New Exodus and Mark* (Tübingen: Mohr Siebeck, 1997), 257–87; Collins, *Mark*, 503; Marcus, *Mark 8–16*, 749–50, 751–57. Jesus is certainly able to forgive sin during his earthly ministry (2:1–12), but the text nowhere mentions that this is a central purpose of his death. The link with sin here can only be maintained by drawing on themes from Isa 52–53 (though the specific term *lytron* is noticeably absent from this passage and Mark does not quote from this particular "servant song"); contrast the discussion in Dodd, *According to the Scriptures*, 123–25, with the much more cautious assessment of M. D. Hooker, *Jesus and the Servant* (London: SPCK, 1959), 62–102. Although the theology of Isa 40–55 as a whole has certainly informed much of Mark's thinking throughout the gospel, Hooker is probably correct in her assessment that the "influence of Isaiah 53 on this saying has . . . been grossly exaggerated"; *Commentary*, 249; see also Kaminouchi, *"But It Is Not So,"* 142–55; and Breytenbach, "Narrating," 164.

41. So Dowd and Malbon, "Significance," who argue that Jesus's death ransoms the majority of people from both "demonic powers and human tyrants" (294).

42. So Breytenbach, "Narrating," who argues that Jesus's life is a ransom for the "doomed

these may be in view. Later, on the eve of his death, as he takes the cup over supper, Jesus declares, "This is my blood of the covenant, which is poured out for many" (14:24). The reference to the "covenant" evokes ideas of God's election of Israel, and looks back to Sinai (Exod 24:8) and the new covenant of Jer 31:31–34,[43] while the phrase "poured out for many" (*to ekchynnomenon hyper pollōn*) lends sacrificial overtones to events.[44] Altogether, Jesus's words seem to imply that his willing (and sacrificial) death will establish a new covenant, so that those who share the cup (through the Eucharist) will form a new community. In sum, although it would be inaccurate to ascribe any clear theories of "atonement" to Mark, Jesus's death clearly has a purpose: it acts as a ransom and offers those who follow him a new way to relate to God.

And this, I suggest, is the reason why the Markan Jesus dies alone. The disciples, as we have seen, play a variety of roles in Mark's biography. Early on, they form a community around Jesus; within the middle section of the work their misunderstanding emphasizes just how difficult Jesus's teaching is to grasp. As we move into the passion narrative, their lack of courage helps to underscore Jesus's unwavering steadfastness to the will of the Father. Once Jesus is on the cross, however, the focus of the narrative is entirely on him: on his act of self-denial, his shameful death, and his participation in the depths of human suffering. It is through this shameful death that Jesus will establish a new covenant with God, and so for Mark it has to be endured alone. Jesus dies in the most miserable way possible—even, apparently, abandoned by God (15:34). Once Jesus has drunk the "cup," however, others can follow in his path, and—despite its shame and ignominy—his death offers a clear model for others to emulate.

Imitation

We have already seen that, like other biographers, Mark was interested not only in presenting an account of Jesus's teaching and way of life, but also in holding it up as a model for others.[45] In ch. 13, Jesus predicted that his followers might

---

life of many" (166); Jesus gives the ransom that no human can give, so that those who follow him need not fear future judgment in the final cosmic catastrophe.

43. The word "new," which is present in some manuscripts, is probably not original here, though the idea is not foreign to the text (see 1 Cor 11:25).

44. The fact that the Markan Jesus dies at the ninth hour (i.e., 3:00 p.m.), the time of the afternoon Tamid (the second daily sacrifice of a lamb in the temple; *Jewish Antiquities* 14.64; 3.237; Acts 3:1), may also suggest that our author interprets his death sacrificially; so Collins, *Mark*, 752–53.

45. See the useful discussions in Hooker, *Not Ashamed*, 47–67; Rhoads, Dewey, and

well find themselves called before governors and kings, handed over by friends and family, and hated by all (13:9–13). In the passion narrative, Jesus provides an illustration of the type of behavior expected of his disciples through a series of contrasts (or *synkrisis*).

First is the scene in Gethsemane (14:32–42). Here our author sets up a striking contrast between Jesus who prays alone to the Father, anxiously awaiting his "hour," and an inner group of disciples (Peter, James, and John). Despite Jesus's repeated admonitions in ch. 13 to "watch," the disciples are unaware of the crisis in which they find themselves and allow themselves to be blissfully overcome by sleep. The anecdote emphasizes Jesus's courage and readiness to die, in contrast to his foolish and uncomprehending followers. Similarly, Jesus's calm acceptance of the arresting party, who have no need of their swords and clubs (14:48), contrasts with the panicked flight of the disciples and even a young man who runs naked into the night (14:50–51). Throughout the scandalously unjust Jewish trial, Jesus stands his ground before the high priest and answers clearly and openly (14:62). Peter, however, outside and accosted by a lowly serving maid, is unable to confess that he is a follower of Jesus and is driven even to curse himself in a desperate attempt to save his life (14:53–72).

If our author wrote for an audience that had experienced persecution, or at least feared that it might be imminent, an emphasis on the paradigmatic death of the leader is not hard to understand. Such an audience may have been particularly interested in Jesus's demise, seeking reassurance that, despite the horror and suffering, Jesus remained true to his teaching until the end. If called upon to make the ultimate sacrifice, his example would provide a blueprint for their own.[46]

Jesus's death for Mark, then, is both a specific means of redemption and a model for followers. It is perhaps the tension between these two rather different concepts that has made it difficult for scholars to pin Mark down to only one meaning. The tension is apparent in Jesus's exchange with the Zebedee brothers in 10:35–40. In response to their bold request, Jesus asks if they are able to drink the cup that he drinks, or to be baptized with the baptism with which he is baptized. Although the brothers answer in the affirmative, it is clear that they cannot really endure the fate that awaits Jesus; the "cup" that Jesus must drink has been prepared for him alone (see 14:36). And yet, once it is over, others will be able to follow, and Zebedee's sons

---

Michie, *Mark as Story*, 113–15; and G. van Oyen, "The Meaning of the Death of Jesus in the Gospel of Mark: A Real Reader Perspective," in van Oyen and Shepherd, *The Trial and Death of Jesus*, 49–68.

46. 1 Tim 6:12–14 similarly remembers Jesus's trial before Pilate in terms of a prototype martyr for followers to emulate; see also 1 Pet 2:20–25; 4:12–14.

will indeed be called upon to give their all (10:39)—an extra-narrative fact perhaps known to Mark's audience.[47] Thus Mark manages to hold together two rather different facets of Jesus's death, one that gives it a specific redemptive purpose, and another in which it subsequently provides an example to follow.

So far we have focused on the most obvious, shameful character of Jesus's death in Mark. This is not, however, the full story, and no ancient reader would come away from Mark's account thinking that Jesus's ignominious death marked the end. Each of Jesus's passion predictions includes his subsequent resurrection (8:31; 9.31; 10:34), and both the transfiguration and Jesus's declaration to the high priest point to his heavenly glory (9:2–8; 14:62). What helps to offset the humiliation and shame of the cross more than anything else, however, is the author's skillful use of irony and reversals: what others see as a shameful death is in fact the triumph of the king—for those with "eyes to see." We shall first trace Jesus's hidden kingship within these chapters before turning to the rather more blatant series of events that surround his death.

"King of the Jews"

Links between Jesus and kingship have been present ever since the prologue to the work, with its evocative use of the royal psalm (1:11, citing Ps 2:7). Early on, Jesus is followed by a great multitude from all regions: Galilee, Judea and Jerusalem, Idumea, beyond the Jordan, and Tyre and Sidon (3:7–8). Those familiar with the story of Israel will recognize these locations as the extent of the kingdom in the great glory days of David and Solomon. Read in conjunction with the specially appointed twelve disciples in the next scene (3:13–19), it would be hard not to see echoes here of the restoration of the twelve tribes and larger themes of the reconstitution of Israel. In ch. 6, the lengthy account of "King" Herod's court serves not only to tell of the Baptist's execution but also to contrast the emerging kingship of Jesus with that of the murderous and spineless Herod—a contrast highlighted all the more by the note that the crowd comes to Jesus like sheep without a shepherd (6:34), a simile commonly found in connection with royal leadership (see 1 Kgs 22:17). Royal imagery appears again in ch. 11, where, in a relatively lengthy exchange at the start of the chapter, Jesus assumes the role of an occupying ruler, requisitioning the colt he will ride into Jerusalem. Jesus's entry into the holy city, amid the crowds strewing

---

47. While the death of James is mentioned in Acts 12:1–12, there is no reference in the New Testament to the death of John. In fact, Irenaeus claimed that he lived to a good old age and died under Trajan (98–117 CE); *Against Heresies* 2.2.5; 3.3.4.

their garments before him and singing their acclamations, imitates the entrance processions of Greco-Roman kings and triumphal warriors—a feature that would have been well known to Mark's audience. Yet the evangelist quickly subverts any expectations his listeners might have: rather than claim his city, the kingly ruler simply leaves (Mark 11:11), and instead of inaugurating his rule through purging the temple, he returns the next day and announces its destruction.[48]

It is in ch. 15, however, that the theme of kingship really comes to the fore. The constant mockery that Jesus undergoes in this chapter is largely on account of his kingly pretensions; he will be mocked by Pilate (15:6–15), by the Roman soldiers (15:16–20a), and by the chief priests and scribes who stand by the cross (15:31–32).[49] Lying behind all of this is a powerful irony: Jesus really is the King for those with eyes to see.[50] He is not a political revolutionary such as those who made a name for themselves in the revolt against Rome: Jesus makes no defense before Pilate, but the carefully constructed contrast between him and Barabbas speaks eloquently for the differences between the two men. Not only will Jesus not "lord it over others" (10:42), but neither is his kingship the warlike despotism of the political insurrectionaries and pseudo-kings who so recently led the nation to disaster.[51] Mark's paradoxical narrative shows that, despite appearances, the crucified Christ is indeed King of the Jews.

Yet Mark's crucifixion scene may go further still. There are, as Thomas Schmidt pointed out some time ago, a number of apparently inconsequential details within the Markan crucifixion scene that serve to link Jesus with the figure of the triumphator: these include the gathering of the whole cohort (mimicking the assembly of the praetorian guard in Rome); the name Golgotha (where the mention of a skull evokes the Capitoline Hill); the refusal of myrrhed wine (aping the triumphator's refusal of wine and casting of it upon the altar), and the placement of the central character between two others (lending the scene a sense of "enthronement").[52] We

---

48. P. D. Duff, "The March of the Divine Warrior and the Advent of the Greco-Roman King: Mark's Account of Jesus's Entry into Jerusalem," *JBL* 111 (1992): 55–71, with many references to Greco-Roman processions (including that of Yahweh in Zech 14).

49. See F. J. Matera, *The Kingship of Jesus: Composition and Theology in Mark 15* (Chico, CA: Scholars, 1982); H. K. Bond, *Pontius Pilate in History and Interpretation* (Cambridge: Cambridge University Press, 1998), 100–101.

50. J. Camery-Hoggatt, *Irony in Mark's Gospel: Text and Subtext* (Cambridge: Cambridge University Press, 1992), 171–77, on the passion narrative.

51. On Barabbas, see above, p. 188; also my article, "Barabbas Remembered," in *Jesus and Paul: Global Perspectives in Honor of James D. G. Dunn for His 70th Birthday*, ed. B. J. Oropeza, C. K. Robertson, and D. Mohrmann (London: T&T Clark, 2009), 59–71.

52. T. E. Schmidt, "Mark 15.6–32: The Crucifixion Narrative and the Roman Triumphal

might read this, with Schmidt, as an "anti-triumph," paradoxically presenting Jesus's procession to Golgotha as the triumph of a victorious general (or, by Mark's day, of course, the emperor). But this overlooks one important element: the triumph always involved the death of the defeated king or military leader. Set within the context of the triumph, then, even a death confers a sense of kingship on the one executed. In a perceptive article, Allan Georgia notes what he calls the "conceptual doubling" of Mark's narrative. Our author presents Jesus as both the victor and the victim, the one who triumphs and also the defeated king who must die. Thus Golgotha becomes both "the culminating place of Jesus's role as triumphal victor and the altar for his execution as triumphal victim."[53]

Georgia struggles to find parallels to Mark's multilayered presentation within contemporary literature, and is forced to conclude that what we have here is "exceptional," perhaps even "unprecedented."[54] More likely, in my opinion, the parallels are found not so much in literature as in the visual world. A common aspect to death in antiquity was its theatricality, its staging and sense of spectacle.[55] This was of course nowhere more obvious than in the gladiatorial displays and staged animal hunts of the arena, which were approaching the height of their popularity when Mark was writing. Simply watching a man's death for its own sake, however, had never

---

Procession," *NTS* 41 (1995): 1–18. On the triumph, see also L. Bonfante Warren, "Roman Triumphs and Etruscan Kings: The Changing Face of the Triumph," *JRS* 60 (1970): 49–66; H. S. Versnel, *Triumphus: An Inquiry into the Origin, Development, and Meaning of the Roman Triumph* (Leiden: Brill, 1970); and M. Beard, *The Roman Triumph* (Cambridge, MA: Harvard University Press, 2009). Christ had been understood as triumphator prior to Mark—cf. 2 Cor 2:14. Although we should beware of pushing details in the narrative too far, Schmidt's overall case has much to recommend it—particularly if Mark's Gospel was written in Rome shortly after the war of 66–70 CE, when the victorious triumph of Vespasian and his sons in 71 CE was still fresh in the memory of his audience (on which, see the lengthy account in Josephus, *Jewish War* 7.123–57).

53. A. T. Georgia, "Translating the Triumph: Reading Mark's Crucifixion Narrative against a Roman Ritual of Power," *JSNT* 36 (2013): 32.

54. Georgia, "Translating," 34. The closest analogy he finds is Chariton's *Callirhoe* 8, which combines an elaborate *parousia* narrative with triumphal themes (pp. 26–29). For broad parallels with Mark's scene, Seneca noted that the crowds that escorted the funeral procession of Drusus (Augustus's stepson) to Rome made the funeral seem more like a triumph (*Consolation to Marcia* 3.2).

55. On the theatricality of Roman death, see Coleman, "Fatale Charades"; V. M. Hope, *Death in Ancient Rome: A Sourcebook* (London: Routledge, 2007), 28–37; and C. Edwards, "Modelling Roman Suicide? The Afterlife of Cato," *Economy and Society* 34 (2005): 200–222.

been popular; death was never represented on the Roman stage,[56] and the midday executions in the arena were initially unpopular. Audiences craved novelty and excitement, or at the very least a display of military skill. In an attempt to enhance the popularity of the midday executions, Nero turned to the declining world of the theater to add an element of drama to the deaths of criminals, creating what Carlin Barton refers to as the "snuff play."[57] The Flavian amphitheater in Rome opened with a number of deaths designed to imitate historical characters or mythological figures (Martial, *On the Spectacles* 7); the condemned criminal might be "dismembered as Orpheus, gored as Prometheus, penetrated as Pasiphae, castrated as Attis, crucified as Laureolus, or burned as Scaevola."[58] As James Harley notes, this was not so much a "play" with the condemned in the lead role (there would hardly be time for that), as suggestive framing of the execution that allowed spectators to make imaginative connections. Exactly how this was done could vary. It might be through music, through a specific costume, or even through suggestive scenery.[59]

Mark, I suggest, offers not so much visual as textual clues to the different levels of meaning within his narrative. His audience would have been culturally programmed to pick up on such clues, to visualize the scene in their minds, and to respond to it on a number of different levels, and in a number of different ways.[60]

56. Edwards, "Modelling," 207. She notes that Romans preferred to read about death than to watch it—*exitus* literature, for example, stayed in the "theatre of the mind." Similarly, death and bloodshed had not appeared on the Greek stage; see A. Henrichs, "Drama and Dromena: Bloodshed, Violence and Sacrificial Metaphor in Euripides," *Harvard Studies in Classical Philology* 100 (2000): 177.

57. C. A. Barton, "Savage Miracles: The Redemption of Lost Honor in Roman Society and the Sacrament of the Gladiator and the Martyr," *Representations* 45 (1994): 41.

58. C. Barton, "Savage Miracles," 41.

59. J. Harley, "The Aesthetics of Death: The Theatrical Elaboration of Ancient Roman Blood Spectacles," *Theatre History Studies* 19 (1998): 89–97.

60. Although different in many respects, the figure of the gladiator showed how shame could be transformed into glory. Gladiators occupied an ambiguous social position: despite being socially despised, it was not only the Stoics who applauded their discipline and military values (*gravitas, disciplina,* etc.). The gladiatorial sacred oath recalled the Roman general's self-consecration (*devotio*), a voluntary pledge to accept death. Those who entertained the masses through the institutionalized spectacles of mass violence in the arena could achieve honor in survival, or glory through death. See Seneca, *Moral Epistles* 70.19–26; also D. G. Kyle, *Spectacles of Death in Ancient Rome* (London: Routledge, 1999), 79–91. The audience in the arena could decide how a show might end. If the gladiator's death-defying valor won him their sympathy and admiration, he could be granted *missio* or reprieve/release. "The criminal remains a *ludibrium*, an object of sport, but one who, through a more-than-human

Unlike the spectacles of death in Roman circles, however, what Mark is doing here is not mocking the victim (who really does deserve the honors given to him) but parodying contemporary notions of greatness. Through the framing device of the triumph, Mark shows that what looked to an outsider to be the depths of suffering, humiliation, and even rejection was in reality the triumph of God's Son. As so frequently in Mark, conventional ideas of power and kingship, even glory and shame, are turned on their heads. Our author seems to play with the idea of Roman power here, destabilizing its meaning and putting in its place highly subversive ways of what it means to be "King of the Jews."[61]

Events around Jesus's Death

So much for the deeper resonances within Mark's account. On the level of the story, however, such a brutal and ignominious end cried out for further explanation. Jesus's cry and the lack of response might suggest that God had abandoned him, but Mark counters this by describing two unusual events closely linked with his death: (1) the darkness that covers the land and (2) the tearing of the temple veil.

Unusual occurrences within the natural word were often linked with the deaths of great men, and were frequently noted by their biographers.[62] A series of prodigies, for example, occurred after the death of Julius Caesar, including a comet that appeared for seven nights in a row and a sun that lost its heat. The meaning of these phenomena, at least as far as ordinary folk were concerned, was that the gods were displeased by Caesar's murder (Plutarch, *Caesar* 69.4–5). Similarly, Augustus's death was heralded by a number of unusual events that were later taken to be omens; these included the mysterious closure of the senate house and a thunderbolt striking Augustus's statue on the Capitol (Dio Cassius, *Roman History* 56.29.3–6). Plutarch tells of a huge serpent that wrapped itself around the head of the dead Spartan king Cleomenes; while some explained the phenomenon in rather more prosaic ways, the vast majority of observers were seized with fear, believing that the incident demonstrated that the king "was of a superior nature and beloved of the gods"

---

courage and determination to embrace his own destruction, has risen above the farce he could not escape" (Barton, "Savage Miracles," 43). Jesus, of course, was not forced to evoke a scene of old, but what is interesting here are the different levels on which the audience can understand the spectacle taking place before them and the degree to which they might confer or withhold their sympathy.

61. H. Leander, "With Homi Bhabha at the Jerusalem City Gates: A Postcolonial Reading of the 'Triumphal' Entry (Mark 11.1–11)," *JSNT* 32 (2010): 323.

62. See above, pp. 61–62.

(Plutarch, *Cleomenes* 39).[63] And Lucian makes fun of both his protagonist and those he dubs "fools and dullards" by mischievously inventing a series of wondrous events that he claims accompanied Peregrinus's death (including an earthquake and a vulture that rose from the funeral pyre toward heaven, shouting, "I am through with the earth; to Olympus I fare").[64] Clearly, then, the association of the death of a great man with unusual natural events was part of the common ancient repertoire, but what specifically did Mark intend his prodigies to demonstrate?

The first unusual occurrence takes place as Jesus hangs on the cross: Mark tells us that darkness covered the whole earth for his last three hours (15:33). This strange phenomenon is often linked to Amos 8:9, which envisages the darkness of the eschatological age along with the associated motifs of judgment and punishment.[65] Similar ideas are found in Mark 13:24-27, but there it is clearly the return of the Son of Man that is envisaged, an event that, from the rest of ch. 13, appears to be still in the future for Mark's audience. Furthermore, if Mark *did* intend to signal the beginning of the eschatological age here in 15:33, it is curious that the darkening of the sun is the only phenomenon mentioned, with no suggestion of the waning of the moon, or the fall of the stars, or any of the other phenomena so frequently mentioned in eschatological writings. More likely, in my view, Mark's audience would have understood the darkness as indicative of a solar eclipse. Pliny the Elder describes eclipses (of both the sun and the moon) as the most marvelous and portentous occurrences in the natural world; while he himself understands how they come about, he knows that ordinary folk fear them, associating them with crime or death.[66] Philo, too, knows that "eclipses announce the death of kings and the destruction of cities."[67] Within the biographical tradition, they are frequently

63. Perrin, LCL 102.

64. Lucian, *The Passing of Peregrinus* 39; Harmon, LCL 302. Lucian returns to the festival to hear an old man already telling the story of the vulture to onlookers (40)!

65. Amos 5:20; Joel 2:31-32; and Isa 60:1-2 also link darkness with the "Day of the Lord." Other scriptural references to darkness include Mic 7:8 (where there is no indication that the darkness is anything out of the ordinary) and Ezek 32:7-8 (where it is part of the graphic description of God's judgment on the Egyptians). Darkness is part of the eschatological repertoire in Testament of Moses 10:5; and, in a similar vein, Pseudo-Philo, *Biblical Antiquities* 19:13, declares that the sun will set quickly when God visits the earth.

66. Pliny, *Natural History* 2.45-46, 53-58.

67. Philo, *On Providence* 2.50 (Colson, LCL 363). Eclipses might also indicate the outcome of a battle: Herodotus, *Persian Wars* 7.37 (here it is a good omen for Xerxes, who goes on to win the battle against the Macedonians); Plutarch, *Aemilius Paulus* 17.7-11 (here it is also a good omen, signifying Aemilius's defeat of the Macedonians); Plutarch, *Pelopidas* 31.1-3 (here Pelopidas wins the battle but loses his life). They might also warn of treachery

associated with the deaths of kings or heroes. An eclipse is said to have occurred at the death of Julius Caesar (Plutarch, *Caesar* 69.4–5),[68] shortly before the deaths of Augustus (Dio Cassius, *Roman History* 56.29.5–6) and Herod (Josephus, *Jewish Antiquities* 17.167),[69] and on the death of the philosopher Carneades (Diogenes Laertius, *Lives* 4.64). The occurrence could be variously interpreted as a sign of divine displeasure, or an indication that God or nature were mourning the deceased.[70]

Closely linked to this is the second portent, which occurs at the moment that Jesus breathes his last.[71] The veil of the temple (*katapetasma*), we are told, was torn in two, from top to bottom (15:38). But what is the meaning of this strange event? Scholarly discussion has become preoccupied with the question of which of the two temple veils Mark has in mind: the inner veil that enclosed the innermost part of the holy of holies, or the outer veil that hung above the golden doors to the sanctuary building?[72] However, as Marinus de Jonge pointed out over thirty years ago, the fact that Mark does not specify which veil he has in mind suggests that

---

to come: Virgil, for example, claims that the sun warns when dark uprisings threaten and when treachery and hidden wars are gaining strength (*Georgics* 1.461–65).

68. An occurrence that Virgil poetically interpreted as the sun being moved to pity (*Georgics* 1.466–68); for a similar sentiment, see Diogenes Laertius, *Lives* 4.64.

69. Josephus briefly notes an eclipse of the moon directly before describing Herod's final illness; *Jewish Antiquities* 17.167.

70. For useful discussions, see Marcus, *Mark 8–16*, 1053–54; Collins, *Mark*, 751–53.

71. The archaic word *ekpneuō* in 15:37 is described by Lee as a "rare euphemism" that "lends dignity and solemnity to the scene." Similarly, the largely obsolescent verb *boaō* in 15:34 (which had largely been replaced by *krazō*) may lend a more dignified tone to these final moments; see J. A. L. Lee, "Some Features of the Speech of Jesus in Mark's Gospel," *NovT* 27 (1985): 25. J. E. Aguilar Chiu probably reads too much into the unusual verb when he sees it as an allusion to the earlier gift of the Spirit, "A Theological Reading of ἐξέπνευσεν in Mark 15:37, 39," *CBQ* 78 (2016): 682–705.

72. In favor of the *inner* veil, see, for example, Collins, *Mark*, 760; J. Marcus, *Mark 1–8: A New Translation with Introduction and Commentary* (New York: Doubleday, 2000), 1057; D. M. Gurtner, "LXX Syntax and the Identity of the NT Veil," *NovT* 47 (2005): 344–53; also his "The Rending of the Veil and Markan Christology: 'Unveiling' the ΥΙΟΣ ΘΕΟΥ (Mark 15:38–39)," *BibInt* 15 (2007): 292–306. In favor of the *outer* veil, see D. Ulansey, "The Heavenly Veil Torn: Mark's Cosmic Inclusio," *JBL* 110 (1991): 123–25; J. B. Chance, "The Cursing of the Temple and the Tearing of the Veil in the Gospel of Mark," *BibInt* 15 (2007): 268–91. Interestingly, tradition associates the veil with Rome (where it perhaps formed part of the Flavian procession); according to *b. Gittin* 56b, Titus slashed the veil with his sword after the defeat of Jerusalem and used it to wrap up the temple vessels in the sanctuary; see D. M. Gurtner, "The Veil of the Temple in History and Legend," *JETS* 49 (2006): 107 and 110.

the matter was of little concern to him.[73] Some argue that the tearing of the veil (usually understood as the innermost one) symbolizes the removal of everything that separates God from humans. According to this reading, Jesus's death enables all people to come to God on an equal basis through Christ.[74] This would not be out of keeping with Mark's theology, especially Jesus's declaration that the temple was to be a "house of prayer for all the nations" (11:17). Yet I doubt that it is Mark's primary meaning here. Much more likely in my view are the readings that interpret the tearing of the veil as a sign of the impending destruction of the temple.[75] Such portents are common in the literature of the period. Despite a certain skepticism, Josephus lists eight portents that were later seen to have foreshadowed the end of the temple; these included voices thought to say, "Let us depart from here"; the huge eastern gate opening by itself in the sixth hour of the night; a bright light shining on the altar in the middle of the night; and a range of strange celestial and natural phenomena (*Jewish War* 6.288–331). Tacitus also reports similar portents, perhaps on the basis of Josephus (*Histories* 5.13), as do rabbinic sources.[76] What all of these strange events indicate is God's departure from the temple in preparation for its destruction. Intriguingly, *The Lives of the Prophets* predicts that the temple will be destroyed by a western nation and that the curtain will be torn into small pieces.[77]

Such a reading would fit well with the theme of the temple's destruction, which is found several times within Mark's Gospel. The clearest prediction is found in 13:2, where, in response to the disciples' amazement at the size of the stones, Jesus remarks, "There will not be left here one stone upon another, that will not be thrown down." The temple incident, sandwiched within the story of the withered fig tree, is clearly an acted prophecy of impending destruction (11:12–21). The story of the tenants in the vineyard, too, ends with the threat of destruction (12:1–9). Finally,

73. M. de Jonge, "Matthew 27:51 in Early Christian Exegesis," *HTR* 79 (1986): 67–79. De Jonge points out that the question was not brought up by interpreters prior to Origen (68, 78).

74. So, for example, H. L. Chronis, "The Torn Veil: Cultus and Christology in Mark 15:37–39," *JBL* 101 (1982): 97–114; and L. W. Hurtado, *Mark* (Peabody, MA: Hendrickson, 1995), 268–69.

75. So J. R. Donahue, *Are You the Christ? The Trial Narrative in the Gospel of Mark* (Missoula: SBL Press, 1973), 203; Hooker, *Commentary*, 377–78; Chance, "Cursing"; Marcus, *Mark 1–8*, 1066–67; Dowd and Malbon, "Significance," 296. A number of these scholars see the breaking down of barriers as a secondary meaning here.

76. See *y. Yoma* 6.3 and *b. Yoma* 4.1. For these texts, see R. L. Plummer, "Something Awry in the Temple? The Rending of the Temple Veil and Early Jewish Sources That Report Unusual Phenomena in the Temple around AD 30," *JETS* 48 (2005): 301–16.

77. This document is usually dated to the early first century; the relevant section is attributed to Hab 12:10–13.

at his trial, Jesus is accused of threatening to destroy the temple and to replace it with one "not made with hands" (14:58). The witnesses are false, but where they err is perhaps not so much in the threat toward the temple as the claim that Jesus will destroy it himself. To interpret the rending of the veil as the beginning of divine judgment against the temple, then, would fit perfectly with these earlier episodes.

Like the account of the baptism (with which it has several verbal and thematic links),[78] this scene is recounted solely for the benefit of Mark's audience; there is no indication that people in the story have any idea of what has happened.[79] What it shows is that Jesus's predictions are about to come true. Jesus is God's Son, his last envoy, and with his death God will come in judgment. All of those failing to produce fruit are to be condemned, starting with the temple and its chief priests. If Mark wrote in the aftermath of the disastrous Jewish war with Rome, then the shocking reality of the temple's destruction would be all the more pressing. It might have been the Romans who actually burned the temple to the ground, but they did it as instruments of God, and the reasons for its destruction, as least as Mark is concerned, can be traced back quite clearly to the authorities' rejection of Jesus.

The torn veil is the first hint within the story-world that Jesus will be vindicated. He has gone to the cross in utter obedience to the divine will, dying as a slave in accordance with his teaching. In contrast to all that the world counts as honorable, Jesus's true majesty is revealed through his ignominious death. The darkness that covers the land shows that, despite his silence, God (and perhaps the whole natural world) cannot remain indifferent to events. With the tearing of the curtain, however, the God who has remained silent in this scene is preparing to judge Jesus's

78. In Mark 10:38, Jesus conceives of his own impending death as a baptism (a connection also made by Paul in Rom 6:3). A number of scholars have noted the close verbal and thematic links between the baptism/adoption scene in 1:9–11 and 15:35–38: the figure of Elijah is common to both, as is the presence of a voice declaring Jesus to be the "Son"; the rare word *ekpneuō* in 15:37 evokes the descent of the Spirit (*pneuma*) in 1:9; and the verb to "tear" (*schizō*) is also found in both scenes, the tearing of the curtain from top to bottom calling to mind the tearing of the heavens in 1:10. (If Mark's audience knew that the curtain was a tapestry depicting the heavens [Josephus, *Jewish War* 5.212–14], as Ulansey suggests, the links would be even greater.) See the studies by S. Motyer, "The Rending of the Veil: A Markan Pentecost," *NTS* 33 (1987): 155–57; H. M. Jackson, "The Death of Jesus in Mark and the Miracle from the Cross," *NTS* 33 (1987): 16–37; Ulansey, "Heavenly Veil"; and L. E. Vaage, "Bird-Watching at the Baptism of Jesus: Early Christian Mythmaking in Mark 1:9–11," in *Reimagining Christian Origins: A Colloquium Honoring Burton L. Mack*, ed. E. A. Castelli and H. Taussig (Valley Forge: Trinity, 1996), 280–94.

79. So also Collins, *Mark*, 760; contra those who suggest that this is what the centurion saw; for example, Marcus, *Mark 1–8*, 1057.

enemies, and the first effects of that judgment—in the form of the devastated land and the desolate temple—are only too well known to Mark's audience.

And this, I suggest, is what the centurion "sees." What prompts his declaration is not the darkness, nor the power of Jesus's dying shout, nor even the tearing of the temple curtain. The Roman's remark is caused, quite simply—and as Mark clearly indicates—by observing the way in which Jesus dies (*idōn . . . hoti houtōs exepneusen*; 15:39).[80] From his vantage point, facing Jesus (*ex evantias autou*), the centurion recognizes Jesus's shameful death for what it "truly" is (*alēthōs*): a perfect expression of his teaching and the means by which humans are to enter into a new relationship with God.[81] The fact that this "confession" is made by an executioner—a hostile character who we would not expect to be sympathetic toward Jesus—is significant. Mark makes use of the trope, common in martyrological literature, whereby the executioner cannot remain unaffected by the one he is ordered to kill (see, for example, Plato, *Phaedo* 116c). The confession comes from the most unlikely source and is for that reason all the more compelling. But this is not quite the end of Jesus's story; one final episode will make the Son's vindication complete.

The Disappearance of the Body

An ancient audience might assume that, as a victim of crucifixion, Jesus would not be buried. One of the horrors of the cross was that the body would remain suspended for several days, serving as carrion for scavenging animals, and a warning to the living.[82] Yet there are indications that victims of crucifixion were sometimes buried in Judea, and Paul's brief allusion to burial in 1 Cor 15:4 does seem to suggest that a tradition regarding Jesus's burial goes back to an early date.[83] The Markan Jesus mentions burial only in connection with his anointing in 14:8, and not in any of his passion predictions, not even in the third and most explicit (10:33–34).

80. Collins argues that the phrase has "resumptive force," stressing that the centurion sees correctly in contrast to the bystanders earlier who do not; she takes this as an example of Markan *synkrisis* (*Mark*, 766–77).

81. On the centurion here, see above, pp. 216–18.

82. Lack of burial was considered a terrible thing, signaling the complete destruction not only of the physical body but also of one's identity; see Hope, *Death*, 109; Kyle, *Spectacles*, 130–33.

83. The evidence suggests to me that the historical Jesus *was* buried. If so, however, the likelihood is that the corpse was disposed of quickly, perhaps in a shallow grave with none of the rituals usually associated with burial—anointing, speeches, a meal at the grave, and a period of mourning (Kyle, *Spectacles*, 128, and Hope, *Death*, 93–120). See further my *The Historical Jesus: A Guide for the Perplexed* (London: Bloomsbury, 2012), 162–65; and for similar views, R. E. Brown, "The Burial of Jesus (Mark 15:42–47)," *CBQ* 50 (1988): 233–45.

Jesus's interment itself does not seem to be of any great interest to Mark. It serves to underscore the important apologetic point that Jesus really was dead. Pilate is surprised at how quickly Jesus expired, but his death is confirmed by the centurion who witnessed his end (15:44–45). The scene also introduces us to Joseph of Arimathea, a "respected member of the council," and three women whom we now find out have been with Jesus throughout his ministry: Mary Magdalene, Mary the mother of James the younger and Joses, and Salome. These women link the cross with the burial, and the burial with the empty grave. The note that Jesus was placed in a rock-hewn tomb with a stone rolled against the door is not, I suggest, primarily designed to dignify Jesus's burial (though some early Christians may have taken comfort in it, and the tradition, especially in John's Gospel, does grow in this direction). More significantly, it provides a *very specific location* for the body in a way that a shallow grave or a mass burial site could not have done. And Mark leaves us in no doubt that when the women come back to this very specific place on the Sunday morning, the tomb is empty (16:1–8).

Odd as it may seem, the disappearance of corpses is by no means unusual in ancient literature, leading Richard Miller to talk of the *topos* of the "missing body" or the "translation fable."[84] The "quintessential translation fable of the Roman world" was the story of Romulus, celebrated throughout the empire on the Nones of July. According to Plutarch, there were various versions of the tale in existence, but the one he seems to favor alleges that the king was found to be missing after a great storm and a darkening of the sky. At his disappearance, the rulers declared that he had been taken up to heaven and was now to be worshiped as a benevolent god, a story confirmed by an eminent patrician who claimed to have met him "arrayed in bright and shining armor" and to have been told that he was now the god Quirinus. From that day on, all honored him not only as a former king but as a god (*Romulus* 27.3–28.4). Plutarch notes that he has found many such fables in his reading, among Greeks as well as Romans. He cites the case of Aristeas of Proconnesus, who died in a fuller's shop, but when his friends came to bury him his corpse was nowhere to be found. Certain travelers claimed to have seen him, and Herodotus notes that he appeared again seven years later and instructed the people to set up a statue of

84. R. C. Miller, "Mark's Empty Tomb and Other Translation Fables in Classical Antiquity," *JBL* 129 (2010): 759–76. See also C. H. Talbert, *What Is a Gospel? The Genre of the Canonical Gospels* (Minneapolis: Fortress, 1977), 25–52; V. K. Robbins, *Jesus the Teacher: A Socio-Rhetorical Interpretation of Mark* (Philadelphia: Fortress, 1984), 192; F. G. Downing, *Doing Things with Words in the First Christian Century* (Sheffield: Sheffield Academic, 2000), 148–51; Collins, *Mark*, 791–93; and G. Petridou, *Divine Epiphany in Greek Literature and Culture* (Oxford: Oxford University Press, 2015), 4.

himself next to an altar to Apollo.[85] Plutarch also mentions the case of the violent Cleomedes of Astypalaea, who killed a large number of young boys by pulling down the pillar supporting the school roof. In an attempt to escape the angry citizens, he hid in a chest within the sanctuary of Athena; when the citizens pulled it apart, however, it was empty. Sending to the Delphic oracle, the message came back (in Pausanias's words):

> Last of the heroes is Cleomedes of Atypalaea;
> Honour him with sacrifices as being no longer a mortal.[86]

Heracles, too, signaled his assumption into heaven by disappearing completely. According to Diodorus Siculus, he ascended a pyre in obedience to the Delphic oracle; once there, Zeus sent down a thunderbolt that completely consumed both the pyre and Heracles himself. When not a single bone from his body could be found, people assumed that "he had passed from among men into the company of the Gods."[87] Diogenes Laertius preserves an earlier tradition that Empedocles tried to mimic the disappearance of Heracles by throwing himself into Mount Etna in the expectation that he would be acclaimed as a god; unfortunately for the philosopher, however, one of his distinctive bronze sandals was thrown from the fiery crater, thus exposing the whole ruse.[88] And Arrian is scandalized by an author who claims that Alexander the Great considered throwing himself into the Euphrates "so that he might disappear from the world and make more credible to posterity the belief that his birth was by a God and thus it was to the Gods that he departed."[89] This is the tradition satirized by Lucian in *The Passing of Peregrinus*, where his antihero similarly steps onto a funeral pyre in the hope that he will be taken up into the divine realm.[90] In a rather different vein, Philostratus tells of Apollonius's reception into heaven from the temple of Athene in Crete; for this author, the absence of a tomb, along with reported visions of the philosopher, confirms his divinity (*Life of Apollonius of*

85. Plutarch, *Romulus* 27.4; Herodotus, *Persian Wars* 4.14.3.

86. Plutarch, *Romulus* 27.4–5; Pausanias, *Descriptions of Greece* 6.9.6–8 (Jones, LCL 272). Plutarch also mentions the case of Alcmene, though rather briefly (*Romulus* 27.6).

87. Diodorus Siculus, *The Library of History* 4.38; Oldfather, LCL 303. Diodorus goes on to note that, after his apotheosis, Zeus persuaded Hera to adopt him as her son (4.39).

88. Diogenes Laertius, *Lives* 8.69.

89. Arrian, *Anabasis* 7.27; Brunt, LCL 269.

90. As we have seen, Lucian mischievously embellishes his account of Peregrinus's end, adding the details of the earthquake and the vulture. Within a short time, however, an old man is telling passersby that he saw Peregrinus/Proteus in white clothes with a garland of wild olive on his head (*The Passing of Peregrinus* 40).

Tyana 8.30–31). Although a number of these authors are skeptical of such stories, it is clear that for most ordinary people the disappearance of a corpse signaled both the translation of a person into the heavenly realm and the appropriateness of offering him divine honors.[91]

Mark's thought-world here seems to be Greco-Roman, with the empty tomb showing decisively that Jesus has achieved postmortem exaltation and deification.[92] Onto this, he superimposes the distinctively Jewish idea of resurrection, *anastasis*, which Jesus three times proclaims. While most people will be raised only at the eschaton, however, for Jesus it takes place straightaway, as was the case with Elijah and Moses.[93] Mark's dramatic scene shows that Jesus is now, as he promised the high priest, seated at the right hand of Power, and readers can be assured that he will soon return to earth with the "clouds of heaven" (14:62). In the circumstances, the fear and trembling of the women are only to be expected in the face of such awesome events.[94] And there was no need for them to tell their story, because Mark has told it for them in the persona of the omniscient narrator. With this final episode, then, the Son's vindication is complete.

Conclusion

Jesus's crucifixion was an attempt by the rulers of his day to consign not only his body but also his memory to oblivion. In many ways, Mark's *bios* can be seen as an act of defiance, a refusal to accept the Roman sentence and an attempt to shape the way in which both his life and death should be remembered. His work takes the place of a funeral ovation, outlining Jesus's way of life and pointing to the family of believers who succeed him.[95] While men of higher class and greater worldly

91. As L. H. Feldman notes, the final scene in Josephus's account of Moses has him disappearing into a cloud, a scene highly reminiscent of Romulus's departure from the earth (*Jewish Antiquities* 4.326–28); *Josephus' Interpretation of the Bible* (Berkeley: University of California Press, 1998), 397.

92. As Miller puts it, "One finds no conventional trait of early Jewish eschatological resurrection, whether literal or conceptual, in Mark's concluding episode"; "Mark's," 767.

93. This is presumably why Jesus is linked with these two figures at the transfiguration scene. See *Jewish Antiquities* 4.315–31 for the popular tradition that Moses simply returned to the deity.

94. On the women's fear, see above, p. 219. Miller notes that the fear of the women echoes the frightened flight of people from the Campus Martius at the translation of Romulus; "Mark's," 773.

95. On the funeral oration, see Kyle, *Spectacles*, 130–33; also Polybius, *Histories* 6.53–54.

distinction might have had their epitaphs set in stone, Mark provides his hero with a written monument to a truly worthy life.[96]

In the highly visual concluding chapters to his work, Mark holds up the death of Jesus to public scrutiny. His Jesus dies a philosopher's death, obedient to God and true to his teaching. There is a consistency between the way of life he advocates and his death: the latter is simply the logical end when a life of humility and service to others is pushed to its extreme. In certain respects, the death of the Markan Jesus is unique: by sinking to the depths of godforsaken shame and despair, Jesus ransoms his people and establishes the possibility of a new covenant with God. And yet for Mark, once Jesus has trodden his lonely path, others will be called to follow him, and Jesus's death provides a model for believers. They too must stand firm, answer charges openly, and willingly take up their cross. There is no room for complacency here, as the examples of Judas and Peter make all too clear, but Jesus promises that the Holy Spirit will be with followers in their hour of need and will speak through them (13:11). Little comfort perhaps, but a full acknowledgment of what is demanded from disciples, and a reassurance that Jesus asks no more than he has undergone himself.

In the end, then, Mark redeems Jesus's death not by casting it as "noble" or conventionally "honorable," but by showing that it conforms perfectly to his counter-cultural teaching. Like the good philosopher, Jesus has a fitting death, an extension of his earlier way of life. Presumably this was Mark's strategy from the start, even as he planned the *bios* and decided which aspects of Jesus's teaching to emphasize in that all-important middle section of the work, as Jesus makes his way to Jerusalem. We might suspect that his account convinced only those who were willing to be convinced by it. But still, as the basis for all subsequent narrative retellings, Mark's attempt to match Jesus's death to his earlier life and teaching was to have a profound effect on the way the Christian church would remember its founder for the next two millennia.

This is where Mark chooses to end his biography. Many have found his final scene abrupt and disquieting: it ends on a note of fear and trembling, and an awkward grammatical construction (the *gar* of 16:8). The doubly promised appearance of the resurrected Jesus to the disciples in Galilee (14:28; 16:7) is not recorded, and the women fail to deliver their message just as the secrecy that hangs over the gospel is finally lifted. Little wonder perhaps that scholars have speculated on

96. Hope notes that the Latin word *monumentum* can mean both a material structure and a written text; *Death*, 71. Tacitus assumes that all undocumented lives are soon forgotten: "Many will be engulfed in oblivion as if they had no name or fame. But Agricola, whose story is told for posterity, will survive" (*Agricola* 46).

whether Mark intended to write more but was prevented from doing so,[97] or (more commonly) propose that a longer ending was lost in antiquity.[98]

I cannot claim that reading Mark as a biography solves the problem of Mark's ending. As a detailed survey of the endings of biographical (or quasi-biographical) works by W. L. Knox demonstrates, no ancient *bios* ends in such an unsatisfactory way. The most common way for a biography to end was with a summary panegyric, briefly outlining the hero's virtues or greatness. This was the conclusion favored by Xenophon's *Memorabilia*, Lucian's *Demonax*, Tacitus's *Agricola*, and two of Plutarch's *Lives* (*Agis* and *Galba*). At other times, a work might end with the hero's burial, a general comment to the effect that everyone lived "happily ever after," or a concluding sentence of the type we find in Philo's *Life of Moses*—"Such, as recorded in the Holy Scriptures, was the life and such the end of Moses, king, lawgiver, high priest, prophet" (2.292). Still others end by clearing up outstanding details—perhaps a note of honors paid to the hero, the subsequent actions of characters in the story, or the fate of the hero's family; when complete, the narrative simply draws to a close (this is the way that both Plutarch and Suetonius typically end their *Lives*).

A couple of points, however, are worth making. First, when Mark was seen as sui generis, belonging to no specific known genre, there seems to have been a general assumption that the work's central topic was the *kerygma*, Christian preaching about Jesus. Such a view would clearly expect an ending in which the crucial news about Jesus's resurrection reached the disciples and was openly proclaimed. On this reading, a communication failure right at the end was highly problematic. Once we see Mark as a biography, though, some of this difficulty is resolved. Having described his hero's death along with some of the unusual things that followed it (the torn veil, the centurion's confession, and the empty tomb), Mark's account is now complete. Furthermore, these unusual portents would quite clearly show an ancient audience that, following his servile death, Jesus has indeed been vindicated

---

97. See W. L. Knox, "The Ending of St Mark's Gospel," *HTR* 35 (1942): 13–23; Knox leaves it unclear as to whether the gospel was unfinished or whether the original was damaged.

98. This view is much less common today than in the past, though see B. Witherington, *The Gospel of Mark: Socio-Rhetorical Commentary* (Grand Rapids: Eerdmans, 2001), 62. For a full discussion, see N. C. Croy, who argues that the original ending was lost (along with the opening paragraphs) because of the fragile nature of the ancient codex; *The Mutilation of Mark's Gospel* (Nashville: Abingdon, 2003). For a recent defense of Mark's ending at 16:8 (which takes the biographical nature of the work seriously), see E. E. Shively, "Recognizing Penguins: Audience Expectation, Cognitive Genre Theory, and the Ending of Mark's Gospel," *CBQ* 80 (2018): 373–92.

THE DEATH OF JESUS

by God and is now in heaven at God's right hand. The words of the angelic young man (16:7) should leave the reader in no doubt on this score.

Second, the fact that Mark's *bios* interacts with what his Christ-following audience already knows is also significant here. We have already seen that Mark's implied audience is favorably disposed toward the disciples and knows that they go on to be revered missionaries ("fishers of people") later on. We can also presume that they are aware that the risen Jesus did appear to his closest followers (so 1 Cor 15:5–8, likely a central feature of Christian preaching from the beginning). The *bios*, then, does not leave them with an enigma—Will the risen Jesus appear to his followers?—but with the promise of events that they know to have been fulfilled. Indeed, the more significance we give to our initial observation that one of Mark's primary reasons for writing a *bios* was to incorporate the life and mission of Jesus into the term "gospel" (see pp. 114–15 above), the less he needed to recount more traditional and commonly accepted material, such as appearances of the risen Lord to the disciples.

Read this way, the women's awestruck fear is still difficult, though it might now function as a warning not to let fear stand in the way of Christian witness. Mark has no happy ending to relate, but perhaps the situation of his primary recipients, who were either experiencing or fearful of persecution, prohibited any glib or naïve resolution to the story of their founding teacher. Mark has continually stressed that following Jesus is hard and that much will be asked of those who would become disciples. Like Jesus, they will be handed over to enemies, delivered to councils, beaten in synagogues, called to stand witness before governors and kings (13:9–13), and even perhaps asked to become martyrs (8:34–38). The situation of Mark's audience is not an easy one, but our author assures them that the story is not yet complete. God's retribution on Jesus's enemies has begun through the fall of Jerusalem and its temple, but listeners need to stand firm and to "watch" as they await the glorious return of the Son (13:24–27). Mark's audience are called upon to join the Christian missionaries and disciples who have gone before them into "Galilee." This is where their own discipleship must begin, with the knowledge of Jesus's salvific death and his example of living and dying before them.

Final Reflections

All biography is a form of autobiography.

—Hermione Lee[1]

The argument of this book is that Mark's *bios* is a very specific reception of earlier Jesus tradition. Our author used the genre of biography to extend Christ-following proclamation (the "gospel") from an earlier narrow focus on the death and resurrection of Jesus so that it now included the way of life of its founding figure. Situating Jesus at the heart of a biography was not an inevitable development but a bold step in outlining a radical form of Christian discipleship patterned on the life—and death—of Jesus. On a fairly basic level, ancient biography immortalizes the memory of the subject, creating a literary monument to his life and teaching. Yet it is also a bid to legitimize a specific view of that figure and to position an author and his audience as appropriate "gatekeepers" of that memory. With its focus on a revered teacher, biography seems particularly well suited to the articulation of shared values and commitments, the formation of group identity, and the binding together of a past story with present concerns and future hopes.

The Earliest Life of Jesus

Whether Mark was the *first* biographer of Jesus we cannot of course say. He is certainly the earliest biographer whose work has survived, and perhaps it is not too much of a stretch to claim that his was the most successful early biography. In the preceding chapters, I have tried to position Mark's work at the very beginning of an emerging Christian book culture. Along with the letters of Paul, selections from the Jewish Scriptures, and perhaps other written collections of sayings and brief reports, Mark's written work helped to create a Christ-following identity around *texts*, rather as the Jewish synagogue similarly focused on revered writings. As we have seen, Mark delib-

1. H. Lee, *Biography: A Very Short Introduction* (Oxford: Oxford University Press, 2009), 12.

erately writes in simple prose with a colloquial style. The *chreia* form, with its lack of circumstantial details, is not a sign of lengthy oral transmission but a commonly used building block in episodic biographies. Some material may have come to Mark already cast in this literary shape, but he may well have worked up many previously oral traditions himself, crafting and arranging earlier material so that it fitted his purposes. These powerful short anecdotes, I argued, were engaging and easily remembered; as Mark's audience took them to heart and retold them, they began to create an early Christian *paideia*, based on sayings, events, and situations from the life of Jesus. What had earlier been free-floating and rather loose tradition was now historicized and linked (for good or ill) to specific times and places in the life of Jesus.

Although Mark adopts a typically Greco-Roman genre, it is clear from the very beginning of his work, with its abrupt start and lack of a prologue, that this will not be a conventional life. With his adoption by the God of Israel, Mark gives his hero a highly prestigious ancestry. The miracles in the first half of the work establish Jesus as the Spirit-filled Son, a force to be reckoned with. In these opening chapters, he is cast as an honorable, even elite, male who constantly reveals his moderation (*sōphrosynē*) and loving concern for others (*philanthrōpia*). Not surprisingly, Jesus's authority and great popularity attract opponents, who try to dishonor him in the public world of male agonistic debate, only to be constantly shamed for their efforts. As the *bios* proceeds, however, it becomes clear that the Markan Jesus holds highly subversive views on contemporary honor and glory. He constantly scorns a life of luxury and associates with those whom others might regard as undesirable. Although he is due great honor, he prefers to keep his true identity secret, demonstrating his modesty and restraint. In the central block of teaching, he completely undermines traditional ideas of honor, urging his hearers to share in a radically different view of the world. Followers are asked to give up everything, to act as slaves to one another, and even perhaps to lose their lives—just as Jesus will do himself. Throughout the *bios*, it is clear that Jesus offers a model to followers—in his concern for others early on, his modesty and restraint, his rejection of contemporary notions of honor and esteem, and finally in his servile death. This comes out clearly in the constant invitation to "follow" Jesus, but also in the work's structure, particularly the threefold parallelism among John the Baptist, Jesus, and the believer, and the work's opening with baptism and closing with a renewed call to discipleship. Even the lack of a physical description, I suggested, plays into this call to imitate Jesus.

Other characters, I argued in Chapter 5, are largely there to enhance Jesus's qualities. Occasionally they might exemplify the values of the kingdom (persistence, extravagant giving, and so on), but more commonly they act as a foil to Jesus. A large part of Markan "characterization" is due to the careful placement and juxtaposition of episodes, a patterning that invites comparison and contrast. We saw, for example, that the elaborate *synkrisis* surrounding "King" Herod contrasts the tyrannical monarch with the emerging portrait of Jesus, establishing the latter even more firmly as an ideal elite male with royal and imperial qualities. I also noted that the function of the Twelve is not to act as model disciples: not only do they frequently fall short on this score, but there is no need for them to do so—Jesus himself stands as the central character to be emulated. Rather, the often conflicting and ambiguous presentation of the Twelve is primarily designed to throw *Jesus's* character and way of life into relief. The Twelve, I suggested, perform three main roles: first, they allow Jesus to be presented as an exemplary and authoritative teacher who gathers a circle of followers around him (here they act as praiseworthy followers); second, they allow Jesus to expand on his teaching, especially as it becomes increasingly difficult (here by allowing the Markan Jesus to continue his instruction by asking questions and misunderstanding what they are told); and, third, they allow Mark to highlight Jesus's courageous and lonely death (through their cowardice and providing *exempla* of the kind of behavior to avoid). As is the case with other *bioi*, Mark will have expected his work to be read alongside other Christian traditions: what might seem to be a harsh portrait of the Twelve has to be read in the context of a Christ-following group who knows of the great missionary exploits of the disciples later on, and interpret Peter's shameful denial in the light of his later martyrdom.

Paradoxically, the only fitting end for the Jesus of Mark's biography is a shameful one. In Chapter 6 we saw that Jesus's death is salvific for our author—as God's beloved Son, he is the only one able to make himself least of all and to go to a lonely death as a "ransom for many." Once he has suffered an ignominious execution and been vindicated by God, however, his servile death serves as a model for others to emulate. Our author turns conventional ideas of a noble death upside down, even as his earlier teaching in chs. 8–10 turned ideas of honor/shame on their head. Indeed, it seems likely that Mark began planning his work from its ending, with his subject's shameful death strongly influencing the countercultural contents of the central body of teaching. In this way, Mark presents Jesus's life and death as all of a piece—the values that he preached to others and by which he lived are also those that define his death. As a good philosopher, he dies in accordance with his preaching.

Automimēsis

One final point has intrigued me throughout the writing of this book. I opened this closing chapter with a quotation from Dame Hermione Lee, professor of English literature at the University of Oxford and a noted expert on biography: "all biography is a form of autobiography."[2] She is of course correct: the choice of biographical

2. Lee, *Biography*, 12.

subject matter is not an arbitrary or random one. Almost by definition, a biographer writes about a subject whom he or she considers important, someone the author admires or can relate to, and a person whose life might have something important to say to readers today. There is usually a deeply personal element, a spark of empathy or a shared situation, that draws the biographer to a particular subject. But it is not only in the choice of subject that personal preference plays a part. The very act of constructing a "life," choosing where to start and where to end, deciding what to include and what to omit, and determining how to link events into a coherent narrative, reveals as much about the biographer as the subject. When the character is no longer alive and primary evidence is all too thin (or perhaps contradictory), the biographer is tempted to fill in the gaps according to his or her own values and interests. This process is not limited to biography but spans the range of artistic and imaginative endeavors. It even has a name: *automimēsis* (self-imitation), or transference.[3]

A clear example of this in biblical scholarship is research into the historical Jesus. One of the commonly acknowledged pitfalls of this particular academic pursuit is the tendency of historians to reconstruct a Jesus in their own likeness. The famous words of George Tyrrell echo with an ominous ring in the mind of all Jesus critics: what Protestant questers found, he quipped, was the face of a Protestant interpreter reflected back at them from the bottom of a deep well.[4] Perhaps more accurately, what Jesus critics all too commonly find is a Jesus who embodies their own values and concerns, a Jesus who stands for what they find important and who believes the things they believe.

The same feature can also be observed in ancient *bioi*. The differing presentations of Socrates in Xenophon's *Memorabilia* and Plato's *Phaedo* provide a good illustration. Both authors seek to absolve Socrates of the charges leveled against him, but both go on to cast him as the mouthpiece of their own distinctive philosophy. In his praise of Agesilaus, too, Xenophon reveals what characteristics he holds dear, and as Tomas Hägg notes, he "may be accused of imposing his own ideals on his object."[5] Similarly, the *Cyropaedia* reveals as much about Xenophon's ideals of leadership as it does about the great Persian king (the greater the distance between the subject and his biographer, the easier it was for the biographer to craft him in his

---

3. T. Hägg, *The Art of Biography in Antiquity* (Cambridge: Cambridge University Press, 2012), 5–6.

4. G. Tyrrell, *Christianity at the Crossroads* (London: Longmans, Green, 1913), 44 (Tyrrell directed his argument specifically against Adolf von Harnack). Similar sentiments were shared by A. Schweitzer, *The Quest of the Historical Jesus* (London: A&C Black, 1954), 4.

5. Hägg, *Art of Biography*, 49.

own image).[6] In stressing Evagoras's mildness and moderation, Isocrates doubtless reflected his own ethical and political ideals. So blatantly does Demonax seem to speak with the voice of Lucian that many have doubted that he really existed.[7] And Philo's note—without any biblical warrant—that Moses applied himself to learning (*Life of Moses* 1.20) has not unreasonably led Louis Feldman to comment that "one is tempted to think that Philo may also have molded his biblical heroes in his own image."[8]

Such comparisons might cause us to reflect a little on Mark. A question rarely asked is, How far has the evangelist cast Jesus in his own image? Put differently, to what extent does the Markan Jesus exhibit the values and concerns of Mark himself? When the evangelists were seen as little more than compilers of units of tradition, these questions would have been meaningless. The more Mark is seen as a biographer, however, engaged in what was fundamentally a creative and imaginative art form, the more these questions become important. As long ago as 1912, George Bernard Shaw could confidently assert that Matthew, "like most biographers, strives to identify the opinions and prejudices of his hero with his own."[9] This would be all the more true for Mark, the first to set out traditional material in biographical form. Clearly our author was a devoted follower of Jesus, someone who had reflected long and hard on his master's shameful exit and who saw significant links between discipleship and servanthood. Whatever was the case for the historical Jesus, the most important aspect of his teaching for our author was his countercultural message, his redefinition of honor and shame, and his call to followers to define themselves through adherence to this new code of service. This is the memory with which our author worked, imposing his own pattern on the chaos of tradition, and crafting it into a powerful story of a great teacher who conquers even the most unjust and humiliating of deaths.

What all of this means is that Mark's own person and situation cannot be entirely divorced from his work. He has chosen to present his story of Jesus in a certain way because of his own particular interests—and presumably he expected his intended audience to share his concerns and to find his work useful. Consequently,

---

6. Hägg, *Art of Biography*, 29, 33–34, 49, 64–66.

7. See the survey in D. Clay, "Lucian of Samosata: Four Philosophical Lives" (Nigrinus, Demonax, Peregrinus, Alexander Pseudomantis), in *ANRW* II 36.5, 3406–50.

8. L. H. Feldman, *Philo's Portrayal of Moses in the Context of Ancient Judaism* (Notre Dame: University of Notre Dame Press, 2007), 48.

9. G. B. Shaw, preface to *Androcles and the Lion* ("On the Prospects of Christianity"), in *The Bodley Head Bernard Shaw: Collected Plays with Their Prefaces* (London: Max Reinhardt/Bodley Head, 1972; orig. 1912), 4:487.

the standard historical-critical way of beginning the study of a gospel by asking about its authorship, date, and place is by no means misguided (however meager our results). We may also have clues here as to why Mark's work was not the final word. It is in the nature of biographies that they are only ever provisional—there can never be a "definitive biography." All bear the impress not only of their author but also of the circumstances of their writing and the people to whom they were directed.[10] It was inevitable therefore that new biographers, taking inspiration from Mark but with their own concerns, and addressing new situations and contexts, would produce their own versions. Hence it is no great surprise to find Mark's work inspiring those of Matthew, Luke, and John.

In the end, literary figures overtake their historical counterparts. Try as we might, we can no longer get behind Mark's account. The lines of communication between the historical Jesus and the Markan creation are too confused, too contradictory, and too fragile. But why would we want anything other than Mark's account? Reconstructing the historical Jesus is a good scholarly enterprise and might even be important in terms of countering perverse claims about him, but the historical man (however reconstructed) will never speak to the hearts of millions of believers in the way that Mark's work has done for two millennia, and will doubtless continue to do. Mark's biography has forever set the contours of how the story of Jesus should be told. Whether we like it or not, the story of Jesus is *Mark's* story of Jesus.

10. So E. Homberger and J. Charmley, *The Troubled Face of Biography* (London: Macmillan, 1988), xi.

Bibliography

Achtemeier, Paul J. *Jesus and the Miracle Tradition*. Eugene, OR: Wipf & Stock, 2008.

———. "Omne Verbum Sonat: The New Testament and the Oral Environment of Late Western Antiquity." *JBL* 109 (1990): 3–27.

Adams, Sean A. *The Genre of Acts and Collected Biography*. Cambridge: Cambridge University Press, 2013.

———. "Luke and Progymnasmata: Rhetorical Handbooks, Rhetorical Sophistication and Genre Selection." Pages 137–54 in *Ancient Education and Early Christianity*. Edited by Matthew Ryan Hauge and Andrew W. Pitts. LNTS 533. London: Bloomsbury T&T Clark, 2016.

———. "Luke's Preface and Its Relationship to Greek Historiography: A Response to Loveday Alexander." *JGRChJ* 3 (2006): 177–91.

———. "What Are *Bioi/Vitae*? Generic Self-Consciousness in Ancient Biography." *The Oxford Handbook to Ancient Biography*. Edited by Koen De Temmerman. Oxford: Oxford University Press, 2020.

Aguilar Chiu, José E. "A Theological Reading of ἐξέπνευσεν in Mark 15:37, 39." *CBQ* 78 (2016): 682–705.

Ahearne-Kroll, Stephen P. "Challenging the Divine: LXX Psalm 21 in the Passion Narrative of the Gospel of Mark." Pages 119–48 in *The Trial and Death of Jesus: Essays on the Passion Narrative in Mark*. Edited by Geert van Oyen and Tom Shepherd. CBET 45. Leuven: Peeters, 2006.

———. *The Psalms of Lament in Mark's Passion: Jesus's Davidic Suffering*. SNTSMS 142. Cambridge: Cambridge University Press, 2007.

Ahearne-Kroll, Stephen P., Paul A. Holloway, and James A. Kelhoffer, eds. *Women and Gender in Ancient Religions*. WUNT 263. Tübingen: Mohr Siebeck, 2010.

Alexander, Loveday. "Ancient Book Production and the Circulation of the Gospels." Pages 71–111 in *The Gospels for All Christians: Rethinking the Gospel Audiences*. Edited by Richard Bauckham. Edinburgh: T&T Clark, 1998.

———. *The Preface to Luke's Gospel: Literary Convention and Social Context in Luke 1.1–4 and Acts 1.1*. SNTSMS 78. Cambridge: Cambridge University Press, 1993.

———. "What Is a Gospel?" Pages 13–33 in *The Cambridge Companion to the Gospels*. Edited by Stephen Barton. Cambridge: Cambridge University Press, 2006.

Alexander, Philip S. "Rabbinic Biography and the Biography of Jesus." Pages 19–50 in *Syn-*

optic Studies: The Ampleforth Conferences of 1982 and 1983. Edited by Christopher M. Tuckett. JSNTSup 7. Sheffield: JSOT Press, 1984.

Anderson, Hugh. "The Old Testament in Mark's Gospel." Pages 280–306 in *The Use of the Old Testament in the New*. Edited by James M. Efird. Durham, NC: Duke University Press, 1972.

Anderson, Janice C., and Stephen D. Moore. "Matthew and Masculinity." Pages 67–92 in *New Testament Masculinities*. Edited by Stephen D. Moore and Janice Capel Anderson. SemeiaSt 45. Atlanta: SBL Press, 2003.

Armstrong, A. M. "The Methods of the Greek Physiognomists." *G&R* 5 (1958): 52–56.

Arnal, William. "Major Episodes in the Biography of Jesus. An Assessment of the Historicity of the Narrative Tradition." *TJT* 13 (1997): 201–26.

Ash, Rhiannon. "Never Say Die! Assassinating Emperors in Suetonius' *Lives*." Pages 200–216 in *Writing Biography in Greece and Rome*. Edited by Koen De Temmerman and Kristoffel Demoen. Cambridge: Cambridge University Press, 2016.

Ash, Rhiannon, Judith Mossman, and Francis B. Titchener, eds. *Fame and Infamy: Essays for Christopher Pelling on Characterization in Greek and Roman Biography*. Oxford: Oxford University Press, 2015.

Assmann, Jan. "Form as a Mnemonic Device: Cultural Texts and Cultural Memory." Pages 67–82 in *Performing the Gospel: Orality, Memory, and Mark; Essays Dedicated to Werner Kelber*. Edited by Richard A. Horsley, Jonathan A. Draper, and John Miles Foley. Minneapolis: Fortress, 2006.

Aune, David E. "Genre Theory and the Genre-Function of Mark and Matthew." Pages 145–75 in *Mark and Matthew I, Comparative Readings: Understanding the Earliest Gospels in Their First Century Settings*. Edited by Eve-Marie Becker and Anders Runesson. WUNT 271. Tübingen: Mohr Siebeck, 2011.

———. "Greco-Roman Biography." Pages 107–26 in *Greco-Roman Literature and the New Testament*. Edited by David E. Aune. Sources for Biblical Study 21. Atlanta: Scholars Press, 1988.

———. *The New Testament in Its Literary Environment*. LEC 8. Philadelphia: Westminster, 1987.

———. "The Problem of Genre of the Gospels: A Critique of C. H. Talbert's *What Is a Gospel?*" Pages 9–60 in *Studies of History and Tradition in the Four Gospels*. Edited by R. T. France and David Wenham. Sheffield: JSOT Press, 1981.

Aune, David E., ed. *Greco-Roman Literature and the New Testament*. Sources for Biblical Study 21. Atlanta: Scholars Press, 1988.

Aus, Roger. *Water into Wine and the Beheading of John the Baptist: Early Jewish-Christian Interpretation of Esther 1 in John 2:1–11 and Mark 6:17–29*. Atlanta: Scholars Press, 1988.

Bacon, Benjamin W. "The Prologue of Mark: A Study of Sources and Structure." *JBL* 26 (1907): 84–106.

Baert, Barbara. "The Dancing Daughter and the Head of John the Baptist (Mark 6:14–29) Revisited: An Interdisciplinary Approach." *Louvain Studies* 38 (2014): 5–29.

Bagnall, Roger. *Everyday Writing in the Graeco-Roman East*. Berkeley: University of California Press, 2011.

Baltzer, Klaus. *Die Biographie der Propheten*. Neukirchen-Vluyn: Neukirchener Verlag, 1975.

Baragwanath, Emily. "Characterization in Herodotus." Pages 17–35 in *Fame and Infamy: Essays on Characterization in Greek and Roman Biography and Historiography*. Edited by Rhiannon Ash, Judith Mossman, and Frances B. Titchener. Oxford: Oxford University Press.

Barton, Stephen, ed. *The Cambridge Companion to the Gospels*. Cambridge: Cambridge University Press, 2006.

———. "Can We Identify the Gospel Audiences?" Pages 173–94 in *The Gospels for All Christians: Rethinking the Gospel Audiences*. Edited by Richard Bauckham. Edinburgh: T&T Clark, 1998.

Bassett, Sherylee R. "The Death of Cyrus the Younger." *ClQ* 49 (1999): 473–83.

Bauckham, Richard. "The Eyewitnesses in the Gospel of Mark." *SEÅ* 74 (2009): 19–39.

———. "For Whom Were the Gospels Written?" Pages 9–48 in *The Gospels for All Christians: Rethinking the Gospel Audiences*. Edited by Richard Bauckham. Edinburgh: T&T Clark, 1998.

———, ed. *The Gospels for All Christians: Rethinking the Gospel Audiences*. Edinburgh: T&T Clark, 1998.

———. *Jesus and the Eyewitnesses: The Gospels as Eyewitness Testimony*. 2nd ed. Grand Rapids: Eerdmans, 2017.

———. "Response to Philip Esler." *SJT* 51 (1998): 249–53.

———. *Testimony of the Beloved Disciple: Narrative, History, and Theology in the Gospel of John*. Grand Rapids: Baker Academic, 2007.

Baumgarten, Roland. "Dangerous Tears? Platonic Provocations and Aristotelian Answers." Pages 85–104 in *Tears in the Graeco-Roman World*. Edited by Thorsten Fögen. Berlin: de Gruyter, 2009.

Beard, Mary. *Literacy in the Roman World*. JRASup 3. Ann Arbor: University of Michigan Press, 1991.

———. *The Roman Triumph*. Cambridge, MA: Harvard University Press, 2009.

Beavis, Mary Ann. *Mark's Audience: The Literary and Social Setting of Mark 4.11–12*. JSNTSup 33. Sheffield: Sheffield Academic, 1989.

Beck, Mark. "Lucian's *Life of Demonax*: The Socratic Paradigm, Individuality, and Personality." Pages 80–96 in *Writing Biography in Greece and Rome*. Edited by Koen De Temmerman and Kristoffel Demoen. Cambridge: Cambridge University Press, 2016.

Becker, Eve-Marie. *Das Markusevangelium im Rahmen Antiker Historiographie*. WUNT 194. Tübingen: Mohr Siebeck, 2006.

———. "Dating Mark and Matthew as Ancient Literature." Pages 123–43 in *Mark and Matthew I, Comparative Readings: Understanding the Earliest Gospels in Their First Century Settings*. Edited by Eve-Marie Becker and Anders Runesson. WUNT 271. Tübingen: Mohr Siebeck, 2011.

Becker, Eve-Marie, and Anders Runesson, eds. *Mark and Matthew I, Comparative Read-*

ings: Understanding the Earliest Gospels in Their First-Century Setting. WUNT 271. Tübingen: Mohr Siebeck, 2011.

Becker, Michael. "Miracle Traditions in Early Rabbinic Literature: Some Questions on Their Pragmatics." Pages 48–69 in *Wonders Never Cease: The Purpose of Narrating Miracle Stories in the New Testament and Its Religious Environment*. Edited by Bert Jan Lietaert Peerbolte and Michael Labahn. LNTS 288. London: T&T Clark, 2006.

Beneker, Jeffrey. "Nepos' Biographical Method in the Lives of Foreign Generals." *CJ* 105 (2009): 109–21.

Bennema, Cornelis. "A Theory of Character in the Fourth Gospel with Reference to Ancient and Modern Literature." *BibInt* 17 (2009): 375–421.

Berger, Klaus. "Hellenistische Gattungen im NT." *ANRW* II 25.2:1031–1432.

Best, Ernest. "Mark's Narrative Technique." *JSNT* 37 (1989): 43–58.

———. "Mark's Readers: A Profile." Pages 839–58 in *The Four Gospels, 1992: Festschrift for Frans Neirynck*. BETL 100. Edited by Frans van Segbroeck, Christopher M. Tuckett, Gilbert Van Belle, and Joseph Verheyden. Leuven: Leuven University Press, 1992.

———. "Peter in the Gospel according to Mark." *CBQ* 40 (1978): 547–58.

———. "The Role of the Disciples in Mark." *NTS* 23 (1976–7): 377–401.

———. *The Temptation and the Passion: The Markan Soteriology*. 2nd ed. SNTSMS 2. Cambridge: Cambridge University Press, 1990.

Betz, Hans D. *Nachfolge und Nachahmung Jesu Christi im Neuen Testament*. BHT 37. Tübingen: Mohr Siebeck, 1967.

Billault, Alain S. "Characterization in the Ancient Novel." Pages 115–29 in *The Novel in the Ancient World*. Edited by Gareth L. Schmeling. Leiden: Brill, 1996.

Bird, Michael. "The Markan Community, Myth or Maze? Bauckham's 'The Gospel for All Christians' Revisited." *JTS* 57 (2006): 474–86.

Black, C. Clifton. *The Disciples according to Mark: Markan Redaction in Current Debate*. 2nd ed. JSNTSup 27 Grand Rapids: Eerdmans, 2012.

———. *Mark: Images of an Apostolic Interpreter*. Studies on Personalities of the New Testament. Edinburgh: T&T Clark, 2001.

———. "Mark as Historian of God's Kingdom." *CBQ* 71 (2009): 64–83.

Black, Matthew. "The Use of Rhetorical Terminology in Papias on Mark and Matthew." *JSNT* 37 (1989): 31–41.

Bloomer, W. Martin. *Valerius Maximus and the Rhetoric of the New Nobility*. Chapel Hill: University of North Carolina Press, 1992.

Bockmuehl, Markus N. A. *Simon Peter in Scripture and Memory: The New Testament Apostle in the Early Church*. Grand Rapids: Baker Academic, 2012.

Boeft, Jan den. "Asclepius' Healings Made Known." Pages 20–31 in *Wonders Never Cease: The Purpose of Narrating Miracle Stories in the New Testament and Its Religious Environment*. Edited by Michael Labahn and B. Jan Lietaert Peerbolte. LNTS 288. London: T&T Clark, 2006.

Bond, Helen K. "Barabbas Remembered." Pages 59–71 in *Jesus and Paul: Global Perspectives in Honor of James D. G. Dunn for His 70th Birthday*. Edited by B. J. Oropeza, C. K.

Robertson, and Douglas Mohrmann. LNTS 414. London: T&T Clark International, 2009.

———. *Caiaphas: Friend of Rome and Judge of Jesus?* Louisville: Westminster John Knox, 2004.

———. *The Historical Jesus: A Guide for the Perplexed.* London: Bloomsbury, 2012.

———. "Josephus on Herod's Domestic Intrigue in the Jewish War." *JSJ* 43 (2012): 295–314.

———. "Paragon of Discipleship? Simon of Cyrene in the Markan Passion Narrative." Pages 18–35 in *Matthew and Mark across Perspectives: Essays in Honour of Stephen C. Barton and William R. Telford.* Edited by Kristian A. Bendoraitis and Nijay K. Gupta. LNTS 538. Edinburgh: T&T Clark, 2016.

———. *Pontius Pilate in History and Interpretation.* SNTSMS 100. Cambridge: Cambridge University Press, 1998.

———. "Was Peter behind Mark's Gospel?" Pages 46–61 in *Peter in Earliest Christianity.* Edited by Bond and Larry W. Hurtado. Grand Rapids: Eerdmans, 2015.

———. "'You'll Probably Get Away with Crucifixion': Laughing at the Cross in the *Life of Brian* and the Ancient World." Pages 113–26 in *Jesus and Brian: Exploring the Historial Jesus and His Times via Monty Python's "Life of Brian."* Edited by Joan E. Taylor. London: Bloomsbury, 2015.

Bonfante Warren, L. "Roman Triumphs and Etruscan Kings: The Changing Face of the Triumph." *JRS* 60 (1970): 49–66.

Boomershine, Thomas E. "Peter's Denial as Polemic or Confession: The Implications of Media Criticism for Biblical Hermeneutics." *Semeia* 39 (1987): 47–68.

Boomershine, Thomas E., and Gilbert L. Bartholomew. "The Narrative Technique of Mark 16:8." *JBL* 100 (1981): 213–23.

Borgen, Peder. "The Place of the Old Testament in the Formation of New Testament Theology: Response." *NTS* 23 (1976): 67–75.

Boring, M. Eugene. *Mark: A Commentary.* Louisville: Westminster John Knox, 2006.

———. "Markan Christology: God-Language for Jesus?" *NTS* 45 (1999): 451–71.

Borrell, Agusti. *The Good News of Peter's Denial: A Narrative and Rhetorical Reading of Mark 14:54, 66–72.* Translated by S. Conlon. Atlanta: Scholars Press, 1998.

Botha, Pieter J. J. "Mark's Story as Oral Traditional Literature." *Hervormde Teologiese Studies* 47 (1991): 304–31.

Bousset, Wilhelm. *Kyrios Christos: A History of the Belief in Christ from the Beginnings of Christianity to Irenaeus.* Translated by J. E. Steely. Nashville: Abingdon, 1970. Translation of *Kyrios Christos: Geschichte des Chirstusglaubens von den Anfängen des Christentums bis Irenaeus.* Göttingen: Vandenhoeck & Ruprecht, 1913.

Branscomb, B. H. *The Gospel of Mark.* London: Hodder and Stoughton, 1937.

Brant, Jo-Ann. "Divine Birth and Apparent Parents: The Plot of the Fourth Gospel." Pages 199–217 in *Ancient Fiction and Early Christian Narrative.* Edited by Ronald F. Hock, J. Bradley Chance, and Judith Perkins. SBLSymS 6. Atlanta: Scholars Press, 1998.

Braund, David C. "Berenice in Rome." *Historia* 33 (1984): 120–23.

Breytenbach, Cilliers. "Das Markusevangelium also Episodische Erzählung." Pages 138–69 in

Der Erzähler des Evangeliums: methodische Neuansätze in der Markusforschung. SBS 118/119. Edited by Ferdinand Hahn. Stuttgart: Verlag Katholisches Bibelwerk, 1985.

———. "Narrating the Death of Jesus in Mark: Utterances of the Main Character, Jesus." *ZNW* 105 (2014): 153–68.

Brown, Raymond E. "The Burial of Jesus (Mark 15:42–47)." *CBQ* 50 (1988): 233–45.

———. *The Death of the Messiah: From Gethsemane to the Grave; A Commentary on the Passion Narratives in the Four Gospels.* 2 vols. New York: Doubleday, 1994.

Brown, Scott G. "Mark 11:1–12:12: A Triple Intercalation?" *CBQ* (2002): 78–89.

Bruce, Iain A. F. "Theopompus and Classical Greek Historiography." *History and Theory* 1 (1970): 86–109.

Bryan, Christopher. *A Preface to Mark: Notes on the Gospel in Its Literary and Cultural Settings.* Oxford: Oxford University Press, 1993.

Bryskog, Samuel. *Story as History—History as Story: The Gospel Tradition in the Context of Ancient Oral History.* WUNT 123. Tübingen: Mohr Siebeck, 2000.

Bultmann, Rudolf. *History of the Synoptic Tradition.* 2nd ed. Translated by J. Marsh. Oxford: Blackwell, 1968. Translation of *Die Geschichte der synoptischen Tradition.* FRLANT 29. Göttingen: Vandenhoeck & Ruprecht, 1921.

———. "The Gospels (Form)." Pages 86–92 in vol. 1 of *Twentieth Century Theology in the Making.* Edited by Jaroslav Pelikan. Translated by R. A. Wilson. London: Collins, 1969.

Burnett, Frederick W. "Characterization and Reader Construction of Characters in the Gospels." *Semeia* 63 (1993): 3–28.

Burridge, Richard A. "About People, by People, for People: Gospel Genre and Audiences." Pages 113–45 in *The Gospels for All Christians: Rethinking the Gospel Audiences.* Edited by Richard Bauckham. Edinburgh: T&T Clark, 1998.

———. *Four Gospels, One Jesus? A Symbolic Reading.* 2nd ed. Grand Rapids: Eerdmans, 2005.

———. *Imitating Jesus: An Inclusive Approach to New Testament Ethics.* Grand Rapids: Eerdmans, 2007.

———. "Reading the Gospels as Biography." Pages 31–49 in *Limits of Ancient Biography.* Edited by Brian McGing and Judith Mossman. Swansea: Classical Press of Wales, 2006.

———. *What Are the Gospels? A Comparison with Graeco-Roman Biography.* Cambridge: Cambridge University Press, 1992; 2nd ed., Grand Rapids: Eerdmans, 2004; 3rd ed., Waco: Baylor University Press, 2018.

Burkett, Delbert R. *The Son of Man Debate: A History and Evaluation.* SNTSMS 107. Cambridge: Cambridge University Press, 1999.

Butts, James R. "The Progymnasmata of Theon: A New Text with Translation and Commentary." PhD diss., Claremont Graduate School, 1987.

Campbell, William S. "Engagement, Disengagement and Obstruction: Jesus's Defense Strategies in Mark's Trial and Execution Scenes (14.53–64; 15.1–39)." *JSNT* 26 (2004): 283–300.

Cancik, Hubert. "Bios und Logos: Formgeschichtliche Untersuchungen zu Lukians 'Demonax.'" Pages 115–30 in *Markus—Philologie. Historische, literargeschichtliche und stilis-*

tische Untersuchungen zum zweiten Evangelium. Edited by Hubert Cancik. WUNT 33. Tübingen: Mohr Siebeck, 1984.

———. "Die Gattung Evangelium: Das Evangelium des Markus im Rahmen der antiken Historiographie." Pages 85–113 in *Markus—Philologie. Historische, literargeschichtliche und stilistische Untersuchungen zum zweiten Evangelium.* Edited by Hubert Cancik. WUNT 33. Tübingen: Mohr Siebeck, 1984.

Capes, David B. "*Imitatio Christi* and the Gospel Genre." *BBR* 13 (2003): 1–19.

Carter, Warren. "Cross-Gendered Romans and Mark's Jesus: Legion Enters the Pigs (Mark 5:1–20)." *JBL* 134 (2015): 139–55.

Castelli, Elizabeth A. *Imitating Paul: A Discourse of Power.* Literary Currents in Biblical Interpretation. Louisville: Westminster John Knox, 1991.

Catchpole, D. "The Fearful Silence of the Women at the Tomb: A Study of Markan Theology." *Journal of Theology for Southern Africa* 19 (1977): 3–10.

Chance, J. Bradley. "The Cursing of the Temple and the Tearing of the Veil in the Gospel of Mark." *BibInt* 15 (2007): 268–91.

———. "Fiction in Ancient Biography: An Approach to a Sensitive Issue in Gospel Interpretation." *Perspectives in Religious Studies* 18 (1991): 125–42.

Charlesworth, James H. "Can One Recover Aramaic Sources behind Mark's Gospel?" *Review of Rabbinic Judaism* 5 (2002): 249–58.

Christ, Matthew R. "Theopompus and Herodotus: A Reassessment." *ClQ* 43 (1993): 47–52.

Chronis, Harry L. "The Torn Veil: Cultus and Christology in Mark 15:37–39." *JBL* 101 (1982): 97–114.

Clark, Donald. L. *Rhetoric in Greco-Roman Education.* New York: Columbia University Press, 1957.

Clay, Diskin. "Lucian of Samosata: Four Philosophical Lives." *ANRW* II 36.5:3406–50.

Collins, Adela Y. *The Beginnings of the Gospel: Probings of Mark in Context.* Minneapolis: Fortress, 1992.

———. "From Noble Death to Crucified Messiah." *NTS* 40 (1994): 481–503.

———. "Genre and the Gospels." *Journal of Religion* (1995): 239–45.

———. "The Genre of the Passion Narrative." *Studia Theologica* 47 (1993): 3–28.

———. *Mark: A Commentary.* Hermeneia. Minneapolis: Fortress, 2007.

———. "Mark and His Readers: The Son of God among Greeks and Romans." *HTR* 93 (2000): 85–100.

———. "Mark and His Readers: The Son of God among Jews." *HTR* 92 (1999): 393–408.

———. "Mark's Interpretation of the Death of Jesus." *JBL* 128 (2009): 545–54.

———. "The Origin of the Designation of Jesus as 'Son of Man.'" *HTR* 80 (1987): 391–407.

Colson, Francis H. "Τάξει in Papias (The Gospels and Rhetorical Schools)." *JTS* 14 (1912): 62–69.

Conzelmann, Hans. "History and Theology in the Passion Narratives of the Synoptic Gospels." *Int* 24 (1970): 178–97.

Cook, John G. "Envisioning Crucifixion: Light from Several Inscriptions and the Palatine Graffito." *NovT* 50 (2008): 262–85.

Combes, I. A. H. *The Metaphor of Slavery in the Writings of the Early Church: From the New Testament to the Beginning of the Fifth Century.* JSNTSup 156. Sheffield: Sheffield Academic, 1998.

Cotter, Wendy. *The Christ of the Miracle Stories: Portrait through Encounter.* Grand Rapids: Baker Academic, 2010.

———. *Miracles in Greco-Roman Antiquity: A Sourcebook for the Study of New Testament Miracle Stories.* The Context of Early Christianity. Oxford: Routledge, 1999.

Cox Miller, Patricia, ed. *Biography in Late Antiquity: A Quest for the Holy Man.* Berkeley: University of California Press, 1983.

Cranfield, Charles E. B. *The Gospel according to Saint Mark: An Introduction and Commentary.* Cambridge: Cambridge University Press, 1959.

Crawford, Barry S., and Merrill P. Miller, eds. *Redescribing the Gospel of Mark.* Early Christianity and Its Literature 22. Atlanta: SBL Press, 2017.

Cribiore, Raffaella. *Gymnastics of the Mind: Greek Education in Hellenistic and Roman Egypt.* Princeton: Princeton University Press, 2001.

Crossan, J. D. *The Historical Jesus: The Life of a Mediterranean Jewish Peasant.* San Francisco: HarperSanFrancisco, 1991.

Crowder, Stephanie R. B. *Simon of Cyrene: A Case of Roman Conscription.* New York: Peter Lang, 2002.

Croy, N. Clayton. *The Mutilation of Mark's Gospel.* Nashville: Abingdon, 2003.

Culpepper, R. Alan. "Mark 6:17–29 in Its Narrative Context: Kingdoms in Conflict." Pages 145–63 in *Mark as Story: Retrospect and Prospect.* Edited by Kelly R. Iverson and Christopher W. Skinner. Atlanta: SBL Press, 2011.

Damm, Alexander. *Ancient Rhetoric and the Synoptic Problem: Clarifying Markan Priority.* BETL 252. Leuven: Peeters, 2013.

D'Angelo, Mary Rose. "Abba and Father: Imperial Theology in the Contexts of Jesus and the Gospels." Pages 64–78 in *The Historical Jesus in Context.* Edited by A.-J. Levine, Dale C. Allison Jr., and J. D. Crossan. Princeton: Princeton University Press, 2006.

Darling Young, Robin. "The 'Woman with the Soul of Abraham': Traditions about the Mother of the Maccabean Martyrs." Pages 67–81 in *"Women Like This": New Perspectives on Jewish Women in the Graeco-Roman World.* Edited A.-J. Levine. Atlanta: Scholars Press, 1991.

Daube, David. "The Responsibilities of Master and Disciples in the Gospels." *NTS* 19 (1972/1973): 1–15.

Davies, Stevan. "Mark's Use of the *Gospel of Thomas*, Part One." *Neot* 30 (1996): 307–34.

Davies, Stevan, and Kevin Johnson. "Mark's Use of the *Gospel of Thomas*, Part Two." *Neot* 31 (1997): 233–61.

Deissmann, Adolf. *Light from the Ancient East: The New Testament Illustrated by Recently Discovered Texts of the Graeco-Roman World.* Translated by L. R. M. Strachan. London: Hodder and Stoughton, 1927.

De Pourcq, Maarten, and Geert Roskam. "Mirroring Virtues in Plutarch's Lives of Agis, Cleomenes and the Gracchi." Pages 163–80 in *Writing Biography in Greece and Rome.*

Edited by Koen De Temmerman and Kristoffel Demoen. Cambridge: Cambridge University Press, 2016.

De Temmerman, Koen. "Ancient Biography and Formalities of Fiction." Pages 3–25 in *Writing Biography in Greece and Rome*. Edited by Koen De Temmerman and Kristoffel Demoen. Cambridge: Cambridge University Press, 2016.

De Temmerman, Koen, and Kristoffel Demoen, eds. *Writing Biography in Greece and Rome: Narrative Technique and Fictionalization*. Cambridge: Cambridge University Press, 2016.

Dewey, Arthur J. "The Locus for Death: Social Memory and the Passion Narratives." Pages 119–28 in *Memory, Tradition, and Text: Uses of the Past in Early Christianity*. Edited by Alan Kirk and Tom Thatcher. Semeia 52. Atlanta: SBL Press, 2005.

———. "'Time to Murder and Create': Visions and Revisions in the Gospel of Peter." *Semeia* 49 (1990): 101–27.

Dewey, Joanna. "Mark as Aural Narrative: Structures as Clues to Understanding." *Sewanee Theological Review* 36 (1992): 45–56.

———. "Mark as Interwoven Tapestry: Forecasts and Echoes for a Listening Audience." *CBQ* 53 (1991): 221–35.

———. "Oral Methods of Structuring in Mark." *Int* 43 (1989): 32–44.

———. "The Survival of Mark's Gospel: A Good Story?" *JBL* 123 (2004): 495–507.

———. "Women in the Gospel of Mark." *Word and World* 26 (2006): 22–29.

Dibelius, Martin. *From Tradition to Gospel*. Translated by B. L. Woolf. New York: Charles Scribner's Sons, 1935. Translation of *Die Formgeschichte des Evangeliums*. 2nd ed. Tübingen: Mohr Siebeck, 1933.

Dickson, John P. "Gospel as News: εὐαγγελ- from Aristophanes to the Apostle Paul." *NTS* 51 (2005): 212–30.

Diehl, Judy A. "What Is a Gospel? Recent Studies in the Gospel Genre." *CR:BS* 9 (2011): 171–99.

Dihle, Albrecht. "The Gospels and Greek Biography." Pages 361–86 in *The Gospel and the Gospels*. Edited by P. Stuhlmacher. Grand Rapids: Eerdmans, 1991.

Dixon, Edward P. "Descending Spirit and Descending Gods: A 'Greek' Interpretation of the Spirit's 'Descent as a Dove' in Mark 1:10." *JBL* 128 (2009): 759–80.

Dodd, Charles H. *According to the Scriptures: The Substructure of New Testament Theology*. London: Nisbet, 1952.

———. *History and the Gospel*. London: Nisbet, 1938.

Donahue, John R. *Are You the Christ? The Trial Narrative in the Gospel of Mark*. Missoula, MT: SBL Press, 1973.

———. "Introduction: From Passion Traditions to Passion Narrative." Pages 1–20 in *The Passion in Mark: Studies on Mark 14–16*. Edited by Werner H. Kelber. Philadelphia: Fortress, 1976.

———. "A Neglected Factor in the Theology of Mark." *JBL* 101 (1982): 563–94.

———. "The Quest for the Community of Mark's Gospel." Pages 817–38 in *The Four Gospels, 1992: Festschrift for Frans Neirynck*. BETL 100. Edited by Frans van Segbroeck,

Christopher M. Tuckett, Gilbert Van Belle, and Joseph Verheyden. Leuven: Leuven University Press, 1992.

———. "Windows and Mirrors: The Setting of Mark's Gospel." *CBQ* 57 (1995): 1–26.

Doran, Robert. "Narratives of Noble Death." Pages 385–99 in *The Historical Jesus in Context*. Edited by A.-J. Levine, Dale C. Allison Jr., and J. D. Crossan. Princeton: Princeton University Press, 2006.

Döring, Klaus. "Sokrates bei Epiktet." Pages 195–226 in *Studia Platónica. Festschrift für Hermann Gundert zu seinem 65; Geburtstag am 30.4.1974*. Edited by Klaus Döring and Wolfgang Kullman. Amsterdam: Grüner, 1974.

Dormeyer, Detlev. "Die Kompositionsmetapher 'Evangelium Jesu Christi, Des Sohnes Gottes' Mk 1.1. Ihre Theologische und Literarische Aufgabe in der Jesus-Biographie des Markus." *NTS* 33 (1987): 452–68.

———. *Das Markusevangelium als idealbiographie von Jesus Christus, dem Nazarener*. 2nd ed. SBB 43. Stuttgart: Verlag Katholishces Bibelwerk, 2002.

———. *The New Testament among the Writings of Antiquity*. Translated by R. Kossov. BS 55. Sheffield: Sheffield Academic, 1998.

———. *Die Passion Jesu als Verhaltensmodell: literarische und theologische Analyse der Traditionsund Redaktionsgeschichte der Markuspassion*. Münster: Aschendorff, 1974.

Dormeyer, Detlev, and Hubert Frankemölle. "Evangelium als literarische Gattung und als theologischer Begriff. Tendenzen und Aufgaben der Evangelienforschung im 20. Jahrhundert, mit einer Untersuchung des Markusevangeliums in seinem Verhältnis zur antiken Biographie." *ANRW* II 25.2 (1984): 1543–1704.

Dowd, Sharyn, and Elizabeth S. Malbon. "The Significance of Jesus's Death in Mark: Narrative Context and Authorial Audience." *JBL* 125 (2006): 271–97.

Downing, F. Gerald. *Doing Things with Words in the First Christian Century*. JSNTSup 200. Sheffield: Sheffield Academic, 2000.

———. "A Genre for Q and a Socio-Cultural Context for Q: Comparing Sets of Similarities with Sets of Differences." *JSNT* 55 (1994): 3–26.

———. "Quite Like Q: A Genre for 'Q': The 'Lives' of Cynic Philosophers." *Bib* 69 (1988): 196–225.

———. "Word Processing in the Ancient World: The Social Production and Performance of Q." *JSNT* 64 (1996): 29–48.

Droge, Arthur J., and James D. Tabor. *A Noble Death: Suicide and Martyrdom among Christians and Jews in Antiquity*. San Francisco: HarperSanFrancisco, 1992.

Duff, Paul B. "The March of the Divine Warrior and the Advent of the Greco-Roman King: Mark's Account of Jesus's Entry into Jerusalem." *JBL* 111 (1992): 55–71.

Duff, Timothy. *Plutarch's Lives: Exploring Virtue and Vice*. Oxford: Oxford University Press, 1999.

Duling, Dennis C. "The Gospel of Matthew." Pages 296–318 in *The Blackwell Companion to the New Testament*. Edited by David E. Aune. Oxford: Wiley-Blackwell, 2010.

Dunn, James D. G. "When Did the Understanding of Jesus's Death as an Atoning Sacrifice First Emerge?" Pages 169–81 in *Israel's God and Rebecca's Children: Christology and*

Community in Early Judaism and Christianity. Edited by D. Capes, A. D. DeConick, H. K. Bond, and T. Miller. Waco: Baylor University Press, 2007.

Duran, Nicole. "Having Men for Dinner: Deadly Banquets and Biblical Women." *BTB* 35 (2005): 117–24.

Driggers, Ira B. "God as Healer of Creation in the Gospel of Mark." Pages 81–106 in *Character Studies and the Gospel of Mark.* Edited by Christopher W. Skinner and Matthew R. Hauge. London: Bloomsbury, 2014.

Drury, John. "What Are the Gospels?" *ExpTim* 87 (1976): 324–28.

Earl, Donald. "Prologue-Form in Ancient Historiography." *ANRW* I 2:842–56.

Easterling, Patricia F. "Constructing Character in Greek Tragedy." Pages 83–99 in *Characterization and Individuality in Greek Literature.* Edited by Christopher B. R. Pelling. Oxford: Clarendon, 1990.

Edwards, Catharine. "Modelling Roman Suicide? The Afterlife of Cato." *Economy and Society* 34 (2005): 200–22.

Edwards, James R. "Markan Sandwiches: The Significance of Interpolations in Markan Narratives." *NovT* 31 (1989): 193–216.

Edwards, Mark J. "Gospel and Genre: Some Reservations." Pages 51–75 in *Limits of Ancient Biography.* Edited by Brian McGing and Judith Mossman. Swansea: Classical Press of Wales, 2006.

———. "A Portrait of Plotinus." *ClQ* 43 (1993): 480–90.

Edwards, Mark J., and Simon Swain, eds. *Portraits: Biographical Representation in the Greek and Latin Literature of the Roman Empire.* Oxford: Clarendon, 1997.

Efird, James M., ed. *The Use of the Old Testament in the New and Other Essays: Studies in Honor of W. F. Stinespring.* Durham, NC: Duke University Press, 1972.

Ehrensperger, Kathy. "Speaking Greek under Rome: Paul, the Power of Language and the Language of Power." *Neot* 46 (2012): 9–28.

Ehrman, Bart. *The New Testament: A Historical Introduction to the Early Christian Writings.* 5th ed. Oxford: Oxford University Press, 2012.

———. *The Orthodox Corruption of Scripture: The Effect of Early Christological Controversies on the Text of the New Testament.* Oxford: Oxford University Press, 1993; 2nd ed., 2011.

Elliott, Scott S. "'Witless in Your Own Cause': Divine Plots and Fractured Characters in the Life of Aesop and the Gospel of Mark." *Religion and Theology* 12 (2005): 397–418.

Ellis, Earl. "The Date and Provenance of Mark's Gospel." Pages 801–15 in *The Four Gospels, 1992: Festschrift for Frans Neirynck.* BETL 100. Edited by Frans van Segbroeck, Christopher M. Tuckett, Gilbert Van Belle, and Joseph Verheyden. Leuven: Leuven University Press, 1992.

Esler, Philip F. "Community and Gospel in Early Christianity: A Response to Richard Bauckham's Gospels for All Christians." *SJT* 51 (1998): 235–48.

Evans, Craig A. "Mark's Incipit and the Priene Calendar Inscription: From Jewish Gospel to Greco-Roman Gospel." *JGRChJ* 1 (2000): 67–81.

Eve, Eric. *Behind the Gospels: Understanding the Oral Tradition.* London: SPCK, 2013.

————. *The Healer from Nazareth: Jesus's Miracles in Historical Context*. London: SPCK, 2009.

————. "Spit in Your Eye: The Blind Man of Bethsaida and the Blind Man of Alexandria." *NTS* 54 (2008): 1–17.

Eyben, Emiel. "The Beginning and End of Youth in Roman Antiquity." *Paedagogica Historica* 29 (1993): 247–85.

Feldman, Louis H. *Josephus' Interpretation of the Bible*. Berkeley: University of California Press, 1998.

————. *Philo's Portrayal of Moses in the Context of Ancient Judaism*. Notre Dame: University of Notre Dame Press, 2007.

————. *Studies in Josephus' Rewritten Bible*. JSJSup 58. Leiden: Brill, 1998.

Fitzgerald, John T. "The Ancient Lives of Aristotle and the Modern Debate about the Genre of the Gospels." *Restoration Quarterly* (1994): 209–21.

Fitzmyer, Joseph A. "4Q Testimonia and the New Testament." *TS* 15 (1957): 513–37.

————. "Crucifixion in Ancient Palestine, Qumran Literature, and the New Testament." *CBQ* 40 (1978): 493–513.

Fleddermann, Harry. "The Flight of a Naked Young Man (Mark 14:51–52)." *CBQ* 41 (1979): 412–18.

Focant, Camille. *The Gospel according to Mark: A Commentary*. Translated by L. R. Keylock. Eugene, OR: Pickwick, 2012. Translation of *L'évangile selon Marc*. Paris: Cerf, 2004.

————. "L'incompréhension des disciples dans le deuxième évangile. Tradition et redaction." *Revue Biblique* 82 (1975): 161–85.

————. "La tête du prophète sur un plat, ou, L'anti-repas d'alliance (Mc 6.14–29)." *NTS* 46 (2001): 334–53.

Focke, F. "Synkrisis." *Hermes* 58 (1923): 327–68.

Fögen, Thorsten, ed. *Tears in the Graeco-Roman World*. Berlin: de Gruyter, 2009.

Fowler, Robert M. *Loaves and Fishes: The Function of the Feeding Stories in the Gospel of Mark*. Chico, CA: Scholars Press, 1981.

Freudenburg, Kirk. "*Recusatio* as Political Theatre: Horace's Letter to Augustus." *JRS* 104 (2014): 105–32.

Freyne, Seán. "The Disciples in Mark and the *maskilim* in Daniel: A Comparison." *JSNT* 16 (1982): 7–23.

————. "Mark's Gospel and Ancient Biography." Pages 51–75 in *The Limits of Ancient Biography*. Edited by Brian McGing and Judith Mossman. Swansea: Classical Press of Wales, 2006.

Frickenschmidt, Dirk. *Evangelium als Biographie: Die vier Evangelien im Rahmen antiker Erzählkunst*. TANZ 22. Tübingen: Francke, 1997.

Fulkerson, Laurel. *No Regrets: Remorse in Classical Antiquity*. Oxford: Oxford University Press, 2013.

Gaiman, Neil. "The Pornography of Genre, or the Genre of Pornography." *Journal of the Fantastic in the Arts* 24 (2013): 401–7.

Galinsky, Karl. "Continuity and Change: Religion in the Augustan Semi-Century." Pages

71–82 in *A Companion to Roman Religion*. Edited by Jörg Rüpke. Oxford: Wiley-Blackwell, 2007.

Gamble, Harry. *Books and Readers in the Early Church: A History of Early Christian Texts*. New Haven: Yale University Press, 1995.

———. "The Book Trade in the Roman Empire." Pages 23–36 in *The Early Text of the New Testament*. Edited by Charles H. Hill and Michael J. Kruger. Oxford: Oxford University Press, 2012.

Geiger, Joseph. "Munatius Rufus and Thrasea Paetus on Cato the Younger." *Athenaeum* 57 (1979): 48–72.

———. "Nepos and Plutarch: From Latin to Greek Political Biography." *Illinois Classical Studies* 13 (1988): 245–56.

Gelardini, Gabriella. "The Contest for a Royal Title: Herod versus Jesus in the *Gospel according to Mark* (6,14–29; 15,6–15)." *ASE* 28 (2011): 93–106.

Georgia, Allan T. "Translating the Triumph: Reading Mark's Crucifixion Narrative against a Roman Ritual of Power." *JSNT* 36 (2013): 17–38.

Georgiadou, Aristoula. "The 'Lives of the Caesars' and Plutarch's Other Lives." *Illinois Classical Studies* 13 (1988): 349–56.

Gibson, Jeffrey B. "The Rebuke of the Disciples in Mark 8:14–21." *JSNT* 27 (1986): 31–47.

Gill, Christopher. "The Character-Personality Distinction." Pages 1–31 in *Characterization and Individuality in Greek Literature*. Edited by Christopher B. R. Pelling. Oxford: Clarendon, 1990.

———. "The Death of Socrates." *ClQ* 23 (1973): 25–28.

———. "The Question of Character Development: Plutarch and Tacitus." *ClQ* 33 (1983): 469–87.

Gilliard, Frank D. "More Silent Reading in Antiquity: Non Omne Verbum Sonabat." *JBL* 112 (1993): 689–96.

Glancy, Jennifer A. "Unveiling Masculinity: The Construction of Gender in Mark 6:17–29." *BibInt* 2 (1994): 34–50.

Glasson, T. Francis. "The Place of the Anecdote: A Note on Form Criticism." *JTS* 32 (1981): 142–50.

Gleason, Maud W. *Making Men: Sophists and Self-Presentation in Ancient Rome*. Princeton: Princeton University Press, 1995.

Glendinning, Victoria. "Lies and Silences." Pages 49–62 in *The Troubled Face of Biography*. Edited by Eric Homberger and John Charmley. London: Macmillan, 1988.

Glicksman, Andrew T. *Wisdom of Solomon 10: A Jewish Hellenistic Reinterpretation of Early Israelite History through Sapiential Lenses*. DCLS 9. Berlin: de Gruyter, 2011.

Goar, Robert J. *The Legend of Cato Uticensis from the First Century BC to the Fifth Century AD: With an Appendix on Dante and Cato*. Brussels: Latomus, 1987.

Goldhill, Simon. "The Anecdote: Exploring the Boundaries between Oral and Literate Performance in the Second Sophistic." Pages 96–112 in *Ancient Literacies: The Culture of Reading in Greece and Rome*. Edited by William A. Johnson and Holt N. Parker. Oxford: Oxford University Press, 2011.

———. *Reading Greek Tragedy*. Cambridge: Cambridge University Press, 1986.

Goldstein, Jonathan A. *II Maccabees: A New Translation, with Introduction and Commentary.* AB 41A. New York: Doubleday, 1983.

Goodacre, Mark. "Scripturalization in Mark's Crucifixion Narrative." Pages 33–47 in *The Trial and Death of Jesus: Essays on the Passion Narrative in Mark.* Edited by Geert van Oyen and Tom Shepherd. CBET 45. Leuven: Peeters, 2006.

Gradel, Ittai. *Emperor Worship and Roman Religion.* Oxford: Oxford University Press, 2002.

Grau, Sergi. "How to Kill a Philosopher: The Narrating of Ancient Greek Philosopher's Deaths in Relation to Their Way of Living." *Ancient Philosophy* 30 (2010): 347–81.

Green, Joel B. *The Death of Jesus: Tradition and Interpretation in the Passion Narrative.* WUNT 2/33. Tübingen: Mohr Siebeck, 1988.

———. "The Gospel according to Mark." Pages 139–47 in *The Cambridge Companion to the Gospels.* Edited by Stephen C. Barton. Cambridge: Cambridge University Press, 2006.

Grobel, Kendrick. "He That Cometh After Me." *JBL* 60 (1941): 397–401.

Guelich, Robert A. *Mark 1–8:26.* WBC 34A. Dallas: Word, 1989.

Gundry, Robert H. "εὐαγγέλιον: Gospel: How Soon a Book?" *JBL* 115 (1996): 321–25.

———. *Mark: A Commentary on His Apology for the Cross.* Grand Rapids: Eerdmans, 1993.

Gurtner, Daniel M. "LXX Syntax and the Identity of the NT Veil." *NovT* 47 (2005): 344–53.

———. "The Rending of the Veil and Markan Christology: 'Unveiling' the ΥΙΟΣ ΘΕΟΥ (Mark 15:38–39)." *BibInt* 15 (2007): 292–306.

———. "The Veil of the Temple in History and Legend." *JETS* 49 (2006): 97–114.

Hadas, Moses. *Hellenistic Culture: Fusion and Difference.* New York: W. W. Norton, 1959.

Hadas, Moses, and Morton Smith. *Heroes and Gods: Spiritual Biographies in Antiquity.* Religious Perspectives 13. New York: Harper & Row, 1965.

Hägg, Tomas. *The Art of Biography in Antiquity.* Cambridge: Cambridge University Press, 2012.

———. *Narrative Technique in Ancient Greek Romances. Studies of Chariton, Xenophon Ephesius and Achilles Tatius.* Acta Instituti Atheniensis Regni Sueciae 8, 13. Stockholm: Svenska institutet i Athen, 1971.

Halliwell, Francis S. "Traditional Greek Conceptions of Character." Pages 32–59 in *Characterization and Individuality in Greek Literature.* Edited by Christopher B. R. Pelling. Oxford: Clarendon, 1990.

Hamilton, Nigel. *Biography: A Brief History.* Cambridge, MA: Harvard University Press, 2007.

Hanson, James. "The Disciples in Mark's Gospel: Beyond the Pastoral/Polemical Debate." *Horizons in Biblical Theology* 20 (1998): 128–55.

Hare, Douglas R. A. "The Lives of the Prophets: A New Translation and Introduction." Pages 379–99 in vol. 2 of *The Old Testament Pseudepigrapha.* Edited by James H. Charlesworth. New York: Doubleday, 1985.

———. *The Son of Man Tradition.* Minneapolis: Fortress, 1990.

Harker, Andrew. *Loyalty and Dissidence in Roman Egypt: The Case of the Acta-Alexandrinorum*. Cambridge: Cambridge University Press, 2008.

Harley, James. "The Aesthetics of Death: The Theatrical Elaboration of Ancient Roman Blood Spectacles." *Theatre History Studies* 18 (1998): 89–97.

Harris, William V. *Ancient Literacy*. Cambridge, MA: Harvard University Press, 1989.

Hauge, Matthew R. "The Creation of Person in Ancient Narrative and the Gospel of Mark." Pages 57–77 in *Character Studies and the Gospel of Mark*. Edited by Christopher W. Skinner and Matthew R. Hauge. London: Bloomsbury, 2014.

———. "Fabulous Narratives: The Storytelling Tradition in the Synoptic Gospels." Pages 89–105 in *Ancient Education and Early Christianity*. LNTS 533. Edited by Matthew R. Hauge and Andrew W. Pitts. London: Bloomsbury, 2016.

Hauge, Matthew R., and Andrew W. Pitts, eds. *Ancient Education and Early Christianity*. LNTS 533. London: Bloomsbury, 2016.

Hawkin, David J. "The Incomprehension of the Disciples in the Marcan Redaction." *JBL* 91 (1972): 491–500.

Hays, Richard B. *The Moral Vision of the New Testament: Community, Cross, New Creation*. London: T&T Clark, 1996.

Henaut, Barry W. *Oral Tradition and the Gospels: The Problem of Mark 4*. JSNTSup 82. Sheffield: Sheffield Academic, 1993.

Henderson, John. "Was Suetonius' Julius a Caesar?" Pages 81–110 in *Suetonius the Biographer: Studies in Roman Lives*. Edited by Tristan Power and Roy K. Gibson. Oxford: Oxford University Press, 2014.

Hengel, Martin. *Crucifixion in the Ancient World and the Folly of the Message of the Cross*. Philadelphia: Fortress, 1977.

———. *Saint Peter: The Underestimated Apostle*. Translated by Thomas H. Trapp. Grand Rapids: Eerdmans, 2010.

———. *Studies in the Gospel of Mark*. Translated by John Bowden. London: SCM, 1985.

Henrichs, Albert. "Drama and Dromena: Bloodshed, Violence and Sacrificial Metaphor in Euripides." *Harvard Studies in Classical Philology* 100 (2000): 173–88.

Henten, Jan-Wilhelm van, and Friedrich Avemarie. *Martyrdom and Noble Death: Selected Texts from Graeco-Roman, Jewish and Christian Antiquity*. London: Routledge, 2002.

Hershbell, Jackson P. "Plutarch's Portrait of Socrates." *Illinois Classical Studies* 13 (1988): 365–81.

Hezser, Catherine. *Jewish Literacy in Roman Palestine*. TSAJ 81. Tübingen: Mohr Siebeck, 2001.

———. "Private and Public Education." Pages 465–81 in *The Oxford Handbook of Jewish Daily Life in Roman Palestine*. Edited by C. Hezser. Oxford: Oxford University Press, 2010.

———. "The Torah versus Homer: Jewish and Greco-Roman Education in Late Roman Palestine." Pages 5–24 in *Ancient Education and Early Christianity*. LNTS 533. Edited by Matthew R. Hauge and Andrew W. Pitts. London: Bloomsbury, 2016.

Hock, Ronald F. "Social Experience and the Beginning of the Gospel of Mark." Pages 311–26 in *Reimagining Christian Origins: A Colloquium Honoring Burton L. Mack*. Edited by Elizabeth A. Castelli and Hal Taussig. Valley Forge, PA: Trinity, 1996.

———. "Why New Testament Scholars Should Read Ancient Novels." Pages 121–38 in *Ancient Fiction and Early Christian Narrative*. Edited by Ronald F. Hock, J. Bradley Chance, and Judith Perkins. SBLSymS 6. Atlanta: Scholars Press, 1998.

Hock, Ronald F., and Edward N. O'Neil. *The Chreia and Ancient Rhetoric: Classroom Exercises*. Writings from the Greco-Roman World 2. Leiden: Brill, 2002.

———. *The Chreia in Ancient Rhetoric*. Vol. 1, *The Progymnasmata*. Atlanta: Scholars Press, 1986.

Hock, Ronald F., J. Bradley Chance, and Judith Perkins, eds. *Ancient Fiction and Early Christian Narrative*. SBLSymS 6. Atlanta: Scholars Press, 1998.

Hoffeditz, David M., and Gary E. Yates. "*Femme Fatale* Redux: Intertextual Connection to the Elijah/Jezebel Narratives in Mark 6:14–29." *BBR* 15 (2005): 199–221.

Homberger, Eric, and John Charmley, eds. *The Troubled Face of Biography*. London: Macmillan, 1988.

Hooker, Morna D. *A Commentary on the Gospel according to St Mark*. London: A&C Black, 1995.

———. "Isaiah in Mark's Gospel." Pages 35–49 in *Isaiah in the New Testament*. Edited by Steve Moyise and Maarten J. J. Menken. London: T&T Clark, 2005.

———. *Jesus and the Servant*. London: SPCK, 1959.

Hope, Valerie M. *Death in Ancient Rome: A Sourcebook*. Routledge Sourcebooks for the Ancient World. London: Routledge, 2007.

Hopkinson, Neil, ed. *Lucian: A Selection*. Cambridge Greek and Latin Classics. Cambridge: Cambridge University Press, 2008.

Horsfall, Nicholas. "Rome without Spectacles." *G&R* 42 (1995): 49–56.

Horsley, Richard A. "Oral Tradition in New Testament Studies." *Oral Tradition* 18 (2003): 34–36.

Horsley, Richard A., with Jonathan A. Draper and J. M. Foley, eds. *Performing the Gospel: Orality, Memory and Mark; Essays Dedicated to Werner Kelber*. Minneapolis: Fortress, 2006.

Hultgren, Arland J. *Jesus and His Adversaries: The Form and Function of the Conflict Stories in the Synoptic Tradition*. Minneapolis: Augsburg, 1979.

Hurley, Donna. "Rhetorics of Assassination: Ironic Reversal and the Emperor Gaius." Pages 146–58 in *Suetonius the Biographer: Studies in Roman Lives*. Edited by Tristan Power and Roy K. Gibson. Oxford: Oxford University Press, 2014.

Hurtado, Larry W. *Earliest Christian Artifacts: Manuscripts and Christian Origins*. Grand Rapids: Eerdmans, 2006.

———. "Fashions, Fallacies and Future Prospects in New Testament Studies." *JSNT* 36 (2014): 299–324.

———. "Following Jesus in the Gospel of Mark—and Beyond." Pages 9–29 in *Patterns of Discipleship in the New Testament*. Edited by Richard N. Longenecker. Grand Rapids: Eerdmans, 1996.

———. "Greco-Roman Textuality and the Gospel of Mark: A Critical Assessment of W. Kelber's *The Oral and the Written Gospel*." *BBR* 7 (1997): 91–106.

———. "Manuscripts and the Sociology of Early Christian Reading." Pages 49–62 in *The Early Text of the New Testament*. Edited by Charles H. Hill and Michael J. Kruger. Oxford: Oxford University Press, 2012.

———. *Mark: Based on the New International Version*. Peabody, MA: Hendrickson, 1995.

———. "Mark's Gospel—Evolutionary or Revolutionary Document?" *JSNT* 40 (1990): 15–32.

———. "Oral Fixation and New Testament Studies? 'Orality,' 'Performance' and Reading Texts in Early Christianity." *NTS* 60 (2014): 321–40.

———. "Summary and Concluding Observations." Pages 159–77 in *Who Is This Son of Man? The Latest Scholarship on a Puzzling Expression of the Historical Jesus*. LNTS 390. Edited by Larry W. Hurtado and Paul W. Owen. London: T&T Clark, 2010.

———. "The Women, the Tomb, and the Climax of Mark." Pages 427–50 in *A Wandering Galilean: Essays in Honour of Sean Freyne*. Edited by Z. Rodgers, M. Daly-Denton, and A. Fitzpatrick-McKinley. Leiden: Brill, 2009.

Hurtado, Larry W., and Paul W. Owen, eds. *Who Is This Son of Man? The Latest Scholarship on a Puzzling Expression of the Historical Jesus*. LNTS 390. London: T&T Clark, 2010.

Hurtado, Larry W., and Chris Keith. "Writing and Book Production in the Hellenistic and Roman Periods." Pages 63–80 in *The New Cambridge History of the Bible: From the Beginning to 600*. Edited by J. Carleton Paget and J. Schaper. Cambridge: Cambridge University Press, 2013.

Huxley, George. "Aristotle's Interest in Biography." *Greek Roman and Byzantine Studies* 15 (1974): 203–13.

Iersel, Bas M. F. van. "Failed Followers in Mark: Mark 13:12 as a Key for the Identification of the Intended Readers." *CBQ* 58 (1996): 244–63.

Incigneri, Brian J. *The Gospel to the Romans: The Setting and Rhetoric of Mark's Gospel*. Leiden: Brill, 2003.

Iverson, Kelly R. "A Centurion's 'Confession': A Performance-Critical Analysis of Mark 15:30." *JBL* 130 (2011): 329–50.

———. "Orality and the Gospels: A Survey of Recent Research." *CR:BS* 8 (2009): 71–106.

Iverson, Kelly R., and Christopher W. Skinner, eds. *Mark as Story: Retrospect and Prospect*. Atlanta: SBL Press, 2011.

———. "The Present Tense of Performance: The Immediacy and Transformative Power in Luke's Passion." Pages 131–57 in *From Text to Performance: Narrative and Performance Criticisms in Dialogue and Debate*. Edited by Kelly R. Iverson. Eugene, OR: Cascade, 2014.

Jackson, Howard M. "The Death of Jesus in Mark and the Miracle from the Cross." *NTS* 33 (1987): 16–37.

Jacobi, Christine. *Jesusüberlieferung bei Paulus? Analogien zwischen den echten Paulusbriefen und den synoptischen Evangelien*. BZNW 213. Berlin: de Gruyter, 2015.

James, Warren. "Diogenes Laertius, Biographer of Philosophers." Pages 133–49 in *Ordering Knowledge in the Roman Empire*. Edited by Jason König and Tim Whitmarsh. Cambridge: Cambridge University Press, 2007.

Janson, Tore. *Latin Prose Prefaces: Studies in Literary Conventions*. Acta Universitatis Stockholmiensis 13. Stockholm: Almqvist and Wiksell, 1964.

Jensen, Robin M. *Living Water: Images, Symbols, and Settings of Early Christian Baptism*. Supplements to Vigiliae Christianae 105. Leiden: Brill, 2011.

Jeremias, Joachim. *The Eucharistic Words of Jesus*. 3rd ed. Translated by Norman Perrin. London: SCM, 1966.

———. *New Testament Theology: Part I, The Proclamation of Jesus*. Translated by John Bowden. London: SCM, 1971.

Johnson, Earl S. "Is Mark 15.39 the Key to Mark's Christology?" *JSNT* 31 (1987): 3–22.

———. "Mark 10:46–52: Blind Bartimaeus." *CBQ* 40 (1978): 191–204.

Johnson, M. D. "*Life of Adam and Eve*: A New Translation and Introduction." Pages 249–95 in vol. 2 of *The Old Testament Pseudepigrapha*. Edited by James H. Charlesworth. New York: Doubleday, 1985.

Johnson, William A. "Constructing Elite Reading Communities in the High Empire." Pages 320–30 in *Ancient Literacies: The Culture of Reading in Greece and Rome*. Edited by William A. Johnson and Holt N. Parker. Oxford: Oxford University Press, 2011.

———. "Towards a Sociology of Reading in Classical Antiquity." *AJP* 121 (2000): 593–627.

Johnson, William A., and Holt N. Parker, eds. *Ancient Literacies: The Culture of Reading in Greece and Rome*. Oxford: Oxford University Press, 2011.

Jones, Christopher P. "The Historicity of the Neronian Persecution: A Response to Brent Shaw." *NTS* 63 (2017): 146–52.

Jonge, Marinus de. "Jesus's Death for Others and the Deaths of the Maccabean Martyrs." Pages 142–51 in *Text and Testimony: Essays in Honour of A. F. J. Klijn*. Edited by T. Baarda, A. Hilhorst, G. P. Luttikhuizen, and A. S. van der Woude. Kampen: Kok, 1988.

———. "Matthew 27:51 in Early Christian Exegesis." *HTR* 79 (1986): 67–79.

Judge, Edwin A. *The Social Pattern of the Christian Groups in the First Century*. London: Tyndale, 1960.

Juel, Donald H. *A Master of Surprise: Mark Interpreted*. Minneapolis: Fortress, 1994.

Kaminouchi, Alberto de M. *"But It Is Not So among You": Echoes of Power in Mark 10.32–45*. JSNTSup 249. London: T&T Clark, 2003.

Karla, Grammatiki A. "*Life of Aesop*: Fictional Biography as Popular Literature?" Pages 47–64 in *Writing Biography in Greece and Rome*. Edited by Koen De Temmerman and Kristoffel Demoen. Cambridge: Cambridge University Press, 2016.

Kechagia, Eleni. "Dying Philosophers in Ancient Biography: Zeno the Stoic and Epicurus." Pages 181–99 in *Writing Biography in Greece and Rome*. Edited by Koen De Temmerman and Kristoffel Demoen. Cambridge: Cambridge University Press, 2016.

Kee, Howard C. "Aretalogy and Gospel." *JBL* 92 (1973): 402–22.

Keefer, Kyle. *The New Testament as Literature: A Very Short Introduction*. Oxford: Oxford University Press, 2008.

Keener, Craig S. "Assumptions in Historical-Jesus Research: Using Ancient Biographies and Disciples' Traditioning as a Control." *JSHJ* 9 (2011): 26–58.

———. *The Gospel of John: A Commentary*. Vol. 1. Peabody, MA: Hendrickson, 2003.

———. "Otho: A Targeted Comparison of Suetonius' Biography and Tacitus' *History*, with Implications for the Gospels' Historical Reliability." *BBR* 21 (2011): 331–56.

Keith, Chris. "Early Christian Book Culture and the Emergence of the First Written Gospel." Pages 22–39 in *Mark, Manuscripts and Monotheism: Essays in Honor of Larry W. Hurtado*. Edited by Chris Keith and Dieter T. Roth. LNTS 528. London: Bloomsbury, 2015.

———. *The Pericope Adulterae, the Gospel of John and the Literacy of Jesus*. NTTSD 38. Leiden: Brill, 2009.

Keith, Chris, and Dieter T. Roth, eds. *Mark, Manuscripts and Monotheism: Essays in Honor of Larry W. Hurtado*. LNTS 528. London: Bloomsbury, 2015.

Kelber, Werner H. "Conclusion: From Passion Narrative to Gospel." Pages 153–80 in *The Passion in Mark: Studies on Mark 14–16*. Edited by Werner H. Kelber. Philadelphia: Fortress, 1976.

———. *Imprints, Voiceprints, and Footprints of Memory: Collected Essays of Werner H. Kelber*. SBLRBS 74. Atlanta: SBL Press, 2013.

———. "Mark 14,32–42: Gethsemane, Passion Christology and Discipleship Failure." *ZNW* 63 (1972): 166–87.

———. *The Oral and the Written Gospel: The Hermeneutics of Speaking and Writing in the Synoptic Tradition, Mark, Paul and Q*. Voices in Performance and Text. Reprinted with new introduction. Bloomington: Indiana University Press, 1997.

———, ed. *The Passion in Mark: Studies on Mark 14–16*. Philadelphia: Fortress, 1976.

Kelber, Werner H., and Samuel Byrskog, eds. *Jesus in Memory: Traditions in Oral and Scribal Perspectives*. Waco: Baylor University Press, 2009.

Kelhoffer, James A. "'How Soon a Book' Revisited: ΕΥΑΓΓΕΛΙΟΝ as a Reference to 'Gospel' Materials in the First Half of the Second Century." *ZNW* 95 (2004): 1–34.

———. "A Tale of Two Markan Characterizations: The Exemplary Woman Who Anointed Jesus's Body for Burial (14:3–9) and the Silent Trio Who Fled the Empty Tomb (16:1–8)." Pages 85–98 in *Women and Gender in Ancient Religions*. Edited by Stephen P. Ahearne-Kroll, Paul A. Holloway, and James A. Kelhoffer. WUNT 263. Tübingen: Mohr Siebeck, 2010.

Kennedy, George A. *Progymnasmata: Greek Textbooks of Prose Composition and Rhetoric*. Writings from the Greco-Roman World 10. Atlanta: SBL Press, 2003.

Ker, James. *The Deaths of Seneca*. Oxford: Oxford University Press, 2009.

Kirk, Alan. "The Memory of Violence and the Death of Jesus in Q." Pages 191–206 in *Memory, Tradition, and Text: Uses of the Past in Early Christianity*. Edited by Alan Kirk and Tom Thatcher. Semeia 52. Atlanta: SBL Press, 2005.

Kirk, Alan, and Tom Thatcher, eds. *Memory, Tradition, and Text: Uses of the Past in Early Christianity*. Semeia 52. Atlanta: SBL Press, 2005.

Klawans, Jonathan. *Josephus and the Theologies of Ancient Judaism*. Oxford: Oxford University Press, 2013.

Klink, Edward W., III. *The Audience of the Gospels: The Origin and Function of the Gospels in Early Christianity*. LNTS 353. London: T&T Clark, 2010.

Kloppenborg (Verbin), John S. "*Evocatio Deorum* and the Date of Mark." *JBL* 124 (2005): 419–50.

———. *Excavating Q: The History and Setting of the Sayings Gospel*. Edinburgh: T&T Clark, 2000.

———. "'Excitus clari viri': The Death of Jesus in Luke." *TJT* 8 (1992): 106–20.

———. "Literate Media in Early Christian Groups: The Creation of a Christian Book Culture." *JECS* 22 (2014): 21–59.

Knox, Wilfred L. "The Ending of St Mark's Gospel." *HTR* 35 (1942): 13–23.

———. *The Sources of the Synoptic Gospels*. Vol. 1. Edited by H. Chadwick. Cambridge: Cambridge University Press, 1953.

Koester, Helmut. "From the Kerygma-Gospel to Written Gospels." *NTS* 35 (1989): 361–81.

———. "One Jesus and Four Gospels." *HTR* 61 (1968): 230–36.

Konstan, David, and Robyn Walsh. "Civic and Subversive Biography in Antiquity." Pages 26–43 in *Writing Biography in Greece and Rome*. Edited by Koen De Temmerman and Kristoffel Demoen. Cambridge: Cambridge University Press, 2016.

Koskenniemi, Erkki. "The Function of the Miracle Stories in Philostratus' *Vita Apollonii Tyanensis*." Pages 70–83 in *Wonders Never Cease: The Purpose of Narrating Miracle Stories in the New Testament and Its Religious Environment*. Edited by Michael Labahn and B. Jan Lietaert Peerbolte. LNTS 288. London: T&T Clark, 2006.

Koskenniemi, Erkki, Kirsi Nisula, and Jorma Toppari. "Wine Mixed with Myrrh (Mark 15:23) and *Crurifragium* (John 19:31–32): Two Details of the Passion Narratives." *JSNT* 27 (2005): 379–91.

Kraemer, Ross S. "Implicating Herodias and Her Daughter in the Death of John the Baptizer: A (Christian) Theological Strategy?" *JBL* 125 (2006): 321–49.

Kurz, William W. "Narrative Models for Imitation in Luke-Acts." Pages 171–89 in *Greeks, Romans, Christians: Essays in Honor of Abraham J. Malherbe*. Edited by D. L. Balch, E. Ferguson, and W. A. Meeks. Minneapolis: Fortress, 1990.

Kürzinger, Josef. *Papias von Hierapolis und die Evangelien des Neuen Testaments*. Eichstatter Materialien 4. Regensburg: Putset, 1983.

Kyle, Donald G. *Spectacles of Death in Ancient Rome*. London: Routledge, 1999.

Labahn, Michael. *Der Gekommene als Wiederkommender: Die Logienquelle als erzählte Geschichte*. ABG 32. Leipzig: Evangelische Verlagsanstalt, 2010.

Labahn, Michael, and B. Jan Lietaert Peerbolte, eds. *Wonders Never Cease: The Purpose of Narrating Miracle Stories in the New Testament and Its Religious Environment*. LNTS 288. London: T&T Clark, 2006.

Larsen, Matthew D. C. "Accidental Publication, Unfinished Texts and the Traditional Goals of New Testament Textual Criticism." *JSNT* 39 (2017): 362–87.

Last, Richard. "Communities That Write: Christ-Groups, Associations, and Gospel Communities." *NTS* 58 (2012): 173–98.

Lee, Hermione. *Biography: A Very Short Introduction.* Oxford: Oxford University Press, 2009.

Lee, John A. L. "Some Features of the Speech of Jesus in Mark's Gospel." *NovT* 27 (1985): 1–26.

Lefkowitz, Mary R. "The Euripides Vita." *Greek, Roman and Byzantine Studies* 20 (1979): 187–210.

———. "Patterns of Fiction in Ancient Biography." *The American Scholar* 52 (1983): 205–18.

Lehtipuu, Outi. "Characterization and Persuasion: The Rich Man and the Poor Man in Luke 16.19–31." Pages 73–105 in *Characterization in the Gospels: Reconceiving Narrative Criticism.* Edited by David M. Rhoads and Kari Syreeni. JSNTSup 184. Sheffield: Sheffield Academic, 1999.

Leivestad, Ragnar. "Exit the Apocalyptic Son of Man." *NTS* (1972): 243–67.

Leo, Friedrich. *Die griechisch-römische Biographie nach ihrer literarischen Form.* Leipzig: Teubner, 1901.

Levene, David. "Defining the Divine in Rome." *TAPA* 142 (2012): 41–81.

Lewis, Philip B. "Indications of a Liturgical Source in the Gospel of Mark." *Encounter* 39 (1978): 385–94.

Lewis, Robert B. *Paul's "Spirit of Adoption" in Its Roman Imperial Context.* LNTS 545. London: T&T Clark, 2016.

Liew, Tat-siong Benny. "Re-Mark-able Masculinities: Jesus, the Son of Man, and the (Sad) Sum of Manhood." Pages 93–135 in *New Testament Masculinities.* Edited by Stephen D. Moore and Janice C. Anderson. Semeia 45. Atlanta: SBL Press, 2003.

———. "Tyranny, Boundary and Might: Colonial Mimicry in Mark's Gospel." *JSNT* 73 (1999): 7–31.

Lincoln, Andrew T. *Born of a Virgin? Reconceiving Jesus in the Bible, Tradition and Theology.* Grand Rapids: Eerdmans, 2013.

———. *The Gospel according to John.* Peabody, MA: Hendrickson, 2005.

———. "The Promise and the Failure: Mark 16:7, 8." *JBL* 108 (1989): 283–300.

Lindars, Barnabas. "The Place of the Old Testament in the Formation of New Testament Theology: Prolegomena." *NTS* 23 (1976): 59–66.

Lindsay, Hugh. *Adoption in the Roman World.* Cambridge: Cambridge University Press, 2009.

Litchfield, Henry W. "National *Exempla Virtutis* in Roman Literature." *HSCP* 25 (1914): 1–71.

Longenecker, Bruce. "Socio-Economic Profiling of the First Urban Christians." Pages 36–59 in *After the First Urban Christians: The Social-Scientific Study of Pauline Christianity Twenty-Five Years Later.* Edited by David G. Horrell and Todd D. Still. London: T&T Clark, 2009.

Luhrmann, Dieter. *Das Markusevangelium*. Tübingen: Mohr Siebeck, 1987.

Lukaszewski, Albert. "Issues concerning the Aramaic behind ὁ υἱὸς τοῦ ἀνθρώπου: A Critical Review of Scholarship." Pages 1–27 *Who Is This Son of Man? The Latest Scholarship on a Puzzling Expression of the Historical Jesus*. Edited by Larry W. Hurtado and Paul W. Owen. LNTS 390. London: T&T Clark, 2010.

Luke, Trevor S. "A Healing Touch for Emperor: Vespasian's Wonders in Domitianic Rome." *G&R* 57 (2010): 77–106.

Lund, Nils W. *Chiasmus in the New Testament: A Study in Formgeschichte*. Chapel Hill: University of North Carolina Press, 1942.

MacDonald, Dennis R. *The Homeric Epics and the Gospel of Mark*. New Haven: Yale University Press, 2003.

Mack, Burton L. *Rhetoric and the New Testament*. Minneapolis: Fortress, 1990.

Mack, Burton L., and Vernon K. Robbins. *Patterns of Persuasion in the Gospels*. Sonoma, CA: Polebridge, 1989.

Malbon, Elizabeth S. "Fallible Followers: Women and Men in the Gospel of Mark." *Semeia* 28 (1983): 29–48.

———. "History, Theology, Story: Re-contextualizing Mark's 'Messianic Secret' as Characterization." Pages 35–56 in *Character Studies and the Gospel of Mark*. Edited by Christopher W. Skinner and Matthew R. Hauge. London: Bloomsbury, 2014.

———. "The Jewish Leaders in the Gospel of Mark: A Literary Study of Marcan Characterization." *JBL* 108 (1989): 259–81.

———. *Mark's Jesus: Characterization as Narrative Christology*. Waco: Baylor University Press, 2009.

———. "'Reflected Christology': An Aspect of Narrative 'Christology' in the Gospel of Mark." *Perspectives in Religious Studies* 26 (1999): 127–45.

Malcolm, Norman. *Ludwig Wittgenstein: A Memoir*. Oxford: Oxford University Press, 1966.

Malherbe, Abraham J. "A Physical Description of Paul." *HTR* 97 (1986): 170–75.

———, ed. *Moral Exhortation: A Greco-Roman Sourcebook*. LEC 4. Philadelphia: Westminster, 1986.

Malina, Bruce J. "Were There 'Authors' in New Testament Times?" Pages 262–71 in *To Set at Liberty: Essays on Early Christianity in Its Social World in Honor of John H. Elliott*. Edited by S. K. Black. SWBA 2/11. Sheffield: Sheffield Phoenix, 2014.

Marcus, Joel. "Crucifixion as Parodic Exaltation." *JBL* 125 (2006): 73–87.

———. "The Jewish War and the Sitz im Leben of Mark." *JBL* 113 (1992): 441–62.

———. *Mark 1–8: A New Translation with Introduction and Commentary*. AYB 27. New York: Doubleday, 2000.

———. *Mark 8–16: A New Translation with Introduction and Commentary*. AYB 27A. New York: Doubleday, 2009.

Markley, John R. *Peter—Apocalyptic Seer*. WUNT 2.348. Tübingen: Mohr Siebeck, 2013.

———. "Reassessing Peter's Imperception in Synoptic Tradition." Pages 99–108 in *Peter in Early Christianity*. Edited by Helen K. Bond and Larry W. Hurtado. Grand Rapids: Eerdmans, 2015.

Martens, Peter W. "'Anyone Hung on a Tree Is under God's Curse' (Deuteronomy 21:23): Jesus's Crucifixion and Interreligious Exegetical Debate in Late Antiquity." *Ex Auditu* 26 (2010): 69–90.

Martin, Dale B. *Slavery as Salvation: The Metaphor of Slavery in Pauline Christianity*. New Haven: Yale University Press, 1990.

Martin, Hubert. "The Concept of Philanthropia in Plutarch's Lives." *AJP* 82 (1961): 164–75.

Martin, Michael W. "Philo's Use of Syncrisis: An Examination of Philonic Composition in the Light of the *Progymnasmata*." *Perspectives in Religious Studies* (2003): 271–97.

———. "Progymnasmatic Topic Lists: A Composition Template for Luke and Other Bioi?" *NTS* 54 (2008): 18–41.

Marx, F. A. "Tacitus und die Literatur der exitus illustrium virorum." *Philologus* 92 (1937): 83–103.

Mason, Steve. *Life of Josephus*. Leiden: Brill, 2003.

Matera, Frank J. "'He Saved Others; He Cannot Save Himself': A Literary-Critical Perspective on the Markan Miracles." *Int* 47 (1993): 15–26.

———. *The Kingship of Jesus: Composition and Theology in Mark 15*. Chico, CA: Scholars Press, 1982.

———. *New Testament Ethics: The Legacies of Jesus and Paul*. Louisville: Westminster John Knox, 1996.

Matilla, Talvikki. "Naming the Nameless: Gender and Discipleship in Matthew's Passion Narrative." Pages 153–79 in *Characterization in the Gospels: Reconceiving Narrative Criticism*. Edited by David M. Rhoads and Kari Syreeni. JSNTSup 184. Sheffield: Sheffield Academic, 1999.

Mattingley, Harold. *Tacitus on Britain and Germany*. Translated by H. Mattingley. Harmondsworth: Penguin, 1948.

Matzko McCarthy, David. "The Gospels Embodied: Saints and Martyrs." Pages 224–44 in *The Cambridge Companion to the Gospels*. Edited by Stephen C. Barton. Cambridge: Cambridge University Press, 2006.

Mayes, Andrew D. H. "Biography in the Ancient World: The Story of the Rise of David." Pages 1–12 in *The Limits of Ancient Biography*. Edited by Brian McGing and Judith Mossman. Swansea: Classical Press of Wales, 2006.

McCracken, David. "Character in the Boundary: Bakhtin's Interdividuality in Biblical Narratives." *Semeia* 63 (1993): 29–42.

McDonnell, Myles. "Writing, Copying and Autograph Manuscripts in Ancient Rome." *ClQ* 46 (1996): 469–91.

McGing, Brian C. "Synkrisis in Tacitus' *Agricola*." *Hermathena* 132 (1982): 15–25.

McGing, Brian C., and Judith Mossman, eds. *The Limits of Ancient Biography*. Swansea: Classical Press of Wales, 2006.

McIver, Robert K. *Memory, Jesus, and the Synoptic Gospels*. SBL Resources for Biblical Study 59. Atlanta: SBL Press, 2011.

McKnight, Scot. "Jesus and His Death: Some Recent Scholarship." *CR:BS* 9 (2001): 185–228.

McLaren, James S. *Power and Politics in Palestine: The Jews and the Governing of Their Land, 100 BC–70 AD*. JSNTSup 63. Sheffield: JSOT Press, 1991.

McVann, Mark. "The 'Passion' of John the Baptist and Jesus before Pilate: Mark's Warnings about Kings and Governors." *BTB* 38 (2008): 152–57.

McWhirter, Jocelyn. "Messianic Exegesis in Mark's Passion Narrative." Pages 69–97 in *The Trial and Death of Jesus*. Edited by Geert van Oyen and Tom Shepherd. CBET 45. Leuven: Peeters, 2006.

Meggitt, Justin J. *Paul, Poverty and Survival*. Studies of the New Testament and Its World. Edinburgh: T&T Clark, 1998.

Meeks, Wayne A. *The First Urban Christians: The Social World of the Apostle Paul*. New Haven: Yale University Press, 1983.

Mendels, Doron. *Memory in Jewish, Pagan and Christian Societies of the Graeco-Roman World. Fragmented Memory–Comprehensive Memory–Collective Memory*. LSTS 45. London: T&T Clark, 2004.

Meyer, Eduard. *Ursprung und Anfänge des Christentums*. Vol. 1, *Die Evangelien*. Stuttgart: Magnus, 1921.

Middleton, Paul. "Suffering and the Creation of Christian Identity in the Gospel of Mark." Pages 173–89 in *T&T Clark Handbook to Social Identity in the New Testament*. Edited by J. Brian Tucker and Coleman A. Baker. London: Bloomsbury, 2014.

Miles, Graeme. "'I, Porphyry': The Narrator and Reader in the Vita Plotini." *Open Access Australasian Society for Classical Studies Proceedings, 2–5 February 2010*. Perth: University of Western Australia, 2010.

Millar, Fergus. "Cornelius Nepos, 'Atticus,' and the Roman Revolution." Pages 346–72 in *Rome, the Greek World, and the East*. Vol. 1, *The Roman Republic and the Augustan Revolution*. Edited by Guy M. Rogers and Hannah M. Cotton. Chapel Hill: University of North Carolina Press, 2002.

Miller, Geoffrey D. "An Intercalation Revisited: Christology, Discipleship and Dramatic Irony in Mark 6.6b–30." *JSNT* 35 (2012): 176–95.

Miller, Richard C. "Mark's Empty Tomb and Other Translation Fables in Classical Antiquity." *JBL* 129 (2010): 759–76.

Mitchell, Margaret. "Patristic Counter-Evidence to the Claim That 'The Gospels Were Written for All Christians.'" *NTS* 51 (2005): 36–79.

Moeser, Marion C. *The Anecdote in Mark, the Classical World and the Rabbis*. JSNTSup 227. Sheffield: Sheffield Academic, 2002.

Moloney, Francis J. "Mark 6:6b–30: Mission, the Baptist, and Failure." *CBQ* 63 (2001): 647–63.

Momigliano, Arnaldo. *The Development of Greek Biography*. Cambridge, MA: Harvard University Press, 1971.

Moo, Douglas J. *The Old Testament in the Gospel Passion Narratives*. Sheffield: Almond, 1983.

Moore, Stephen D. "Why There Are No Humans or Animals in the Gospel of Mark." Pages 71–93 in *Mark as Story: Retrospect and Prospect*. Edited by Kelly R. Iverson and Christopher W. Skinner. Atlanta: SBL Press, 2011.

Moore, Stephen D., and Janice C. Anderson, eds. *New Testament Masculinities*. SemeiaSt 45. Atlanta: SBL Press, 2003.

Morgan, Teresa. *Literate Education in the Hellenistic and Roman Worlds*. Cambridge: Cambridge University Press, 1998.

———. "Not the Whole Story? Moralizing Biography and *Imitatio Christi*." Pages 353–66 in *Fame and Infamy: Essays for Christopher Pelling on Characterization in Greek and Roman Biography*. Edited by Rhiannon Ash, Judith Mossman, and Francis B. Titchener. Oxford: Oxford University Press, 2015.

Moss, Candida R. *The Other Christs: Imitating Jesus in Ancient Christian Ideologies of Martyrdom*. Oxford: Oxford University Press, 2010.

———. "The Transfiguration: An Exercise in Markan Accommodation." *BibInt* 12 (2004): 69–89.

Most, Glen W. "A Cock for Asclepius." *ClQ* 43 (1993): 96–111.

Motyer, Steve. "The Rending of the Veil: A Markan Pentecost." *NTS* 33 (1987): 155–57.

Moyise, Steve. *The Old Testament in the New: An Introduction*. T&T Clark Approaches to Biblical Studies. London: Continuum, 2001.

Müller, Mogens. *The Expression "Son of Man" and the Development of Christology: A History of Interpretation*. London: Equinox, 2008.

Musurillo, Herbert A. *The Acts of the Pagan Martyrs, Acta Alexandrinorum*. Oxford: Clarendon, 1954.

Naluparayil, Jacob C. "Jesus of the Gospel of Mark: Present State of Research." *CR:BS* 8 (2000): 191–226.

Neirynck, Frans. *Duality in Mark: Contributions to the Study of the Markan Redaction*. BETL 31. Leuven: Leuven University Press, 1988.

Neufeld, Dietmar. *Mockery and Secretism in the Social World of Mark's Gospel*. LNTS 503. London: Bloomsbury, 2014.

Neyrey, Jerome H. "Jesus, Gender and the Gospel of Matthew." Pages 43–66 in *New Testament Masculinities*. Edited by Stephen D. Moore and Janice Capel Anderson. SemeiaSt 45. Atlanta: SBL Press, 2003.

———. "Josephus' *Vita* and the Encomium: A Native Model of Personality." *JSJ* 25 (1994): 177–206.

———. "Questions, Chreiai and Challenges to Honor: The Interface of Rhetoric and Culture in Mark's Gospel." *CBQ* 60 (1998): 657–81.

Nineham, Dennis E. "Eye-Witness Testimony and the Gospel Tradition I." *JTS* 9 (1958): 13–25.

———. "Eye-Witness Testimony and the Gospel Tradition III." *JTS* 11 (1960): 253–64.

———. *The Gospel of Saint Mark*. Pelican NT Commentaries. Harmondsworth: Penguin, 1963.

Norden, Eduard. *Die antike Kunstprosa: vom VI. Jahrhundert v. Chr. bis in die Zeit der Renaissance*. 2 vols. Leipzig: Teubner, 1898. Reprint, Darmstadt: Wissenschaftliche Buchgesellschaft, 1958.

O'Brien, Kelli S. *The Use of Scripture in the Markan Passion Narrative*. LNTS 384. London: T&T Clark, 2010.

Ong, Walter. *Orality and Literacy: The Technologizing of the Word*. London: Methuen, 1982.

Overbeck, Franz. "Über die Anfänge der patristischen Literatur." *Historische Zeitschrift* 12 (1882): 417–72.

Oyen, Geert van. "The Meaning of the Death of Jesus in the Gospel of Mark: A Real Reader Perspective." Pages 49–68 in *The Trial and Death of Jesus: Essays on the Passion Narrative in Mark*. Edited by Geert van Oyen and Tom Shepherd. CBET 45. Leuven: Peeters, 2006.

Oyen, Geert van, and Tom Shepherd, eds. *The Trial and Death of Jesus: Essays on the Passion Narrative in Mark*. CBET 45. Leuven: Peeters, 2006.

Parker, David. *The Living Text of the Gospels*. Cambridge: Cambridge University Press, 1997.

Parker, Holt N. "Books and Reading Latin Poetry." Pages 186–230 in *Ancient Literacies: The Culture of Reading in Greece and Rome*. Edited by William A. Johnson and Holt N. Parker. Oxford: Oxford University Press, 2011.

Parris, David P. "Imitating the Parables: Allegory, Narrative and the Role of Mimesis." *JSNT* 25 (2002): 33–53.

Pelling, Christopher B. R. "Aspects of Plutarch's Characterization." *Illinois Classical Studies* 13 (1988): 257–74.

———. "Childhood and Personality in Greek Biography." Pages 213–44 in *Characterization and Individuality in Greek Literature*. Edited by Christopher B. R. Pelling. Oxford: Clarendon, 1990.

———. *Plutarch: Life of Antony*. Cambridge: Cambridge University Press, 1988.

———. "Plutarch's Method of Work in the Roman Lives." *Journal of Hellenic Studies* 99 (1979): 74–96.

Pelling, Christopher B. R., ed. *Characterization and Individuality in Greek Literature*. Oxford: Clarendon, 1990.

Peppard, Michael. "The Eagle and the Dove: Roman Imperial Sonship and the Baptism of Jesus (Mark 1.9–11)." *NTS* 56 (2010): 431–51.

———. *The Son of God in the Roman World: Divine Sonship in Its Social and Political Context*. Oxford: Oxford Univeristy Press, 2011.

Pervo, Richard. "A Nihilist Fabula: Introducing the *Life of Aesop*." Pages 77–120 in *Ancient Fiction and Early Christian Narrative*. Edited by Ronald F. Hock, J. Bradley Chance, and Judith Perkins. SBLSymS 6. Atlanta: Scholars Press, 1998.

Pesch, Rudolf. *Das Markusevangelium. I. Teil. Einleitung und Kommentar zu Kap. 1, 1–8,26*. Freiburg: Herder, 1976.

———. *Das Markusevangelium. II. Teil. Kommentar zu Kap. 8,27–16,20*. Freiburg: Herder, 1977.

Petersen, Norman R. "Can One Speak of a Gospel Genre?" *Neot* 28 (1994): 137–58.

———. "'Point of View' in Mark's Narrative." *Semeia* 12 (1978): 97–121.

Peterson, Dwight N. *The Origins of Mark: The Marcan Community in Current Debate*. Biblical Interpretation 48. Leiden: Brill, 2000.

Petridou, Georgia. *Divine Epiphany in Greek Literature and Culture.* Oxford: Oxford University Press, 2015.

Pilch, John J. "Secrecy in the Gospel of Mark." *PACE* 21 (1992): 150–53.

———. "Secrecy in the Mediterranean World: An Anthropological Perspective." *BTB* 24 (1994): 51–57.

Pitts, Andrew W. "The Origins of Greek Mimesis and the Gospel of Mark: Genre as a Potential Constraint in Assessing Markan Imitation." Pages 107–36 in *Ancient Education and Early Christianity.* LNTS 533. Edited by Matthew R. Hauge and Andrew W. Pitts. London: Bloomsbury, 2016.

Plummer, Robert L. "Something Awry in the Temple? The Rending of the Temple Veil and Early Jewish Sources That Report Unusual Phenomena in the Temple around AD 30." *JETS* 48 (2005): 301–16.

Pobee, John. "The Cry of the Centurion—A Cry of Defeat." Pages 91–102 in *The Trial of Jesus: Cambridge Studies in Honour of C. F. D. Moule.* Edited by E. Bammel. SBT 13. London: SCM, 1970.

Porter, Stanley. "The Use of Authoritative Citations in Mark's Gospel and Ancient Biography: A Study of P.Oxy. 1176." Pages 116–30 in *Biblical Interpretation in Early Christian Gospels.* Vol. 1, *The Gospel of Mark.* Edited by Thomas R. Hatina. LNTS 304. London: T&T Clark, 2006.

Price, Simon R. F. "Gods and Emperors: The Greek Language of the Roman Imperial Cult." *JHS* 104 (1984): 79–95.

———. *Rituals and Power: The Roman Imperial Cult in Asia Minor.* Cambridge: Cambridge University Press, 1984.

Pryzwansky, Molly M. "Cornelius Nepos: Key Issues and Critical Approaches." *CJ* 105 (2009): 97–108.

Radcliffe, Timothy. "'The Coming of the Son of Man': Mark's Gospel and the Subversion of the Apocalyptic Image." Pages 15–36 in *Language, Meaning and God: Essays in Honour of Herbert McCabe, OP.* Edited by B. Davies. London: Chapman, 1987.

Räisänen, Heikki. *The "Messianic Secret" in Mark's Gospel.* Translated by C. Tuckett. SNTW. Edinburgh: T&T Clark, 1990.

Rawson, Elizabeth. *Intellectual Life in the Late Roman Republic.* London: Duckworth, 1985.

Redman, Judith C. S. "How Accurate Are Eyewitnesses? Bauckham and the Eyewitnesses in the Light of Psychological Research." *JBL* 129 (2010): 177–97.

Reinach, Salomon. "Simon de Cyrène." Pages 181–88, in vol. 4 of Reinach, *Cultes, Mythes et Religions,* 5 vols. Paris: Leroux, 1904–23.

Renan, J. Ernest. *The History of the Origins of Christianity.* Vol. 1, *Life of Jesus.* Woodstock, Ont.: Devoted Publishing, 2016; orig. English ed. 1890. Translation of *Vie de Jésus.* 13th ed. Paris: Michel Lévy, 1864.

Rengstorf, Karl. "μαθητής." *TDNT* 4:415–60.

Rhoads, David M. "Narrative Criticism: Practices and Prospects." Pages 264–85 in *Characterization in the Gospels: Reconceiving Narrative Criticism.* Edited by David M. Rhoads and Kari Syreeni. JSNTSup 184. Sheffield: Sheffield Academic, 1999.

———. "Performance Criticism: An Emerging Methodology in Second Testament Studies—Part 1." *BTB* 36 (2006): 18–33.

———. "Performance Criticism: An Emerging Methodology in Second Testament Studies—Part 2." *BTB* 36 (2006): 164–84.

Rhoads, David M., and Donald Michie. *Mark as Story: An Introduction to the Narrative of a Gospel.* Philadelphia: Fortress, 1982.

Rhoads, David M., and Kari Syreeni, eds. *Characterization in the Gospels: Reconceiving Narrative Criticism.* JSNTSup 184. Sheffield: Sheffield Academic, 1999.

Rhoads, David M., Joanna Dewey, and Donald Michie. *Mark as Story: An Introduction to the Narrative of a Gospel.* 3rd ed. Minneapolis: Fortress, 2012.

Riddle, Donald W. "Mark 4.1–34: The Evolution of a Gospel Source." *JBL* 56 (1937): 77–90.

Riemer, Ulrike. "Miracle Stories and Their Narrative Intent in the Context of the Ruler Cult of Classical Antiquity." Pages 32–47 in *Wonders Never Cease: The Purpose of Narrating Miracle Stories in the New Testament and Its Religious Environment.* Edited by Michael Labahn and B. Jan Lietaert Peerbolte. LNTS 288. London: T&T Clark, 2006.

Robbins, Vernon K. "The Chreia." Pages 1–23 in *Greco-Roman Literature and the New Testament: Selected Forms and Genres.* Edited by David E. Aune. Sources for Biblical Study 21. Atlanta: Scholars Press, 1988.

———. "Classifying Pronouncement Stories in Plutarch's Parallel Lives." *Semeia* 20 (1998): 29–52.

———. "Interfaces of Orality and Literature in the Gospel of Mark." Pages 125–46 in *Performing the Gospel: Orality, Memory and Mark; Essays Dedicated to Werner Kelber.* Edited by Richard A. Horsley, Jonathan A. Draper, and J. M. Foley. Minneapolis: Fortress, 2006.

———. *Jesus the Teacher: A Socio-Rhetorical Interpretation of Mark.* Philadelphia: Fortress, 1984.

———. "Pronouncement Stories and Jesus's Blessing of the Children: A Rhetorical Approach." *Semeia* 29 (1983): 43–74.

———, ed. *The Rhetoric of Pronouncement.* Semeia 64. Atlanta: SBL Press, 1993.

Rodriguez, Rafael. *Oral Tradition and the New Testament: A Guide for the Perplexed.* London: Bloomsbury, 2014.

Rohrbaugh, Richard L. "Methodological Considerations in the Debate over the Social Class Status of Early Christians." *JAAR* 52 (1984): 519–46.

Ronconi, Alessandro. "Exitus illustrium virorum." *RAC* 6 (1966): 1258–68.

Rose, Herbert J. "Herakles and the Gospels." *ARW* 34 (1937): 42–60.

Roskam, Hendrika N. *The Purpose of the Gospel of Mark in Its Historical and Social Context.* NovTSup 114. Leiden: Brill, 2004.

Ruppert, Lothar. *Jesus als der leidende Gerechte? Der Weg Jesu im Lichte eines alt- und zwischentestamentlichen Motivs.* SBS 59. Stuttgart: Verlag Katholisches Bibelwerk, 1972.

Russell, Donald A. "On Reading Plutarch's Lives." *G&R* 13 (1966): 139–54.

———. *Plutarch.* London: Duckworth, 1973.

Sailor, Dylan. "The Agricola." Pages 23–44 in *A Companion to Tacitus*. Edited by Victoria E. Pagan. Chichester: Wiley-Blackwell, 2012.

Sanders, Edward P. *The Tendencies of the Synoptic Tradition*. Cambridge: Cambridge University Press, 1969.

Sanders, Edward P., and Margaret Davies. *Studying the Synoptic Gospels*. London: SCM, 1989.

Sandnes, Karl Olaf. "Imitatio Homeri? An Appraisal of Dennis R. MacDonald's 'Mimesis Criticism.'" *JBL* 124 (2005): 715–32.

Scaer, Peter. *The Lukan Passion and the Praiseworthy Death*. NTM 10. Sheffield: Sheffield Phoenix, 2005.

Schenkeveld, Dirk M. "The Intended Public of Demetrius' *On Style*: The Place of the Treatise in the Hellenistic Educational System." *Rhetorica* 18 (2000): 29–48.

Schmidt, Karl L. *Der Rahmen der Geschichte Jesu: Literarkritische Untersuchungen zur ältesten Jesusüberlieferung*. Berlin: Trowitzsch, 1919.

———. *The Place of the Gospels in the General History of Literature*. Translated by B. R. McCane. Columbia: University of South Carolina Press, 2002.

Schmidt, Thomas E. "Mark 15.6–32: The Crucifixion Narrative and the Roman Triumphal Procession." *NTS* 41 (1995): 1–18.

Schnelle, Udo. *The History and Theology of the New Testament Writings*. Translated by M. Eugene Boring. Minneapolis: Fortress, 1998.

Schröter, Jens. "Jesus and the Canon: The Early Jesus Traditions in the Context of the Origins of the New Testament Canon." Pages 104–22 in *Performing the Gospel: Orality, Memory and Mark; Essays Dedicated to Werner Kelber*. Edited by Richard A. Horsley, Jonathan A. Draper, and J. M. Foley. Minneapolis: Fortress, 2006.

Schüssler Fiorenza, Elisabeth. *In Memory of Her: A Feminist Theological Reconstruction of Christian Origins*. New York: Crossroad, 1983.

Schwartz, Daniel R. "The Pauline Allusions to the Redemptive Mechanism of the Crucifixion." *JBL* 102 (1983): 259–68.

Schweitzer, A. *The Quest of the Historical Jesus: A Critical Study of Its Progress from Reimarus to Wrede*. 3rd ed. Translated by W. Montgomery. London: A&C Black, 1954.

Schwiebert, Jonathan. "Jesus's Question to Pilate in Mark 15:2." *JBL* 136 (2017): 937–47.

Scobie, Alex. "Storytellers, Storytelling, and the Novel in Graeco-Roman Antiquity." *Rheinisches Museum für Philologie* 122 (1979): 229–59.

Scroggs, Robin, and Kent I. Groff. "Baptism in Mark: Dying and Rising with Christ." *JBL* 92 (1973): 531–48.

Seeley, David. *The Noble Death: Graeco-Roman Martyrology and Paul's Concept of Salvation*. JSNTSup 28. Sheffield: Sheffield Academic, 1990.

———. "Rulership and Service in Mark 10:41–5." *NovT* 35 (1993): 234–50.

Segbroeck, Frans van, Christopher M. Tuckett, Gilbert Van Belle, and Joseph Verheyden, eds. *The Four Gospels 1992: Festschrift for Frans Neirynck*. BETL 100. Leuven: Leuven University Press, 1992.

Sellew, Philip. "Composition of Didactic Scenes in Mark's Gospel." *JBL* 108 (1989): 613–34.

Shaw, Brent D. "The Myth of the Neronian Persecution." *JRS* 105 (2015): 73–100.

Shaw, George B. *The Bodley Head Bernard Shaw: Collected Plays with Their Prefaces*. Vol. 4. London: Max Reinhardt/Bodley Head, 1972.

Sheerin, Daniel J. "Rhetorical and Hermeneutic *Synkrisis* in Patristic Typology." Pages 22–30 in *Nova et Vetera: Patristic Studies in Honor of Thomas Patrick Halton*. Edited by J. Petruccione. Washington, DC: Catholic University of America Press, 1998.

Shelston, Alan. *Biography*. The Critical Idiom 34. London: Methuen, 1977.

Shepherd, Tom. "The Narrative Function of Markan Intercalation." *NTS* 41 (1995): 522–40.

Shiner, Whitney T. "The Ambiguous Pronouncement of the Centurion and the Shrouding of Meaning in Mark." *JSNT* 78 (2000): 3–22.

———. "Creating Plot in Episodic Narrative." Pages 155–76 in *Ancient Fiction and Early Christian Narrative*. Edited by Ronald F. Hock, J. Bradley Chance, and Judith Perkins. SBLSym 6. Atlanta: Scholars Press, 1998.

———. *Follow Me! Disciples in Markan Rhetoric*. SBLDS 145. Atlanta: Scholars Press, 1995.

———. *Proclaiming the Gospel: First Century Performance of the Gospel of Mark*. Eugene, OR: Cascade, 2001.

Shively, Elizabeth E. "Characterizing the Non-human: Satan in the Gospel of Mark." Pages 127–51 in *Character Studies and the Gospel of Mark*. Edited by Christopher W. Skinner and Matthew R. Hauge. London: Bloomsbury, 2014.

———. "Recognizing Penguins: Audience Expectation, Cognitive Genre Theory, and the Ending of Mark's Gospel." *CBQ* 80 (2018): 373–92.

Shrimpton, Gordon. "Theopompus' Treatment of Philip in the 'Philippica.'" *Phoenix* 31 (1977): 123–44.

Shuler, Philip L. *A Genre for the Gospels: The Biographical Character of Matthew*. Philadelphia: Fortress, 1982.

Sick, David H. "The Symposium of the 5,000." *JTS* 66 (2015): 1–27.

Sim, David. "The Gospels for All Christians?" *JSNT* 84 (2001): 3–27.

Simmonds, Andrew. "Mark's and Matthew's *Sub Rosa* Message in the Scene of Pilate and the Crowd." *JBL* 131 (2012): 733–54.

Simon, Uriel. "Minor Characters in Biblical Narrative." *JSOT* 46 (1990): 11–19.

Skidelsky, Robert. "Only Connect: Biography and Truth." Pages 1–16 in *The Troubled Face of Biography*. Edited by Eric Homberger and John Charmley. London: Macmillan, 1988.

Skinner, Christopher W. "The Study of Character(s) in the Gospel of Mark: A Survey of Research from Wrede to the Performance Critics (1901 to 2014)." Pages 3–34 in *Character Studies and the Gospel of Mark*. Edited by Christopher W. Skinner and Matthew R. Hauge. London: Bloomsbury, 2014.

Skinner, Christopher W., and Matthew R. Hauge, eds. *Character Studies and the Gospel of Mark*. London: Bloomsbury, 2014.

Smith, Abraham. "Tyranny Exposed: Mark's Typological Characterization of Herod Antipas (Mark 6:14–29)." *BibInt* 14 (2006): 259–93.

Smith, Dennis E. "Messianic Banquet." *ABD* 4:788–91.

Smith, D. Moody. "The Use of the Old Testament in the New." Pages 3–65 in *The Use of the*

Bibliography

Old Testament in the New. Edited by James M. Efird. Durham, NC: Duke University Press, 1972.

Smith, Justin M. "Famous (or Not So Famous) Last Words." Paper given to the Markan Literary Sources Section of the SBL Annual Meeting. Atlanta, 2016.

———. *Why Βίος? On the Relationship between Gospel Genre and Implied Audience*. LNTS 518. London: Bloomsbury, 2015.

Smith, Morton. "Prolegomena to a Discussion of Aretalogies, Divine Men, the Gospels and Jesus." *JBL* 90 (1971): 174–99.

Smith, Stephen H. "The Role of Jesus's Opponents in the Markan Drama." *NTS* 35 (1989): 161–82.

Soards, Marion L. "Appendix IX: The Question of a Pre-Markan Passion Narrative." Pages 1492–524 in vol. 2 of *The Death of the Messiah: From Gethsemane to the Grave; A Commentary on the Passion Narratives in the Four Gospels*. Edited by Raymond E. Brown. AYBRL. New Haven: Yale University Press, 1994.

Standaert, Benoit H. M. G. M. *L'Evangile selon Marc: Composition et Genre Litteraire*. Nijmegen: Stichting Studentenpers, 1978.

Stanton, Graham. *Jesus and Gospel*. Cambridge: Cambridge University Press, 2004.

———. *Jesus of Nazareth in New Testament Preaching*. Cambridge: Cambridge University Press, 1974.

———. "Matthew: βίβλιος, εὐαγγέλιον, βίος?" Pages 1187–1201 in *The Four Gospels, 1992: Festschrift for Frans Neirynck*. BETL 100. Edited by Frans van Segbroeck, Christopher M. Tuckett, Gilbert Van Belle, and Joseph Verheyden. Leuven: Leuven University Press, 1992.

Stark, Rodney. "The Class Basis of Early Christianity: Inferences from a Sociological Model." *Sociological Analysis* 47 (1986): 216–25.

Starr, Raymond J. "Reading Aloud: Lectores and Roman Reading." *CJ* 86 (1990–91): 337–43.

Stein, Robert H. *Mark*. BECNT. Grand Rapids: Baker Academic, 2008.

Sterling, Gregory. *Historiography and Self-Definition: Josephus, Luke-Acts and Apologetic Historiography*. NovTSup 64. Leiden: Brill, 1991.

———. "Mors philosophi: The Death of Jesus in Luke." *HTR* 94 (2001): 383–402.

Stern, Rex. *The Political Biographies of Cornelius Nepos*. Ann Arbor: University of Michigan Press, 2012.

———. "Shared Virtues and the Limits of Relativism in Nepos' Epaminondas and Atticus." *CJ* 105 (2009): 123–36.

Stock, Augustine. *Call to Discipleship: A Literary Study of Mark's Gospel*. Wilmington, DE: Michael Glazier, 1982.

Strecker, Georg. *History of New Testament Literature*. Translated by Calvin Katter with Hans-Joachim Mollenhauer. Harrisburg, PA: Trinity Press International, 1997.

Strelan, Rick. "The Fallen Watchers and the Disciples in Mark." *JSP* 20 (1999): 73–92.

Suhl, Alfred. *Die Funktion der alttestamentlichen Zitate und Anspielungen im Markusevangelium*. Gütersloh: Gerd Mohn, 1965.

Talbert, Charles H. *What Is a Gospel? The Genre of the Canonical Gospels*. Philadelphia: Fortress, 1977.

Tannehill, Robert C. "The Disciples in Mark: The Function of a Narrative Role." Pages 169–95 in *The Interpretation of Mark*. Edited by W. R. Telford. Edinburgh: T&T Clark, 1995.

———. "The Gospel of Mark as Narrative Christology." *Semeia* 16 (1979): 57–95.

Taylor, Joan E. *What Did Jesus Look Like?* London: Bloomsbury, 2018.

Taylor, Justin. "The Acts of the Apostles as Biography." Pages 77–88 in *The Limits of Ancient Biography*. Edited by Brian McGing and Judith Mossman. Swansea: Classical Press of Wales, 2006.

———. "The Role of Rhetorical Elaboration in the Formation of Mark's Passion Narrative (Mark 14.43–16.8): An Enquiry." Pages 11–26 in *Greco-Roman Culture and the New Testament: Studies Commemorating the Centennial of the Pontifical Biblical Institute*. Edited by David E. Aune and Frederick E. Brent. NovTSup 143. Leiden: Brill, 2012.

Taylor, R. O. P. "Form Criticism in the First Centuries." *ExpTim* 55 (1944): 218–20.

Taylor, Vincent. *The Formation of the Gospel Tradition*. 2nd ed. London: Macmillan, 1953.

———. *The Gospel according to St Mark*. London: Macmillan, 1952.

Telford, William R. "The Pre-Markan Tradition in Recent Research (1980–1990)." Pages 693–723 in *The Four Gospels, 1992: Festschrift for Frans Neirynck*. BETL 100. Edited by Frans van Segbroeck, Christopher M. Tuckett, Gilbert Van Belle, and Joseph Verheyden. Leuven: Leuven University Press, 1992.

———. *The Theology of the Gospel of Mark*. New Testament Theology. Cambridge: Cambridge University Press, 1999.

———. *Writing on the Gospel of Mark*. Guides to Advanced Biblical Research. Dorchester: Deo, 2009.

Telford, W. R., ed. *The Interpretation of Mark*. 2nd ed. Edinburgh: T&T Clark, 1995.

Thatcher, Tom. "Jesus, Judas and Peter: Character by Contrast in the Fourth Gospel." *BSac* 153 (1996): 435–48.

———. "(Re)Mark(s) on the Cross." *BibInt* 4 (1996): 346–61.

———. "Why John Wrote a Gospel: Memory and History in an Early Christian Community." Pages 79–97 in *Memory, Tradition, and Text: Uses of the Past in Early Christianity*. Edited by Alan Kirk and Tom Thatcher. Semeia 52. Atlanta: SBL Press, 2005.

Theissen, Gerd. *The Gospels in Context: Social and Political History in the Synoptic Tradition*. Translated by L. M. Maloney. Edinburgh: T&T Clark, 1992.

———. *The Social Setting of Pauline Christianity: Essays on Corinth*. Translated and edited by John H. Schültz. Philadelphia: Fortress, 1978.

Thomas, Rosalind. "Writing, Reading, Public and Private 'Literacies': Functional Literacy and Democratic Literacy in Greece." Pages 13–42 in *Ancient Literacies: The Culture of Reading in Greece and Rome*. Edited by William A. Johnson and Holt N. Parker. Oxford: Oxford University Press, 2011.

Thompson, Michael B. "The Holy Internet: Communication between Churches in the First

Bibliography

Christian Generation." Pages 49–70 in *The Gospels for All Christians: Rethinking the Gospel Audiences.* Edited by Richard Bauckham. Edinburgh: T&T Clark, 1998.

Thwaite, Ann. "Writing Lives." Pages 17–32 in *The Troubled Face of Biography.* Edited by Eric Homberger and John Charmley. London: Macmillan, 1988.

Toher, Mark. "Characterizing Augustus." Pages 226–53 in *Fame and Infamy: Essays for Christopher Pelling on Characterization in Greek and Roman Biography.* Edited by Rhiannon Ash, Judith Mossman, and Francis B. Titchener. Oxford: Oxford University Press, 2015.

———. "The 'Exitus' of Augustus." *Hermes* 140 (2012): 37–44.

Tolbert, Mary Ann. "How the Gospel of Mark Builds Character." *Int* 47 (1993): 347–57.

———. *Sowing the Gospel: Mark's World in Literary-Historical Perspective.* Minneapolis: Fortress, 1989.

Tuckett, Christopher M. "Form Criticism." Pages 21–38 in *Jesus in Memory: Traditions in Oral and Scribal Perspectives.* Waco: Baylor University Press, 2009.

Tuckett, Christopher M., ed. *The Messianic Secret.* Issues in Religion and Theology 1. Philadelphia: Fortress, 1983.

Turner, Cuthbert H., and J. Keith Elliott. *The Language and Style of the Gospel of Mark: An Edition of C. H. Turner's "Notes on Marcan Usage" Together with Other Comparable Studies.* NovTSup 71. Leiden: Brill, 1993.

Turpin, William. "Tacitus, Stoic *Exempla,* and the *Praecipuum Munus Annalium.*" *Classical Antiquity* 27 (2008): 359–404.

Tyrrell, George. *Christianity at the Crossroads.* London: Longmans, Green, 1913.

Tyson, Joseph B. "The Blindness of the Disciples in Mark." *JBL* 80 (1961): 261–68.

Ulansey, David. "The Heavenly Veil Torn: Mark's Cosmic Inclusio." *JBL* 110 (1991): 123–25.

Vaage, Lief. E. "Bird-Watching at the Baptism of Jesus: Early Christian Mythmaking in Mark 1:9–11." Pages 280–94 in *Reimagining Christian Origins: A Colloquium Honoring Burton L. Mack.* Edited by Elizabeth A. Castelli and Hal Taussig. Valley Forge, PA: Trinity, 1996.

Versnel, Henk S. *Triumphus: An Inquiry into the Origin, Development, and Meaning of the Roman Triumph.* Leiden: Brill, 1970.

Vines, Michael E. *The Problem of Markan Genre: The Gospel of Mark and the Jewish Novel.* Academia Biblical 3. Atlanta: Scholars Press, 2002.

Votaw, Clyde W. "The Gospels and Contemporary Biographies." *American Journal of Theology* 19 (1915): 45–73, 217–49. Reprinted as *The Gospels and Contemporary Biographies in the Greco-Roman World.* Philadelphia: Fortress, 1970.

Walker, Henry J. *Valerius Maximus, Memorable Deeds and Sayings: One Thousand Tales from Ancient Rome.* Indianapolis: Hackett, 2004.

Wallace-Hadrill, Andrew. "*Civilis Princeps*: Between Citizen and King." *JRS* 72 (1982): 32–48.

Walton, Steve. "What Are the Gospels? Richard Burridge's Impact on Scholarly Understanding of the Genre of the Gospels." *CBQ* 14 (2015): 81–93.

Wardle, Timothy. "Mark, the Jerusalem Temple and Jewish Sectarianism: Why Geographical Proximity Matters in Determining the Provenance of Mark." *NTS* 62 (2016): 60–78.

Watson, David F. *Honor among Christians: The Cultural Key to the Messianic Secret.* Minneapolis: Fortress, 2010.

Watson, Francis. *Gospel Writing: A Canonical Perspective.* Grand Rapids: Eerdmans, 2013.

———. "The Social Function of Mark's Secrecy Theme." *JSNT* 24 (1985): 49–69.

———. "Towards a Literal Reading of the Gospels." Pages 195–217 in *The Gospels for All Christians: Rethinking the Gospel Audiences.* Edited by Richard Bauckham. Edinburgh: T&T Clark, 1998.

Watt, Ian. *The Rise of the Novel: Studies in Defoe, Richardson and Fielding.* London: Chatto and Windus, 1957.

Watts, Rikki E. "The Psalms in Mark's Gospel." Pages 25–45 in *The Psalms in the New Testament.* Edited by Steve Moyise and Maarten J. J. Menken. London: T&T Clark, 2004.

Weder, Hans. "Disciple, Discipleship." *ABD* 2:207–10. Translated by Dennis Martin.

Weeden, Theodore J. "The Heresy That Necessitated Mark's Gospel." *ZNW* 59 (1968): 145–58.

Wehrli, Fritz. "Gnōme, Anekdote und Biographie." *MH* 30 (1973): 193–208.

Weinfeld, Moshe. "The King as the Servant of the People." *JJS* 33 (1982): 189–94.

Wendland, Paul. *Die Urchristliche Literaturformen.* 2nd ed. HNT 1/3. Tübingen: Mohr Siebeck, 1912.

Whitaker, Robyn. "Rebuke or Recall? Rethinking the Role of Peter in Mark's Gospel." *CBQ* 75 (2013): 666–82.

Whitmarsh, Tim, ed. *The Cambridge Companion to the Greek and Roman Novel.* Cambridge Companions to Literature. Cambridge: Cambridge University Press, 2008.

Wiarda, Timothy. "Peter as Peter in the Gospel of Mark." *NTS* 45 (1999): 19–37.

Williams, Joel F. "The Character of Jesus as Lord in Mark's Gospel." Pages 107–26 in *Character Studies and the Gospel of Mark.* Edited by Christopher W. Skinner and Matthew R. Hauge. London: Bloomsbury, 2014.

———. "Discipleship and Minor Characters in Mark's Gospel." *BSac* 153 (1996): 332–43.

Williams, Peter J. "An Examination of Ehrman's Case for *orgistheis* in Mark 1.41." *NovT* 54 (2012): 1–12.

Wilson, Brittany E. *Unmanly Men: Refigurations of Masculinity in Luke-Acts.* Oxford: Oxford University Press, 2015.

Winter, Paul. "Marginal Notes on the Trial of Jesus." *ZNW* 50 (1959): 221–51.

Wire, Antoinette Clark. *The Case for Mark Composed in Performance.* BPCS 3. Eugene, OR: Cascade, 2001.

Wischmeyer, O. "Forming Identity through Literature: The Impact of Mark for the Building of Christ-Believing Communities in the Second Half of the First Century CE." Pages 355–78 in *Mark and Matthew I, Comparative Readings: Understanding the Earliest Gospels in Their First-Century Setting.* Edited by Eve-Marie Becker and Anders Runesson. WUNT 271. Tübingen: Mohr Siebeck, 2011.

———. "Herrschen als Dienen—Mk 10,41–45." *ZNW* 90 (1999): 28–44.

Witherington, Ben, III. *The Gospel of Mark: Socio-Rhetorical Commentary*. Grand Rapids: Eerdmans, 2001.

Wrede, William. *The Messianic Secret*. Translated by J. C. G. Grieg. Cambridge: Clarke, 1971.

Wright, Arthur. "Τάξει in Papias." *JTS* 14 (1913): 298–300.

Wright, William M. "Greco-Roman Character Typing and the Presentation of Judas in the Fourth Gospel." *CBQ* 71 (2009): 544–59.

Yamada, Kota. "The Preface to the Lukan Writings and Rhetorical Historiography." Pages 154–72 in *The Rhetorical Interpretation of Scripture*. Edited by Stanley E. Porter and Dennis L. Stamps. JSNTSup 180. Sheffield: Sheffield Academic, 1999.

Zemler-Cizewski, Wanda. "The Apocryphal Life of Adam and Eve: Recent Scholarly Work." *AThR* 86 (2004): 671–77.

Index of Authors

Index of Subjects

Index of Scripture and Other Ancient Sources

Index of Scripture and Other Ancient Sources